Optimizing Java

*Practical Techniques for Improving
JVM Application Performance*

*Benjamin J. Evans, James Gough,
and Chris Newland*

Beijing · Boston · Farnham · Sebastopol · Tokyo

Optimizing Java

by Benjamin J. Evans, James Gough, and Chris Newland

Copyright © 2018 Benjamin J. Evans, James Gough, and Chris Newland. All rights reserved.

Published by O'Reilly Media, Inc., 1005 Gravenstein Highway North, Sebastopol, CA 95472.

O'Reilly books may be purchased for educational, business, or sales promotional use. Online editions are also available for most titles (*http://oreilly.com/safari*). For more information, contact our corporate/institutional sales department: 800-998-9938 or *corporate@oreilly.com*.

Editors: Susan Conant and Virginia Wilson
Production Editor: Colleen Cole
Copyeditor: Rachel Monaghan
Proofreader: Rachel Head
Indexer: Ellen Troutman-Zaig

Interior Designer: David Futato
Cover Designer: Randy Comer
Illustrator: Anna Evans
Technical Reviewers: Julian Templeman, Michael Hsu, Alex Blewitt, Dmitry Vyazelenko

May 2018:   First Edition

Revision History for the First Edition
2018-04-12:   First Release

See *http://oreilly.com/catalog/errata.csp?isbn=9781492025795* for release details.

978-1-492-02579-5

[LSI]

This book is dedicated to my wife, Anna, who not only illustrated it beautifully, but also helped edit portions and, crucially, was often the first person I bounced ideas off.

—Benjamin J. Evans

This book is dedicated to my incredible family Megan, Emily, and Anna. Writing would not have been possible without their help and support. I'd also like to thank my parents, Heather and Paul, for encouraging me to learn and their constant support.

I'd also like to thank Benjamin Evans for his guidance and friendship—it's been a pleasure working together again.

—James Gough

This book is dedicated to my wife, Reena, who supported and encouraged my efforts and to my sons, Joshua and Hugo, may they grow up with inquisitive minds.

—Chris Newland

Table of Contents

Foreword

How do you define performance?

Most developers, when asked about the performance of their application, will assume some measure of speed is requested. Something like transactions per second, or gigabytes of data processed...getting a lot of work done in the shortest amount of time possible. If you're an application architect, you may measure performance in broader metrics. You may be more concerned about resource utilization than straight-line execution. You might pay more attention to the performance of connections between services than of the services themselves. If you make business decisions for your company, application performance will probably not be measured in time as often as it is measured in dollars. You may argue with developers and architects about resource allocation, weighing the cost of devops against the time it takes to do the company's work.

And regardless of which role you identify with, all these metrics are important.

I started out developing Java applications in 1996. I had just moved from my first job writing AppleScript CGIs for the University of Minnesota's business school to maintaining server-side Perl applications for the web development team. Java was very new then—the first stable version, 1.0.2, was released earlier that year—and I was tasked with finding something useful to build.

Back in those days, the best way to get performance out of a Java application was to write it in some other language. This was before Java had a Just-in-Time (JIT) compiler, before parallel and concurrent garbage collectors, and long before the server side would become dominated by Java technology. But many of us wanted to use Java, and we developed all sorts of tricks to make our code run well. We wrote gigantic methods to avoid method dispatch overhead. We pooled and reused objects because garbage collection was slow and disruptive. We used lots of global state and static methods. We wrote truly awful Java code, but it worked...for a little while.

In 1999, things started to change.

After years struggling to use Java for anything demanding speed, JIT technologies started to reach us. With compilers that could inline methods, the number of method calls became less important than breaking up our giant monoliths into smaller pieces. We gleefully embraced object-oriented design, splitting our methods into tiny chunks and wrapping interfaces around everything. We marveled at how every release of Java would run things just a little bit better, because we were writing good Java code and the JIT compiler loved it. Java soared past other technologies on the server, leading us to build larger and more complex apps with richer abstractions.

At the same time, garbage collectors were rapidly improving. Now the overhead of pooling would very frequently overshadow the cost of allocation. Many garbage collectors offered multithreaded operation, and we started to see low-pause, nearly concurrent GCs that stayed out of our applications' way. The standard practice moved toward a carefree creating and throwing away of objects with the promise that a sufficiently smart GC would eventually make it all OK. And it worked…for a little while.

The problem with technology is that it always invalidates itself. As JIT and GC technologies have improved, the paths to application performance have become tricky to navigate. Even though JVMs can optimize our code and make objects almost free, the demands of applications and users continue to grow.

Some of the time, maybe even most of the time, the "good" coding patterns prevail: small methods inline properly, interface and type checks become inexpensive, native code produced by the JIT compiler is compact and efficient. But other times we need to hand-craft our code, dial back abstractions and architecture in deference to the limitations of the compiler and CPU. Some of the time, objects really are free and we can ignore the fact that we're consuming memory bandwidth and GC cycles. Other times we're dealing with terabyte-scale (or larger) datasets that put stress on even the best garbage collectors and memory subsystems.

The answer to the performance question these days is to know your tools. And frequently, that means knowing not just how Java the language works, but also how JVM libraries, memory, the compiler, GCs, and the hardware your apps run on are interacting. In my work on the JRuby project, I've learned an immutable truth about the JVM: there's no single solution for all performance problems, but for all performance problems there are solutions. The trick is finding those solutions and piecing together the ones that meet your needs best. Now you have a secret weapon in these performance battles: the book you are about to read.

Turn the page, friends, and discover the wealth of tools and techniques available to you. Learn how to balance application design with available resources. Learn how to monitor and tune the JVM. Learn how to make use of the latest Java technologies that are more efficient than old libraries and patterns. Learn how to make Java fly.

It's an exciting time to be a Java developer, and there have never been so many opportunities to build efficient and responsive applications on the Java platform. Let's get started.

— Charlie Nutter
Principal Software Engineer,
Red Hat Middleware

Preface

Conventions Used in This Book

The following typographical conventions are used in this book:

Italic
> Indicates new terms, URLs, email addresses, filenames, and file extensions.

`Constant width`
> Used for program listings, as well as within paragraphs to refer to program elements such as variable or function names, databases, data types, environment variables, statements, and keywords.

`<constant width>` *in angle brackets*
> Shows text that should be replaced with user-supplied values or by values determined by context.

 This element signifies a tip or suggestion.

 This element signifies a general note.

 This element indicates a warning or caution.

Using Code Examples

Supplemental material (code examples, exercises, etc.) is available for download at *http://bit.ly/optimizing-java-1e-code-examples*.

This book is here to help you get your job done. In general, if example code is offered with this book, you may use it in your programs and documentation. You do not need to contact us for permission unless you're reproducing a significant portion of the code. For example, writing a program that uses several chunks of code from this book does not require permission. Selling or distributing a CD-ROM of examples from O'Reilly books does require permission. Answering a question by citing this book and quoting example code does not require permission. Incorporating a significant amount of example code from this book into your product's documentation does require permission.

We appreciate, but do not require, attribution. An attribution usually includes the title, author, publisher, and ISBN. For example: "*Optimizing Java* by Benjamin J. Evans, James Gough, and Chris Newland (O'Reilly). Copyright 2018 Benjamin J. Evans, James Gough, and Chris Newland, 978-1-492-02579-5."

If you feel your use of code examples falls outside fair use or the permission given above, feel free to contact us at *permissions@oreilly.com*.

O'Reilly Safari

Safari (formerly Safari Books Online) is a membership-based training and reference platform for enterprise, government, educators, and individuals.

Members have access to thousands of books, training videos, Learning Paths, interactive tutorials, and curated playlists from over 250 publishers, including O'Reilly Media, Harvard Business Review, Prentice Hall Professional, Addison-Wesley Professional, Microsoft Press, Sams, Que, Peachpit Press, Adobe, Focal Press, Cisco Press, John Wiley & Sons, Syngress, Morgan Kaufmann, IBM Redbooks, Packt, Adobe Press, FT Press, Apress, Manning, New Riders, McGraw-Hill, Jones & Bartlett, and Course Technology, among others.

For more information, please visit *http://oreilly.com/safari*.

How to Contact Us

Please address comments and questions concerning this book to the publisher:

O'Reilly Media, Inc.
1005 Gravenstein Highway North
Sebastopol, CA 95472
800-998-9938 (in the United States or Canada)
707-829-0515 (international or local)
707-829-0104 (fax)

We have a web page for this book, where we list errata, examples, and any additional information. You can access this page at *http://bit.ly/optimizing-java*.

To comment or ask technical questions about this book, send email to *bookquestions@oreilly.com*.

For more information about our books, courses, conferences, and news, see our website at *http://www.oreilly.com*.

Find us on Facebook: *http://facebook.com/oreilly*

Follow us on Twitter: *http://twitter.com/oreillymedia*

Watch us on YouTube: *http://www.youtube.com/oreillymedia*

Acknowledgments

The authors would like to thank a large number of people for their invaluable assistance.

For writing the foreword:

- Charlie Nutter

For providing highly specialist technical help, including information and knowledge not available anywhere else:

- Christine Flood
- Chris Seaton
- Kirk Pepperdine
- Simon Ritter
- Monica Beckwith
- David Jones

- Richard Warburton
- Stephen Connolly
- Jaroslav Tulach

For general detail, encouragement, advice and introductions:

- George Ball
- Steve Poole
- Richard Pollock
- Andrew Binstock

Our technical reviewers:

- Michael Hsu
- Dmitry Vyazelenko
- Julian Templeman
- Alex Blewitt

The O'Reilly Team:

- Virginia Wilson
- Susan Conant
- Colleen Cole
- Rachel Monaghan
- Nan Barber
- Brian Foster
- Lindsay Ventimiglia
- Maureen Spencer
- Heather Scherer

## CHAPTER 1

Optimization and Performance Defined

Optimizing the performance of Java (or any other sort of code) is often seen as a Dark Art. There's a mystique about performance analysis—it's commonly viewed as a craft practiced by the "lone hacker, who is tortured and deep thinking" (one of Hollywood's favorite tropes about computers and the people who operate them). The image is one of a single individual who can see deeply into a system and come up with a magic solution that makes the system work faster.

This image is often coupled with the unfortunate (but all-too-common) situation where performance is a second-class concern of the software teams. This sets up a scenario where analysis is only done once the system is already in trouble, and so needs a performance "hero" to save it. The reality, however, is a little different.

The truth is that performance analysis is a weird blend of hard empiricism and squishy human psychology. What matters is, at one and the same time, the absolute numbers of observable metrics and how the end users and stakeholders *feel* about them. The resolution of this apparent paradox is the subject of the rest of this book.

Java Performance—The Wrong Way

For many years, one of the top three hits on Google for "Java performance tuning" was an article from 1997–8, which had been ingested into the index very early in Google's history. The page had presumably stayed close to the top because its initial ranking served to actively drive traffic to it, creating a feedback loop.

The page housed advice that was completely out of date, no longer true, and in many cases detrimental to applications. However, its favored position in the search engine results caused many, many developers to be exposed to terrible advice.

For example, very early versions of Java had terrible method dispatch performance. As a workaround, some Java developers advocated avoiding writing small methods and instead writing monolithic methods. Of course, over time, the performance of virtual dispatch greatly improved. Not only that, but with modern Java Virtual Machines (JVMs) and especially automatic managed inlining, virtual dispatch has now been eliminated at the majority of call sites. Code that followed the "lump everything into one method" advice is now at a substantial disadvantage, as it is very unfriendly to modern Just-in-Time (JIT) compilers.

There's no way of knowing how much damage was done to the performance of applications that were subjected to the bad advice, but this case neatly demonstrates the dangers of not using a quantitative and verifiable approach to performance. It also provides another excellent example of why you shouldn't believe everything you read on the internet.

The execution speed of Java code is highly dynamic and fundamentally depends on the underlying Java Virtual Machine. An old piece of Java code may well execute faster on a more recent JVM, even without recompiling the Java source code.

As you might imagine, for this reason (and others we will discuss later) this book is not a cookbook of performance tips to apply to your code. Instead, we focus on a range of aspects that come together to produce good performance engineering:

- Performance methodology within the overall software lifecycle
- Theory of testing as applied to performance
- Measurement, statistics, and tooling
- Analysis skills (both systems and data)
- Underlying technology and mechanisms

Later in the book, we will introduce some heuristics and code-level techniques for optimization, but these all come with caveats and tradeoffs that the developer should be aware of before using them.

Please do not skip ahead to those sections and start applying the techniques detailed without properly understanding the context in which the advice is given. All of these techniques are capable of doing more harm than good if you lack a proper understanding of how they should be applied.

In general, there are:

- No magic "go faster" switches for the JVM
- No "tips and tricks" to make Java run faster
- No secret algorithms that have been hidden from you

As we explore our subject, we will discuss these misconceptions in more detail, along with some other common mistakes that developers often make when approaching Java performance analysis and related issues. Still here? Good. Then let's talk about performance.

Java Performance Overview

To understand why Java performance is the way that it is, let's start by considering a classic quote from James Gosling, the creator of Java:

> Java is a blue collar language. It's not PhD thesis material but a language for a job.

That is, Java has always been an extremely practical language. Its attitude to performance was initially that as long as the environment was *fast enough*, then raw performance could be sacrificed if developer productivity benefited. It was therefore not until relatively recently, with the increasing maturity and sophistication of JVMs such as HotSpot, that the Java environment became suitable for high-performance computing applications.

This practicality manifests itself in many ways in the Java platform, but one of the most obvious is the used of *managed subsystems*. The idea is that the developer gives up some aspects of low-level control in exchange for not having to worry about some of the details of the capability under management.

The most obvious example of this is, of course, memory management. The JVM provides automatic memory management in the form of a pluggable garbage collection subsystem, so that memory does not have to be manually tracked by the programmer.

 Managed subsystems occur throughout the JVM and their existence introduces extra complexity into the runtime behavior of JVM applications.

As we will discuss in the next section, the complex runtime behavior of JVM applications requires us to treat our applications as experiments under test. This leads us to think about the statistics of observed measurements, and here we make an unfortunate discovery.

The observed performance measurements of JVM applications are very often not normally distributed. This means that elementary statistical techniques (e.g., *standard deviation* and *variance*) are ill-suited for handling results from JVM applications. This is because many basic statistics methods contain an implicit assumption about the normality of results distributions.

One way to understand this is that for JVM applications outliers can be very significant—for a low-latency trading application, for example. This means that sampling of measurements is also problematic, as it can easily miss the exact events that have the most importance.

Finally, a word of caution. It is very easy to be misled by Java performance measurements. The complexity of the environment means that it is very hard to isolate individual aspects of the system.

Measurement also has an overhead, and frequent sampling (or recording every result) can have an observable impact on the performance numbers being recorded. The nature of Java performance numbers requires a certain amount of statistical sophistication, and naive techniques frequently produce incorrect results when applied to Java/JVM applications.

Performance as an Experimental Science

Java/JVM software stacks are, like most modern software systems, very complex. In fact, due to the highly optimizing and adaptive nature of the JVM, production systems built on top of the JVM can have some incredibly subtle and intricate performance behavior. This complexity has been made possible by Moore's Law and the unprecedented growth in hardware capability that it represents.

> The most amazing achievement of the computer software industry is its continuing cancellation of the steady and staggering gains made by the computer hardware industry.
>
> —Henry Petroski

While some software systems have squandered the historical gains of the industry, the JVM represents something of an engineering triumph. Since its inception in the late 1990s the JVM has developed into a very high-performance, general-purpose execution environment that puts those gains to very good use. The tradeoff, however, is that like any complex, high-performance system, the JVM requires a measure of skill and experience to get the absolute best out of it.

> A measurement not clearly defined is worse than useless.
>
> —Eli Goldratt

JVM performance tuning is therefore a synthesis between technology, methodology, measurable quantities, and tools. Its aim is to effect measurable outputs in a manner desired by the owners or users of a system. In other words, performance is an experimental science—it achieves a desired result by:

- Defining the desired outcome
- Measuring the existing system
- Determining what is to be done to achieve the requirement
- Undertaking an improvement exercise
- Retesting
- Determining whether the goal has been achieved

The process of defining and determining desired performance outcomes builds a set of quantitative objectives. It is important to establish what should be measured and record the objectives, which then form part of the project's artifacts and deliverables. From this, we can see that performance analysis is based upon defining, and then achieving, nonfunctional requirements.

This process is, as has been previewed, not one of reading chicken entrails or another divination method. Instead, we rely upon statistics and an appropriate handling of results. In Chapter 5 we will introduce a primer on the basic statistical techniques that are required for accurate handling of data generated from a JVM performance analysis project.

For many real-world projects, a more sophisticated understanding of data and statistics will undoubtedly be required. You are encouraged to view the statistical techniques found in this book as a starting point, rather than a definitive statement.

A Taxonomy for Performance

In this section, we introduce some basic performance metrics. These provide a vocabulary for performance analysis and will allow you to frame the objectives of a tuning project in quantitative terms. These objectives are the nonfunctional requirements that define performance goals. One common basic set of performance metrics is:

- Throughput
- Latency
- Capacity
- Utilization
- Efficiency
- Scalability

- Degradation

We will briefly discuss each in turn. Note that for most performance projects, not every metric will be optimized simultaneously. The case of only a few metrics being improved in a single performance iteration is far more common, and this may be as many as can be tuned at once. In real-world projects, it may well be the case that optimizing one metric comes at the detriment of another metric or group of metrics.

Throughput

Throughput is a metric that represents the rate of work a system or subsystem can perform. This is usually expressed as number of units of work in some time period. For example, we might be interested in how many transactions per second a system can execute.

For the throughput number to be meaningful in a real performance exercise, it should include a description of the reference platform it was obtained on. For example, the hardware spec, OS, and software stack are all relevant to throughput, as is whether the system under test is a single server or a cluster. In addition, transactions (or units of work) should be the same between tests. Essentially, we should seek to ensure that the workload for throughput tests is kept consistent between runs.

Latency

Performance metrics are sometimes explained via metaphors that evoke plumbing. If a water pipe can produce 100 liters per second, then the volume produced in 1 second (100 liters) is the throughput. In this metaphor, the latency is effectively the length of the pipe. That is, it's the time taken to process a single transaction and see a result at the other end of the pipe.

It is normally quoted as an end-to-end time. It is dependent on workload, so a common approach is to produce a graph showing latency as a function of increasing workload. We will see an example of this type of graph in "Reading Performance Graphs" on page 9.

Capacity

The capacity is the amount of work parallelism a system possesses—that is, the number of units of work (e.g., transactions) that can be simultaneously ongoing in the system.

Capacity is obviously related to throughput, and we should expect that as the concurrent load on a system increases, throughput (and latency) will be affected. For this reason, capacity is usually quoted as the processing available at a given value of latency or throughput.

Utilization

One of the most common performance analysis tasks is to achieve efficient use of a system's resources. Ideally, CPUs should be used for handling units of work, rather than being idle (or spending time handling OS or other housekeeping tasks).

Depending on the workload, there can be a huge difference between the utilization levels of different resources. For example, a computation-intensive workload (such as graphics processing or encryption) may be running at close to 100% CPU but only be using a small percentage of available memory.

Efficiency

Dividing the throughput of a system by the utilized resources gives a measure of the overall efficiency of the system. Intuitively, this makes sense, as requiring more resources to produce the same throughput is one useful definition of being less efficient.

It is also possible, when one is dealing with larger systems, to use a form of cost accounting to measure efficiency. If solution A has a total dollar cost of ownership (TCO) twice that of solution B for the same throughput then it is, clearly, half as efficient.

Scalability

The throughout or capacity of a system depends upon the resources available for processing. The change in throughput as resources are added is one measure of the scalability of a system or application. The holy grail of system scalability is to have throughput change exactly in step with resources.

Consider a system based on a cluster of servers. If the cluster is expanded, for example, by doubling in size, then what throughput can be achieved? If the new cluster can handle twice the volume of transactions, then the system is exhibiting "perfect linear scaling." This is very difficult to achieve in practice, especially over a wide range of possible loads.

System scalability is dependent upon a number of factors, and is not normally a simple constant factor. It is very common for a system to scale close to linearly for some range of resources, but then at higher loads to encounter some limitation that prevents perfect scaling.

Degradation

If we increase the load on a system, either by increasing the number of requests (or clients) or by increasing the speed requests arrive at, then we may see a change in the observed latency and/or throughput.

Note that this change is dependent on utilization. If the system is underutilized, then there should be some slack before observables change, but if resources are fully utilized then we would expect to see throughput stop increasing, or latency increase. These changes are usually called the degradation of the system under additional load.

Connections Between the Observables

The behavior of the various performance observables is usually connected in some manner. The details of this connection will depend upon whether the system is running at peak utility. For example, in general, the utilization will change as the load on a system increases. However, if the system is underutilized, then increasing load may not appreciably increase utilization. Conversely, if the system is already stressed, then the effect of increasing load may be felt in another observable.

As another example, scalability and degradation both represent the change in behavior of a system as more load is added. For scalability, as the load is increased, so are available resources, and the central question is whether the system can make use of them. On the other hand, if load is added but additional resources are not provided, degradation of some performance observable (e.g., latency) is the expected outcome.

In rare cases, additional load can cause counterintuitive results. For example, if the change in load causes some part of the system to switch to a more resource-intensive but higher-performance mode, then the overall effect can be to reduce latency, even though more requests are being received.

To take one example, in Chapter 9 we will discuss HotSpot's JIT compiler in detail. To be considered eligible for JIT compilation, a method has to be executed in interpreted mode "sufficiently frequently." So it is possible at low load to have key methods stuck in interpreted mode, but for those to become eligible for compilation at higher loads due to increased calling frequency on the methods. This causes later calls to the same method to run much, much faster than earlier executions.

Different workloads can have very different characteristics. For example, a trade on the financial markets, viewed end to end, may have an execution time (i.e., latency) of hours or even days. However, millions of them may be in progress at a major bank at any given time. Thus, the capacity of the system is very large, but the latency is also large.

However, let's consider only a single subsystem within the bank. The matching of a buyer and a seller (which is essentially the parties agreeing on a price) is known as *order matching*. This individual subsystem may have only hundreds of pending orders at any given time, but the latency from order acceptance to completed match may be as little as 1 millisecond (or even less in the case of "low-latency" trading).

In this section we have met the most frequently encountered performance observables. Occasionally slightly different definitions, or even different metrics, are used, but in most cases these will be the basic system numbers that will normally be used to guide performance tuning, and act as a taxonomy for discussing the performance of systems of interest.

Reading Performance Graphs

To conclude this chapter, let's look at some common patterns of behavior that occur in performance tests. We will explore these by looking at graphs of real observables, and we will encounter many other examples of graphs of our data as we proceed.

The graph in Figure 1-1 shows sudden, unexpected degradation of performance (in this case, latency) under increasing load—commonly called a *performance elbow*.

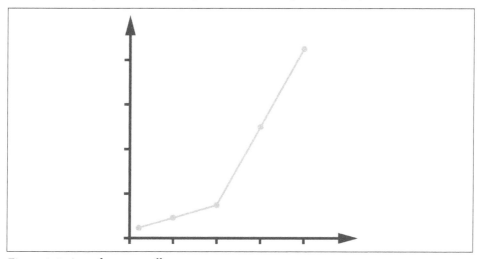

Figure 1-1. A performance elbow

By contrast, Figure 1-2 shows the much happier case of throughput scaling almost linearly as machines are added to a cluster. This is close to ideal behavior, and is only likely to be achieved in extremely favorable circumstances—e.g., scaling a stateless protocol with no need for session affinity with a single server.

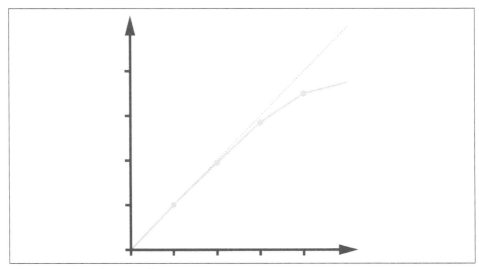

Figure 1-2. Near-linear scaling

In Chapter 12 we will meet Amdahl's Law, named for the famous computer scientist (and "father of the mainframe") Gene Amdahl of IBM. Figure 1-3 shows a graphical representation of his fundamental constraint on scalability; it shows the maximum possible speedup as a function of the number of processors devoted to the task.

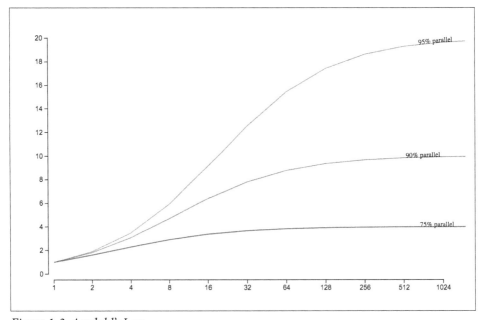

Figure 1-3. Amdahl's Law

We display three cases: where the underlying task is 75%, 90%, and 95% paralleliza-
ble. This clearly shows that whenever the workload has any piece at all that must be
performed serially, linear scalability is impossible, and there are strict limits on how
much scalability can be achieved. This justifies the commentary around Figure 1-2—
even in the best cases linear scalability is all but impossible to achieve.

The limits imposed by Amdahl's Law are surprisingly restrictive. Note in particular
that the x-axis of the graph is logarithmic, and so even with an algorithm that is
(only) 5% serial, 32 processors are needed for a factor-of-12 speedup. Even worse, no
matter how many cores are used, the maximum speedup is only a factor of 20 for that
algorithm. In practice, many algorithms are far more than 5% serial, and so have a
more constrained maximum possible speedup.

As we will see in Chapter 6, the underlying technology in the JVM's garbage collection subsystem naturally gives rise to a "sawtooth" pattern of memory used for
healthy applications that aren't under stress. We can see an example in Figure 1-4.

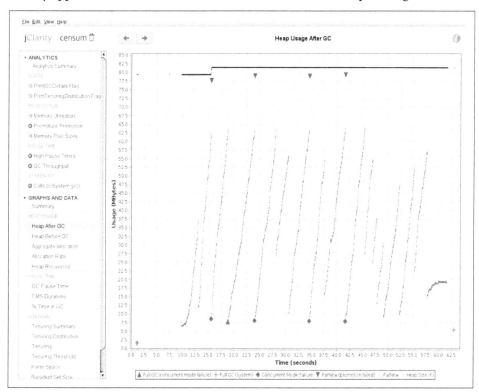

Figure 1-4. Healthy memory usage

In Figure 1-5, we show another memory graph that can be of great importance when performance tuning an application's memory allocation rate. This short example shows a sample application (calculating Fibonnaci numbers). It clearly displays a sharp drop in the allocation rate at around the 90 second mark.

Other graphs from the same tool (jClarity Censum) show that the application starts to suffer from major garbage collection problems at this time, and so the application is unable to allocate sufficient memory due to CPU contention from the garbage collection threads.

We can also spot that the allocation subsystem is running hot—allocating over 4 GB per second. This is well above the recommended maximum capacity of most modern systems (including server class hardware). We will have much more to say about the subject of allocation when we discuss garbage collection in Chapter 6.

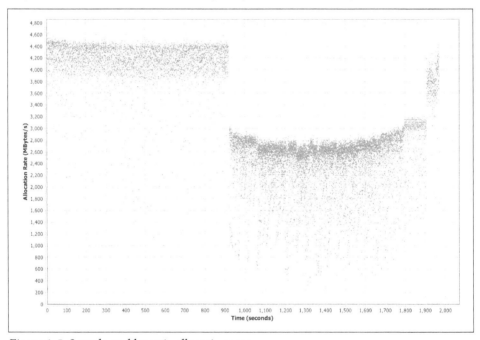

Figure 1-5. Sample problematic allocation rate

In the case where a system has a resource leak, it is far more common for it to manifest in a manner like that shown in Figure 1-6, where an observable (in this case latency) slowly degrades as the load is ramped up, before hitting an inflection point where the system rapidly degrades.

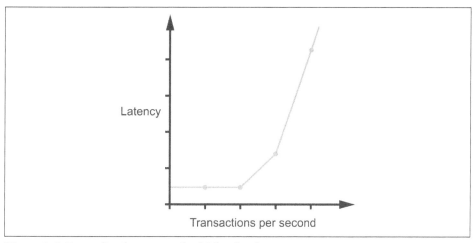

Figure 1-6. Degrading latency under higher load

Summary

In this chapter we have started to discuss what Java performance is and is not. We have introduced the fundamental topics of empirical science and measurement, and the basic vocabulary and observables that a good performance exercise will use. Finally, we have introduced some common cases that are often seen within the results obtained from performance tests. Let's move on and begin our discussion of some of the major aspects of the JVM, and set the scene for understanding what makes JVM-based performance optimization a particularly complex problem.

## CHAPTER 2

Overview of the JVM

There is no doubt that Java is one of the largest technology platforms on the planet, boasting roughly 9–10 million developers (according to Oracle). By design, many developers do not need to know about the low-level intricacies of the platform they work with. This leads to a situation where developers only meet these aspects when a customer complains about performance for the first time.

For developers interested in performance, however, it is important to understand the basics of the JVM technology stack. Understanding JVM technology enables developers to write better software and provides the theoretical background required for investigating performance-related issues.

This chapter introduces how the JVM executes Java in order to provide a basis for deeper exploration of these topics later in the book. In particular, Chapter 9 has an in-depth treatment of bytecode. One strategy for the reader could be to read this chapter now, and then reread it in conjunction with Chapter 9, once some of the other topics have been understood.

Interpreting and Classloading

According to the specification that defines the Java Virtual Machine (usually called the VM Spec), the JVM is a stack-based interpreted machine. This means that rather than having registers (like a physical hardware CPU), it uses an execution stack of partial results and performs calculations by operating on the top value (or values) of that stack.

The basic behavior of the JVM interpreter can be thought of as essentially "a `switch` inside a `while` loop"—processing each opcode of the program independently of the last, using the evaluation stack to hold intermediate values.

As we will see when we delve into the internals of the Oracle/ OpenJDK VM (HotSpot), the situation for real production-grade Java interpreters can be more complex, but *switch-inside-while* is an acceptable mental model for the moment.

When we launch our application using the `java HelloWorld` command, the operating system starts the virtual machine process (the `java` binary). This sets up the Java virtual environment and initializes the stack machine that will actually execute the user code in the *HelloWorld* class file.

The entry point into the application will be the `main()` method of *HelloWorld.class*. In order to hand over control to this class, it must be loaded by the virtual machine before execution can begin.

To achieve this, the Java classloading mechanism is used. When a new Java process is initializing, a chain of classloaders is used. The initial loader is known as the Bootstrap classloader and contains classes in the core Java runtime. In versions of Java up to and including 8, these are loaded from *rt.jar*. In version 9 and later, the runtime has been modularised and the concepts of classloading are somewhat different.

The main point of the Bootstrap classloader is to get a minimal set of classes (which includes essentials such as `java.lang.Object`, `Class`, and `Classloader`) loaded to allow other classloaders to bring up the rest of the system.

Java models classloaders as objects within its own runtime and type system, so there needs to be some way to bring an initial set of classes into existence. Otherwise, there would be a circularity problem in defining what a classloader is.

The Extension classloader is created next; it defines its parent to be the Bootstrap classloader and will delegate to its parent if needed. Extensions are not widely used, but can supply overrides and native code for specific operating systems and platforms. Notably, the Nashorn JavaScript runtime introduced in Java 8 is loaded by the Extension loader.

Finally, the Application classloader is created; it is responsible for loading in user classes from the defined classpath. Some texts unfortunately refer to this as the "System" classloader. This term should be avoided, for the simple reason that it doesn't load the system classes (the Bootstrap classloader does). The Application classloader is encountered extremely frequently, and it has the Extension loader as its parent.

Java loads in dependencies on new classes when they are first encountered during the execution of the program. If a classloader fails to find a class, the behavior is usually to delegate the lookup to the parent. If the chain of lookups reaches the Bootstrap

classloader and it isn't found, a `ClassNotFoundException` will be thrown. It is important that developers use a build process that effectively compiles with the exact same
classpath that will be used in production, as this helps to mitigate this potential issue.

Under normal circumstances Java only loads a class once and a `Class` object is created to represent the class in the runtime environment. However, it is important to
realize that the same class can potentially be loaded twice by different classloaders. As
a result, a class in the system is identified by the classloader used to load it as well as
the fully qualified class name (which includes the package name).

Executing Bytecode

It is important to appreciate that Java source code goes through a significant number
of transformations before execution. The first is the compilation step using the Java
compiler `javac`, often invoked as part of a larger build process.

The job of `javac` is to convert Java code into *.class* files that contain bytecode. It achieves this by doing a fairly straightforward translation of the Java source code, as
shown in Figure 2-1. Very few optimizations are done during compilation by `javac`,
and the resulting bytecode is still quite readable and recognizable as Java code when
viewed in a disassembly tool, such as the standard `javap`.

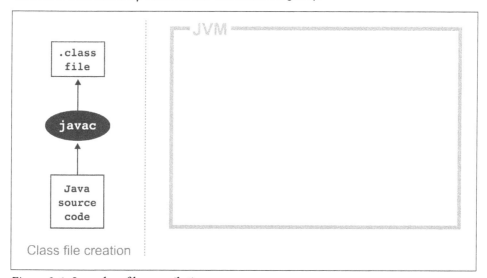

Figure 2-1. Java class file compilation

Bytecode is an intermediate representation that is not tied to a specific machine
architecture. Decoupling from the machine architecture provides portability, meaning already developed (or compiled) software can run on any platform supported by

the JVM and provides an abstraction from the Java language. This provides our first important insight into the way the JVM executes code.

 The Java language and the Java Virtual Machine are now to a degree independent, and so the J in JVM is potentially a little misleading, as the JVM can execute any JVM language that can produce a valid class file. In fact, Figure 2-1 could just as easily show the Scala compiler `scalac` generating bytecode for execution on the JVM.

Regardless of the source code compiler used, the resulting class file has a very well-defined structure specified by the VM specification (Table 2-1). Any class that is loaded by the JVM will be verified to conform to the expected format before being allowed to run.

Table 2-1. Anatomy of a class file

Component	Description
Magic number	0xCAFEBABE
Version of class file format	The minor and major versions of the class file
Constant pool	The pool of constants for the class
Access flags	Whether the class is abstract, static, and so on
This class	The name of the current class
Superclass	The name of the superclass
Interfaces	Any interfaces in the class
Fields	Any fields in the class
Methods	Any methods in the class
Attributes	Any attributes of the class (e.g., name of the source file, etc.)

Every class file starts with the magic number 0xCAFEBABE, the first 4 bytes in hexadecimal serving to denote conformance to the class file format. The following 4 bytes represent the minor and major versions used to compile the class file, and these are checked to ensure that the target JVM is not of a lower version than the one used to compile the class file. The major and minor version are checked by the classloader to ensure compatibility; if these are not compatible an UnsupportedClassVersionError will be thrown at runtime, indicating the runtime is a lower version than the compiled class file.

Magic numbers provide a way for Unix environments to identify the type of a file (whereas Windows will typically use the file extension). For this reason, they are difficult to change once decided upon. Unfortunately, this means that Java is stuck using the rather embarrassing and sexist 0xCAFEBABE for the foreseeable future, although Java 9 introduces the magic number 0xCAFEDADA for module files.

The constant pool holds constant values in code: for example, names of classes, interfaces, and fields. When the JVM executes code, the constant pool table is used to refer to values rather than having to rely on the layout of memory at runtime.

Access flags are used to determine the modifiers applied to the class. The first part of the flag identifies general properties, such as whether a class is public, followed by whether it is final and cannot be subclassed. The flag also determines whether the class file represents an interface or an abstract class. The final part of the flag indicates whether the class file represents a synthetic class that is not present in source code, an annotation type, or an enum.

The this class, superclass, and interface entries are indexes into the constant pool to identify the type hierarchy belonging to the class. Fields and methods define a signature-like structure, including the modifiers that apply to the field or method. A set of attributes is then used to represent structured items for more complicated and non-fixed-size structures. For example, methods make use of the Code attribute to represent the bytecode associated with that particular method.

Figure 2-2 provides a mnemonic for remembering the structure.

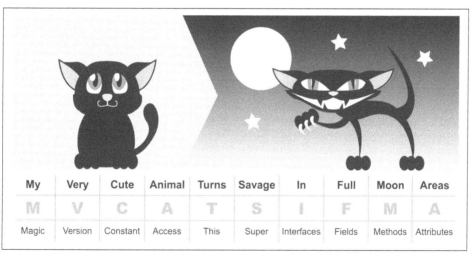

My	Very	Cute	Animal	Turns	Savage	In	Full	Moon	Areas
M	V	C	A	T	S	I	F	M	A
Magic	Version	Constant	Access	This	Super	Interfaces	Fields	Methods	Attributes

Figure 2-2. Mnemonic for class file structure

In this very simple code example, it is possible to observe the effect of running `javac`:

```java
public class HelloWorld {
    public static void main(String[] args) {
        for (int i = 0; i < 10; i++) {
            System.out.println("Hello World");
        }
    }
}
```

Java ships with a class file disassembler called `javap`, allowing inspection of *.class* files. Taking the *HelloWorld* class file and running `javap -c HelloWorld` gives the following output:

```
public class HelloWorld {
  public HelloWorld();
    Code:
       0: aload_0
       1: invokespecial #1     // Method java/lang/Object."<init>":()V
       4: return

  public static void main(java.lang.String[]);
    Code:
       0: iconst_0
       1: istore_1
       2: iload_1
       3: bipush        10
       5: if_icmpge     22
       8: getstatic     #2     // Field java/lang/System.out ...
      11: ldc           #3     // String Hello World
      13: invokevirtual #4     // Method java/io/PrintStream.println ...
      16: iinc          1, 1
      19: goto          2
      22: return
}
```

This layout describes the bytecode for the file *HelloWorld.class*. For more detail `javap` also has a `-v` option that provides the full class file header information and constant pool details. The class file contains two methods, although only the single `main()` method was supplied in the source file; this is the result of `javac` automatically adding a default constructor to the class.

The first instruction executed in the constructor is `aload_0`, which places the `this` reference onto the first position in the stack. The `invokespecial` command is then called, which invokes an instance method that has specific handling for calling super-constructors and creating objects. In the default constructor, the invoke matches the default constructor for `Object`, as an override was not supplied.

Opcodes in the JVM are concise and represent the type, the operation, and the interaction between local variables, the constant pool, and the stack.

Moving on to the `main()` method, `iconst_0` pushes the integer constant 0 onto the evaluation stack. `istore_1` stores this constant value into the local variable at offset 1 (represented as `i` in the loop). Local variable offsets start at 0, but for instance methods, the 0th entry is always `this`. The variable at offset 1 is then loaded back onto the stack and the constant `10` is pushed for comparison using `if_icmpge` ("if integer compare greater or equal"). The test only succeeds if the current integer is >= 10.

For the first few iterations, this comparison test fails and so we continue to instruction 8. Here the static method from `System.out` is resolved, followed by the loading of the "Hello World" string from the constant pool. The next invoke, `invokevirtual`, invokes an instance method based on the class. The integer is then incremented and `goto` is called to loop back to instruction 2.

This process continues until the `if_icmpge` comparison eventually succeeds (when the loop variable is >= 10); on that iteration of the loop, control passes to instruction 22 and the method returns.

Introducing HotSpot

In April 1999 Sun introduced one of the biggest changes to Java in terms of performance. The HotSpot virtual machine is a key feature of Java that has evolved to enable performance that is comparable to (or better than) languages such as C and C++ (see Figure 2-3). To explain how this is possible, let's delve a little deeper into the design of languages intended for application development.

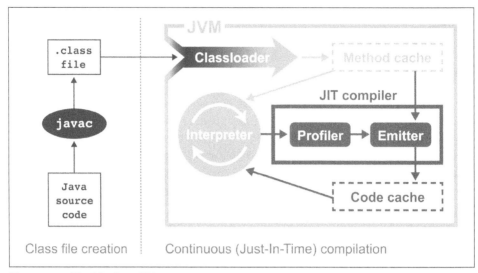

Figure 2-3. The HotSpot JVM

Language and platform design frequently involves making decisions and tradeoffs between desired capabilities. In this case, the division is between languages that stay "close to the metal" and rely on ideas such as "zero-cost abstractions," and languages that favor developer productivity and "getting things done" over strict low-level control.

> C++ implementations obey the zero-overhead principle: What you don't use, you don't pay for. And further: What you do use, you couldn't hand code any better.
>
> —Bjarne Stroustrup

The zero-overhead principle sounds great in theory, but it requires all users of the language to deal with the low-level reality of how operating systems and computers actually work. This is a significant extra cognitive burden that is placed upon developers who may not care about raw performance as a primary goal.

Not only that, but it also requires the source code to be compiled to platform-specific machine code at build time—usually called *Ahead-of-Time* (AOT) compilation. This is because alternative execution models such as interpreters, virtual machines, and portablity layers all are most definitely not zero-overhead.

The principle also hides a can of worms in the phrase "what you do use, you couldn't hand code any better." This presupposes a number of things, not least that the developer is able to produce better code than an automated system. This is not a safe assumption at all. Very few people want to code in assembly language anymore, so the use of automated systems (such as compilers) to produce code is clearly of some benefit to most programmers.

Java has never subscribed to the zero-overhead abstraction philosophy. Instead, the approach taken by the HotSpot virtual machine is to analyze the runtime behavior of your program and intelligently apply optimizations where they will benefit performance the most. The goal of the HotSpot VM is to allow you to write idiomatic Java and follow good design principles rather then contort your program to fit the VM.

Introducing Just-in-Time Compilation

Java programs begin their execution in the bytecode interpreter, where instructions are performed on a virtualized stack machine. This abstraction from the CPU gives the benefit of class file portability, but to get maximum performance your program must execute directly on the CPU, making use of its native features.

HotSpot achieves this by compiling units of your program from interpreted bytecode into native code. The units of compilation in the HotSpot VM are the method and the loop. This is known as *Just-in-Time* (JIT) compilation.

JIT compilation works by monitoring the application while it is running in interpreted mode and observing the parts of code that are most frequently executed. During this analysis process, programmatic trace information is captured that allows for more sophisticated optimization. Once execution of a particular method passes a threshold, the profiler will look to compile and optimize that particular section of code.

There are many advantages to the JIT approach to compilation, but one of the main ones is that it bases compiler optimization decisions on trace information that is collected during the interpreted phase, enabling HotSpot to make more informed optimizations.

Not only that, but HotSpot has had hundreds of engineering years (or more) of development attributed to it and new optimizations and benefits are added with almost every new release. This means that any Java application that runs on top of a new release of HotSpot will be able to take advantage of new performance optimizations present in the VM, without even needing to be recompiled.

After being translated from Java source to bytecode and now going through another step of (JIT) compilation, the code actually being executed has changed very significantly from the source code as written. This is a key insight, and it will drive our approach to dealing with performance-related investigations. JIT-compiled code executing on the JVM may well look nothing like the original Java source code.

The general picture is that languages like C++ (and the up-and-coming Rust) tend to have more predictable performance, but at the cost of forcing a lot of low-level complexity onto the user.

Note that "more predictable" does not necessarily mean "better." AOT compilers produce code that may have to run across a broad class of processors, and may not be able to assume that specific processor features are available.

Environments that use profile-guided optimization (PGO), such as Java, have the potential to use runtime information in ways that are simply impossible to most AOT platforms. This can offer improvements to performance, such as dynamic inlining and optimizing away virtual calls. HotSpot can even detect the precise CPU type it is running on at VM startup, and can use this information to enable optimizations designed for specific processor features if available.

The technique of detecting precise processor capabilities is known as *JVM intrinsics*, and is not to be confused with the intrinsic locks introduced by the synchronized keyword.

A full discussion of PGO and JIT compilation can be found in Chapters 9 and 10.

The sophisticated approach that HotSpot takes is a great benefit to the majority of ordinary developers, but this tradeoff (to abandon zero-overhead abstractions) means that in the specific case of high-performance Java applications, the developer must be very careful to avoid "common sense" reasoning and overly simplistic mental models of how Java applications actually execute.

Analyzing the performance of small sections of Java code (*micro-benchmarks*) is usually actually harder than analyzing entire applications, and is a very specialized task that the majority of developers should not undertake. We will return to this subject in Chapter 5.

HotSpot's compilation subsystem is one of the two most important subsystems that the virtual machine provides. The other is automatic memory management, which was one of the major selling points of Java in the early years.

JVM Memory Management

In languages such as C, C++, and Objective-C the programmer is responsible for managing the allocation and release of memory. The benefits of managing memory and lifetime of objects yourself are more deterministic performance and the ability to tie resource lifetime to the creation and deletion of objects. But these benefits come at a huge cost—for correctness, developers must be able to accurately account for memory.

Unfortunately, decades of practical experience showed that many developers have a poor understanding of idioms and patterns for memory management. Later versions of C++ and Objective-C have improved this using smart pointer idioms in the standard library. However, at the time Java was created poor memory management was a major cause of application errors. This led to concern among developers and managers about the amount of time spent dealing with language features rather than delivering value for the business.

Java looked to help resolve the problem by introducing automatically managed heap memory using a process known as *garbage collection* (GC). Simply put, garbage collection is a nondeterministic process that triggers to recover and reuse no-longer-needed memory when the JVM requires more memory for allocation.

However, the story behind GC is not quite so simple, and various algorithms for garbage collection have been developed and applied over the course of Java's history. GC comes at a cost: when it runs, it often *stops the world*, which means while GC is in progress the application pauses. Usually these pause times are designed to be incredibly small, but as an application is put under pressure they can increase.

Garbage collection is a major topic within Java performance optimization, so we will devote Chapters 6, 7, and 8 to the details of Java GC.

Threading and the Java Memory Model

One of the major advances that Java brought in with its first version was built-in support for multithreaded programming. The Java platform allows the developer to create new threads of execution. For example, in Java 8 syntax:

```
Thread t = new Thread(() -> {System.out.println("Hello World!");});
t.start();
```

Not only that, but the Java environment is inherently multithreaded, as is the JVM. This produces additional, irreducible complexity in the behavior of Java programs, and makes the work of the performance analyst even harder.

In most mainstream JVM implementations, each Java application thread corresponds precisely to a dedicated operating system thread. The alternative, using a shared pool of threads to execute all Java application threads (an approach known as *green threads*), proved not to provide an acceptable performance profile and added needless complexity.

It is safe to assume that every JVM application thread is backed by a unique OS thread that is created when the start() method is called on the corresponding Thread object.

Java's approach to multithreading dates from the late 1990s and has these fundamental design principles:

- All threads in a Java process share a single, common garbage-collected heap.
- Any object created by one thread can be accessed by any other thread that has a reference to the object.
- Objects are mutable by default; that is, the values held in object fields can be changed unless the programmer explicitly uses the final keyword to mark them as immutable.

The Java Memory Model (JMM) is a formal model of memory that explains how different threads of execution see the changing values held in objects. That is, if threads A and B both have references to object obj, and thread A alters it, what happens to the value observed in thread B?

This seemingly simple question is actually more complicated than it seems, because the operating system scheduler (which we will meet in Chapter 3) can forcibly evict threads from CPU cores. This can lead to another thread starting to execute and accessing an object before the original thread had finished processing it, and potentially seeing the object in a damaged or invalid state.

The only defense the core of Java provides against this potential object damage during concurrent code execution is the mutual exclusion lock, and this can be very complex to use in real applications. Chapter 12 contains a detailed look at how the JMM works, and the practicalities of working with threads and locks.

Meet the JVMs

Many developers may only be immediately familiar with the Java implementation produced by Oracle. We have already met the virtual machine that comes from the Oracle implementation, HotSpot. However, there are several other implementations that we will discuss in this book, to varying degrees of depth:

OpenJDK
OpenJDK is an interesting special case. It is an open source (GPL) project that provides the reference implementation of Java. The project is led and supported by Oracle and provides the basis of its Java releases.

Oracle

Oracle's Java is the most widely known implementation. It is based on OpenJDK, but relicensed under Oracle's proprietary license. Almost all changes to Oracle Java start off as commits to an OpenJDK public repository (with the exception of security fixes that have not yet been publicly disclosed).

Zulu

Zulu is a free (GPL-licensed) OpenJDK implementation that is fully Java-certified and provided by Azul Systems. It is unencumbered by proprietary licenses and is freely redistributable. Azul is one of the few vendors to provide paid support for OpenJDK.

IcedTea

Red Hat was the first non-Oracle vendor to produce a fully certified Java implementation based on OpenJDK. IcedTea is fully certified and redistributable.

Zing

Zing is a high-performance proprietary JVM. It is a fully certified implementation of Java and is produced by Azul Systems. It is 64-bit Linux only, and is designed for server-class systems with large heaps (10s of 100s of GB) and a lot of CPU.

J9

IBM's J9 started life as a proprietary JVM but was open-sourced partway through its life (just like HotSpot). It is now built on top of an Eclipse open runtime project (OMR), and forms the basis of IBM's proprietary product. It is fully compliant with Java certification.

Avian

The Avian implementation is not 100% Java conformant in terms of certification. It is included in this list because it is an interesting open source project and a great learning tool for developers interested in understanding the details of how a JVM works, rather than as a 100% production-ready solution.

Android

Google's Android project is sometimes thought of as being "based on Java." However, the picture is actually a little more complicated. Android originally used a different implementation of Java's class libraries (from the clean-room Harmony project) and a cross compiler to convert to a different (*.dex*) file format for a non-JVM virtual machine.

Of these implementations, the great majority of the book focuses on HotSpot. This material applies equally to Oracle Java, Azul Zulu, Red Hat IcedTea, and all other OpenJDK-derived JVMs.

There are essentially no performance-related differences between the various HotSpot-based implementations, when comparing like-for-like versions.

We also include some material related to IBM J9 and Azul Zing. This is intended to provide an awareness of these alternatives rather than a definitive guide. Some readers may wish to explore these technologies more deeply, and they are encouraged to proceed by setting performance goals, and then measuring and comparing, in the usual manner.

Android is moving to use the OpenJDK 8 class libraries with direct support in the Android runtime. As this technology stack is so far from the other examples, we won't consider Android any further in this book.

A Note on Licenses

Almost all of the JVMs we will discuss are open source, and in fact, most of them are derived from the GPL-licensed HotSpot. The exceptions are IBM's Open J9, which is Eclipse-licensed, and Azul Zing, which is commercial (although Azul's Zulu product is GPL).

The situation with Oracle Java (as of Java 9) is slightly more complex. Despite being derived from the OpenJDK code base, it is proprietary, and is *not* open source software. Oracle achieves this by having all contributors to OpenJDK sign a license agreement that permits dual licensing of their contribution to both the GPL of OpenJDK and Oracle's proprietary license.

Each update release to Oracle Java is taken as a branch off the OpenJDK mainline, which is not then patched on-branch for future releases. This prevents divergence of Oracle and OpenJDK, and accounts for the lack of meaningful difference between Oracle JDK and an OpenJDK binary based on the same source.

This means that the only real difference between Oracle JDK and OpenJDK is the license. This may seem an irrelevance, but the Oracle license contains a few clauses that developers should be aware of:

- Oracle does not grant the right to redistribute its binaries outside of your own organization (e.g., as a Docker image).
- You are not permitted to apply a binary patch to an Oracle binary without its agreement (which will usually mean a support contract).

There are also several other commercial features and tools that Oracle makes available that will only work with Oracle's JDK, and within the terms of its license. This situation will be changing with future releases of Java from Oracle, however, as we will discuss in Chapter 15.

When planning a new greenfield deployment, developers and architects should consider carefully their choice of JVM vendor. Some large organizations, notably Twitter and Alibaba, even maintain their own private builds of OpenJDK, although the engineering effort required for this is beyond the reach of many companies.

Monitoring and Tooling for the JVM

The JVM is a mature execution platform, and it provides a number of technology alternatives for instrumentation, monitoring, and observability of running applications. The main technologies available for these types of tools for JVM applications are:

- Java Management Extensions (JMX)
- Java agents
- The JVM Tool Interface (JVMTI)
- The Serviceability Agent (SA)

JMX is a powerful, general-purpose technology for controlling and monitoring JVMs and the applications running on them. It provides the ability to change parameters and call methods in a general way from a client application. A full treatment is, unfortunately, outside the scope of this book. However, JMX (and its associated network transport, RMI) is a fundamental aspect of the management capabilities of the JVM.

A Java agent is a tooling component, written in Java (hence the name), that makes use of the interfaces in `java.lang.instrument` to modify the bytecode of methods. To install an agent, provide a startup flag to the JVM:

```
-javaagent:<path-to-agent-jar>=<options>
```

The agent JAR must contain a manifest and include the attribute `Premain-Class`. This attribute contains the name of the agent class, which must implement a public static `premain()` method that acts as the registration hook for the Java agent.

If the Java instrumentation API is not sufficient, then the JVMTI may be used instead. This is a native interface of the JVM, so agents that make use of it must be written in a native compiled language—essentially, C or C++. It can be thought of as a communication interface that allows a native agent to monitor and be informed of events by the JVM. To install a native agent, provide a slightly different flag:

```
-agentlib:<agent-lib-name>=<options>
```

or:

```
-agentpath:<path-to-agent>=<options>
```

The requirement that JVMTI agents be written in native code means that it is much easier to write code that can damage running applications and even crash the JVM.

Where possible, it is usually preferable to write a Java agent over JVMTI code. Agents are much easier to write, but some information is not available through the Java API, and to access that data JVMTI may be the only possibility available.

The final approach is the Serviceability Agent. This is a set of APIs and tools that can expose both Java objects and HotSpot data structures.

The SA does not require any code to be run in the target VM. Instead, the HotSpot SA uses primitives like symbol lookup and reading of process memory to implement debugging capability. The SA has the ability to debug live Java processes as well as core files (also called *crash dump files*).

VisualVM

The JDK ships with a number of useful additional tools along with the well-known binaries such as javac and java. One tool that is often overlooked is VisualVM, which is a graphical tool based on the NetBeans platform.

jvisualvm is a replacement for the now obsolete jconsole tool from earlier Java versions. If you are still using jconsole, you should move to VisualVM (there is a compatibility plug-in to allow jconsole plug-ins to run inside VisualVM).

Recent versions of Java have shipped solid versions of VisualVM, and the version present in the JDK is now usually sufficient. However, if you need to use a more recent version, you can download the latest version from *http://visualvm.java.net/*. After downloading, you will have to ensure that the visualvm binary is added to your path or you'll get the JRE default binary.

From Java 9 onward, VisualVM is being removed from the main distribution, so developers will have to download the binary separately.

When VisualVM is started for the first time it will calibrate the machine it is running on, so there should be no other applications running that might affect the performance calibration. After calibration, VisualVM will finish starting up and show a splash screen. The most familiar view of VisualVM is the Monitor screen, which is similar to that shown in Figure 2-4.

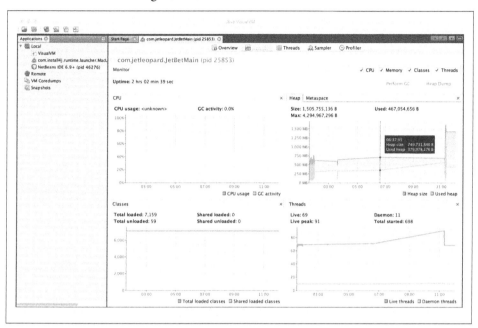

Figure 2-4. VisualVM Monitor screen

VisualVM is used for live monitoring of a running process, and it uses the JVM's *attach mechanism*. This works slightly differently depending on whether the process is local or remote.

Local processes are fairly straightforward. VisualVM lists them down the lefthand side of the screen. Double-clicking on one of them causes it to appear as a new tab in the righthand pane.

To connect to a remote process, the remote side must accept inbound connections (over JMX). For standard Java processes, this means `jstatd` must be running on the remote host (see the manual page for `jstatd` for more details).

 Many application servers and execution containers provide an equivalent capability to `jstatd` directly in the server. Such processes do not need a separate `jstatd` process.

To connect to a remote process, enter the hostname and a display name that will be used on the tab. The default port to connect to is 1099, but this can be changed easily.

Out of the box, VisualVM presents the user with five tabs:

Overview

Provides a summary of information about your Java process. This includes the full flags that were passed in and all system properties. It also displays the exact Java version executing.

Monitor

This is the tab that is the most similar to the legacy JConsole view. It shows high-level telemetry for the JVM, including CPU and heap usage. It also shows the number of classes loaded and unloaded, and an overview of the numbers of threads running.

Threads

Each thread in the running application is displayed with a timeline. This includes both application threads and VM threads. The state of each thread can be seen, with a small amount of history. Thread dumps can also be generated if needed.

Sampler and Profiler

In these views, simplified sampling of CPU and memory utilization can be accessed. This will be discussed more fully in Chapter 13.

The plug-in architecture of VisualVM allows additional tools to be easily added to the core platform to augment the core functionality. These include plug-ins that allow interaction with JMX consoles and bridging to legacy JConsole, and a very useful garbage collection plug-in, VisualGC.

Summary

In this chapter we have taken a quick tour through the overall anatomy of the JVM. It has only been possible to touch on some of the most important subjects, and virtually every topic mentioned here has a rich, full story behind it that will reward further investigation.

In Chapter 3 we will discuss some details of how operating systems and hardware work. This is to provide necessary background for the Java performance analyst to understand observed results. We will also look at the timing subsystem in more detail, as a complete example of how the VM and native subsystems interact.

Hardware and Operating Systems

Why should Java developers care about hardware?

For many years the computer industry has been driven by Moore's Law, a hypothesis made by Intel founder Gordon Moore about long-term trends in processor capability. The law (really an observation or extrapolation) can be framed in a variety of ways, but one of the most usual is:

> The number of transistors on a mass-produced chip roughly doubles every 18 months.

This phenomenon represents an exponential increase in computer power over time. It was originally cited in 1965, so represents an incredible long-term trend, almost unparalleled in the history of human development. The effects of Moore's Law have been transformative in many (if not most) areas of the modern world.

 The death of Moore's Law has been repeatedly proclaimed for decades now. However, there are very good reasons to suppose that, for all practical purposes, this incredible progress in chip technology has (finally) come to an end.

Hardware has become increasingly complex in order to make good use of the "transistor budget" available in modern computers. The software platforms that run on that hardware have also increased in complexity to exploit the new capabilities, so while software has far more power at its disposal it has come to rely on complex underpinnings to access that performance increase.

The net result of this huge increase in the performance available to the ordinary application developer has been the blossoming of complex software. Software applications now pervade every aspect of global society.

Or, to put it another way:

> Software is eating the world.
>
> —Marc Andreessen

As we will see, Java has been a beneficiary of the increasing amount of computer power. The design of the language and runtime has been well suited (or lucky) to make use of this trend in processor capability. However, the truly performance-conscious Java programmer needs to understand the principles and technology that underpin the platform in order to make best use of the available resources.

In later chapters, we will explore the software architecture of modern JVMs and techniques for optimizing Java applications at the platform and code levels. But before turning to those subjects, let's take a quick look at modern hardware and operating systems, as an understanding of those subjects will help with everything that follows.

Introduction to Modern Hardware

Many university courses on hardware architectures still teach a simple-to-understand, classical view of hardware. This "motherhood and apple pie" view of hardware focuses on a simple view of a register-based machine, with arithmetic, logic, and load and store operations. As a result, it overemphasizes C programming as the source of truth as compared to what a CPU actually does. This is, simply, a factually incorrect worldview in modern times.

Since the 1990s the world of the application developer has, to a large extent, revolved around the Intel x86/x64 architecture. This is an area of technology that has undergone radical change, and many advanced features now form important parts of the landscape. The simple mental model of a processor's operation is now completely incorrect, and intuitive reasoning based on it is liable to lead to utterly wrong conclusions.

To help address this, in this chapter, we will discuss several of these advances in CPU technology. We will start with the behavior of memory, as this is by far the most important to a modern Java developer.

Memory

As Moore's Law advanced, the exponentially increasing number of transistors was initially used for faster and faster clock speed. The reasons for this are obvious: faster clock speed means more instructions completed per second. Accordingly, the speed of processors has advanced hugely, and the 2+ GHz processors that we have today are hundreds of times faster than the original 4.77 MHz chips found in the first IBM PC.

However, the increasing clock speeds uncovered another problem. Faster chips require a faster stream of data to act upon. As Figure 3-1 shows,[1] over time main memory could not keep up with the demands of the processor core for fresh data.

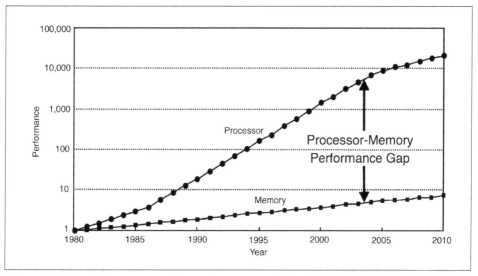

Figure 3-1. Speed of memory and transistor counts (Hennessy and Patterson, 2011)

This results in a problem: if the CPU is waiting for data, then faster cycles don't help, as the CPU will just have to idle until the required data arrives.

Memory Caches

To solve this problem, CPU caches were introduced. These are memory areas on the CPU that are slower than CPU registers, but faster than main memory. The idea is for the CPU to fill the cache with copies of often-accessed memory locations rather than constantly having to re-address main memory.

Modern CPUs have several layers of cache, with the most-often-accessed caches being located close to the processing core. The cache closest to the CPU is usually called *L1* (for "level 1 cache"), with the next being referred to as *L2*, and so on. Different processor architectures have a varying number and configuration of caches, but a common choice is for each execution core to have a dedicated, private L1 and L2 cache, and an L3 cache that is shared across some or all of the cores. The effect of these caches in speeding up access times is shown in Figure 3-2.[2]

---

1 John L. Hennessy and David A. Patterson, *From Computer Architecture: A Quantitative Approach*, 5th ed. (Burlington, MA: Morgan Kaufmann, 2011).

2 Access times shown in terms of number of clock cycles per operation; data provided by Google.

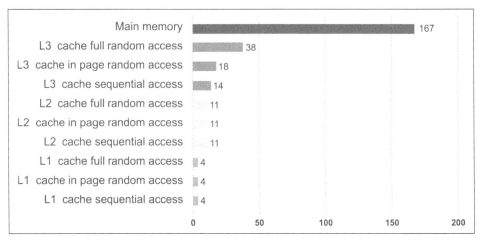

Figure 3-2. Access times for various types of memory

This approach to cache architecture improves access times and helps keep the core fully stocked with data to operate on. Due to the clock speed versus access time gap, more transistor budget is devoted to caches on a modern CPU.

The resulting design can be seen in Figure 3-3. This shows the L1 and L2 caches (private to each CPU core) and a shared L3 cache that is common to all cores on the CPU. Main memory is accessed over the Northbridge component, and it is traversing this bus that causes the large drop-off in access time to main memory.

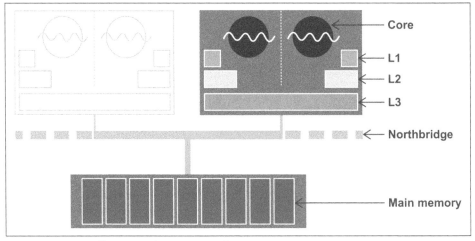

Figure 3-3. Overall CPU and memory architecture

Although the addition of a caching architecture hugely improves processor through-put, it introduces a new set of problems. These problems include determining how memory is fetched into and written back from the cache. The solutions to this prob-lem are usually referred to as *cache consistency protocols*.

 There are other problems that crop up when this type of caching is applied in a parallel processing environment, as we will see later in this book.

At the lowest level, a protocol called MESI (and its variants) is commonly found on a wide range of processors. It defines four states for any line in a cache. Each line (usu-ally 64 bytes) is either:

- Modified (but not yet flushed to main memory)
- Exclusive (present only in this cache, but does match main memory)
- Shared (may also be present in other caches; matches main memory)
- Invalid (may not be used; will be dropped as soon as practical)

The idea of the protocol is that multiple processors can simultaneously be in the Shared state. However, if a processor transitions to any of the other valid states (Exclusive or Modified), then this will force all the other processors into the Invalid state. This is shown in Table 3-1.

Table 3-1. MESI allowable states between processors

	M	E	S	I
M	-	-	-	Y
E	-	-	-	Y
S	-	-	Y	Y
I	Y	Y	Y	Y

The protocol works by broadcasting the intention of a processor to change state. An electrical signal is sent across the shared memory bus, and the other processors are made aware. The full logic for the state transitions is shown in Figure 3-4.

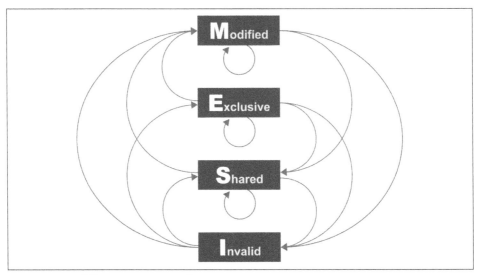

Figure 3-4. MESI state transition diagram

Originally, processors wrote every cache operation directly into main memory. This was called *write-through* behavior, but it was and is very inefficient, and required a large amount of bandwidth to memory. More recent processors also implement *write-back* behavior, where traffic back to main memory is significantly reduced by processors writing only modified (dirty) cache blocks to memory when the cache blocks are replaced.

The overall effect of caching technology is to greatly increase the speed at which data can be written to, or read from, memory. This is expressed in terms of the bandwidth to memory. The *burst rate*, or theoretical maximum, is based on several factors:

- Clock frequency of memory
- Width of the memory bus (usually 64 bits)
- Number of interfaces (usually two in modern machines)

This is multiplied by two in the case of DDR RAM (DDR stands for "double data rate" as it communicates on both edges of a clock signal). Applying the formula to 2015 commodity hardware gives a theoretical maximum write speed of 8–12 GB/s. In practice, of course, this could be limited by many other factors in the system. As it stands, this gives a modestly useful value to allow us to see how close the hardware and software can get.

Let's write some simple code to exercise the cache hardware, as seen in Example 3-1.

Example 3-1. Caching example

```java
public class Caching {

    private final int ARR_SIZE = 2 * 1024 * 1024;
    private final int[] testData = new int[ARR_SIZE];

    private void run() {
        System.err.println("Start: "+ System.currentTimeMillis());
        for (int i = 0; i < 15_000; i++) {
            touchEveryLine();
            touchEveryItem();
        }
        System.err.println("Warmup finished: "+ System.currentTimeMillis());
        System.err.println("Item      Line");
        for (int i = 0; i < 100; i++) {
            long t0 = System.nanoTime();
            touchEveryLine();
            long t1 = System.nanoTime();
            touchEveryItem();
            long t2 = System.nanoTime();
            long elItem = t2 - t1;
            long elLine = t1 - t0;
            double diff = elItem - elLine;
            System.err.println(elItem + " " + elLine +" "+  (100 * diff / elLine));
        }
    }

    private void touchEveryItem() {
        for (int i = 0; i < testData.length; i++)
            testData[i]++;
    }

    private void touchEveryLine() {
        for (int i = 0; i < testData.length; i += 16)
            testData[i]++;
    }

    public static void main(String[] args) {
        Caching c = new Caching();
        c.run();
    }
}
```

Intuitively, touchEveryItem() does 16 times as much work as touchEveryLine(), as 16 times as many data items must be updated. However, the point of this simple example is to show how badly intuition can lead us astray when dealing with JVM performance. Let's look at some sample output from the Caching class, as shown in Figure 3-5.

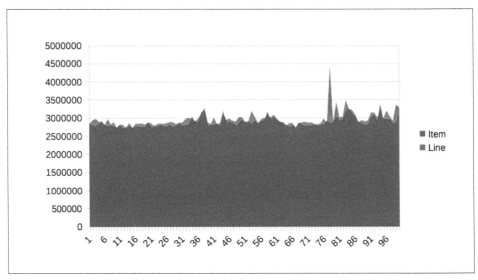

Figure 3-5. Time elapsed for Caching example

The graph shows 100 runs of each function, and is intended to show several different effects. Firstly, notice that the results for both functions are remarkably similar in terms of time taken, so the intuitive expectation of "16 times as much work" is clearly false.

Instead, the dominant effect of this code is to exercise the memory bus, by transferring the contents of the array from main memory into the cache to be operated on by touchEveryItem() and touchEveryLine().

In terms of the statistics of the numbers, although the results are reasonably consistent, there are individual outliers that are 30–35% different from the median value.

Overall, we can see that each iteration of the simple memory function takes around 3 milliseconds (2.86 ms on average) to traverse a 100 MB chunk of memory, giving an effective memory bandwidth of just under 3.5 GB/s. This is less than the theoretical maximum, but is still a reasonable number.

 Modern CPUs have a hardware prefetcher that can detect predictable patterns in data access (usually just a regular "stride" through the data). In this example, we're taking advantage of that fact in order to get closer to a realistic maximum for memory access bandwidth.

One of the key themes in Java performance is the sensitivity of applications to object allocation rates. We will return to this point several times, but this simple example gives us a basic yardstick for how high allocation rates could rise.

Modern Processor Features

Hardware engineers sometimes refer to the new features that have become possible as a result of Moore's Law as "spending the transistor budget." Memory caches are the most obvious use of the growing number of transistors, but other techniques have also appeared over the years.

Translation Lookaside Buffer

One very important use is in a different sort of cache, the Translation Lookaside Buffer (TLB). This acts as a cache for the page tables that map virtual memory addresses to physical addresses, which greatly speeds up a very frequent operation— access to the physical address underlying a virtual address.

There's a memory-related software feature of the JVM that also has the acronym TLB (as we'll see later). Always check which feature is being discussed when you see TLB mentioned.

Without the TLB, all virtual address lookups would take 16 cycles, even if the page table was held in the L1 cache. Performance would be unacceptable, so the TLB is basically essential for all modern chips.

Branch Prediction and Speculative Execution

One of the advanced processor tricks that appear on modern processors is branch prediction. This is used to prevent the processor from having to wait to evaluate a value needed for a conditional branch. Modern processors have multistage instruction pipelines. This means that the execution of a single CPU cycle is broken down into a number of separate stages. There can be several instructions in flight (at different stages of execution) at once.

In this model a conditional branch is problematic, because until the condition is evaluated, it isn't known what the next instruction after the branch will be. This can cause the processor to stall for a number of cycles (in practice, up to 20), as it effectively empties the multistage pipeline behind the branch.

Speculative execution was, famously, the cause of major security problems discovered to affect very large numbers of CPUs in early 2018.

To avoid this, the processor can dedicate transistors to building up a heuristic to decide which branch is more likely to be taken. Using this guess, the CPU fills the pipeline based on a gamble. If it works, then the CPU carries on as though nothing had happened. If it's wrong, then the partially executed instructions are dumped, and the CPU has to pay the penalty of emptying the pipeline.

Hardware Memory Models

The core question about memory that must be answered in a multicore system is "How can multiple different CPUs access the same memory location consistently?"

The answer to this question is highly hardware-dependent, but in general, javac, the JIT compiler, and the CPU are all allowed to make changes to the order in which code executes. This is subject to the provision that any changes don't affect the outcome as observed by the current thread.

For example, let's suppose we have a piece of code like this:

```
myInt = otherInt;
intChanged = true;
```

There is no code between the two assignments, so the executing thread doesn't need to care about what order they happen in, and thus the environment is at liberty to change the order of instructions.

However, this could mean that in another thread that has visibility of these data items, the order could change, and the value of myInt read by the other thread could be the old value, despite intChanged being seen to be true.

This type of reordering (stores moved after stores) is not possible on x86 chips, but as Table 3-2 shows, there are other architectures where it can, and does, happen.

Table 3-2. Hardware memory support

	ARMv7	POWER	SPARC	x86	AMD64	zSeries
Loads moved after loads	Y	Y	-	-	-	-
Loads moved after stores	Y	Y	-	-	-	-
Stores moved after stores	Y	Y	-	-	-	-
Stores moved after loads	Y	Y	Y	Y	Y	Y
Atomic moved with loads	Y	Y	-	-	-	-
Atomic moved with stores	Y	Y	-	-	-	-
Incoherent instructions	Y	Y	Y	Y	-	Y

In the Java environment, the Java Memory Model (JMM) is explicitly designed to be a weak model to take into account the differences in consistency of memory access between processor types. Correct use of locks and volatile access is a major part of ensuring that multithreaded code works properly. This is a very important topic that we will return to in Chapter 12.

There has been a trend in recent years for software developers to seek greater understanding of the workings of hardware in order to derive better performance. The term *mechanical sympathy* has been coined by Martin Thompson and others to describe this approach, especially as applied to the low-latency and high-performance spaces. It can be seen in recent research into lock-free algorithms and data structures, which we will meet toward the end of the book.

Operating Systems

The point of an operating system is to control access to resources that must be shared between multiple executing processes. All resources are finite, and all processes are greedy, so the need for a central system to arbitrate and meter access is essential. Among these scarce resources, the two most important are usually memory and CPU time.

Virtual addressing via the memory management unit (MMU) and its page tables is the key feature that enables access control of memory, and prevents one process from damaging the memory areas owned by another.

The TLBs that we met earlier in the chapter are a hardware feature that improves lookup times to physical memory. The use of the buffers improves performance for software's access time to memory. However, the MMU is usually too low-level for developers to directly influence or be aware of. Instead, let's take a closer look at the OS process scheduler, as this controls access to the CPU and is a far more user-visible piece of the operating system kernel.

The Scheduler

Access to the CPU is controlled by the process scheduler. This uses a queue known as the *run queue* as a waiting area for threads or processes that are eligible to run but which must wait their turn for the CPU. On a modern system there are effectively always more threads/processes that want to run than can, and so this CPU contention requires a mechanism to resolve it.

The job of the scheduler is to respond to interrupts, and to manage access to the CPU cores. The lifecycle of a Java thread is shown in Figure 3-6. In theory, the Java specification permits threading models whereby Java threads do not necessarily correspond to operating system threads. However, in practice, such "green threads" approaches have not proved to be useful, and have been abandoned in mainstream operating environments.

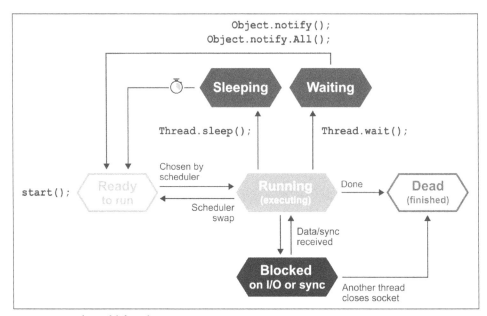

Figure 3-6. Thread lifecycle

In this relatively simple view, the OS scheduler moves threads on and off the single core in the system. At the end of the time quantum (often 10 ms or 100 ms in older operating systems), the scheduler moves the thread to the back of the run queue to wait until it reaches the front of the queue and is eligible to run again.

If a thread wants to voluntarily give up its time quantum it can do so either for a fixed amount of time (via `sleep()`) or until a condition is met (using `wait()`). Finally, a thread can also block on I/O or a software lock.

When you are meeting this model for the first time, it may help to think about a machine that has only a single execution core. Real hardware is, of course, more complex, and virtually any modern machine will have multiple cores, which allows for true simultaneous execution of multiple execution paths. This means that reasoning about execution in a true multiprocessing environment is very complex and counterintuitive.

An often-overlooked feature of operating systems is that by their nature, they introduce periods of time when code is not running on the CPU. A process that has completed its time quantum will not get back on the CPU until it arrives at the front of the run queue again. Combined with the fact that CPU is a scarce resource, this means that code is waiting more often than it is running.

This means that the statistics we want to generate from processes that we actually want to observe are affected by the behavior of other processes on the systems. This "jitter" and the overhead of scheduling is a primary cause of noise in observed results. We will discuss the statistical properties and handling of real results in Chapter 5.

One of the easiest ways to see the action and behavior of a scheduler is to try to observe the overhead imposed by the OS to achieve scheduling. The following code executes 1,000 separate 1 ms sleeps. Each of these sleeps will involve the thread being sent to the back of the run queue, and having to wait for a new time quantum. So, the total elapsed time of the code gives us some idea of the overhead of scheduling for a typical process:

```
long start = System.currentTimeMillis();
for (int i = 0; i < 2_000; i++) {
    Thread.sleep(2);
}
long end = System.currentTimeMillis();
System.out.println("Millis elapsed: " + (end - start) / 4000.0);
```

Running this code will cause wildly divergent results, depending on the operating system. Most Unixes will report roughly 10–20% overhead. Earlier versions of Windows had notoriously bad schedulers, with some versions of Windows XP reporting up to 180% overhead for scheduling (so that 1,000 sleeps of 1 ms would take 2.8 s). There are even reports that some proprietary OS vendors have inserted code into their releases in order to detect benchmarking runs and cheat the metrics.

Timing is of critical importance to performance measurements, to process scheduling, and to many other parts of the application stack, so let's take a quick look at how timing is handled by the Java platform (and a deeper dive into how it is supported by the JVM and the underlying OS).

A Question of Time

Despite the existence of industry standards such as POSIX, different OSs can have very different behaviors. For example, consider the os::javaTimeMillis() function. In OpenJDK this contains the OS-specific calls that actually do the work and ultimately supply the value to be eventually returned by Java's System.currentTimeMillis() method.

As we discussed in "Threading and the Java Memory Model" on page 25, as it relies on functionality that has to be provided by the host operating system, os::javaTimeMillis() has to be implemented as a native method. Here is the function as implemented on BSD Unix (e.g., for Apple's macOS operating system):

```
jlong os::javaTimeMillis() {
  timeval time;
  int status = gettimeofday(&time, NULL);
  assert(status != -1, "bsd error");
  return jlong(time.tv_sec) * 1000  + jlong(time.tv_usec / 1000);
}
```

The versions for Solaris, Linux, and even AIX are all incredibly similar to the BSD case, but the code for Microsoft Windows is completely different:

```
jlong os::javaTimeMillis() {
  if (UseFakeTimers) {
    return fake_time++;
  } else {
    FILETIME wt;
    GetSystemTimeAsFileTime(&wt);
    return windows_to_java_time(wt);
  }
}
```

Windows uses a 64-bit `FILETIME` type to store the time in units of 100 ns elapsed since the start of 1601, rather than the Unix `timeval` structure. Windows also has a notion of the "real accuracy" of the system clock, depending on which physical timing hardware is available. So, the behavior of timing calls from Java can be highly variable on different Windows machines.

The differences between the operating systems do not end with timing, as we will see in the next section.

Context Switches

A *context switch* is the process by which the OS scheduler removes a currently running thread or task and replaces it with one that is waiting. There are several different types of context switch, but broadly speaking, they all involve swapping the executing instructions and the stack state of the thread.

A context switch can be a costly operation, whether between user threads or from user mode into kernel mode (sometimes called a *mode switch*). The latter case is particularly important, because a user thread may need to swap into kernel mode in order to perform some function partway through its time slice. However, this switch will force instruction and other caches to be emptied, as the memory areas accessed by the user space code will not normally have anything in common with the kernel.

A context switch into kernel mode will invalidate the TLBs and potentially other caches. When the call returns, these caches will have to be refilled, and so the effect of a kernel mode switch persists even after control has returned to user space. This causes the true cost of a system call to be masked, as can be seen in Figure 3-7.[3]

---

3 Livio Stoares and Michael Stumm, "FlexSC: Flexible System Call Scheduling with Exception-Less System Calls," in OSDI'10, *Proceedings of the 9th USENIX Conference on Operating Systems Design and Implementation* (Berkeley, CA: USENIX Association, 2010), 33–46.

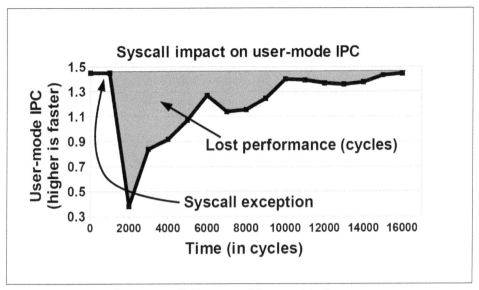

Figure 3-7. Impact of a system call (Soares and Stumm, 2010)

To mitigate this when possible, Linux provides a mechanism known as the *vDSO* (virtual dynamically shared object). This is a memory area in user space that is used to speed up syscalls that do not really require kernel privileges. It achieves this speed increase by not actually performing a context switch into kernel mode. Let's look at an example to see how this works with a real syscall.

A very common Unix system call is `gettimeofday()`. This returns the "wallclock time" as understood by the operating system. Behind the scenes, it is actually just reading a kernel data structure to obtain the system clock time. As this is side-effect-free, it does not actually need privileged access.

If we can use the vDSO to arrange for this data structure to be mapped into the address space of the user process, then there's no need to perform the switch to kernel mode. As a result, the refill penalty shown in Figure 3-7 does not have to be paid.

Given how often most Java applications need to access timing data, this is a welcome performance boost. The vDSO mechanism generalizes this example slightly and can be a useful technique, even if it is available only on Linux.

A Simple System Model

In this section we cover a simple model for describing basic sources of possible performance problems. The model is expressed in terms of operating system observables of fundamental subsystems and can be directly related back to the outputs of standard Unix command-line tools.

The model is based on a simple conception of a Java application running on a Unix or Unix-like operating system. Figure 3-8 shows the basic components of the model, which consist of:

- The hardware and operating system the application runs on
- The JVM (or container) the application runs in
- The application code itself
- Any external systems the application calls
- The incoming request traffic that is hitting the application

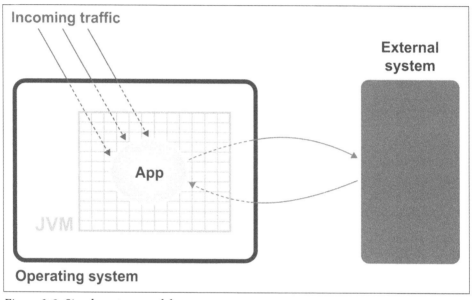

Figure 3-8. Simple system model

Any of these aspects of a system can be responsible for a performance problem. There are some simple diagnostic techniques that can be used to narrow down or isolate particular parts of the system as potential culprits for performance problems, as we will see in the next section.

Basic Detection Strategies

One definition for a well-performing application is that efficient use is being made of system resources. This includes CPU usage, memory, and network or I/O bandwidth.

If an application is causing one or more resource limits to be hit, then the result will be a performance problem.

The first step in any performance diagnosis is to recognize which resource limit is being hit. We cannot tune the appropriate performance metrics without dealing with the resource shortage—by increasing either the available resources or the efficiency of use.

It is also worth noting that the operating system itself should not normally be a major contributing factor to system utilization. The role of an operating system is to manage resources on behalf of user processes, not to consume them itself. The only real exception to this rule is when resources are so scarce that the OS is having difficulty allocating anywhere near enough to satisfy user requirements. For most modern server-class hardware, the only time this should occur is when I/O (or occasionally memory) requirements greatly exceed capability.

Utilizing the CPU

A key metric for application performance is CPU utilization. CPU cycles are quite often the most critical resource needed by an application, and so efficient use of them is essential for good performance. Applications should be aiming for as close to 100% usage as possible during periods of high load.

When you are analyzing application performance, the system must be under enough load to exercise it. The behavior of an idle application is usually meaningless for performance work.

Two basic tools that every performance engineer should be aware of are vmstat and iostat. On Linux and other Unixes, these command-line tools provide immediate and often very useful insight into the current state of the virtual memory and I/O subsystems, respectively. The tools only provide numbers at the level of the entire host, but this is frequently enough to point the way to more detailed diagnostic approaches. Let's take a look at how to use vmstat as an example:

```
$ vmstat 1
 r  b swpd   free    buff   cache   si  so  bi  bo   in   cs us sy  id wa st
 2  0    0 759860 248412 2572248    0   0   0  80   63  127  8  0  92  0  0
 2  0    0 759002 248412 2572248    0   0   0   0   55  103 12  0  88  0  0
 1  0    0 758854 248412 2572248    0   0   0  80   57  116  5  1  94  0  0
 3  0    0 758604 248412 2572248    0   0   0  14   65  142 10  0  90  0  0
 2  0    0 758932 248412 2572248    0   0   0  96   52  100  8  0  92  0  0
 2  0    0 759860 248412 2572248    0   0   0   0   60  112  3  0  97  0  0
```

The parameter 1 following vmstat indicates that we want vmstat to provide ongoing output (until interrupted via Ctrl-C) rather than a single snapshot. New output lines are printed every second, which enables a performance engineer to leave this output running (or capture it into a log) while an initial performance test is performed.

The output of vmstat is relatively easy to understand and contains a large amount of useful information, divided into sections:

1. The first two columns show the number of runnable (r) and blocked (b) processes.

2. In the memory section, the amount of swapped and free memory is shown, followed by the memory used as buffer and as cache.

3. The swap section shows the memory swapped in from and out to disk (si and so). Modern server-class machines should not normally experience very much swap activity.

4. The block in and block out counts (bi and bo) show the number of 512-byte blocks that have been received from and sent to a block (I/O) device.

5. In the system section, the number of interrupts (in) and the number of context switches per second (cs) are displayed.

6. The CPU section contains a number of directly relevant metrics, expressed as percentages of CPU time. In order, they are user time (us), kernel time (sy, for "system time"), idle time (id), waiting time (wa), and "stolen time" (st, for virtual machines).

Over the course of the remainder of this book, we will meet many other, more sophisticated tools. However, it is important not to neglect the basic tools at our disposal. Complex tools often have behaviors that can mislead us, whereas the simple tools that operate close to processes and the operating system can convey clear and uncluttered views of how our systems are actually behaving.

Let's consider an example. In "Context Switches" on page 46 we discussed the impact of a context switch, and we saw the potential impact of a full context switch to kernel space in Figure 3-7. However, whether between user threads or into kernel space, context switches introduce unavoidable wastage of CPU resources.

A well-tuned program should be making maximum possible use of its resources, especially CPU. For workloads that are primarily dependent on computation ("CPU-bound" problems), the aim is to achieve close to 100% utilization of CPU for userland work.

To put it another way, if we observe that the CPU utilization is not approaching 100% user time, then the next obvious question is, "Why not?" What is causing the program to fail to achieve that? Are involuntary context switches caused by locks the problem? Is it due to blocking caused by I/O contention?

The vmstat tool can, on most operating systems (especially Linux), show the number of context switches occurring, so a vmstat 1 run allows the analyst to see the real-time effect of context switching. A process that is failing to achieve 100% userland CPU usage and is also displaying a high context switch rate is likely to be either blocked on I/O or experiencing thread lock contention.

However, vmstat output is not enough to fully disambiguate these cases on its own. vmstat can help analysts detect I/O problems, as it provides a crude view of I/O operations, but to detect thread lock contention in real time, tools like VisualVM that can show the states of threads in a running process should be used. An additional common tool is the statistical thread profiler that samples stacks to provide a view of blocking code.

Garbage Collection

As we will see in Chapter 6, in the HotSpot JVM (by far the most commonly used JVM) memory is allocated at startup and managed from within user space. That means that system calls (such as sbrk()) are not needed to allocate memory. In turn, this means that kernel-switching activity for garbage collection is quite minimal.

Thus, if a system is exhibiting high levels of system CPU usage, then it is definitely not spending a significant amount of its time in GC, as GC activity burns user space CPU cycles and does not impact kernel space utilization.

On the other hand, if a JVM process is using 100% (or close to that) of CPU in user space, then garbage collection is often the culprit. When analyzing a performance problem, if simple tools (such as vmstat) show consistent 100% CPU usage, but with almost all cycles being consumed by user space, then we should ask, "Is it the JVM or user code that is responsible for this utilization?" In almost all cases, high user space utilization by the JVM is caused by the GC subsystem, so a useful rule of thumb is to check the GC log and see how often new entries are being added to it.

Garbage collection logging in the JVM is incredibly cheap, to the point that even the most accurate measurements of the overall cost cannot reliably distinguish it from random background noise. GC logging is also incredibly useful as a source of data for analytics. It is therefore imperative that GC logs be enabled for all JVM processes, especially in production.

We will have a great deal to say about GC and the resulting logs later in the book. However, at this point, we would encourage the reader to consult with their operations staff and confirm whether GC logging is on in production. If not, then one of the key points of Chapter 7 is to build a strategy to enable this.

I/O

File I/O has traditionally been one of the murkier aspects of overall system performance. Partly this comes from its closer relationship with messy physical hardware, with engineers making quips about "spinning rust" and similar, but it is also because I/O lacks abstractions as clean as we see elsewhere in operating systems.

In the case of memory, the elegance of virtual memory as a separation mechanism works well. However, I/O has no comparable abstraction that provides suitable isolation for the application developer.

Fortunately, while most Java programs involve some simple I/O, the class of applications that make heavy use of the I/O subsystems is relatively small, and in particular, most applications do not simultaneously try to saturate I/O at the same time as either CPU or memory.

Not only that, but established operational practice has led to a culture in which production engineers are already aware of the limitations of I/O, and actively monitor processes for heavy I/O usage.

For the performance analyst/engineer, it suffices to have an awareness of the I/O behavior of our applications. Tools such as `iostat` (and even `vmstat`) have the basic counters (e.g., blocks in or out), which are often all we need for basic diagnosis, especially if we make the assumption that only one I/O-intensive application is present per host.

Finally, it's worth mentioning one aspect of I/O that is becoming more widely used across a class of Java applications that have a dependency on I/O but also stringent performance applications.

Kernel bypass I/O

For some high-performance applications, the cost of using the kernel to copy data from, for example, a buffer on a network card and place it into a user space region is prohibitively high. Instead, specialized hardware and software is used to map data directly from a network card into a user-accessible area. This approach avoids a "double copy" as well as crossing the boundary between user space and kernel, as we can see in Figure 3-9.

However, Java does not provide specific support for this model, and instead applications that wish to make use of it rely upon custom (native) libraries to implement the required semantics. It can be a very useful pattern and is increasingly commonly implemented in systems that require very high-performance I/O.

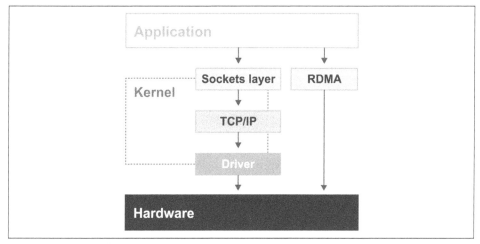

Figure 3-9. Kernel bypass I/O

 In some ways, this is reminiscent of Java's New I/O (NIO) API that was introduced to allow Java I/O to bypass the Java heap and work directly with native memory and underlying I/O.

In this chapter so far we have discussed operating systems running on top of "bare metal." However, increasingly, systems run in virtualized environments, so to conclude this chapter, let's take a brief look at how virtualization can fundamentally change our view of Java application performance.

Mechanical Sympathy

Mechanical sympathy is the idea that having an appreciation of the hardware is invaluable for those cases where we need to squeeze out extra performance.

> You don't have to be an engineer to be a racing driver, but you do have to have mechanical sympathy.
>
> —Jackie Stewart

The phrase was originally coined by Martin Thompson, as a direct reference to Jackie Stewart and his car. However, as well as the extreme cases, it is also useful to have a baseline understanding of the concerns outlined in this chapter when dealing with production problems and looking at improving the overall performance of your application.

For many Java developers, mechanical sympathy is a concern that it is possible to ignore. This is because the JVM provides a level of abstraction away from the hardware to unburden the developer from a wide range of performance concerns. Developers can use Java and the JVM quite successfully in the high-performance and low-latency space, by gaining an understanding of the JVM and the interaction it has with hardware. One important point to note is that the JVM actually makes reasoning about performance and mechanical sympathy harder, as there is more to consider. In Chapter 14 we will describe how high-performance logging and messaging systems work and how mechanical sympathy is appreciated.

Let's look at an example: the behavior of cache lines.

In this chapter we have discussed the benefit of processor caching. The use of cache lines enables the fetching of blocks of memory. In a multithreaded environment cache lines can cause a problem when you have two threads attempting to read or write to a variable located on the same cache line.

A race essentially occurs where two threads now attempt to modify the same cache line. The first one will invalidate the cache line on the second thread, causing it to be reread from memory. Once the second thread has performed the operation, it will then invalidate the cache line in the first. This ping-pong behavior results in a drop-off in performance known as *false sharing*—but how can this be fixed?

Mechanical sympathy would suggest that first we need to understand that this is happening and only after that determine how to resolve it. In Java the layout of fields in an object is not guaranteed, meaning it is easy to find variables sharing a cache line. One way to get around this would be to add padding around the variables to force them onto a different cache line. "Queues" on page 361 will demonstrate one way we can achieve this using a low-level queue in the Agrona project.

Virtualization

Virtualization comes in many forms, but one of the most common is to run a copy of an operating system as a single process on top of an already running OS. This leads to the situation represented in Figure 3-10, where the virtual environment runs as a process inside the unvirtualized (or "real") operating system that is executing on bare metal.

A full discussion of virtualization, the relevant theory, and its implications for application performance tuning would take us too far afield. However, some mention of the differences that virtualization causes seems appropriate, especially given the increasing amount of applications running in virtual, or cloud, environments.

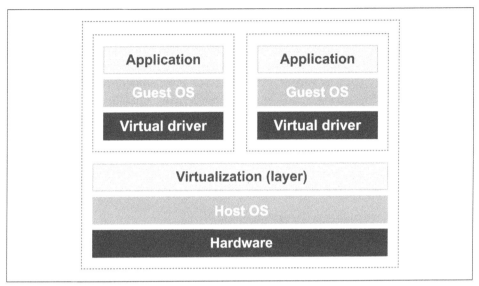

Figure 3-10. Virtualization of operating systems

Although virtualization was originally developed in IBM mainframe environments as early as the 1970s, it was not until recently that x86 architectures were capable of supporting "true" virtualization. This is usually characterized by these three conditions:

- Programs running on a virtualized OS should behave essentially the same as when running on bare metal (i.e., unvirtualized).

- The hypervisor must mediate all access to hardware resources.

- The overhead of the virtualization must be as small as possible, and not a significant fraction of execution time.

In a normal, unvirtualized system, the OS kernel runs in a special, privileged mode (hence the need to switch into kernel mode). This gives the OS direct access to hardware. However, in a virtualized system, direct access to hardware by a guest OS is prohibited.

One common approach is to rewrite the privileged instructions in terms of unprivileged instructions. In addition, some of the OS kernel's data structures need to be "shadowed" to prevent excessive cache flushing (e.g., of TLBs) during context switches.

Some modern Intel-compatible CPUs have hardware features designed to improve the performance of virtualized OSs. However, it is apparent that even with hardware assists, running inside a virtual environment presents an additional level of complexity for performance analysis and tuning.

The JVM and the Operating System

The JVM provides a portable execution environment that is independent of the operating system, by providing a common interface to Java code. However, for some fundamental services, such as thread scheduling (or even something as mundane as getting the time from the system clock), the underlying operating system must be accessed.

This capability is provided by native methods, which are denoted by the keyword native. They are written in C, but are accessible as ordinary Java methods. This interface is referred to as the Java Native Interface (JNI). For example, java.lang.Object declares these nonprivate native methods:

```
public final native Class<?> getClass();
public native int hashCode();
protected native Object clone() throws CloneNotSupportedException;
public final native void notify();
public final native void notifyAll();
public final native void wait(long timeout) throws InterruptedException;
```

As all these methods deal with relatively low-level platform concerns, let's look at a more straightforward and familiar example: getting the system time.

Consider the os::javaTimeMillis() function. This is the (system-specific) code responsible for implementing the Java System.currentTimeMillis() static method. The code that does the actual work is implemented in C++, but is accessed from Java via a "bridge" of C code. Let's look at how this code is actually called in HotSpot.

As you can see in Figure 3-11, the native System.currentTimeMillis() method is mapped to the JVM entry point method JVM_CurrentTimeMillis(). This mapping is achieved via the JNI Java_java_lang_System_registerNatives() mechanism contained in *java/lang/System.c*.

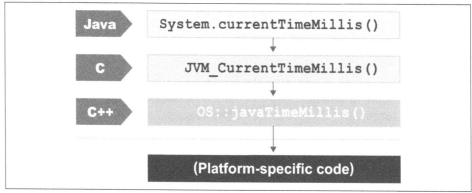

Figure 3-11. The HotSpot calling stack

`JVM_CurrentTimeMillis()` is a call to the VM entry point method. This presents as a C function but is really a C++ function exported with a C calling convention. The call boils down to the call `os::javaTimeMillis()` wrapped in a couple of OpenJDK macros.

This method is defined in the `os` namespace, and is unsurprisingly operating system–dependent. Definitions for this method are provided by the OS-specific subdirectories of source code within OpenJDK. This provides a simple demonstration of how the platform-independent parts of Java can call into services that are provided by the underlying operating system and hardware.

Summary

Processor design and modern hardware have changed enormously over the last 20 years. Driven by Moore's Law and by engineering limitations (notably the relatively slow speed of memory), advances in processor design have become somewhat esoteric. The cache miss rate has become the most obvious leading indicator of how performant an application is.

In the Java space, the design of the JVM allows it to make use of additional processor cores even for single-threaded application code. This means that Java applications have received significant performance advantages from hardware trends, compared to other environments.

As Moore's Law fades, attention will turn once again to the relative performance of software. Performance-minded engineers need to understand at least the basic points of modern hardware and operating systems to ensure that they can make the most of their hardware and not fight against it.

In the next chapter we will introduce the core methodology of performance tests. We will discuss the primary types of performance tests, the tasks that need to be undertaken, and the overall lifecycle of performance work. We will also catalogue some common best practices (and antipatterns) in the performance space.

## CHAPTER 4

Performance Testing Patterns and Antipatterns

Performance testing is undertaken for a variety of reasons. In this chapter we will introduce the different types of test that a team may wish to execute, and discuss best practices for each type.

In the second half of the chapter, we will outline some of the more common antipatterns that can plague a performance test or team, and explain refactored solutions to help prevent them from becoming a problem for teams.

Types of Performance Test

Performance tests are frequently conducted for the wrong reasons, or conducted badly. The reasons for this vary widely, but are often rooted in a failure to understand the nature of performance analysis and a belief that "something is better than nothing." As we will see repeatedly, this belief is often a dangerous half-truth at best.

One of the more common mistakes is to speak generally of "performance testing" without engaging with the specifics. In fact, there are many different types of large-scale performance tests that can be conducted on a system.

 Good performance tests are quantitative. They ask questions that produce a numeric answer that can be handled as an experimental output and subjected to statistical analysis.

The types of performance tests we will discuss in this book usually have mostly independent (but somewhat overlapping) goals, so you should take care when thinking about the domain of any given single test. A good rule of thumb when planning a performance test is simply to write down (and confirm to management/the customer) the quantitative questions that the test is intended to answer, and why they are important for the application under test.

Some of the most common test types, and an example question for each, are as follows:

Latency test
    What is the end-to-end transaction time?

Throughput test
    How many concurrent transactions can the current system capacity deal with?

Load test
    Can the system handle a specific load?

Stress test
    What is the breaking point of the system?

Endurance test
    What performance anomalies are discovered when the system is run for an extended period?

Capacity planning test
    Does the system scale as expected when additional resources are added?

Degradation
    What happens when the system is partially failed?

Let's look in more detail at each of these test types in turn.

Latency Test

This is one of the most common types of performance test, usually because it can be closely related to a system observable that is of direct interest to management: how long are our customers waiting for a transaction (or a page load)? This is a double-edged sword, because the quantitative question that a latency test seeks to answer seems so obvious that it can obscure the necessity of identifying quantitative questions for other types of performance tests.

The goal of a latency tuning exercise is usually to directly improve the user experience, or to meet a service-level agreement.

However, even in the simplest of cases, a latency test has some subtleties that must be treated carefully. One of the most noticeable is that (as we will discuss fully in "Statistics for JVM Performance" on page 99) a simple mean (average) is not very useful as a measure of how well an application is reacting to requests.

Throughput Test

Throughput is probably the second most common quantity to be performance-tested. It can even be thought of as equivalent to latency, in some senses.

For example, when we are conducting a latency test, it is important to state (and control) the concurrent transactions ongoing when producing a distribution of latency results.

 The observed latency of a system should be stated at known and controlled throughput levels.

Equally, we usually conduct a throughput test while monitoring latency. We determine the "maximum throughput" by noticing when the latency distribution suddenly changes—effectively a "breaking point" (also called an *inflection point*) of the system. The point of a stress test, as we will see, is to locate such points and the load levels at which they occur.

A throughput test, on the other hand, is about measuring the observed maximum throughput before the system starts to degrade.

Load Test

A load test differs from a throughput test (or a stress test) in that it is usually framed as a binary test: "Can the system handle this projected load or not?" Load tests are sometimes conducted in advance of expected business events—for example, the onboarding of a new customer or market that is expected to drive greatly increased traffic to the application. Other examples of possible events that could warrant performing this type of test include advertising campaigns, social media events, and "viral content."

Stress Test

One way to think about a stress test is as a way to determine how much spare headroom the system has. The test typically proceeds by placing the system into a steady state of transactions—that is, a specified throughput level (often the current peak).

The test then ramps up the concurrent transactions slowly, until the system observables start to degrade.

The value just before the observables started to degrade determines the maximum throughput achieved in a throughput test.

Endurance Test

Some problems manifest only over much longer periods of time (often measured in days). These include slow memory leaks, cache pollution, and memory fragmentation (especially for applications that use the Concurrent Mark and Sweep garbage collector, which may eventually suffer concurrent mode failure; see "CMS" on page 148 for more details).

To detect these types of issues, an endurance test (also known as a soak test) is the usual approach. These are run at average (or high) utilization, but within observed loads for the system. During the test, resource levels are closely monitored to spot any breakdowns or exhaustions of resources.

This type of test is very common in fast-response (or low-latency) systems, as it is very common that those systems will not be able to tolerate the length of a stop-the-world event caused by a full GC cycle (see Chapter 6 and subsequent chapters for more on stop-the-world events and related GC concepts).

Capacity Planning Test

Capacity planning tests bear many similarities to stress tests, but they are a distinct type of test. The role of a stress test is to find out what the current system will cope with, whereas a capacity planning test is more forward-looking and seeks to find out what load an upgraded system could handle.

For this reason, capacity planning tests are often carried out as part of a scheduled planning exercise, rather than in response to a specific event or threat.

Degradation Test

A degradation test is also known as a partial failure test. A general discussion of resilience and fail-over testing is outside the scope of this book, but suffice it to say that in the most highly regulated and scrutinized environments (including banks and financial institutions), failover and recovery testing is taken extremely seriously and is usually planned in meticulous depth.

For our purposes, the only type of resilience test we consider is the degradation test. The basic approach to this test is to see how the system behaves when a component or entire subsystem suddenly loses capacity while the system is running at simulated loads equivalent to usual production volumes. Examples could be application server clusters that suddenly lose members, databases that suddenly lose RAID disks, or network bandwidth that suddenly drops.

Key observables during a degradation test include the transaction latency distribution and throughput.

One particularly interesting subtype of partial failure test is known as the *Chaos Monkey*. This is named after a project at Netflix that was undertaken to verify the robustness of its infrastructure.

The idea behind Chaos Monkey is that in a truly resilient architecture, the failure of a single component should not be able to cause a cascading failure or have a meaningful impact on the overall system.

Chaos Monkey attempts to demonstrate this by randomly killing off live processes that are actually in use in the production environment.

In order to successfully implement Chaos Monkey–type systems, an organization must have the highest levels of system hygiene, service design, and operational excellence. Nevertheless, it is an area of interest and aspiration for an increasing number of companies and teams.

Best Practices Primer

When deciding where to focus your effort in a performance tuning exercise, there are three golden rules that can provide useful guidance:

- Identify what you care about and figure out how to measure it.
- Optimize what matters, not what is easy to optimize.
- Play the big points first.

The second point has a converse, which is to remind yourself not to fall into the trap of attaching too much significance to whatever quantity you can easily measure. Not every observable is significant to a business, but it is sometimes tempting to report on an easy measure, rather than the right measure.

Top-Down Performance

One of the aspects of Java performance that many engineers miss at first encounter is that large-scale benchmarking of Java applications is usually easier than trying to get accurate numbers for small sections of code. We will discuss this in detail in Chapter 5.

The approach of starting with the performance behavior of an entire application is usually called *top-down* performance.

To make the most of the top-down approach, a testing team needs a test environment, a clear understanding of what it needs to measure and optimize, and an understanding of how the performance exercise will fit into the overall software development lifecycle.

Creating a Test Environment

Setting up a test environment is one of the first tasks most performance testing teams will need to undertake. Wherever possible, this should be an exact duplicate of the production environment, in all aspects. This includes not only application servers (which servers should have the same number of CPUs, same version of the OS and Java runtime, etc.), but web servers, databases, load balancers, network firewalls, and so on. Any services (e.g., third-party network services that are not easy to replicate, or do not have sufficient QA capacity to handle a production-equivalent load) will need to be mocked for a representative performance testing environment.

Sometimes teams try to reuse or time-share an existing QA environment for performance testing. This can be possible for smaller environments or for one-off testing, but the management overhead and scheduling and logistical problems that it can cause should not be underestimated.

Performance testing environments that are significantly different from the production environments that they attempt to represent often fail to achieve results that have any usefulness or predictive power in the live environment.

For traditional (i.e., non-cloud-based) environments, a production-like performance testing environment is relatively straightforward to achieve: the team simply buys as many physical machines as are in use in the production environment and then configures them in exactly the same way as production is configured.

Management is sometimes resistant to the additional infrastructure cost that this represents. This is almost always a false economy, but sadly many organizations fail to account correctly for the cost of outages. This can lead to a belief that the savings from not having an accurate performance testing environment are meaningful, as it fails to properly account for the risks introduced by having a QA environment that does not mirror production.

Recent developments, notably the advent of cloud technologies, have changed this rather traditional picture. On-demand and autoscaling infrastructure means that an increasing number of modern architectures no longer fit the model of "buy servers, draw network diagram, deploy software on hardware." The devops approach of treating server infrastructure as "livestock, not pets" means that much more dynamic approaches to infrastructure management are becoming widespread.

This makes the construction of a performance testing environment that looks like production potentially more challenging. However, it raises the possibility of setting up a testing environment that can be turned off when not in use. This can bring significant cost savings to the project, but it requires a proper process for starting up and shutting down the environment as scheduled.

Identifying Performance Requirements

Let's recall the simple system model that we met in "A Simple System Model" on page 47. This clearly shows that the overall performance of a system is not solely determined by your application code. The container, operating system, and hardware all have a role to play.

Therefore, the metrics that we will use to evaluate performance should not be thought about solely in terms of the code. Instead, we must consider systems as a whole and the observable quantities that are important to customers and management. These are usually referred to as performance *nonfunctional requirements* (NFRs), and are the key indicators that we want to optimize.

Some goals are obvious:

- Reduce 95% percentile transaction time by 100 ms.
- Improve system so that 5x throughput on existing hardware is possible.
- Improve average response time by 30%.

Others may be less apparent:

- Reduce resource cost to serve the average customer by 50%.
- Ensure system is still within 25% of response targets, even when application clusters are degraded by 50%.
- Reduce customer "drop-off" rate by 25% per 25 ms of latency.

An open discussion with the stakeholders as to exactly what should be measured and what goals are to be achieved is essential. Ideally, this discussion should form part of the first kick-off meeting for the performance exercise.

Java-Specific Issues

Much of the science of performance analysis is applicable to any modern software system. However, the nature of the JVM is such that there are certain additional complications that the performance engineer should be aware of and consider carefully. These largely stem from the dynamic self-management capabilities of the JVM, such as the dynamic tuning of memory areas.

One particularly important Java-specific insight is related to JIT compilation. Modern JVMs analyze which methods are being run to identify candidates for JIT compilation to optimized machine code. This means that if a method is not being JIT-compiled, then one of two things is true about the method:

- It is not being run frequently enough to warrant being compiled.
- The method is too large or complex to be analyzed for compilation.

The second condition is much rarer than the first. However, one early performance exercise for JVM-based applications is to switch on simple logging of which methods are being compiled and ensure that the important methods for the application's key code paths are being compiled.

In Chapter 9 we will discuss JIT compilation in detail, and show some simple techniques for ensuring that the important methods of applications are targeted for JIT compilation by the JVM.

Performance Testing as Part of the SDLC

Some companies and teams prefer to think of performance testing as an occasional, one-off activity. However, more sophisticated teams tend to make ongoing performance tests, and in particular performance regression testing, an integral part of their software development lifecycle (SDLC).

This requires collaboration between developers and infrastructure teams to control which versions of code are present in the performance testing environment at any given time. It is also virtually impossible to implement without a dedicated testing environment.

Having discussed some of the most common best practices for performance, let's now turn our attention to the pitfalls and antipatterns that teams can fall prey to.

Introducing Performance Antipatterns

An antipattern is an undesired behavior of a software project or team that is observed across a large number of projects.[1] The frequency of occurrence leads to the conclusion (or suspicion) that some underlying factor is responsible for creating the unwanted behavior. Some antipatterns may at first sight seem to be justified, with their nonideal aspects not immediately obvious. Others are the result of negative project practices slowly accreting over time.

In some cases the behavior may be driven by social or team constraints, or by common misapplied management techniques, or by simple human (and developer) nature. By classifying and categorizing these unwanted features, we develop a "pattern language" for discussing them, and hopefully eliminating them from our projects.

Performance tuning should always be treated as a very objective process, with precise goals set early in the planning phase. This is easier said than done: when a team is under pressure or not operating under reasonable circumstances, this can simply fall by the wayside.

Many readers will have seen the situation where a new client is going live or a new feature is being launched, and an unexpected outage occurs—in user acceptance testing (UAT) if you are lucky, but often in production. The team is then left scrambling to find and fix what has caused the bottleneck. This usually means performance testing has not been carried out, or the team "ninja" made an assumption and has now disappeared (ninjas are good at this).

A team that works in this way will likely fall victim to antipatterns more often than a team that follows good performance testing practices and has open and reasoned conversations. As with many development issues, it is often the human elements, such as communication problems, rather than any technical aspect that leads to an application having problems.

One interesting possibility for classification was provided in a blog post by Carey Flichel called "Why Developers Keep Making Bad Technology Choices" (*http://www.carfey.com/blog/why-developers-keep-making-bad-technology-choices/*). The post specifically calls out five main reasons that cause developers to make bad choices. Let's look at each in turn.

---

[1] The term was popularized by the book *AntiPatterns: Refactoring Software, Architectures, and Projects in Crisis*, by William J. Brown, Raphael C. Malvo, Hays W. McCormick III, and Thomas J. Malbray (New York: Wiley, 1998).

Boredom

Most developers have experienced boredom in a role, and for some this doesn't have to last very long before they are seeking a new challenge or role either in the company or elsewhere. However, other opportunities may not be present in the organization, and moving somewhere else may not be possible.

It is likely many readers have come across a developer who is simply riding it out, perhaps even actively seeking an easier life. However, bored developers can harm a project in a number of ways. For example, they might introduce code complexity that is not required, such as writing a sorting algorithm directly in code when a simple `Collections.sort()` would be sufficient. They might also express their boredom by looking to build components with technologies that are unknown or perhaps don't fit the use case just as an opportunity to use them—which leads us to the next section.

Résumé Padding

Occasionally the overuse of technology is not tied to boredom, but rather represents the developer exploiting an opportunity to boost their experience with a particular technology on their résumé (or CV). In this scenario, the developer is making an active attempt to increase their potential salary and marketability as they're about to re-enter the job market. It's unlikely that many people would get away with this inside a well-functioning team, but it can still be the root of a choice that takes a project down an unnecessary path.

The consequences of an unnecessary technology being added due to a developer's boredom or résumé padding can be far-reaching and very long-lived, lasting for many years after the original developer has left for greener pastures.

Peer Pressure

Technical decisions are often at their worst when concerns are not voiced or discussed at the time choices are being made. This can manifest in a few ways; for example, perhaps a junior developer doesn't want to make a mistake in front of more senior members of their team ("imposter syndrome"), or perhaps a developer fears coming across as uninformed on a particular topic. Another particularly toxic type of peer pressure is for competitive teams, wanting to be seen as having high development velocity, to rush key decisions without fully exploring all of the consequences.

Lack of Understanding

Developers may look to introduce new tools to help solve a problem because they are not aware of the full capability of their current tools. It is often tempting to turn to a new and exciting technology component because it is great at performing one specific task. However, introducing more technical complexity must be taken on balance with what the current tools can actually do.

For example, Hibernate is sometimes seen as the answer to simplifying translation between domain objects and databases. If there is only limited understanding of Hibernate on the team, developers can make assumptions about its suitability based on having seen it used in another project.

This lack of understanding can cause overcomplicated usage of Hibernate and unrecoverable production outages. By contrast, rewriting the entire data layer using simple JDBC calls allows the developer to stay on familiar territory. One of the authors taught a Hibernate course that contained a delegate in exactly this position; he was trying to learn enough Hibernate to see if the application could be recovered, but ended up having to rip out Hibernate over the course of a weekend—definitely not an enviable position.

Misunderstood/Nonexistent Problem

Developers may often use a technology to solve a particular issue where the problem space itself has not been adequately investigated. Without having measured performance values, it is almost impossible to understand the success of a particular solution. Often collating these performance metrics enables a better understanding of the problem.

To avoid antipatterns it is important to ensure that communication about technical issues is open to all participants in the team, and actively encouraged. Where things are unclear, gathering factual evidence and working on prototypes can help to steer team decisions. A technology may look attractive; however, if the prototype does not measure up then the team can make a more informed decision.

Performance Antipatterns Catalogue

In this section we will present a short catalogue of performance antipatterns. The list is by no means exhaustive, and there are doubtless many more still to be discovered.

Distracted by Shiny

Description

The newest or coolest tech is often the first tuning target, as it can be more exciting to explore how newer technology works than to dig around in legacy code. It may also be that the code accompanying the newer technology is better written and easier to maintain. Both of these facts push developers toward looking at the newer components of the application.

Example comment

"It's teething trouble—we need to get to the bottom of it."

Reality

- This is often just a shot in the dark rather than an effort at targeted tuning or measuring of the application.
- The developer may not fully understand the new technology yet, and will tinker around rather than examine the documentation—often in reality causing other problems.
- In the case of new technologies, examples online are often for small or sample datasets and don't discuss good practice about scaling to an enterprise size.

Discussion

This antipattern is common in newly formed or less experienced teams. Eager to prove themselves, or to avoid becoming tied to what they see as *legacy* systems, they are often advocates for newer, "hotter" technologies—which may, coincidentally, be exactly the sort of technologies that would confer a salary uptick in any new role.

Therefore, the logical subconscious conclusion is that any performance issue should be approached by first taking a look at the new tech. After all, it's not properly understood, so a fresh pair of eyes would be helpful, right?

Resolutions

- Measure to determine the real location of the bottleneck.
- Ensure adequate logging around the new component.
- Look at best practices as well as simplified demos.
- Ensure the team understands the new technology and establish a level of best practice across the team.

Distracted by Simple

Description

The team targets the simplest parts of the system first, rather than profiling the application overall and objectively looking for pain points in it. There may be parts of the system deemed "specialist" that only the original wizard who wrote them can edit.

Example comments

"Let's get into this by starting with the parts we understand."

"John wrote that part of the system, and he's on holiday. Let's wait until he's back to look at the performance."

Reality

- The original developer understands how to tune (only?) that part of the system.
- There has been no knowledge sharing or pair programming on the various system components, creating single experts.

Discussion

The dual of Distracted by Shiny, this antipattern is often seen in a more established team, which may be more used to a maintenance or keep-the-lights-on role. If the application has recently been merged or paired with newer technology, the team may feel intimidated or not want to engage with the new systems.

Under these circumstances, developers may feel more comfortable profiling only those parts of the system that are familiar, hoping that they will be able to achieve the desired goals without going outside of their comfort zone.

Of particular note is that both of these first two antipatterns are driven by a reaction to the unknown. In Distracted by Shiny, this manifests as a desire by the developer (or team) to learn more and gain advantage—essentially an offensive play. By contrast, Distracted by Simple is a defensive reaction, playing to the familiar rather than engaging with a potentially threatening new technology.

Resolutions

- Measure to determine the real location of the bottleneck.
- Ask for help from domain experts if the problem is in an unfamiliar component.
- Ensure that developers understand all components of the system.

Performance Tuning Wizard

Description

Management has bought into the Hollywood image of a "lone genius" hacker and hired someone who fits the stereotype, to move around the company and fix all performance issues, by using their perceived superior performance tuning skills.

There are genuine performance tuning experts and companies out there, but most would agree that you have to measure and investigate any problem. It's unlikely the same solution will apply to all uses of a particular technology in all situations.

Example comment

"I'm sure I know just where the problem is..."

Reality

- The only thing a perceived wizard or superhero is likely to do is challenge the dress code.

Discussion

This antipattern can alienate developers in the team who perceive themselves to not be good enough to address performance issues. It's concerning, as in many cases a small amount of profiler-guided optimization can lead to good performance increases (see Chapter 13).

That is not to say that there aren't specialists that can help with specific technologies, but the thought that there is a lone genius who will understand all performance issues from the beginning is absurd. Many technologists that are performance experts are specialists at measuring and problem solving based on those measurements.

Superhero types in teams can be very counterproductive if they are not willing to share knowledge or the approaches that they took to resolving a particular issue.

Resolutions

- Measure to determine the real location of the bottleneck.
- Ensure that any experts hired onto a team are willing to share and act as part of the team.

Tuning by Folklore

Description

While desperate to try to find a solution to a performance problem in production, a team member finds a "magic" configuration parameter on a website. Without testing the parameter the team applies it to production, because it must improve things exactly as it has for the person on the internet...

Example comment

"I found these great tips on Stack Overflow. This changes *everything*."

Reality

- The developer does not understand the context or basis of the performance tip, and the true impact is unknown.

- It may have worked for that specific system, but that doesn't mean the change will even have a benefit in another. In reality, it could make things worse.

Discussion

A performance tip is a workaround for a known problem—essentially a solution looking for a problem. Performance tips have a shelf life and usually age badly; someone will come up with a solution that will render the tip useless (at best) in a later release of the software or platform.

One source of performance advice that is usually particularly bad is admin manuals. They contain general advice devoid of context. Lawyers often insist on this vague advice and "recommended configurations" as an additional line of defense if the vendor is sued.

Java performance happens in a specific context, with a large number of contributing factors. If we strip away this context, then what is left is almost impossible to reason about, due to the complexity of the execution environment.

 The Java platform is also constantly evolving, which means a parameter that provided a performance workaround in one version of Java may not work in another.

For example, the switches used to control garbage collection algorithms frequently change between releases. What works in an older VM (version 7 or 6) may not be applied in the current version (Java 8). There are even switches that are valid and useful in version 7 that will cause the VM not to start up in the forthcoming version 9.

Configuration can be a one- or two-character change, but have significant impact in a production environment if not carefully managed.

Resolutions

- Only apply well-tested and well-understood techniques that directly affect the most important aspects of the system.

- Look for and try out parameters in UAT, but as with any change it is important to prove and profile the benefit.
- Review and discuss configuration with other developers and operations staff or devops.

The Blame Donkey

Description

Certain components are always identified as the issue, even if they had nothing to do with the problem.

For example, one of the authors saw a massive outage in UAT the day before go-live. A certain path through the code caused a table lock on one of the central database tables. An error occurred in the code and the lock was retained, rendering the rest of the application unusable until a full restart was performed. Hibernate was used as the data access layer and immediately blamed for the issue. However, in this case, the culprit wasn't Hibernate but an empty `catch` block for the timeout exception that did not clean up the database connection. It took a full day for developers to stop blaming Hibernate and to actually look at their code to find the real bug.

Example comment

"It's always JMS/Hibernate/A_N_OTHER_LIB."

Reality

- Insufficient analysis has been done to reach this conclusion.
- The usual suspect is the only suspect in the investigation.
- The team is unwilling to look wider to establish a true cause.

Discussion

This antipattern is often displayed by management or the business, as in many cases they do not have a full understanding of the technical stack and have acknowledged cognitive biases, so they are proceeding by pattern matching. However, technologists are far from immune to it.

Technologists often fall victim to this antipattern when they have little understanding about the code base or libraries outside of the ones usually blamed. It is often easier to name a part of the application that is commonly the problem, rather than perform a new investigation. It can be the sign of a tired team, with many production issues at hand.

Hibernate is the perfect example of this; in many situations, Hibernate grows to the point where it is not set up or used correctly. The team then has a tendency to bash the technology, as they have seen it fail or not perform in the past. However, the problem could just as easily be the underlying query, use of an inappropriate index, the physical connection to the database, the object mapping layer, or something else. Profiling to isolate the exact cause is essential.

Resolutions

- Resist the pressure to rush to conclusions.
- Perform analysis as normal.
- Communicate the results of the analysis to all stakeholders (to encourage a more accurate picture of the causes of problems).

Missing the Bigger Picture

Description

The team becomes obsessed with trying out changes or profiling smaller parts of the application without fully appreciating the full impact of the changes. Engineers start tweaking JVM switches in an effort to gain better performance, perhaps based on an example or a different application in the same company.

The team may also look to profile smaller parts of the application using micro-benchmarking (which is notoriously difficult to get right, as we will explore in Chapter 5).

Example comments

"If I just change these settings, we'll get better performance."

"If we can just speed up method dispatch time…"

Reality

- The team does not fully understand the impact of changes.
- The team has not profiled the application fully under the new JVM settings.
- The overall system impact from a microbenchmark has not been determined.

Discussion

The JVM has literally hundreds of switches. This gives a very highly configurable runtime, but also gives rise to a great temptation to make use of all of this configurability. This is usually a mistake—the defaults and self-management capabilities are usually sufficient. Some of the switches also combine with each other in unexpected ways, which makes blind changes even more dangerous. Applications even in the same company are likely to operate and profile in a completely different way, so it's important to spend time trying out settings that are recommended.

Performance tuning is a statistical activity, which relies on a highly specific context for execution. This implies that larger systems are usually easier to benchmark than smaller ones—because with larger systems, the law of large numbers works in the engineer's favor, helping to correct for effects in the platform that distort individual events.

By contrast, the more we try to focus on a single aspect of the system, the harder we have to work to unweave the separate subsystems (e.g., threading, GC, scheduling, JIT compilation) of the complex environment that makes up the platform (at least in the Java/C# case). This is extremely hard to do, and handling the statistics is sensitive and is not often a skillset that software engineers have acquired along the way. This makes it very easy to produce numbers that do not accurately represent the behavior of the system aspect that the engineer believed they were benchmarking.

This has an unfortunate tendency to combine with the human bias to see patterns even when none exist. Together, these effects lead us to the spectacle of a performance engineer who has been deeply seduced by bad statistics or a poor control—an engineer arguing passionately for a performance benchmark or effect that their peers are simply not able to replicate.

There are a few other points to be aware of here. First, it's difficult to evaluate the effectiveness of optimizations without a UAT environment that fully emulates production. Second, there's no point in having an optimization that helps your application only in high-stress situations and kills performance in the general case—but obtaining sets of data that are typical of general application usage but also provide a meaningful test under load can be difficult.

Resolutions

Before making any change to switches live:

1. Measure in production.
2. Change one switch at a time in UAT.
3. Ensure that your UAT environment has the same stress points as production.
4. Ensure that test data is available that represents normal load in the production system.
5. Test the change in UAT.
6. Retest in UAT.

7. Have someone recheck your reasoning.

8. Pair with them to discuss your conclusions.

UAT Is My Desktop

Description

UAT environments often differ significantly from production, although not always in a way that's expected or fully understood. Many developers will have worked in situations where a low-powered desktop is used to write code for high-powered production servers. However, it's also becoming more common that a developer's machine is massively more powerful than the small servers deployed in production. Low-powered micro-environments are usually not a problem, as they can often be virtualized for a developer to have one of each. This is not true of high-powered production machines, which will often have significantly more cores, RAM, and efficient I/O than a developer's machine.

Example Comment

"A full-size UAT environment would be too expensive."

Reality

- Outages caused by differences in environments are almost always more expensive than a few more boxes.

Discussion

The UAT Is My Desktop antipattern stems from a different kind of cognitive bias than we have previously seen. This bias insists that doing some sort of UAT must be better than doing none at all. Unfortunately, this hopefulness fundamentally misunderstands the complex nature of enterprise environments. For any kind of meaningful extrapolation to be possible, the UAT environment must be production-like.

In modern adaptive environments, the runtime subsystems will make best use of the available resources. If these differ radically from those in the target deployment, they will make different decisions under the differing circumstances—rendering our hopeful extrapolation useless at best.

Resolutions

- Track the cost of outages and opportunity cost related to lost customers.
- Buy a UAT environment that is identical to production.

- In most cases, the cost of the first far outweighs the second, and sometimes the right case needs to be made to managers.

Production-Like Data Is Hard

Description

Also known as the DataLite antipattern, this antipattern relates to a few common pitfalls that people encounter while trying to represent production-like data. Consider a trade processing plant at a large bank that processes futures and options trades that have been booked but need to be settled. Such a system would typically handle millions of messages a day. Now consider the following UAT strategies and their potential issues:

1. To make things easy to test, the mechanism is to capture a small selection of these messages during the course of the day. The messages are then all run through the UAT system.

   This approach fails to capture burst-like behavior that the system could see. It may also not capture the warmup caused by more futures trading on a particular market before another market opens that trades options.

2. To make the scenario easier to test, the trades and options are updated to use only simple values for assertion.

   This does not give us the "realness" of production data. Considering that we are using an external library or system for options pricing, it would be impossible for us to determine with our UAT dataset that this production dependency has not now caused a performance issue, as the range of calculations we are performing is a simplified subset of production data.

3. To make things easier, all values are pushed through the system at once.
   This is often done in UAT, but misses key warmup and optimizations that may happen when the data is fed at a different rate.

Most of the time in UAT the test dataset is simplified to make things easier. However, it rarely makes results *useful*.

Example comments

"It's too hard to keep production and UAT in sync."

"It's too hard to manipulate data to match what the system expects."

"Production data is protected by security considerations. Developers should not have access to it."

Reality

Data in UAT must be production-like for accurate results. If data is not available for security reasons, then it should be scrambled (aka masked or obfuscated) so it can still be used for a meaningful test. Another option is to partition UAT so developers still don't see the data, but can see the output of the performance tests to be able to identify problems.

Discussion

This antipattern also falls into the trap of "something must be better than nothing." The idea is that testing against even out-of-date and unrepresentative data is better than not testing.

As before, this is an extremely dangerous line of reasoning. While testing against *something* (even if it is nothing like production data) at scale can reveal flaws and omissions in the system testing, it provides a false sense of security.

When the system goes live, and the usage patterns fail to conform to the expected norms that have been anchored by UAT data, the development and ops teams may well find that they have become complacent due to the warm glow that UAT has provided, and are unprepared for the sheer terror that can quickly follow an at-scale production release.

Resolutions

- Consult data domain experts and invest in a process to migrate production data back into UAT, scrambling or obfuscating data if necessary.
- Overprepare for releases for which you expect high volumes of customers or transactions.

Cognitive Biases and Performance Testing

Humans can be bad at forming accurate opinions quickly, even when faced with a problem where they can draw upon past experiences and similar situations.

 A cognitive bias is a psychological effect that causes the human brain to draw incorrect conclusions. It is especially problematic because the person exhibiting the bias is usually unaware of it and may believe they are being rational.

Many of the antipatterns that have been explored in this chapter are caused, in whole or in part, by one or more cognitive biases that are in turn based on an unconscious assumptions.

For example, with the Blame Donkey antipattern, if a component has caused several recent outages the team may be biased to expect that same component to be the cause of any new performance problem. Any data that's analyzed may be more likely to be considered credible if it confirms the idea that the Blame Donkey is responsible. The antipattern combines aspects of the biases known as confirmation bias and recency bias (a tendency to assume that whatever has been happening recently will keep happening).

 A single component in Java can behave differently from application to application depending on how it is optimized at runtime. In order to remove any pre-existing bias, it is important to look at the application as a whole.

Biases can be complementary or dual to each other. For example, some developers may be biased to assume that the problem is not software-related at all, and the cause must be the infrastructure the software is running on; this is common in the Works for Me antipattern, characterized by statements like "This worked fine in UAT, so there must be a problem with the production kit." The converse is to assume that every problem must be caused by software, because that's the part of the system the developer knows about and can directly affect.

Reductionist Thinking

This cognitive bias is based on an analytical approach that insists that if you break a system into small enough pieces, you can understand it by understanding its constituent parts. Understanding each part means reducing the chance of incorrect assumptions being made.

The problem with this view is that in complex systems it just isn't true. Nontrivial software (or physical) systems almost always display emergent behavior, where the whole is greater than a simple summation of its parts would indicate.

Confirmation Bias

Confirmation bias can lead to significant problems when it comes to performance testing or attempting to look at an application subjectively. A confirmation bias is introduced, usually not intentionally, when a poor test set is selected or results from the test are not analyzed in a statistically sound way. Confirmation bias is quite hard to counter, because there are often strong motivational or emotional factors at play (such as someone in the team trying to prove a point).

Consider an antipattern such as Distracted by Shiny, where a team member is looking to bring in the latest and greatest NoSQL database. They run some tests against data that isn't like production data, because representing the full schema is too complicated for evaluation purposes. They quickly prove that on a test set the NoSQL database produces superior access times on their local machine. The developer has already told everyone this would be the case, and on seeing the results they proceed with a full implementation. There are several antipatterns at work here, all leading to new unproved assumptions in the new library stack.

Fiddling with Switches

Tuning by Folklore and Missing the Bigger Picture (abuse of microbenchmarks) are all examples of antipatterns that are caused at least in part by a combination of the reductionism and confirmation biases. One particularly egregious example is a subtype of Tuning by Folklore known as *Fiddling with Switches*.

This antipattern arises because, although the VM attempts to choose settings appropriate for the detected hardware, there are some circumstances where the engineer will need to manually set flags to tune the performance of code. This is not harmful in itself, but there is a hidden cognitive trap here, in the extremely configurable nature of the JVM with command-line switches.

To see a list of the VM flags, use the following switch:

```
-XX:+PrintFlagsFinal
```

As of Java 8u131, this produces over 700 possible switches. Not only that, but there are also additional tuning options available only when the VM is running in diagnostic mode. To see these, add this switch:

```
-XX:+UnlockDiagnosticVMOptions
```

This unlocks around another 100 switches. There is no way that any human can correctly reason about the aggregate effect of applying the possible combinations of these switches. Moreover, in most cases, experimental observations will show that the effect of changing switch values is small—often much smaller than developers expect.

Fog of War (Action Bias)

This bias usually manifests itself during outages or situations where the system is not performing as expected. The most common causes include:

- Changes to infrastructure that the system runs on, perhaps without notification or realizing there would be an impact
- Changes to libraries that the system is dependent on

- A strange bug or race condition the manifests itself on the busiest day of the year

In a well-maintained application with sufficient logging and monitoring, these should generate clear error messages that will lead the support team to the cause of the problem.

However, too many applications have not tested failure scenarios and lack appropriate logging. Under these circumstances even experienced engineers can fall into the trap of needing to feel that they're doing something to resolve the outage and mistaking motion for velocity—the "fog of war" descends.

At this time, many of the human elements discussed in this chapter can come into play if participants are not systematic about their approach to the problem. For example, an antipattern such as the Blame Donkey may shortcut a full investigation and lead the production team down a particular path of investigation—often missing the bigger picture. Similarly, the team may be tempted to break the system down into its constituent parts and look through the code at a low level without first establishing in which subsystem the problem truly resides.

In the past it may always have paid to use a systematic approach to dealing with outage scenarios, leaving anything that did not require a patch to a postmortem. However, this is the realm of human emotion, and it can be very difficult to take the tension out of the situation, especially during an outage.

Risk Bias

Humans are naturally risk averse and resistant to change. Mostly this is because people have seen examples of how change can go wrong. This leads them to attempt to avoid that risk. This can be incredibly frustrating when taking small, calculated risks could move the product forward. We can reduce risk bias significantly by having a robust set of unit tests and production regression tests. If either of these is not trusted, change becomes extremely difficult and the risk factor is not controlled.

This bias often manifests in a failure to learn from application problems (even service outages) and implement appropriate mitigation.

Ellsberg's Paradox

As an example of how bad humans are at understanding probability, consider Ellsberg's Paradox. Named for the famous US investigative journalist and whistleblower Daniel Ellsberg, the paradox deals with the human desire for "known unknowns" over "unknown unknowns."[2]

---

2 To reuse the phrase made famous by Donald Rumsfeld.

The usual formulation of Ellsberg's Paradox is as a simple probability thought experiment. Consider a barrel, containing 90 colored balls—30 are known to be blue, and the rest are either red or green. The exact distribution of red and green balls is not known, but the barrel, the balls, and therefore the odds are fixed throughout.

The first step of the paradox is expressed as a choice of wagers. The player can choose to take either of two bets:

1. The player will win $100 if a ball drawn at random is blue.
2. The player will win $100 if a ball drawn at random is red.

Most people choose A), as it represents known odds: the likelihood of winning is exactly 1/3. However, (assuming that when a ball is removed it is placed back in the same barrel and then rerandomized), when the player is presented with a second bet something surprising happens. In this case the options are:

1. The player will win $100 if a ball drawn at random is blue or green.
2. The player will win $100 if a ball drawn at random is red or green.

In this situation, bet D corresponds to known odds (2/3 chance of winning), so virtually everyone picks this option.

The paradox is that the set of choices A and D is irrational. Choosing A implicitly expresses an opinion about the distribution of red and green balls—effectively that "there are more green balls than red balls." Therefore, if A is chosen, then the logical strategy is to pair it with C, as this would provide better odds than the safe choice of D.

Summary

When you are evaluating performance results, it is essential to handle the data in an appropriate manner and avoid falling into unscientific and subjective thinking. In this chapter, we have met some of the types of test, testing best practices, and antipatterns that are native to performance analysis.

In the next chapter, we're going to move on to looking at low-level performance measurements, the pitfalls of microbenchmarks, and some statistical techniques for handling raw results obtained from JVM measurements.

## CHAPTER 5

Microbenchmarking and Statistics

In this chapter, we will consider the specifics of measuring Java performance numbers directly. The dynamic nature of the JVM means that performance numbers are often harder to handle than many developers expect. As a result, there are a lot of inaccurate or misleading performance numbers floating around on the internet.

A primary goal of this chapter is to ensure that you are aware of these possible pitfalls and only produce performance numbers that you and others can rely upon. In particular, the measurement of small pieces of Java code (*microbenchmarking*) is notoriously subtle and difficult to do correctly, and this subject and its proper usage by performance engineers is a major theme throughout the chapter.

> The first principle is that you must not fool yourself—and you are the easiest person to fool.
>
> —Richard Feynman

The second portion of the chapter describes how to use the gold standard of microbenchmarking tools: JMH. If, even after all the warnings and caveats, you really feel that your application and use cases warrant the use of microbenchmarks, then you will avoid numerous well-known pitfalls and "bear traps" by starting with the most reliable and advanced of the available tools.

Finally, we turn to the subject of statistics. The JVM routinely produces performance numbers that require somewhat careful handling. The numbers produced by microbenchmarks are usually especially sensitive, and so it is incumbent upon the performance engineer to treat the observed results with a degree of statistical sophistication. The last sections of the chapter explain some of the techniques for working with JVM performance data, and problems of interpreting data.

Introduction to Measuring Java Performance

In "Java Performance Overview" on page 3, we described performance analysis as a synthesis between different aspects of the craft that has resulted in a discipline that is fundamentally an experimental science.

That is, if we want to write a good benchmark (or microbenchmark), then it can be very helpful to consider it as though it were a science experiment.

This approach leads us to view the benchmark as a "black box"—it has inputs and outputs, and we want to collect data from which we can conjecture or infer results. However, we must be cautious—it is not enough to simply *collect* data. We need to ensure that we are not *deceived* by our data.

> Benchmark numbers don't matter on their own. It's important what models you derive from those numbers.
>
> —Aleksey Shipilëv

Our ideal goal is therefore to make our benchmark a fair test—meaning that as far as possible we only want to change a single aspect of the system and ensure any other external factors in our benchmark are controlled. In an ideal world, the other possibly changeable aspects of the system would be completely invariant between tests, but we are rarely so fortunate in practice.

 Even if the goal of a scientifically pure fair test is unachievable in practice, it is essential that our benchmarks are at least repeatable, as this is the basis of any empirical result.

One central problem with writing a benchmark for the Java platform is the sophistication of the Java runtime. A considerable portion of this book is devoted to illuminating the automatic optimizations that are applied to a developer's code by the JVM. When we think of our benchmark as a scientific test in the context of these optimizations, then our options become limited.

That is, to fully understand and account for the precise impact of these optimizations is all but impossible. Accurate models of the "real" performance of our application code are difficult to create and tend to be limited in their applicability.

Put another way, we cannot truly divorce the executing Java code from the JIT compiler, memory management, and other subsystems provided by the Java runtime. Neither can we ignore the effects of operating system, hardware, or runtime conditions (e.g., load) that are current when our tests are run.

> No man is an island, Entire of itself
>
> —John Donne

It is easier to smooth out these effects by dealing with a larger aggregate (a whole system or subsystem). Conversely, when we are dealing with small-scale or micro-benchmarks, it is much more difficult to truly isolate application code from the background behavior of the runtime. This is the fundamental reason why micro-benchmarking is so hard, as we will discuss.

Let's consider what appears to be a very simple example—a benchmark of code that sorts a list of 100,000 numbers. We want to examine it with the point of view of trying to create a truly fair test:

```java
public class ClassicSort {

    private static final int N = 1_000;
    private static final int I = 150_000;
    private static final List<Integer> testData = new ArrayList<>();

    public static void main(String[] args) {
        Random randomGenerator = new Random();
        for (int i = 0; i < N; i++) {
            testData.add(randomGenerator.nextInt(Integer.MAX_VALUE));
        }

        System.out.println("Testing Sort Algorithm");

        double startTime = System.nanoTime();

        for (int i = 0; i < I; i++) {
            List<Integer> copy = new ArrayList<Integer>(testData);
            Collections.sort(copy);
        }

        double endTime = System.nanoTime();
        double timePerOperation = ((endTime - startTime) / (1_000_000_000L * I));
        System.out.println("Result: " + (1 / timePerOperation) + " op/s");
    }
}
```

The benchmark creates an array of random integers and, once this is complete, logs the start time of the benchmark. The benchmark then loops around, copying the template array, and then runs a sort over the data. Once this has run for I times, the duration is converted to seconds and divided by the number of iterations to give us the time taken per operation.

The first concern with the benchmark is that it goes straight into testing the code, without any consideration for warming up the JVM. Consider the case where the sort is running in a server application in production. It is likely to have been running for hours, maybe even days. However, we know that the JVM includes a Just-in-Time compiler that will convert interpreted bytecode to highly optimized machine code. This compiler only kicks in after the method has been run a certain number of times.

The test we are therefore conducting is not representative of how it will behave in production. The JVM will spend time optimizing the call while we are trying to benchmark. We can see this effect by running the sort with a few JVM flags:

```
java -Xms2048m -Xmx2048m -XX:+PrintCompilation ClassicSort
```

The -Xms and -Xmx options control the size of the heap, in this case pinning the heap size to 2 GB. The PrintCompilation flag outputs a log line whenever a method is compiled (or some other compilation event happens). Here's a fragment of the output:

```
Testing Sort Algorithm
   73   29   3   java.util.ArrayList::ensureExplicitCapacity (26 bytes)
   73   31   3   java.lang.Integer::valueOf (32 bytes)
   74   32   3   java.util.concurrent.atomic.AtomicLong::get (5 bytes)
   74   33   3   java.util.concurrent.atomic.AtomicLong::compareAndSet (13 bytes)
   74   35   3   java.util.Random::next (47 bytes)
   74   36   3   java.lang.Integer::compareTo (9 bytes)
   74   38   3   java.lang.Integer::compare (20 bytes)
   74   37   3   java.lang.Integer::compareTo (12 bytes)
   74   39   4   java.lang.Integer::compareTo (9 bytes)
   75   36   3   java.lang.Integer::compareTo (9 bytes) made not entrant
   76   40   3   java.util.ComparableTimSort::binarySort (223 bytes)
   77   41   3   java.util.ComparableTimSort::mergeLo (656 bytes)
   79   42   3   java.util.ComparableTimSort::countRunAndMakeAscending (123 bytes)
   79   45   3   java.util.ComparableTimSort::gallopRight (327 bytes)
   80   43   3   java.util.ComparableTimSort::pushRun (31 bytes)
```

The JIT compiler is working overtime to optimize parts of the call hierarchy to make our code more efficient. This means the performance of the benchmark changes over the duration of our timing capture, and we have inadvertently left a variable uncontrolled in our experiment. A warmup period is therefore desirable—it will allow the JVM to settle down before we capture our timings. Usually this involves running the code we are about to benchmark for a number of iterations without capturing the timing details.

Another external factor that we need to consider is garbage collection. Ideally we want GC to be prevented from running during our time capturing, and also to be normalized after setup. Due to the nondeterministic nature of garbage collection, this is incredibly difficult to control.

One improvement we could definitely make is to ensure that we are not capturing timings while GC is likely to be running. We could potentially ask the system for a GC to be run and wait a short time, but the system could decide to ignore this call. As it stands, the timing in this benchmark is far too broad, so we need more detail about the garbage collection events that could be occurring.

Not only that, but as well as selecting our timing points we also want to select a reasonable number of iterations, which can be tricky to figure out through trial and improvement. The effects of garbage collection can be seen with another VM flag (for the detail of the log format, see Chapter 7):

```
java -Xms2048m -Xmx2048m -verbose:gc ClassicSort
```

This will produce GC log entries similar to the following:

```
Testing Sort Algorithm
[GC (Allocation Failure)  524800K->632K(2010112K), 0.0009038 secs]
[GC (Allocation Failure)  525432K->672K(2010112K), 0.0008671 secs]
Result: 9838.556465303362 op/s
```

Another common mistake that is made in benchmarks is to not actually use the result generated from the code we are testing. In the benchmark copy is effectively dead code, and it is therefore possible for the JIT compiler to identify it as a dead code path and optimize away what we are in fact trying to benchmark.

A further consideration is that looking at a single timed result, even though averaged, does not give us the full story of how our benchmark performed. Ideally we want to capture the margin of error to understand the reliability of the collected value. If the error margin is high, it may point to an uncontrolled variable or indeed that the code we have written is not performant. Either way, without capturing the margin of error there is no way to identify there is even an issue.

Benchmarking even a very simple sort can have pitfalls that mean the benchmark is wildly thrown out; however, as the complexity increases things rapidly get much, much worse. Consider a benchmark that looks to assess multithreaded code. Multithreaded code is extremely difficult to benchmark, as it requires ensuring that all the threads are held until each has fully started up, from the beginning of the benchmark to making certain accurate results. If this is not the case, the margin of error will be high.

There are also hardware considerations when it comes to benchmarking concurrent code, and they go beyond simply the hardware configuration. Consider if power management were to kick in or there were other contentions on the machine.

Getting the benchmark code correct is complicated and involves considering a lot of factors. As developers our primary concern is the code we are looking to profile, rather than all the issues just highlighted. All the aforementioned concerns combine to create a situation in which, unless you are a JVM expert, it is extremely easy to miss something and get an erroneous benchmark result.

There are two ways to deal with this problem. The first is to only benchmark systems as a whole. In this case, the low-level numbers are simply ignored and not collected. The overall outcome of so many copies of separate effects is to average out and allow meaningful large-scale results to be obtained. This approach is the one that is needed in most situations and by most developers.

The second approach is to try to address many of the aforementioned concerns by using a common framework, to allow meaningful comparison of related low-level results. The ideal framework would take away some of the pressures just discussed. Such a tool would have to follow the mainline development of OpenJDK to ensure that new optimizations and other external control variables were managed.

Fortunately, such a tool does actually exist, and it is the subject of our next section. For most developers it should be regarded purely as reference material, however, and it can be safely skipped in favor of "Statistics for JVM Performance" on page 99.

Introduction to JMH

We open with an example (and a cautionary tale) of how and why microbenchmarking can easily go wrong if it is approached naively. From there, we introduce a set of heuristics that indicate whether your use case is one where microbenchmarking is appropriate. For the vast majority of applications, the outcome will be that the technique is not suitable.

Don't Microbenchmark If You Can Help It (A True Story)

After a very long day in the office one of the authors was leaving the building when he passed a colleague still working at her desk, staring intensely at a single Java method. Thinking nothing of it, he left to catch a train home. However, two days later a very similar scenario played out—with a very similar method on the colleague's screen and a tired, annoyed look on her face. Clearly some deeper investigation was required.

The application that she was renovating had an easily observed performance problem. The new version was not performing as well as the version that the team was looking to replace, despite using newer versions of well-known libraries. She had been spending some of her time removing parts of the code and writing small benchmarks in an attempt to find where the problem was hiding.

The approach somehow felt wrong, like looking for a needle in a haystack. Instead, the pair worked together on another approach, and quickly confirmed that the application was maxing out CPU utilization. As this is a known good use case for execution profilers (see Chapter 13 for the full details of when to use profilers), 10 minutes profiling the application found the true cause. Sure enough, the problem wasn't in the application code at all, but in a new infrastructure library the team was using.

This war story illustrates an approach to Java performance that is unfortunately all too common. Developers can become obsessed with the idea that their own code must be to blame, and miss the bigger picture.

Developers often want to start hunting for problems by looking closely at small-scale code constructs, but benchmarking at this level is extremely difficult and has some dangerous "bear traps."

Heuristics for When to Microbenchmark

As we discussed briefly in Chapter 2, the dynamic nature of the Java platform, and features like garbage collection and aggressive JIT optimization, lead to performance that is hard to reason about directly. Worse still, performance numbers are frequently dependent on the exact runtime circumstances in play when the application is being measured.

It is almost always easier to analyze the true performance of an entire Java application than a small Java code fragment.

However, there are occasionally times when we need to directly analyze the performance of an individual method or even a single code fragment. This analysis should not be undertaken lightly, though. In general, there are three main use cases for low-level analysis or microbenchmarking:

- You're developing general-purpose library code with broad use cases.
- You're a developer on OpenJDK or another Java platform implementation.
- You're developing extremely latency-sensitive code (e.g., for low-latency trading).

The rationale for each of the three use cases is slightly different.

General-purpose libraries (by definition) have limited knowledge about the contexts in which they will be used. Examples of these types of libraries include Google Guava or the Eclipse Collections (originally contributed by Goldman Sachs). They need to provide acceptable or better performance across a very wide range of use cases—from datasets containing a few dozen elements up to hundreds of millions of elements.

Due to the broad nature of how they will be used, general-purpose libraries are sometimes forced to use microbenchmarking as a proxy for more conventional performance and capacity testing techniques.

Platform developers are a key user community for microbenchmarks, and the JMH tool was created by the OpenJDK team primarily for its own use. The tool has proved to be useful to the wider community of performance experts, though.

Finally, there are some developers who are working at the cutting edge of Java performance, who may wish to use microbenchmarks for the purpose of selecting algorithms and techniques that best suit their applications and extreme use cases. This would include low-latency financial trading, but relatively few other cases.

While it should be apparent if you are a developer who is working on OpenJDK or a general-purpose library, there may be developers who are confused about whether their performance requirements are such that they should consider microbenchmarks.

> The scary thing about microbenchmarks is that they always produce a number, even if that number is meaningless. They measure something; we're just not sure what.
>
> —Brian Goetz

Generally, only the most extreme applications should use microbenchmarks. There are no definitive rules, but unless your application meets most or all of these criteria, you are unlikely to derive genuine benefit from microbenchmarking your application:

- Your total code path execution time should certainly be less than 1 ms, and probably less than 100 µs.
- You should have measured your memory (object) allocation rate (see Chapters 6 and 7 for details), and it should be <1 MB/s and ideally very close to zero.
- You should be using close to 100% of available CPU, and the system utilization rate should be consistently low (under 10%).
- You should have already used an execution profiler (see Chapter 13) to understand the distribution of methods that are consuming CPU. There should be at most two or three dominant methods in the distribution.

With all of this said, it is hopefully obvious that microbenchmarking is an advanced, and rarely to be used, technique. However, it is useful to understand some of the basic theory and complexity that it reflects, as it leads to a better understanding of the difficulties of performance work in less extreme applications on the Java platform.

> Any nanobenchmark test that does not feature disassembly/codegen analysis is not to be trusted. Period.
>
> —Aleksey Shipilëv

The rest of this section explores microbenchmarking more thoroughly and introduces some of the tools and the considerations developers must take into account in order to produce results that are reliable and don't lead to incorrect conclusions. It should be useful background for all performance analysts, regardless of whether it is directly relevant to your current projects.

The JMH Framework

JMH is designed to be the framework that resolves the issues that we have just discussed.

> JMH is a Java harness for building, running, and analyzing nano/micro/milli/macro benchmarks written in Java and other languages targeting the JVM.
>
> —OpenJDK

There have been several attempts at simple benchmarking libraries in the past, with Google Caliper being one of the most well-regarded among developers. However, all of these frameworks have had their challenges, and often what seems like a rational way of setting up or measuring code performance can have some subtle bear traps to contend with. This is especially true with the continually evolving nature of the JVM as new optimizations are applied.

JMH is very different in that regard, and has been worked on by the same engineers that build the JVM. Therefore, the JMH authors know how to avoid the gotchas and optimization bear traps that exist within each version of the JVM. JMH evolves as a benchmarking harness with each release of the JVM, allowing developers to simply focus on using the tool and on the benchmark code itself.

JMH takes into account some key benchmark harness design issues, in addition to some of the problems already highlighted.

A benchmark framework has to be dynamic, as it does not know the contents of the benchmark at compile time. One obvious choice to get around this would be to execute benchmarks the user has written using reflection. However, this involves another complex JVM subsystem in the benchmark execution path. Instead, JMH operates by generating additional Java source from the benchmark, via annotation processing.

 Many common annotation-based Java frameworks (e.g., JUnit) use reflection to achieve their goals, so the use of a processor that generates additional source may be somewhat unexpected to some Java developers.

One issue is that if the benchmark framework were to call the user's code for a large number of iterations, loop optimizations might be triggered. This means the actual process of running the benchmark can cause issues with reliable results.

In order to avoid hitting loop optimization constraints JMH generates code for the benchmark, wrapping the benchmark code in a loop with the iteration count carefully set to a value that avoids optimization.

Executing Benchmarks

The complexities involved in JMH execution are mostly hidden from the user, and setting up a simple benchmark using Maven is straightforward. We can set up a new JMH project by executing the following command:

```
$ mvn archetype:generate \
        -DinteractiveMode=false \
        -DarchetypeGroupId=org.openjdk.jmh \
        -DarchetypeArtifactId=jmh-java-benchmark-archetype \
        -DgroupId=org.sample \
        -DartifactId=test \
        -Dversion=1.0
```

This downloads the required artifacts and creates a single benchmark stub to house the code.

The benchmark is annotated with `@Benchmark`, indicating that the harness will execute the method to benchmark it (after the framework has performed various setup tasks):

```
public class MyBenchmark {
    @Benchmark
    public void testMethod() {
        // Stub for code
    }
}
```

The author of the benchmark can configure parameters to set up the benchmark execution. The parameters can be set either on the command line or in the `main()` method of the benchmark as shown here:

```
public class MyBenchmark {

    public static void main(String[] args) throws RunnerException {
        Options opt = new OptionsBuilder()
                .include(SortBenchmark.class.getSimpleName())
                .warmupIterations(100)
                .measurementIterations(5).forks(1)
                .jvmArgs("-server", "-Xms2048m", "-Xmx2048m").build();

        new Runner(opt).run();
    }
}
```

The parameters on the command line override any parameters that have been set in the `main()` method.

Usually a benchmark requires some setup—for example, creating a dataset or setting up the conditions required for an orthogonal set of benchmarks to compare performance.

State, and controlling state, is another feature that is baked into the JMH framework. The @State annotation can be used to define that state, and accepts the Scope enum to define where the state is visible: Benchmark, Group, or Thread. Objects that are annotated with @State are reachable for the lifetime of the benchmark; it may be necessary to perform some setup.

Multithreaded code also requires careful handling in order to ensure that benchmarks are not skewed by state that is not well managed.

In general, if the code executed in a method has no side effects and the result is not used, then the method is a candidate for removal by the JVM. JMH needs to prevent this from occurring, and in fact makes this extremely straightforward for the benchmark author. Single results can be returned from the benchmark method, and the framework ensures that the value is implicitly assigned to a blackhole, a mechanism developed by the framework authors to have negligible performance overhead.

If a benchmark performs multiple calculations, it may be costly to combine and return the results from the benchmark method. In that scenario it may be necessary for the author to use an explicit blackhole, by creating a benchmark that takes a Blackhole as a parameter, which the benchmark will inject.

Blackholes provide four protections related to optimizations that could potentially impact the benchmark. Some protections are about preventing the benchmark from overoptimizing due to its limited scope, and the others are about avoiding predictable runtime patterns of data, which would not happen in a typical run of the system. The protections are:

- Remove the potential for dead code to be removed as an optimization at runtime.
- Prevent repeated calculations from being folded into constants.
- Prevent false sharing, where the reading or writing of a value can cause the current cache line to be impacted.
- Protect against "write walls."

The term *wall* in performance generally refers to a point at which your resources become saturated and the impact to the application is effectively a bottleneck. Hitting the write wall can impact caches and pollute buffers that are being used for writing. If you do this within your benchmark, you are potentially impacting it in a big way.

As documented in the Blackhole JavaDoc (and as noted earlier), in order to provide these protections you must have intimate knowledge of the JIT compiler so you can build a benchmark that avoids optimizations.

Let's take a quick look at the two `consume()` methods used by blackholes to give us insight into some of the tricks JMH uses (feel free to skip this bit if you're not interested in how JMH is implemented):

```
public volatile int i1 = 1, i2 = 2;

/**
 * Consume object. This call provides a side effect preventing JIT to eliminate
 * dependent computations.
 *
 * @param i int to consume.
 */
public final void consume(int i) {
    if (i == i1 & i == i2) {
      // SHOULD NEVER HAPPEN
        nullBait.i1 = i; // implicit null pointer exception
    }
}
```

We repeat this code for consuming all primitives (changing `int` for the corresponding primitive type). The variables `i1` and `i2` are declared as `volatile`, which means the runtime must re-evaluate them. The `if` statement can never be `true`, but the compiler must allow the code to run. Also note the use of the bitwise AND operator (`&`) inside the `if` statement. This avoids additional branch logic being a problem and results in a more uniform performance.

Here is the second method:

```
public int tlr = (int) System.nanoTime();

/**
 * Consume object. This call provides a side effect preventing JIT to eliminate
 * dependent computations.
 *
 * @param obj object to consume.
 */
public final void consume(Object obj) {
        int tlr = (this.tlr = (this.tlr * 1664525 + 1013904223));
    if ((tlr & tlrMask) == 0) {
      // SHOULD ALMOST NEVER HAPPEN IN MEASUREMENT
        this.obj1 = obj;
        this.tlrMask = (this.tlrMask << 1) + 1;
    }
}
```

When it comes to objects it would seem at first the same logic could be applied, as nothing the user has could be equal to objects that the `Blackhole` holds. However, the compiler is also trying to be smart about this. If the compiler asserts that the object is never equal to something else due to escape analysis, it is possible that comparison itself could be optimized to return `false`.

Instead, objects are consumed under a condition that executes only in rare scenarios. The value for `tlr` is computed and bitwise compared to the `tlrMask` to reduce the chance of a 0 value, but not outright eliminate it. This ensures objects are consumed largely without the requirement to assign the objects. Benchmark framework code is extremely fun to review, as it is so different from real-world Java applications. In fact, if code like that were found anywhere in a production Java application, the developer responsible should probably be fired.

As well as writing an extremely accurate microbenchmarking tool, the authors have also managed to create impressive documentation on the classes. If you're interested in the magic going on behind the scenes, the comments explain it well.

It doesn't take much with the preceding information to get a simple benchmark up and running, but JMH also has some fairly advanced features. The official documentation (*http://openjdk.java.net/projects/code-tools/jmh/*) has examples of each, all of which are worth reviewing.

Interesting features that demonstrate the power of JMH and its relative closeness to the JVM include:

- Being able to control the compiler
- Simulating CPU usage levels during a benchmark

Another cool feature is using blackholes to actually consume CPU cycles to allow you to simulate a benchmark under various CPU loads.

The `@CompilerControl` annotation can be used to ask the compiler not to inline, explicitly inline, or exclude the method from compilation. This is extremely useful if you come across a performance issue where you suspect that the JVM is causing specific problems due to inlining or compilation:

```
@State(Scope.Benchmark)
@BenchmarkMode(Mode.Throughput)
@Warmup(iterations = 5, time = 1, timeUnit = TimeUnit.SECONDS)
@Measurement(iterations = 5, time = 1, timeUnit = TimeUnit.SECONDS)
@OutputTimeUnit(TimeUnit.SECONDS)
@Fork(1)
public class SortBenchmark {

    private static final int N = 1_000;
    private static final List<Integer> testData = new ArrayList<>();

    @Setup
    public static final void setup() {
        Random randomGenerator = new Random();
        for (int i = 0; i < N; i++) {
            testData.add(randomGenerator.nextInt(Integer.MAX_VALUE));
        }
```

```
        System.out.println("Setup Complete");
    }

    @Benchmark
    public List<Integer> classicSort() {
        List<Integer> copy = new ArrayList<Integer>(testData);
        Collections.sort(copy);
        return copy;
    }

    @Benchmark
    public List<Integer> standardSort() {
        return testData.stream().sorted().collect(Collectors.toList());
    }

    @Benchmark
    public List<Integer> parallelSort() {
        return testData.parallelStream().sorted().collect(Collectors.toList());
    }

    public static void main(String[] args) throws RunnerException {
        Options opt = new OptionsBuilder()
                .include(SortBenchmark.class.getSimpleName())
                .warmupIterations(100)
                .measurementIterations(5).forks(1)
                .jvmArgs("-server", "-Xms2048m", "-Xmx2048m")
                .addProfiler(GCProfiler.class)
                .addProfiler(StackProfiler.class)
                .build();

        new Runner(opt).run();
    }
}
```

Running the benchmark produces the following output:

```
Benchmark                       Mode  Cnt     Score      Error   Units
optjava.SortBenchmark.classicSort   thrpt  200  14373.039 ±  111.586  ops/s
optjava.SortBenchmark.parallelSort  thrpt  200   7917.702 ±   87.757  ops/s
optjava.SortBenchmark.standardSort  thrpt  200  12656.107 ±   84.849  ops/s
```

Looking at this benchmark, you could easily jump to the quick conclusion that a classic method of sorting is more effective than using streams. Both code runs use one array copy and one sort, so it should be OK. Developers may look at the low error rate and high throughput and conclude that the benchmark must be correct.

But let's consider some reasons why our benchmark might not be giving an accurate picture of performance—basically trying to answer the question, "Is this a controlled test?" To begin with, let's look at the impact of garbage collection on the classicSort test:

```
Iteration    1:
[GC (Allocation Failure)  65496K->1480K(239104K), 0.0012473 secs]
[GC (Allocation Failure)  63944K->1496K(237056K), 0.0013170 secs]
10830.105 ops/s
Iteration    2:
[GC (Allocation Failure)  62936K->1680K(236032K), 0.0004776 secs]
10951.704 ops/s
```

In this snapshot it is clear that there is one GC cycle running per iteration (approximately). Comparing this to parallel sort is interesting:

```
Iteration    1:
[GC (Allocation Failure)  52952K->1848K(225792K), 0.0005354 secs]
[GC (Allocation Failure)  52024K->1848K(226816K), 0.0005341 secs]
[GC (Allocation Failure)  51000K->1784K(223744K), 0.0005509 secs]
[GC (Allocation Failure)  49912K->1784K(225280K), 0.0003952 secs]
9526.212 ops/s
Iteration    2:
[GC (Allocation Failure)  49400K->1912K(222720K), 0.0005589 secs]
[GC (Allocation Failure)  49016K->1832K(223744K), 0.0004594 secs]
[GC (Allocation Failure)  48424K->1864K(221696K), 0.0005370 secs]
[GC (Allocation Failure)  47944K->1832K(222720K), 0.0004966 secs]
[GC (Allocation Failure)  47400K->1864K(220672K), 0.0005004 secs]
```

So, by adding in flags to see what is causing this unexpected disparity, we can see that something else in the benchmark is causing noise—in this case, garbage collection.

The takeaway is that it is easy to assume that the benchmark represents a controlled environment, but the truth can be far more slippery. Often the uncontrolled variables are hard to spot, so even with a harness like JMH, caution is still required. We also need to take care to correct for our confirmation biases and ensure we are measuring the observables that truly reflect the behavior of our system.

In Chapter 9 we will meet JITWatch, which will give us another view into what the JIT compiler is doing with our bytecode. This can often help lend insight into why bytecode generated for a particular method may be causing the benchmark to not perform as expected.

Statistics for JVM Performance

If performance analysis is truly an experimental science, then we will inevitably find ourselves dealing with distributions of results data. Statisticians and scientists know that results that stem from the real world are virtually never represented by clean, stand-out signals. We must deal with the world as we find it, rather than the overidealized state in which we would like to find it.

> In God we trust. Everyone else, bring data.
>
> —Michael Bloomberg

All measurements contain some amount of error. In the next section we'll describe the two main types of error that a Java developer may expect to encounter when doing performance analysis.

Types of Error

There are two main sources of error that an engineer may encounter. These are:

Random error
> A measurement error or an unconnected factor is affecting results in an uncorrelated manner.

Systematic error
> An unaccounted factor is affecting measurement of the observable in a correlated way.

There are specific words associated with each type of error. For example, *accuracy* is used to describe the level of systematic error in a measurement; high accuracy corresponds to low systematic error. Similarly, *precision* is the term corresponding to random error; high precision is low random error.

The graphics in Figure 5-1 show the effect of these two types of error on a measurement. The extreme left image shows a clustering of measurements around the true result (the "center of the target"). These measurements have both high precision and high accuracy. The second image has a systematic effect (miscalibrated sights perhaps?) that is causing all the shots to be off-target, so these measurements have high precision, but low accuracy. The third image shows shots basically on target but loosely clustered around the center, so low precision but high accuracy. The final image shows no clear signal, as a result of having both low precision and low accuracy.

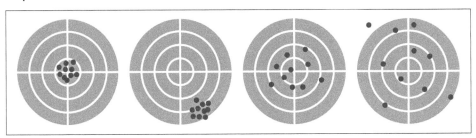

Figure 5-1. Different types of error

Systematic error

As an example, consider a performance test running against a group of backend Java web services that send and receive JSON. This type of test is very common when it is problematic to directly use the application frontend for load testing.

Figure 5-2 was generated from the JP GC extension pack for the Apache JMeter load-generation tool. In it, there are actually two systematic effects at work. The first is the linear pattern observed in the top line (the outlier service), which represents slow exhaustion of some limited server resource. This type of pattern is often associated with a memory leak, or some other resource being used and not released by a thread during request handling, and represents a candidate for investigation—it looks like it could be a genuine problem.

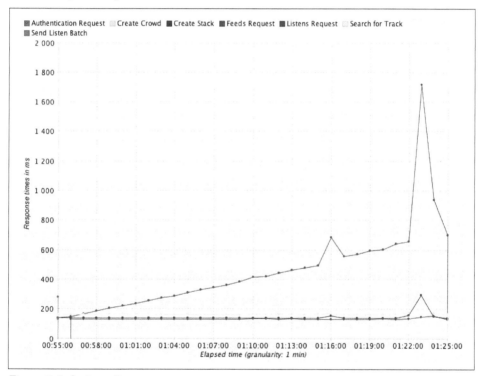

Figure 5-2. Systematic error

Further analysis would be needed to confirm the type of resource that was being affected; we can't just conclude that it's a memory leak.

The second effect that should be noticed is the consistency of the majority of the other services at around the 180 ms level. This is suspicious, as the services are doing very different amounts of work in response to a request. So why are the results so consistent?

The answer is that while the services under test are located in London, this load test was conducted from Mumbai, India. The observed response time includes the irreducible round-trip network latency from Mumbai to London. This is in the range 120–150 ms, and so accounts for the vast majority of the observed time for the services other than the outlier.

This large, systematic effect is drowning out the differences in the actual response time (as the services are actually responding in much less than 120 ms). This is an example of a systematic error that does not represent a problem with our application. Instead, this error stems from a problem in our test setup, and the good news is that this artifact completely disappeared (as expected) when the test was rerun from London.

Random error

The case of random error deserves a mention here, although it is a very well-trodden path.

 The discussion assumes readers are familiar with basic statistical handling of normally distributed measurements (mean, mode, standard deviation, etc.); readers who aren't should consult a basic textbook, such as *The Handbook of Biological Statistics* (*http://biosta thandbook.com/*).[1]

Random errors are caused by unknown or unpredictable changes in the environment. In general scientific usage, these changes may occur in either the measuring instrument or the environment, but for software we assume that our measuring harness is reliable, and so the source of random error can only be the operating environment.

Random error is usually considered to obey a Gaussian (aka normal) distribution. A couple of typical examples are shown in Figure 5-3. The distribution is a good model for the case where an error is equally likely to make a positive or negative contribution to an observable, but as we will see, this is not a good fit for the JVM.

---

1 John H. McDonald, *Handbook of Biological Statistics*, 3rd ed. (Baltimore, MD: Sparky House Publishing, 2014).

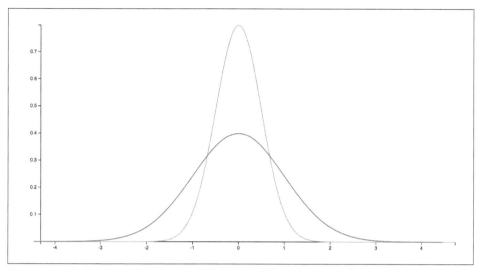

Figure 5-3. A Gaussian distribution (aka normal distribution or bell curve)

Spurious correlation

One of the most famous aphorisms about statistics is "correlation does not imply causation"—that is, just because two variables appear to behave similarly does not imply that there is an underlying connection between them.

In the most extreme examples, if a practitioner looks hard enough, then a correlation can be found between entirely unrelated measurements (*http://tylervigen.com/spurious-correlations*). For example, in Figure 5-4 we can see that consumption of chicken in the US is well correlated with total import of crude oil.[2]

---

2 The spurious correlations in this section come from Tyler Vigen's site and are reused here with permission under a Creative Commons license. If you enjoy them, Vigen has a book with many more amusing examples, available from the link.

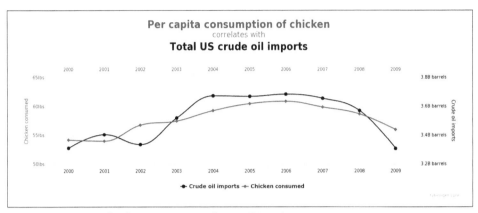

Figure 5-4. A completely spurious correlation (Vigen)

These numbers are clearly not causally related; there is no factor that drives both the import of crude oil and the eating of chicken. However, it isn't the absurd and ridiculous correlations that the practitioner needs to be wary of.

In Figure 5-5, we see the revenue generated by video arcades correlated to the number of computer science PhDs awarded. It isn't too much of a stretch to imagine a sociological study that claimed a link between these observables, perhaps arguing that "stressed doctoral students were finding relaxation with a few hours of video games." These types of claim are depressingly common, despite no such common factor actually existing.

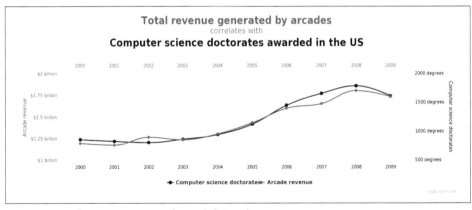

Figure 5-5. A less spurious correlation? (Vigen)

In the realm of the JVM and performance analysis, we need to be especially careful not to attribute a causal relationship between measurements based solely on correlation and that the connection "seems plausible." This can be seen as one aspect of Feynman's "you must not fool yourself" maxim.

We've met some examples of sources of error and mentioned the notorious bear trap of spurious correlation, so let's move on to discuss an aspect of JVM performance measurement that requires some special care and attention to detail.

Non-Normal Statistics

Statistics based on the normal distribution do not require much mathematical sophistication. For this reason, the standard approach to statistics that is typically taught at pre-college or undergraduate level focuses heavily on the analysis of normally distributed data.

Students are taught to calculate the mean and the standard deviation (or variance), and sometimes higher moments, such as skew and kurtosis. However, these techniques have a serious drawback, in that the results can easily become distorted if the distribution has even a few far-flung outlying points.

In Java performance, the outliers represent slow transactions and unhappy customers. We need to pay special attention to these points, and avoid techniques that dilute the importance of outliers.

To consider it from another viewpoint: unless a large number of customers are already complaining, it is unlikely that improving the average response time is the goal. For sure, doing so will improve the experience for everyone, but it is far more usual for a few disgruntled customers to be the cause of a latency tuning exercise. This implies that the outlier events are likely to be of more interest than the experience of the majority who are receiving satisfactory service.

In Figure 5-6 we can see a more realistic curve for the likely distribution of method (or transaction) times. It is clearly not a normal distribution.

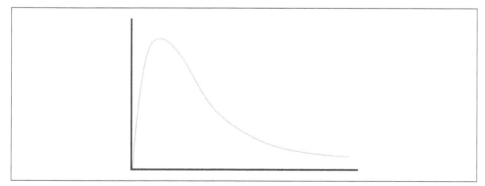

Figure 5-6. A more realistic view of the distribution of transaction times

The shape of the distribution in Figure 5-6 shows something that we know intuitively about the JVM: it has "hot paths" where all the relevant code is already JIT-compiled, there are no GC cycles, and so on. These represent a best-case scenario (albeit a common one); there simply are no calls that are randomly a bit faster.

This violates a fundamental assumption of Gaussian statistics and forces us to consider distributions that are non-normal.

 For distributions that are non-normal, many "basic rules" of normally distributed statistics are violated. In particular, standard deviation/variance and other higher moments are basically useless.

One technique that is very useful for handling the non-normal, "long-tail" distributions that the JVM produces is to use a modified scheme of percentiles. Remember that a distribution is a whole graph—it is a shape of data, and is not represented by a single number.

Instead of computing just the mean, which tries to express the whole distribution in a single result, we can use a sampling of the distribution at intervals. When used for normally distributed data, the samples are usually taken at regular intervals. However, a small adaptation means that the technique can be used for JVM statistics.

The modification is to use a sampling that takes into account the long-tail distribution by starting from the mean, then the 90th percentile, and then moving out logarithmically, as shown in the following method timing results. This means that we're sampling according to a pattern that better corresponds to the shape of the data:

```
50.0% level was 23 ns
90.0% level was 30 ns
99.0% level was 43 ns
99.9% level was 164 ns
99.99% level was 248 ns
99.999% level was 3,458 ns
99.9999% level was 17,463 ns
```

The samples show us that while the average time was 23 ns to execute a getter method, for 1 request in 1,000 the time was an order of magnitude worse, and for 1 request in 100,000 it was *two* orders of magnitude worse than average.

Long-tail distributions can also be referred to as *high dynamic range* distributions. The dynamic range of an observable is usually defined as the maximum recorded value divided by the minimum (assuming it's nonzero).

Logarithmic percentiles are a useful simple tool for understanding the long tail. However, for more sophisticated analysis, we can use a public domain library for handling datasets with high dynamic range. The library is called HdrHistogram and is available from GitHub (*https://github.com/HdrHistogram/HdrHistogram*). It was originally created by Gil Tene (Azul Systems), with additional work by Mike Barker, Darach Ennis, and Coda Hale.

 A histogram is a way of summarizing data by using a finite set of ranges (called *buckets*) and displaying how often data falls into each bucket.

HdrHistogram is also available on Maven Central. At the time of writing, the current version is 2.1.9, and you can add it to your projects by adding this dependency stanza to *pom.xml*:

```
<dependency>
    <groupId>org.hdrhistogram</groupId>
    <artifactId>HdrHistogram</artifactId>
    <version>2.1.9</version>
</dependency>
```

Let's look at a simple example using HdrHistogram. This example takes in a file of numbers and computes the HdrHistogram for the difference between successive results:

```
public class BenchmarkWithHdrHistogram {
    private static final long NORMALIZER = 1_000_000;

    private static final Histogram HISTOGRAM
            = new Histogram(TimeUnit.MINUTES.toMicros(1), 2);

    public static void main(String[] args) throws Exception {
        final List<String> values = Files.readAllLines(Paths.get(args[0]));
        double last = 0;
        for (final String tVal : values) {
            double parsed = Double.parseDouble(tVal);
            double gcInterval = parsed - last;
            last = parsed;
            HISTOGRAM.recordValue((long)(gcInterval * NORMALIZER));
        }
        HISTOGRAM.outputPercentileDistribution(System.out, 1000.0);
    }
}
```

The output shows the times between successive garbage collections. As we'll see in Chapters 6 and 8, GC does do not occur at regular intervals, and understanding the distribution of how frequently it occurs could be useful. Here's what the histogram plotter produces for a sample GC log:

```
Value     Percentile TotalCount 1/(1-Percentile)
```

```
     14.02 0.000000000000              1        1.00
   1245.18 0.100000000000             37        1.11
   1949.70 0.200000000000             82        1.25
   1966.08 0.300000000000            126        1.43
   1982.46 0.400000000000            157        1.67

...

  28180.48 0.996484375000            368      284.44
  28180.48 0.996875000000            368      320.00
  28180.48 0.997265625000            368      365.71
  36438.02 0.997656250000            369      426.67
  36438.02 1.000000000000            369
#[Mean    =        2715.12, StdDeviation   =       2875.87]
#[Max     =       36438.02, Total count    =            369]
#[Buckets =             19, SubBuckets     =            256]
```

The raw output of the formatter is rather hard to analyze, but fortunately, the HdrHistogram project includes an online formatter (*http://hdrhistogram.github.io/HdrHistogram/plotFiles.html*) that can be used to generate visual histograms from the raw output.

For this example, it produces output like that shown in Figure 5-7.

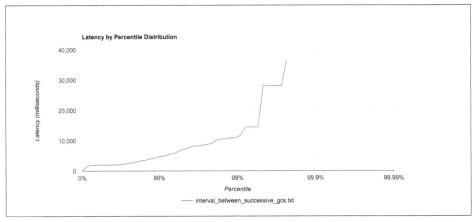

Figure 5-7. Example HdrHistogram visualization

For many observables that we wish to measure in Java performance tuning, the statistics are often highly non-normal, and HdrHistogram can be a very useful tool in helping to understand and visualize the shape of the data.

Interpretation of Statistics

Empirical data and observed results do not exist in a vacuum, and it is quite common that one of the hardest jobs lies in interpreting the results that we obtain from measuring our applications.

> No matter what they tell you, it's always a people problem.
>
> —Gerald Weinberg

In Figure 5-8 we show an example memory allocation rate for a real Java application. This example is for a reasonably well-performing application. The screenshot comes from the Censum garbage collection analyzer, which we will meet in Chapter 8.

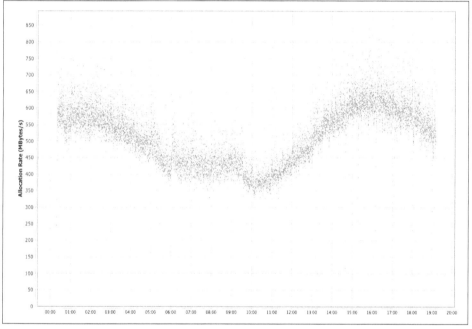

Figure 5-8. Example allocation rate

The interpretation of the allocation data is relatively straightforward, as there is a clear signal present. Over the time period covered (almost a day), allocation rates were basically stable between 350 and 700 MB per second. There is a downward trend starting approximately 5 hours after the JVM started up, and a clear minimum between 9 and 10 hours, after which the allocation rate starts to rise again.

These types of trends in observables are very common, as the allocation rate will usually reflect the amount of work an application is actually doing, and this will vary widely depending on the time of day. However, when we are interpreting real observables, the picture can rapidly become more complicated. This can lead to what is sometimes called the "Hat/Elephant" problem, after a passage in *The Little Prince* by Antoine de Saint-Exupéry.

The problem is illustrated by Figure 5-9. All we can initially see is a complex histogram of HTTP request-response times. However, just like the narrator of the book, if we can imagine or analyze a bit more, we can see that the complex picture is actually made up of several fairly simple pieces.

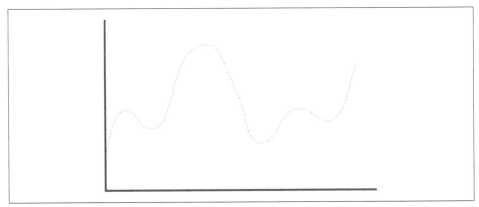

Figure 5-9. Hat, or elephant eaten by a boa?

The key to decoding the response histogram is to realize that "web application responses" is a very general category, including successful requests (so-called 2xx responses), client errors (4xx, including the ubiquitous 404 error), and server errors (5xx, especially 500 Internal Server Error).

Each type of response has a different characteristic distribution for response times. If a client makes a request for a URL that has no mapping (a 404), then the web server can immediately reply with a response. This means that the histogram for only client error responses looks more like Figure 5-10.

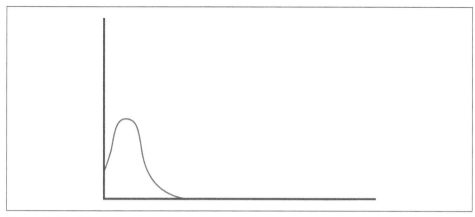

Figure 5-10. Client errors

By contrast, server errors often occur after a large amount of processing time has been expended (for example, due to backend resources being under stress or timing out). So, the histogram for server error responses might look like Figure 5-11.

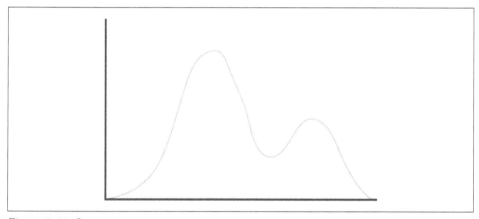

Figure 5-11. Server errors

The successful requests will have a long-tail distribution, but in reality we may expect the response distribution to be "multimodal" and have several local maxima. An example is shown in Figure 5-12, and represents the possibility that there could be two common execution paths through the application with quite different response times.

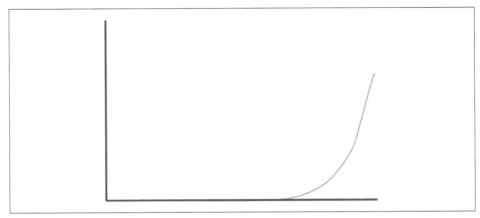

Figure 5-12. Successful requests

Combining these different types of responses into a single graph results in the structure shown in Figure 5-13. We have rederived our original "hat" shape from the separate histograms.

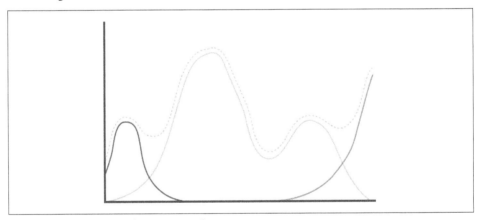

Figure 5-13. Hat or elephant revisited

The concept of breaking down a general observable into more meaningful subpopulations is a very useful one, and shows that we need to make sure that we understand our data and domain well enough before trying to infer conclusions from our results. We may well want to further break down our data into smaller sets; for example, the successful requests may have very different distributions for requests that are predominantly read, as opposed to requests that are updates or uploads.

The engineering team at PayPal have written extensively about their use of statistics and analysis; they have a blog (*https://www.paypal-engineering.com/*) that contains excellent resources. In particular, the piece "Statistics for Software" (*https://www.paypal-engineering.com/2016/04/11/statistics-for-software/*) by Mahmoud

Hashemi is a great introduction to their methodologies, and includes a version of the Hat/Elephant problem discussed earlier.

Summary

Microbenchmarking is the closest that Java performance comes to a "Dark Art." While this characterization is evocative, it is not wholly deserved. It is still an engineering discipline undertaken by working developers. However, microbenchmarks should be used with caution:

- Do not microbenchmark unless you know you are a known use case for it.
- If you must microbenchmark, use JMH.
- Discuss your results as publicly as you can, and in the company of your peers.
- Be prepared to be wrong a lot and to have your thinking challenged repeatedly.

One of the positive aspects of working with microbenchmarks is that it exposes the highly dynamic behavior and non-normal distributions that are produced by low-level subsystems. This, in turn, leads to a better understanding and mental models of the complexities of the JVM.

In the next chapter, we will move on from methodology and start our technical deep dive into the JVM's internals and major subsystems, by beginning our examination of garbage collection.

## CHAPTER 6

Understanding Garbage Collection

The Java environment has several iconic or defining features, and garbage collection is one of the most immediately recognizable. However, when the platform was first released, there was considerable hostility to GC. This was fueled by the fact that Java deliberately provided no language-level way to control the behavior of the collector (and continues not to, even in modern versions).[1]

This meant that in the early days, there was a certain amount of frustration over the performance of Java's GC, and this fed into perceptions of the platform as a whole.

However, the early vision of mandatory, non-user-controllable GC has been more than vindicated, and these days very few application developers would attempt to defend the opinion that memory should be managed by hand. Even modern takes on systems programming languages (e.g., Go and Rust) regard memory management as the proper domain of the compiler and runtime rather than the programmer (in anything other than exceptional circumstances).

The essence of Java's garbage collection is that rather than requiring the programmer to understand the precise lifetime of every object in the system, the runtime should keep track of objects on the programmer's behalf and automatically get rid of objects that are no longer required. The automatically reclaimed memory can then be wiped and reused.

---

1 The `System.gc()` method exists, but is basically useless for any practical purpose.

There are two fundamental rules of garbage collection that all implementations are subject to:

- Algorithms must collect all garbage.
- No live object must ever be collected.

Of these two rules, the second is by far the most important. Collecting a live object could lead to segmentation faults or (even worse) silent corruption of program data. Java's GC algorithms need to be sure that they will never collect an object the program is still using.

The idea of the programmer surrendering some low-level control in exchange for not having to account for every low-level detail by hand is the essence of Java's managed approach and expresses James Gosling's conception of Java as a blue-collar language for getting things done.

In this chapter, we will meet some of the basic theory that underpins Java garbage collection, and explain why it is one of the hardest parts of the platform to fully understand and to control. We will also introduce the basic features of HotSpot's runtime system, including such details as how HotSpot represents objects in the heap at runtime.

Toward the end of the chapter, we will introduce the simplest of HotSpot's production collectors, the parallel collectors, and explain some of the details that make them so useful for many workloads.

Introducing Mark and Sweep

Most Java programmers, if pressed, can recall that Java's GC relies on an algorithm called *mark and sweep*, but most also struggle to recall any details as to how the process actually operates.

In this section we will introduce a basic form of the algorithm and show how it can be used to reclaim memory automatically. This is a deliberately simplified form of the algorithm and is only intended to introduce a few basic concepts—it is not representative of how production JVMs actually carry out GC.

This introductory form of the mark-and-sweep algorithm uses an allocated object list to hold a pointer to each object that has been allocated, but not yet reclaimed. The overall GC algorithm can then be expressed as:

1. Loop through the allocated list, clearing the mark bit.
2. Starting from the GC roots, find the live objects.
3. Set a mark bit on each object reached.

4. Loop through the allocated list, and for each object whose mark bit hasn't been set:

   a. Reclaim the memory in the heap and place it back on the free list.

   b. Remove the object from the allocated list.

The live objects are usually located depth-first, and the resulting graph of objects is called *the live object graph*. It is sometimes also called the *transitive closure of reachable objects*, and an example can be seen in Figure 6-1.

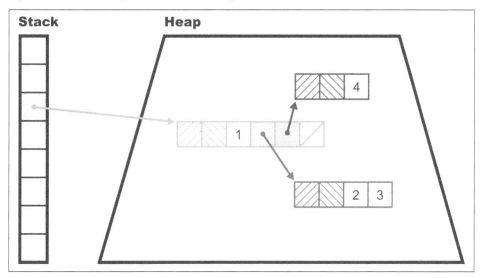

Figure 6-1. Simple view of memory layout

The state of the heap can be hard to visualize, but fortunately there are some simple tools to help us. One of the simplest is the `jmap -histo` command-line tool. This shows the number of bytes allocated per type, and the number of instances that are collectively responsible for that memory usage. It produces output like the following:

```
 num     #instances         #bytes  class name
----------------------------------------------
   1:          20839       14983608  [B
   2:         118743       12370760  [C
   3:          14528        9385360  [I
   4:            282        6461584  [D
   5:         115231        3687392  java.util.HashMap$Node
   6:         102237        2453688  java.lang.String
   7:          68388        2188416  java.util.Hashtable$Entry
   8:           8708        1764328  [Ljava.util.HashMap$Node;
   9:          39047        1561880  jdk.nashorn.internal.runtime.CompiledFunction
  10:          23688        1516032  com.mysql.jdbc.Co...$BooleanConnectionProperty
  11:          24217        1356152  jdk.nashorn.internal.runtime.ScriptFunction
  12:          27344        1301896  [Ljava.lang.Object;
```

```
13:       10040    1107896  java.lang.Class
14:       44090    1058160  java.util.LinkedList$Node
15:       29375     940000  java.util.LinkedList
16:       25944     830208  jdk.nashorn.interna...FinalScriptFunctionData
17:          20     655680  [Lscala.concurrent.forkjoin.ForkJoinTask;
18:       19943     638176  java.util.concurrent.ConcurrentHashMap$Node
19:         730     614744  [Ljava.util.Hashtable$Entry;
20:       24022     578560  [Ljava.lang.Class;
```

There is also a GUI tool available: the Sampling tab of VisualVM, introduced in Chapter 2. The VisualGC plug-in to VisualVM provides a real-time view of how the heap is changing, but in general the moment-to-moment view of the heap is not sufficient for accurate analysis and instead we should use GC logs for better insight—this will be a major theme of Chapter 8.

Garbage Collection Glossary

The jargon used to describe GC algorithms is sometimes a bit confusing (and the meaning of some of the terms has changed over time). For the sake of clarity, we include a basic glossary of how we use specific terms:

Stop-the-world (STW)
The GC cycle requires all application threads to be paused while garbage is collected. This prevents application code from invalidating the GC thread's view of the state of the heap. This is the usual case for most simple GC algorithms.

Concurrent
GC threads can run while application threads are running. This is very, very difficult to achieve, and very expensive in terms of computation expended. Virtually no algorithms are truly concurrent. Instead, complex tricks are used to give most of the benefits of concurrent collection. In "CMS" on page 148 we'll meet HotSpot's Concurrent Mark and Sweep (CMS) collector, which, despite its name, is perhaps best described as a "mostly concurrent" collector.

Parallel
Multiple threads are used to execute garbage collection.

Exact
An exact GC scheme has enough type information about the state of the heap to ensure that all garbage can be collected on a single cycle. More loosely, an exact scheme has the property that it can always tell the difference between an int and a pointer.

Conservative
A conservative scheme lacks the information of an exact scheme. As a result, conservative schemes frequently fritter away resources and are typically far less

efficient due to their fundamental ignorance of the type system they purport to represent.

Moving

In a moving collector, objects can be relocated in memory. This means that they do not have stable addresses. Environments that provide access to raw pointers (e.g., C++) are not a natural fit for moving collectors.

Compacting

At the end of the collection cycle, allocated memory (i.e., surviving objects) is arranged as a single contiguous region (usually at the start of the region), and there is a pointer indicating the start of empty space that is available for objects to be written into. A compacting collector will avoid memory fragmentation.

Evacuating

At the end of the collection cycle, the collected region is totally empty, and all live objects have been moved (evacuated) to another region of memory.

In most other languages and environments, the same terms are used. For example, the JavaScript runtime of the Firefox web browser (SpiderMonkey) also makes use of garbage collection, and in recent years has been adding features (e.g., exactness and compaction) that are already present in GC implementations in Java.

Introducing the HotSpot Runtime

In addition to the general GC terminology, HotSpot introduces terms that are more specific to the implementation. To obtain a full understanding of how garbage collection works on this JVM, we need to get to grips with some of the details of HotSpot's internals.

For what follows it will be very helpful to remember that Java has only two sorts of value:

- Primitive types (`byte`, `int`, etc.)
- Object references

Many Java programmers loosely talk about *objects*, but for our purposes it is important to remember that, unlike C++, Java has no general address dereference mechanism and can only use an *offset operator* (the . operator) to access fields and call methods on *object references*. Also keep in mind that Java's method call semantics are purely call-by-value, although for object references this means that the value that is copied is the address of the object in the heap.

Representing Objects at Runtime

HotSpot represents Java objects at runtime via a structure called an *oop*. This is short for *ordinary object pointer*, and is a genuine pointer in the C sense. These pointers can be placed in local variables of reference type where they point from the stack frame of the Java method into the memory area comprising the Java heap.

There are several different data structures that comprise the family of oops, and the sort that represent instances of a Java class are called *instanceOops*.

The memory layout of an instanceOop starts with two machine words of header present on every object. The *mark word* is the first of these, and is a pointer that points at instance-specific metadata. Next is the *klass word*, which points at class-wide metadata.

In Java 7 and before, the klass word of an instanceOop points into an area of memory called *PermGen*, which was a part of the Java heap. The general rule is that anything in the Java heap must have an object header. In these older versions of Java we refer to the metadata as a *klassOop*. The memory layout of a klassOop is simple—it's just the object header immediately followed by the klass metadata.

From Java 8 onward, the klasses are held outside of the main part of the Java heap (but not outside the C heap of the JVM process). Klass words in these versions of Java do not require an object header, as they point outside the Java heap.

 The *k* at the start is used to help disambiguate the klassOop from an instanceOop representing the Java Class<?> object; they are not the same thing.

In Figure 6-2 we can see the difference: fundamentally the klassOop contains the virtual function table (vtable) for the class, whereas the Class object contains an array of references to Method objects for use in reflective invocation. We will have more to say on this subject in Chapter 9 when we discuss JIT compilation.

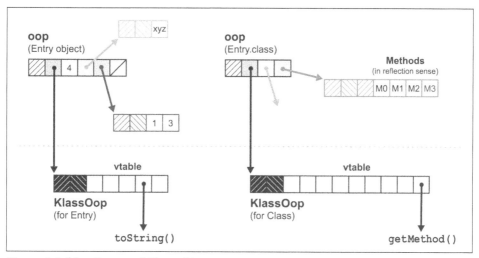

Figure 6-2. klassOops and Class objects

Oops are usually machine words, so 32 bits on a legacy 32-bit machine, and 64 bits on a modern processor. However, this has the potential to waste a possibly significant amount of memory. To help mitigate this, HotSpot provides a technique called *compressed oops*. If the option:

```
-XX:+UseCompressedOops
```

is set (and it is the default for 64-bit heaps from Java 7 and upward), then the following oops in the heap will be compressed:

- The klass word of every object in the heap
- Instance fields of reference type
- Every element of an array of objects

This means that, in general, a HotSpot object header consists of:

- Mark word at full native size
- Klass word (possibly compressed)
- Length word if the object is an array—always 32 bits
- A 32-bit gap (if required by alignment rules)

The instance fields of the object then follow immediately after the header. For klassOops, the vtable of methods follows directly after the klass word. The memory layout for compressed oops can be seen in Figure 6-3.

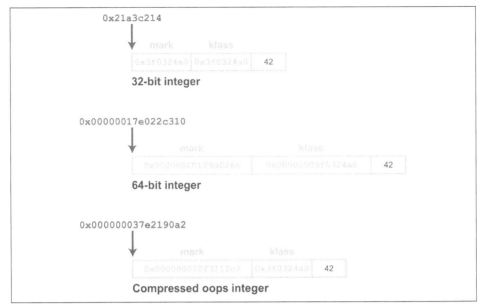

Figure 6-3. Compressed oops

In the past, some extremely latency-sensitive applications could occasionally see improvements by switching off the compressed oops feature—at the cost of increased heap size (typically an increase of 10–50%). However, the class of applications for which this would yield measurable performance benefits is very small, and for most modern applications this would be a classic example of the Fiddling with Switches antipattern we saw in Chapter 4.

As we remember from basic Java, arrays are objects. This means that the JVM's arrays are represented as oops as well. This is why arrays have a third word of metadata as well as the usual mark and klass words. This third word is the array's length—which also explains why array indices in Java are limited to 32-bit values.

The use of additional metadata to carry an array's length alleviates a whole class of problems present in C and C++ where not knowing the length of the array means that additional parameters must be passed to functions.

The managed environment of the JVM does not allow a Java reference to point anywhere but at an instanceOop (or null). This means that at a low level:

- A Java value is a bit pattern corresponding either to a primitive value or to the address of an instanceOop (a reference).

- Any Java reference considered as a pointer refers to an address in the main part of the Java heap.

- Addresses that are the targets of Java references contain a mark word followed by a klass word as the next machine word.

- A klassOop and an instance of Class<?> are different (as the former lives in the metadata area of the heap), and a klassOop cannot be placed into a Java variable.

HotSpot defines a hierarchy of oops in *.hpp* files that are kept in *hotspot/src/share/vm/oops* in the OpenJDK 8 source tree. The overall inheritance hierarchy for oops looks like this:

```
oop (abstract base)
 instanceOop (instance objects)
 methodOop (representations of methods)
 arrayOop (array abstract base)
 symbolOop (internal symbol / string class)
 klassOop (klass header) (Java 7 and before only)
 markOop
```

This use of oop structures to represent objects at runtime, with one pointer to house class-level metadata and another to house instance metadata, is not particularly unusual. Many other JVMs and other execution environments use a related mechanism. For example, Apple's iOS uses a similar scheme for representing objects.

GC Roots and Arenas

Articles and blog posts about HotSpot frequently refer to *GC roots*. These are "anchor points" for memory, essentially known pointers that originate from outside a memory pool of interest and point into it. They are *external* pointers as opposed to *internal* pointers, which originate inside the memory pool and point to another memory location within the memory pool.

We saw an example of a GC root in Figure 6-1. However, as we will see, there are other sorts of GC root, including:

- Stack frames
- JNI
- Registers (for the hoisted variable case)
- Code roots (from the JVM code cache)
- Globals
- Class metadata from loaded classes

If this definition seems rather complex, then the simplest example of a GC root is a local variable of reference type that will always point to an object in the heap (provided it is not null).

The HotSpot garbage collector works in terms of areas of memory called *arenas*. This is a very low-level mechanism, and Java developers usually don't need to consider the operation of the memory system in such detail. However, performance specialists sometimes need to delve deeper into the internals of the JVM, and so a familiarity with the concepts and terms used in the literature is helpful.

One important fact to remember is that HotSpot does not use system calls to manage the Java heap. Instead, as we discussed in "Basic Detection Strategies" on page 48, HotSpot manages the heap size from user space code, so we can use simple observables to determine whether the GC subsystem is causing some types of performance problems.

In the next section, we'll take a closer look at two of the most important characteristics that drive the garbage collection behavior of any Java or JVM workload. A good understanding of these characteristics is essential for any developer who wants to really grasp the factors that drive Java GC (which is one of the key overall drivers for Java performance).

Allocation and Lifetime

There are two primary drivers of the garbage collection behavior of a Java application:

- Allocation rate
- Object lifetime

The allocation rate is the amount of memory used by newly created objects over some time period (usually measured in MB/s). This is not directly recorded by the JVM, but is a relatively easy observable to estimate, and tools such as Censum can determine it precisely.

By contrast, the object lifetime is normally a lot harder to measure (or even estimate). In fact, one of the major arguments against using manual memory management is the complexity involved in truly understanding object lifetimes for a real application. As a result, object lifetime is if anything even more fundamental than allocation rate.

Garbage collection can also be thought of as "memory reclamation and reuse." The ability to use the same physical piece of memory over and over again, because objects are short-lived, is a key assumption of garbage collection techniques.

The idea that objects are created, they exist for a time, and then the memory used to store their state can be reclaimed is essential; without it, garbage collection would not work at all. As we will see in Chapter 7, there are a number of different tradeoffs that garbage collectors must balance—and some of the most important of these tradeoffs are driven by lifetime and allocation concerns.

Weak Generational Hypothesis

One key part of the JVM's memory management relies upon an observed runtime effect of software systems, the Weak Generational Hypothesis:

> The distribution of object lifetimes on the JVM and similar software systems is bimodal—with the vast majority of objects being very short-lived and a secondary population having a much longer life expectancy.

This hypothesis, which is really an experimentally observed rule of thumb about the behavior of object-oriented workloads, leads to an obvious conclusion: garbage-collected heaps should be structured in such a way as to allow short-lived objects to be easily and quickly collected, and ideally for long-lived objects to be separated from short-lived objects.

HotSpot uses several mechanisms to try to take advantage of the Weak Generational Hypothesis:

- It tracks the "generational count" of each object (the number of garbage collections that the object has survived so far).

- With the exception of large objects, it creates new objects in the "Eden" space (also called the "Nursery") and expects to move surviving objects.

- It maintains a separate area of memory (the "old" or "Tenured" generation) to hold objects that are deemed to have survived long enough that they are likely to be long-lived.

This approach leads to the view shown in simplified form in Figure 6-4, where objects that have survived a certain number of garbage collection cycles are promoted to the Tenured generation. Note the continuous nature of the regions, as shown in the diagram.

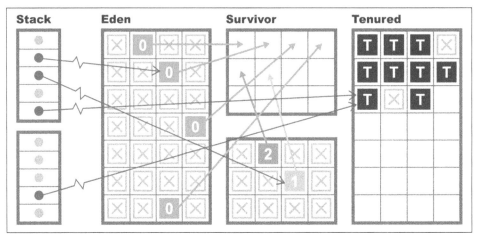

Figure 6-4. Generational collection

Dividing up memory into different regions for purposes of generational collection has some additional consequences in terms of how HotSpot implements a mark-and-sweep collection. One important technique involves keeping track of pointers that point into the young generation from outside. This saves the GC cycle from having to traverse the entire object graph in order to determine the young objects that are still live.

 "There are few references from old to young objects" is sometimes cited as a secondary part of the Weak Generational Hypothesis.

To facilitate this process, HotSpot maintains a structure called a *card table* to help record which old-generation objects could potentially point at young objects. The card table is essentially an array of bytes managed by the JVM. Each element of the array corresponds to a 512-byte area of old-generation space.

The central idea is that when a field of reference type on an old object o is modified, the card table entry for the card containing the instanceOop corresponding to o is marked as dirty. HotSpot achieves this with a simple *write barrier* when updating reference fields. It essentially boils down to this bit of code being executed after the field store:

```
cards[*instanceOop >> 9] = 0;
```

Note that the dirty value for the card is 0, and the right-shift by 9 bits gives the size of the card table as 512 bytes.

Finally, we should note that the description of the heap in terms of old and young areas is historically the way that Java's collectors have managed memory. With the arrival of Java 8u40, a new collector ("Garbage First," or G1) reached production quality. G1 has a somewhat different view of how to approach heap layout, as we will see in "CMS" on page 148. This new way of thinking about heap management will be increasingly important, as Oracle's intention is for G1 to become the default collector from Java 9 onward.

Garbage Collection in HotSpot

Recall that unlike C/C++ and similar environments, Java does not use the operating system to manage dynamic memory. Instead, the JVM allocates (or reserves) memory up front, when the JVM process starts, and manages a single, contiguous memory pool from user space.

As we have seen, this pool of memory is made up of different regions with dedicated purposes, and the address that an object resides at will very often change over time as the collector relocates objects, which are normally created in Eden. Collectors that perform relocation are known as "evacuating" collectors, as mentioned in the "Garbage Collection Glossary" on page 118. Many of the collectors that HotSpot can use are evacuating.

Thread-Local Allocation

The JVM uses a performance enhancement to manage Eden. This is a critical region to manage efficiently, as it is where most objects are created, and very short-lived objects (those with lifetimes less than the remaining time to the next GC cycle) will never be located anywhere else.

For efficiency, the JVM partitions Eden into buffers and hands out individual regions of Eden for application threads to use as allocation regions for new objects. The advantage of this approach is that each thread knows that it does not have to consider the possibility that other threads are allocating within that buffer. These regions are called *thread-local allocation buffers* (TLABs).

 HotSpot dynamically sizes the TLABs that it gives to application threads, so if a thread is burning through memory it can be given larger TLABs to reduce the overhead in providing buffers to the thread.

The exclusive control that an application thread has over its TLABs means that allocation is O(1) for JVM threads. This is because when a thread creates a new object, storage is allocated for the object, and the thread-local pointer is updated to the next free memory address. In terms of the C runtime, this is a simple pointer bump—that is, one additional instruction to move the "next free" pointer onward.

This behavior can be seen in Figure 6-5, where each application thread holds a buffer to allocate new objects. If the application thread fills the buffer, then the JVM provides a pointer to a new area of Eden.

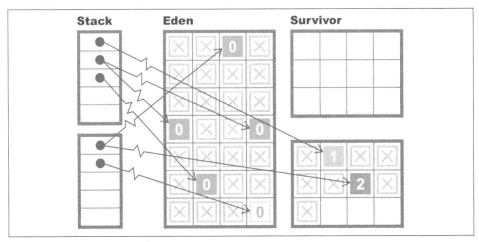

Figure 6-5. Thread-local allocation

Hemispheric Collection

One particular special case of the evacuating collector is worth noting. Sometimes referred to as a *hemispheric evacuating collector*, this type of collector uses two (usually equal-sized) spaces. The central idea is to use the spaces as a temporary holding area for objects that are not actually long-lived. This prevents short-lived objects from cluttering up the Tenured generation and reduces the frequency of full GCs. The spaces have a couple of basic properties:

- When the collector is collecting the currently live hemisphere, objects are moved in a compacting fashion to the other hemisphere and the collected hemisphere is emptied for reuse.
- One half of the space is kept completely empty at all times.

This approach does, of course, use twice as much memory as can actually be held within the hemispheric part of the collector. This is somewhat wasteful, but it is often a useful technique if the size of the spaces is not excessive. HotSpot uses this hemispheric approach in combination with the Eden space to provide a collector for the young generation.

The hemispheric part of HotSpot's young heap is referred to as the *survivor spaces*. As we can see from the view of VisualGC shown in Figure 6-6, the survivor spaces are normally relatively small as compared to Eden, and the role of the survivor spaces swaps with each young generational collection. We will discuss how to tune the size of the survivor spaces in Chapter 8.

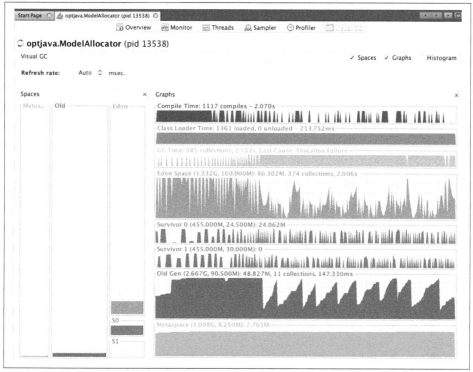

Figure 6-6. The VisualGC plug-in

The VisualGC plug-in for VisualVM, introduced in "VisualVM" on page 30, is a very useful initial GC debugging tool. As we will discuss in Chapter 7, the GC logs contain far more useful information and allow a much deeper analysis of GC than is possible from the moment-to-moment JMX data that VisualGC uses. However, when starting a new analysis, it is often helpful to simply eyeball the application's memory usage.

Using VisualGC it is possible to see some aggregate effects of garbage collection, such as objects being relocated in the heap, and the cycling between survivor spaces that happens at each young collection.

The Parallel Collectors

In Java 8 and earlier versions, the default collectors for the JVM are the parallel collectors. These are fully STW for both young and full collections, and they are optimized for throughput. After stopping all application threads the parallel collectors use all available CPU cores to collect memory as quickly as possible. The available parallel collectors are:

Parallel GC
    The simplest collector for the young generation

ParNew
    A slight variation of Parallel GC that is used with the CMS collector

ParallelOld
    The parallel collector for the old (aka Tenured) generation

The parallel collectors are in some ways similar to each other—they are designed to use multiple threads to identify live objects as quickly as possible and to do minimal bookkeeping. However, there are some differences between them, so let's take a look at the two main types of collections.

Young Parallel Collections

The most common type of collection is young generational collection. This usually occurs when a thread tries to allocate an object into Eden but doesn't have enough space in its TLAB, and the JVM can't allocate a fresh TLAB for the thread. When this occurs, the JVM has no choice other than to stop all the application threads—because if one thread is unable to allocate, then very soon every thread will be unable.

 Threads can also allocate outside of TLABs (e.g., for large blocks of memory). The desired case is when the rate of non-TLAB allocation is low.

Once all application (or user) threads are stopped, HotSpot looks at the young generation (which is defined as Eden and the currently nonempty survivor space) and identifies all objects that are not garbage. This will utilize the GC roots (and the card table to identify GC roots coming from the old generation) as starting points for a parallel marking scan.

The Parallel GC collector then evacuates all of the surviving objects into the currently empty survivor space (and increments their generational count as they are relocated). Finally, Eden and the just-evacuated survivor space are marked as empty, reusable space and the application threads are started so that the process of handing out TLABs to application threads can begin again. This process is shown in Figures 6-7 and 6-8.

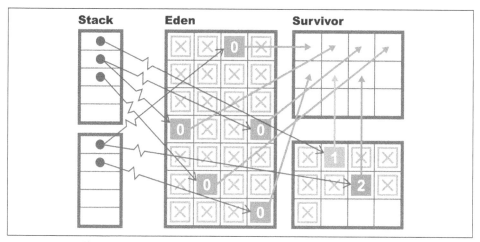

Figure 6-7. Collecting the young generation

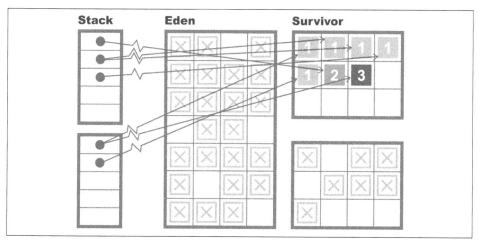

Figure 6-8. Evacuating the young generation

This approach attempts to take full advantage of the Weak Generational Hypothesis by touching only live objects. It also wants to be as efficient as possible and run using all cores as much as possible to shorten the STW pause time.

Old Parallel Collections

The ParallelOld collector is currently (as of Java 8) the default collector for the old generation. It has some strong similarities to Parallel GC, but also some fundamental differences. In particular, Parallel GC is a hemispheric evacuating collector, whereas ParallelOld is a compacting collector with only a single continuous memory space.

This means that as the old generation has no other space to be evacuated to, the parallel collector attempts to relocate objects within the old generation to reclaim space that may have been left by old objects dying. Thus, the collector can potentially be very efficient in its use of memory, and will not suffer from memory fragmentation.

This results in a very efficient memory layout at the cost of using a potentially large amount of CPU during full GC cycles. The difference between the two approaches can be seen in Figure 6-9.

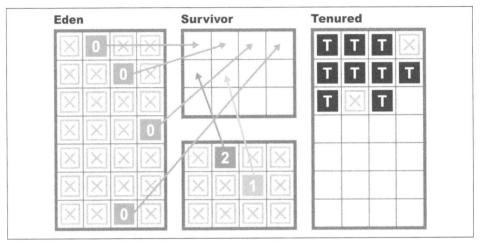

Figure 6-9. Evacuating versus compacting

The behavior of the two memory spaces is quite radically different, as they are serving different purposes. The purpose of the young collections is to deal with the short-lived objects, so the occupancy of the young space is changing radically with allocation and clearance at GC events.

By contrast, the old space does not change as obviously. Occasional large objects will be created directly in Tenured, but apart from that, the space will only change at collections—either by objects being promoted from the young generation, or by a full rescan and rearrangement at an old or full collection.

Limitations of Parallel Collectors

The parallel collectors deal with the entire contents of a generation at once, and try to collect as efficiently as possible. However, this design has some drawbacks. Firstly, they are fully stop-the-world. This is not usually an issue for young collections, as the Weak Generational Hypothesis means that very few objects should survive.

The design of the young parallel collectors is such that dead objects are never touched, so the length of the marking phase is proportional to the (small) number of surviving objects.

This basic design, coupled with the usually small size of the young regions of the heap, means that the pause time of young collections is very short for most workloads. A typical pause time for a young collection on a modern 2 GB JVM (with default sizing) might well be just a few milliseconds, and is very frequently under 10 ms.

However, collecting the old generation is often a very different story. For one thing, the old generation is by default seven times the size of the young generation. This fact alone will make the expected STW length of a full collection much longer than for a young collection.

Another key fact is that the marking time is proportional to the number of live objects in a region. Old objects may be long-lived, so a potentially larger number of old objects may survive a full collection.

This behavior also explains a key weakness of parallel old collection—the STW time will scale roughly linearly with the size of the heap. As heap sizes continue to increase, ParallelOld starts to scale badly in terms of pause time.

Newcomers to GC theory sometimes entertain private theories that minor modifications to mark-and-sweep algorithms might help to alleviate STW pauses. However, this is not the case. Garbage collection has been a very well-studied research area of computer science for over 40 years, and no such "can't you just…" improvement has ever been found.

As we will see in Chapter 7, mostly concurrent collectors do exist and they can run with greatly reduced pause times. However, they are not a panacea, and several fundamental difficulties with garbage collection remain.

As an example of one of the central difficulties with the naive approach to GC, let's consider TLAB allocation. This provides a great boost to allocation performance but is of no help to collection cycles. To see why, consider this code:

```
public static void main(String[] args) {
    int[] anInt = new int[1];
    anInt[0] = 42;
    Runnable r = () -> {
        anInt[0]++;
        System.out.println("Changed: "+ anInt[0]);
    };
```

```
    new Thread(r).start();
}
```

The variable anInt is an array object containing a single int. It is allocated from a TLAB held by the main thread but immediately afterward is passed to a new thread. To put it another way, the key property of TLABs—that they are private to a single thread—is true only at the point of allocation. This property can be violated basically as soon as objects have been allocated.

The Java environment's ability to trivially create new threads is a fundamental, and extremely powerful, part of the platform. However, it complicates the picture for garbage collection considerably, as new threads imply execution stacks, each frame of which is a source of GC roots.

The Role of Allocation

Java's garbage collection process is most commonly triggered when memory allocation is requested but there is not enough free memory on hand to provide the required amount. This means that GC cycles do not occur on a fixed or predictable schedule but purely on an as-needed basis.

This is one of the most critical aspects of garbage collection: it is not deterministic and does not occur at a regular cadence. Instead, a GC cycle is triggered when one or more of the heap's memory spaces are essentially full, and further object creation would not be possible.

 This as-needed nature makes garbage collection logs hard to process using traditional time series analysis methods. The lack of regularity between GC events is an aspect that most time series libraries cannot easily accommodate.

When GC occurs, all application threads are paused (as they cannot create any more objects, and no substantial piece of Java code can run for very long without producing new objects). The JVM takes over all of the cores to perform GC, and reclaims memory before restarting the application threads.

To better understand why allocation is so critical, let's consider the following highly simplified case study. The heap parameters are set up as shown, and we assume that they do not change over time. Of course a real application would normally have a dynamically resizing heap, but this example serves as a simple illustration.

Heap area	Size
Overall	2 GB
Old generation	1.5 GB
Young generation	500 MB
Eden	400 MB
S1	50 MB
S2	50 MB

After the application has reached its steady state, the following GC metrics are observed:

Allocation rate	100 MB/s
Young GC time	2 ms
Full GC time	100 ms
Object lifetime	200 ms

This shows that Eden will fill in 4 seconds, so at steady state, a young GC will occur every 4 seconds. Eden has filled, and so GC is triggered. Most of the objects in Eden are dead, but any object that is still alive will be evacuated to a survivor space (SS1, for the sake of discussion). In this simple model, any objects that were created in the last 200 ms have not had time to die, so they will survive. So, we have:

GC0 @ 4 s   20 MB Eden → SS1 (20 MB)

After another 4 seconds, Eden refills and will need to be evacuated (to SS2 this time). However, in this simplified model, no objects that were promoted into SS1 by GC0 survive—their lifetime is only 200 ms and another 4 s has elapsed, so all of the objects allocated prior to GC0 are now dead. We now have:

GC1 @ 8.002 s   20 MB Eden → SS2 (20 MB)

Another way of saying this is that after GC1, the contents of SS2 consist solely of objects newly arrived from Eden and no object in SS2 has a generational age > 1. Continuing for one more collection, the pattern should become clear:

GC2 @ 12.004 s   20 MB Eden → SS1 (20 MB)

This idealized, simple model leads to a situation where no objects ever become eligible for promotion to the Tenured generation, and the space remains empty throughout the run. This is, of course, very unrealistic.

Instead, the Weak Generational Hypothesis indicates that object lifetimes will be a distribution, and due to the uncertainty of this distribution, some objects will end up surviving to reach Tenured.

Let's look at a very simple simulator for this allocation scenario. It allocates objects, most of which are very short-lived but some of which have a considerably longer life span. It has a couple of parameters that define the allocation: x and y, which between them define the size of each object; the allocation rate (mbPerSec); the lifetime of a short-lived object (shortLivedMS) and the number of threads that the application should simulate (nThreads). The default values are shown in the next listing:

```java
public class ModelAllocator implements Runnable {
    private volatile boolean shutdown = false;

    private double chanceOfLongLived = 0.02;
    private int multiplierForLongLived = 20;
    private int x = 1024;
    private int y = 1024;
    private int mbPerSec = 50;
    private int shortLivedMs = 100;
    private int nThreads = 8;
    private Executor exec = Executors.newFixedThreadPool(nThreads);
```

Omitting `main()` and any other startup/parameter-setting code, the rest of the ModelAllocator looks like this:

```java
public void run() {
    final int mainSleep = (int) (1000.0 / mbPerSec);

    while (!shutdown) {
        for (int i = 0; i < mbPerSec; i++) {
            ModelObjectAllocation to =
                new ModelObjectAllocation(x, y, lifetime());
            exec.execute(to);
            try {
                Thread.sleep(mainSleep);
            } catch (InterruptedException ex) {
                shutdown = true;
            }
        }
    }
}

// Simple function to model Weak Generational Hypothesis
// Returns the expected lifetime of an object - usually this
// is very short, but there is a small chance of an object
// being "long-lived"
```

```
public int lifetime() {
    if (Math.random() < chanceOfLongLived) {
        return multiplierForLongLived * shortLivedMs;
    }

    return shortLivedMs;
    }
}
```

The allocator main runner is combined with a simple mock object used to represent the object allocation performed by the application:

```
public class ModelObjectAllocation implements Runnable {
    private final int[][] allocated;
    private final int lifeTime;

    public ModelObjectAllocation(final int x, final int y, final int liveFor) {
        allocated = new int[x][y];
        lifeTime = liveFor;
    }

    @Override
    public void run() {
        try {
            Thread.sleep(lifeTime);
            System.err.println(System.currentTimeMillis() +": "+ allocated.length);
        } catch (InterruptedException ex) {
        }
    }
}
```

When seen in VisualVM, this will display the simple sawtooth pattern that is often observed in the memory behavior of Java applications that are making efficient use of the heap. This pattern can be seen in Figure 6-10.

We will have a great deal more to say about tooling and visualization of memory effects in Chapter 7. The interested reader can steal a march on the tuning discussion by downloading the allocation and lifetime simulator referenced in this chapter, and setting parameters to see the effects of allocation rates and percentages of long-lived objects.

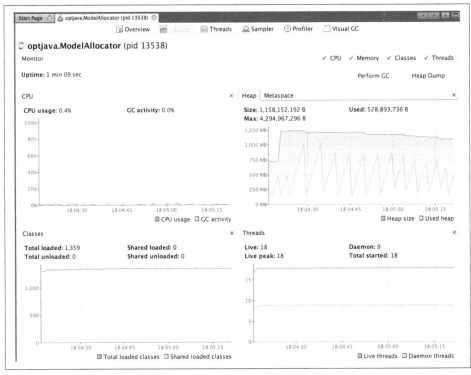

Figure 6-10. Simple sawtooth

To finish this discussion of allocation, we want to shift focus to a very common aspect of allocation behavior. In the real world, allocation rates can be highly changeable and "bursty." Consider the following scenario for an application with a steady-state behavior as previously described:

2 s	Steady-state allocation	100 MB/s
1 s	Burst/spike allocation	1 GB/s
100 s	Back to steady-state	100 MB/s

The initial steady-state execution has allocated 200 MB in Eden. In the absence of long-lived objects, all of this memory has a lifetime of 100 ms. Next, the allocation spike kicks in. This allocates the other 200 MB of Eden space in just 0.2 s, and of this, 100 MB is under the 100 ms age threshold. The size of the surviving cohort is larger than the survivor space, and so the JVM has no option but to promote these objects directly into Tenured. So we have:

```
GC0   @ 2.2 s   100 MB Eden → Tenured (100 MB)
```

The sharp increase in allocation rate has produced 100 MB of surviving objects, although note that in this model all of the "survivors" are in fact short-lived and will very quickly become dead objects cluttering up the Tenured generation. They will not be reclaimed until a full collection occurs.

Continuing for a few more collections, the pattern becomes clear:

```
GC1   @ 2.602 s   200 MB Eden → Tenured (300 MB)

GC2   @ 3.004 s   200 MB Eden → Tenured (500 MB)

GC2   @ 7.006 s   20 MB Eden → SS1 (20 MB) [+ Tenured (500 MB)]
```

Notice that, as discussed, the garbage collector runs as needed, and not at regular intervals. The bigger the allocation rate, the more frequent GCs are. If the allocation rate is too high, then objects will end up being forced to be promoted early.

This phenomenon is called *premature promotion*; it is one of the most important indirect effects of garbage collection and a starting point for many tuning exercises, as we will see in the next chapter.

Summary

The subject of garbage collection has been a live topic of discussion within the Java community since the platform's inception. In this chapter, we have introduced the key concepts that performance engineers need to understand to work effectively with the JVM's GC subsystem. These included:

- Mark-and-sweep collection
- HotSpot's internal runtime representation for objects
- The Weak Generational Hypothesis
- Practicalities of HotSpot's memory subsystems
- The parallel collectors
- Allocation and the central role it plays

In the next chapter, we will discuss GC tuning, monitoring, and analysis. Several of the topics we met in this chapter—especially allocation, and specific effects such as premature promotion—will be of particular significance to the upcoming goals and topics, and it may be helpful to refer back to this chapter frequently.

## CHAPTER 7

Advanced Garbage Collection

In the last chapter we introduced the basic theory of Java garbage collection. From that starting point, we will move forward to introduce the theory of modern Java garbage collectors. This is an area that has unavoidable tradeoffs that guide the engineer's choice of collector.

To begin with we'll introduce and delve into the other collectors the HotSpot JVM provides. These include the ultra low-pause, mostly concurrent collector (CMS) and the modern general-purpose collector (G1).

We will also consider some more rarely seen collectors. These are:

- Shenandoah
- C4
- Balanced
- Legacy HotSpot collectors

Not all of these collectors are used in the HotSpot virtual machine—we will also be discussing the collectors of two other virtual machines: IBM J9 (a formerly closed source JVM that IBM is in the process of opening) and Azul Zing (a proprietary JVM). We have previously introduced both of these VMs in "Meet the JVMs" on page 26.

Tradeoffs and Pluggable Collectors

One aspect of the Java platform that beginners don't always immediately recognize is that while Java has a garbage collector, the language and VM specifications do not say how GC should be implemented. In fact, there have been Java implementations (e.g., Lego Mindstorms) that didn't implement any kind of GC at all![1]

Within the Sun (now Oracle) environment, the GC subsystem is treated as a pluggable subsystem. This means that the same Java program can execute with different garbage collectors without changing the semantics of the program, although the performance of the program may vary considerably based on which collector is in use.

The primary reason for having pluggable collectors is that GC is a very general computing technique. In particular, the same algorithm may not be appropriate for every workload. As a result, GC algorithms represent a compromise or tradeoff between competing concerns.

> There is no single general-purpose GC algorithm that can optimize for all GC concerns simultaneously.

The main concerns that developers often need to consider when choosing a garbage collector include:

- Pause time (aka pause length or duration)
- Throughput (as a percentage of GC time to application runtime)
- Pause frequency (how often the collector needs to stop the application)
- Reclamation efficiency (how much garbage can be collected on a single GC duty cycle)
- Pause consistency (are all pauses roughly the same length?)

Of these, pause time often attracts a disproportionate amount of attention. While important for many applications, it should not be considered in isolation.

> For many workloads pause time is not an effective or useful performance characteristic.

For example, a highly parallel batch processing or Big Data application is likely to be much more concerned with throughput rather than pause length. For many batch

---

1 Such a system is very difficult to program in, as every object that's created has to be reused, and any object that goes out of scope effectively leaks memory.

jobs, pause times of even tens of seconds are not really relevant, so a GC algorithm that favors CPU efficiency of GC and throughput is greatly preferred to an algorithm that is low-pause at any cost.

The performance engineer should also note that there are a number of other tradeoffs and concerns that are sometimes important when considering the choice of collector. However, in the case of HotSpot, the choice is constrained by the available collectors.

Within Oracle/OpenJDK, as of version 10, there are three mainstream collectors for general production use. We have already met the parallel (aka throughput) collectors, and they are the easiest to understand from a theoretical and algorithmic point of view. In this chapter, we will meet the two other mainstream collectors and explain how they differ from Parallel GC.

Toward the end of the chapter, in "Shenandoah" on page 156 and beyond, we will also meet some other collectors that are available, but please note that not all of them are recommended for production use, and some are now deprecated. We also provide a short discussion of collectors available in non-HotSpot JVMs.

Concurrent GC Theory

In specialized systems, such as graphics or animation display systems, there is often a fixed frame rate, which provides a regular, fixed opportunity for GC to be performed.

However, garbage collectors intended for general-purpose use have no such domain knowledge with which to improve the determinism of their pauses. Worse still, non-determinism is directly caused by allocation behavior, and many of the systems that Java is used for exhibit highly variable allocation.

> The minor disadvantage of this arrangement is the delay of the computation proper; its major disadvantage is the unpredictability of these garbage collecting interludes.
>
> —Edsger Dijkstra

The starting point for modern GC theory is to try to address Dijkstra's insight that the nondeterministic nature of STW pauses (both in duration and in frequency) is the major annoyance of using GC techniques.

One approach is to use a collector that is concurrent (or at least partially or mostly concurrent) in order to reduce pause time by doing some of the work needed for collection while the application threads are running. This inevitably reduces the processing power available for the actual work of the application, as well as complicating the code needed to perform collection.

Before discussing concurrent collectors, though, there is an important piece of GC terminology and technology that we need to address, as it is essential to understanding the nature and behavior of modern garbage collectors.

JVM Safepoints

In order to carry out an STW garbage collection, such as those performed by Hot-Spot's parallel collectors, all application threads must be stopped. This seems almost a tautology, but until now we have not discussed exactly *how* the JVM achieves this.

> The JVM is not actually a fully preemptive multithreading environment.
>
> —A Secret

This does not mean that it is purely a cooperative environment—quite the opposite. The operating system can still preempt (remove a thread from a core) at any time. This is done, for example, when a thread has exhausted its timeslice or put itself into a `wait()`.

As well as this core OS functionality, the JVM also needs to perform coordinated actions. In order to facilitate this, the runtime requires each application thread to have special execution points, called *safepoints*, where the thread's internal data structures are in a known-good state. At these times, the thread is able to be suspended for coordinated actions.

 We can see the effects of safepoints in STW GC (the classic example) and thread synchronization, but there are others as well.

To understand the point of safepoints, consider the case of a fully STW garbage collector. For this to run, it requires a stable object graph. This means that all application threads must be paused. There is no way for a GC thread to demand that the OS enforces this demand on an application thread, so the application threads (which are executing as part of the JVM process) must cooperate to achieve this. There are two primary rules that govern the JVM's approach to safepointing:

- The JVM cannot force a thread into the safepoint state.
- The JVM can prevent a thread from leaving the safepoint state.

This means that the implementation of the JVM interpreter must contain code to yield at a barrier if safepointing is required. For JIT-compiled methods, equivalent barriers must be inserted into the generated machine code. The general case for reaching safepoints then looks like this:

1. The JVM sets a global "time to safepoint" flag.
2. Individual application threads poll and see that the flag has been set.

---

3. They pause and wait to be woken up again.

When this flag is set, all app threads must stop. Threads that stop quickly must wait for slower stoppers (and this time may not be fully accounted for in the pause time statistics).

Normal app threads use this polling mechanism. They will always check in between executing any two bytecodes in the interpreter. In compiled code, the most common cases where the JIT compiler has inserted a poll for safepoints are exiting a compiled method and when a loop branches backward (e.g., to the top of the loop).

It is possible for a thread to take a long time to safepoint, and even theoretically to never stop (but this is a pathological case that must be deliberately provoked).

The idea that all threads must be fully stopped before the STW phase can commence is similar to the use of latches, such as that implemented by `CountDownLatch` in the `java.util.concurrent` library.

Some specific cases of safepoint conditions are worth mentioning here.

A thread is automatically at a safepoint if it:

- Is blocked on a monitor
- Is executing JNI code

A thread is *not* necessarily at a safepoint if it:

- Is partway through executing a bytecode (interpreted mode)
- Has been interrupted by the OS

We will meet the safepointing mechanism again later on, as it is a critical piece of the internal workings of the JVM.

Tri-Color Marking

Dijkstra and Lamport's 1978 paper describing their *tri-color marking* algorithm was a landmark for both correctness proofs of concurrent algorithms and GC, and the basic algorithm it describes remains an important part of garbage collection theory.[2]

---

2 Edsger Dijkstra, Leslie Lamport, A. J. Martin, C. S. Scholten, and E. F. M. Steffens, "On-the-Fly Garbage Collection: An Exercise in Cooperation," *Communications of the ACM* 21 (1978): 966–975.

The algorithm works like this:

- GC roots are colored gray.
- All other objects are colored white.
- A marking thread moves to a random gray node.
- If the node has any white children, the marking thread first colors them gray, then colors the node black.
- This process is repeated until there are no gray nodes left.
- All black objects have been proven to be reachable and must remain alive.
- White nodes are eligible for collection and correspond to objects that are no longer reachable.

There are some complications, but this is the basic form of the algorithm. An example is shown in Figure 7-1.

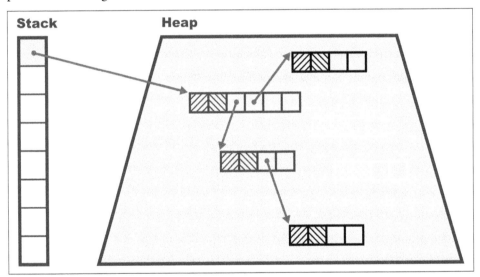

Figure 7-1. Tri-color marking

Concurrent collection also frequently makes use of a technique called *snapshot at the beginning* (SATB). This means that the collector regards objects as live if they were reachable at the start of the collection cycle or have been allocated since. This adds some minor wrinkles to the algorithm, such as mutator threads needing to create new objects in the black state if a collection is running, and in the white state if no collection is in progress.

The tri-color marking algorithm needs to be combined with a small amount of additional work in order to ensure that the changes introduced by the running application threads do not cause live objects to be collected. This is because in a concurrent collector, application (mutator) threads are changing the object graph, while marking threads are executing the tri-color algorithm.

Consider the situation where an object has already been colored black by a marking thread, and then is updated to point at a white object by a mutator thread. This is the situation shown in Figure 7-2.

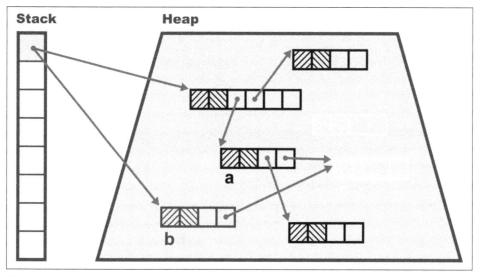

Figure 7-2. A mutator thread could invalidate tri-color marking

If all references from gray objects to the new white object are now deleted, we have a situation where the white object should still be reachable but will be deleted, as it will not be found, according to the rules of the algorithm.

This problem can be solved in several different ways. We could, for example, change the color of the black object back to gray, adding it back to the set of nodes that need processing as the mutator thread processes the update.

That approach, using a "write barrier" for the update, would have the nice algorithmic property that it would maintain the *tri-color invariant* throughout the whole of the marking cycle.

> No black object node may hold a reference to a white object node during concurrent marking.
>
> —Tri-color invariant

An alternative approach would be to keep a queue of all changes that could potentially violate the invariant, and then have a secondary "fixup" phase that runs after the main phase has finished. Different collectors can resolve this problem with tri-color marking in different ways, based on criteria such as performance or the amount of locking required.

In the next section we will meet the low-pause collector, CMS. We are introducing this collector before the others despite it being a collector with only a limited range of applicability. This is because developers are frequently unaware of the extent to which GC tuning requires tradeoffs and compromises.

By considering CMS first, we can showcase some of the practical issues that performance engineers should be aware of when thinking about garbage collection. The hope is that this will lead to a more evidence-based approach to tuning and the inherent tradeoffs in the choice of collector, and a little less Tuning by Folklore.

CMS

The Concurrent Mark and Sweep (CMS) collector is designed to be an extremely low-pause collector for the Tenured (aka old generation) space only. It is usually paired with a slightly modified parallel collector for collecting the young generation (called ParNew rather than Parallel GC).

CMS does as much work as possible while application threads are still running, so as to minimize pause time. The marking algorithm used is a form of tri-color marking, and this means, of course, that the object graph may be mutating while the collector is scanning the heap. As a result, CMS must fix up its records to avoid violating the second rule of garbage collectors, and collecting an object that is still alive.

This leads to a more complex set of phases in CMS than is seen in the parallel collectors. These phases are usually referred to as follows:

1. Initial Mark (STW)
2. Concurrent Mark
3. Concurrent Preclean
4. Remark (STW)
5. Concurrent Sweep
6. Concurrent Reset

For most of the phases, GC runs alongside application threads. However, for two phases (Initial Mark and Remark), all application threads must be stopped. The overall effect should be to replace a single long STW pause with two STW pauses, which are usually very short.

The purpose of the Initial Mark phase is to provide a stable set of starting points for GC that are within the region; these are known as the *internal pointers* and provide an equivalent set to the GC roots for the purposes of the collection cycle. The advantage of this approach is that it allows the marking phase to focus on a single GC pool without having to consider other memory regions.

After the Initial Mark has concluded, the Concurrent Mark phase commences. This essentially runs the tri-color marking algorithm on the heap, keeping track of any changes that might later require fixup.

The Concurrent Preclean phase appears to try to reduce the length of the STW Remark phase as much as possible. The Remark phase uses the card tables to fix up the marking that might have been affected by mutator threads during the Concurrent Mark phase.

The observable effects of using CMS are as follows, for most workloads:

- Application threads don't stop for as long.
- A single full GC cycle takes longer (in wallclock time).
- Application throughput is reduced while a CMS GC cycle is running.
- GC uses more memory for keeping track of objects.
- Considerably more CPU time is needed overall to perform GC.
- CMS does not compact the heap, so Tenured can become fragmented.

The careful reader will note that not all of these characteristics are positive. Remember that with GC there is no silver bullet, merely a set of choices that are appropriate (or acceptable) to the specific workload an engineer is tuning.

How CMS Works

One of the most often overlooked aspects of CMS is, bizarrely, its great strength. CMS mostly runs concurrently with application threads. By default, CMS will use half of the available threads to perform the concurrent phases of GC, and leave the other half for application threads to execute Java code—*and this inevitably involves allocating new objects.* This sounds like a flash of the blindingly obvious, but it has an immediate consequence. What happens if Eden fills up while CMS is running?

The answer is, unsurprisingly, that because application threads cannot continue, they pause and a (STW) young GC runs while CMS is running. This young GC run will usually take longer than in the case of the parallel collectors, because it only has half the cores available for young generation GC (the other half of the cores are running CMS).

At the end of this young collection, some objects will usually be eligible for promotion to Tenured. These promoted objects need to be moved into Tenured while CMS is still running, which requires some coordination between the two collectors. This is why CMS requires a slightly different young collector.

Under normal circumstances, the young collection promotes only a small amount of objects to Tenured, and the CMS old collection completes normally, freeing up space in Tenured. The application then returns to normal processing, with all cores released for application threads.

However, consider the case of very high allocation, perhaps causing premature promotion (discussed at the end of "The Role of Allocation" on page 134) in the young collection. This can cause a situation in which the young collection has too many objects to promote for the available space in Tenured. This can be seen in Figure 7-3.

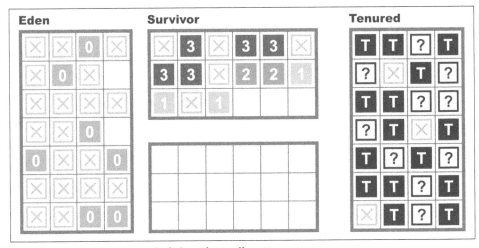

Figure 7-3. Concurrent mode failure from allocation pressure

This is known as a *concurrent mode failure* (CMF), and the JVM has no choice at this point but to fall back to a collection using ParallelOld, which is fully STW. Effectively, the allocation pressure was so high that CMS did not have time to finish processing the old generation before all the "headroom" space to accommodate newly promoted objects filled up.

To avoid frequent concurrent mode failures, CMS needs to start a collection cycle before Tenured is completely full. The heap occupancy level of Tenured at which CMS will start to collect is controlled by the observed behavior of the heap. It can be affected by switches, and starts off defaulted to 75% of Tenured.

There is one other situation that can lead to a concurrent mode failure, and this is heap fragmentation. Unlike ParallelOld, CMS does not compact Tenured as it runs. This means that after a completed run of CMS, the free space in Tenured is not a single contiguous block, and objects that are promoted have to be filled into the gaps between existing objects.

At some point, a young collection may encounter a situation where an object can't be promoted into Tenured due to a lack of sufficient contiguous space to copy the object into. This can be seen in Figure 7-4.

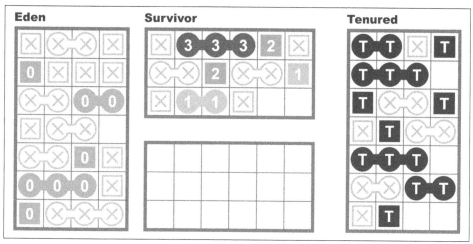

Figure 7-4. Concurrent mode failure from fragmentation

This is a concurrent mode failure caused by heap fragmentation, and as before, the only solution is to fall back to a full collection using ParallelOld (which *is* compacting), as this should free up enough contiguous space to allow the object to be promoted.

In both the heap fragmentation case and the case where young collections outpace CMS, the need to fall back to a fully STW ParallelOld collection can be a major event for an application. In fact, the tuning of low-latency applications that use CMS in order to avoid ever suffering a CMF is a major topic in its own right.

Internally, CMS uses a free list of *chunks* of memory to manage the available free space. During the final phase, Concurrent Sweep, contiguous free blocks will be coalesced by the sweeper threads. This is to provide larger blocks of free space and try to avoid CMFs caused by fragmentation.

However, the sweeper runs concurrently with mutators. Thus, unless the sweeper and the allocator threads synchronize properly, a freshly allocated block might get incorrectly swept up. To prevent this, the sweeper locks the free lists while it is sweeping.

Basic JVM Flags for CMS

The CMS collector is activated with this flag:

```
-XX:+UseConcMarkSweepGC
```

On modern versions of HotSpot, this flag will activate `ParNewGC` (a slight variation of the parallel young collector) as well.

In general, CMS provides a very large number of flags (over 60) that can be adjusted. It can sometimes be tempting to engage in benchmarking exercises that attempt to optimize performance by carefully adjusting the various options that CMS provides. This should be resisted, as in most cases this is actually the Missing the Bigger Picture or Tuning by Folklore (see the "Performance Antipatterns Catalogue" on page 69) antipattern in disguise.

We will cover CMS tuning in more detail in "Tuning Parallel GC" on page 188.

G1

G1 (the "Garbage First" collector) is a very different style of collector than either the parallel collectors or CMS. It was first introduced in a highly experimental and unstable form in Java 6, but was extensively rewritten throughout the lifetime of Java 7, and only really became stable and production-ready with the release of Java 8u40.

We do not recommend using G1 with any version of Java prior to 8u40, regardless of the type of workload being considered.

G1 was originally intended to be a replacement low-pause collector that was:

- Much easier to tune than CMS
- Less susceptible to premature promotion
- Capable of better scaling behavior (especially pause time) on big heaps
- Able to eliminate (or greatly reduce the need to fall back to) full STW collections

However, over time, G1 evolved into being thought of as more of a general-purpose collector that had better pause times on larger heaps (which are increasingly thought of as "the new normal").

Oracle insisted that G1 became the default collector in Java 9, taking over from the parallel collectors, regardless of the impact on end users. It is therefore very important that performance analysts have a good understanding of G1, and that any applications moving from 8 to 9 are properly retested as part of the move.

The G1 collector has a design that rethinks the notion of generations as we have met them so far. Unlike the parallel or CMS collectors, G1 does not have dedicated, contiguous memory spaces per generation. In addition, it does not follow the hemispherical heap layout, as we will see.

G1 Heap Layout and Regions

The G1 heap is based upon the concept of regions. These are areas which are by default 1 MB in size (but are larger on bigger heaps). The use of regions allows for noncontiguous generations and makes it possible to have a collector that does not need to collect all garbage on each run.

 The overall G1 heap is still contiguous in memory—it's just that the memory that makes up each generation no longer has to be.

The region-based layout of the G1 heap can be seen in Figure 7-5.

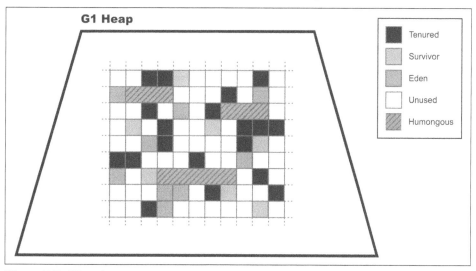

Figure 7-5. G1 regions

G1's algorithm allows regions of either 1, 2, 4, 8, 16, 32, or 64 MB. By default, it expects between 2,048 and 4,095 regions in the heap and will adjust the region size to achieve this.

To calculate the region size, we compute this value:

```
<Heap size> / 2048
```

and then round it down to the nearest permitted region size value. Then the number of regions can be calculated:

```
Number of regions = <Heap size> / <region size>
```

As usual, we can change this value by applying a runtime switch.

G1 Algorithm Design

The high-level picture of the collector is that G1:

- Uses a concurrent marking phase
- Is an evacuating collector
- Provides "statistical compaction"

While warming up, the collector keeps track of the statistics of how many "typical" regions can be collected per GC duty cycle. If enough memory can be collected to balance the new objects that have been allocated since the last GC, then G1 is not losing ground to allocation.

The concepts of TLAB allocation, evacuation to survivor space, and promoting to Tenured are broadly similar to the other HotSpot GCs that we've already met.

 Objects that occupy more space than half a region size are considered humongous objects. They are directly allocated in special *humongous regions*, which are free, contiguous regions that are immediately made part of the Tenured generation (rather than Eden).

G1 still has a concept of a young generation made up of Eden and survivor regions, but of course the regions that make up a generation are not contiguous in G1. The size of the young generation is adaptive and is based on the overall pause time goal.

Recall that when we met the ParallelOld collector, the heuristic "few references from old to young objects" was discussed, in "Weak Generational Hypothesis" on page 125. HotSpot uses a mechanism called card tables to help take advantage of this phenomenon in the parallel and CMS collectors.

The G1 collector has a related feature to help with region tracking. The *Remembered Sets* (usually just called *RSets*) are per-region entries that track outside references that point into a heap region. This means that instead of tracing through the entire heap for references that point into a region, G1 just needs to examine the RSets and then scan those regions for references.

Figure 7-6 shows how the RSets are used to implement G1's approach to dividing up the work of GC between allocator and collector.

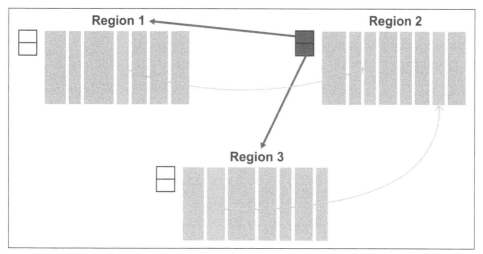

Figure 7-6. Remembered Sets

Both RSets and card tables are approaches that can help with a GC problem called *floating garbage*. This is an issue that is caused when objects that are otherwise dead are kept alive by references from dead objects outside the current collection set. That is, on a global mark they can be seen to be dead, but a more limited local marking may incorrectly report them as alive, depending on the root set used.

G1 Phases

G1 has a collection of phases that are somewhat similar to the phases we've already met, especially in CMS:

1. Initial Mark (STW)

2. Concurrent Root Scan

3. Concurrent Mark

4. Remark (STW)

5. Cleanup (STW)

The Concurrent Root Scan is a concurrent phase that scans survivor regions of the Initial Mark for references to the old generation. This phase must complete before the next young GC can start. In the Remark phase, the marking cycle is completed. This phase also performs reference processing (including weak and soft references) and handles cleanup relating to implementing the SATB approach.

Cleanup is mostly STW, and comprises accounting and RSet "scrubbing." The accounting task identifies regions that are now completely free and ready to be reused (e.g., as Eden regions).

Basic JVM Flags for G1

The switch that you need to enable G1 (in Java 8 and before) is:

```
+XX:UseG1GC
```

Recall that G1 is based around *pause goals*. These allow the developer to specify the desired maximum amount of time that the application should pause on each garbage collection cycle. This is expressed as a goal, and there is no guarantee that the application will be able to meet it. If this value is set too low, then the GC subsystem will be unable to meet the goal.

 Garbage collection is driven by allocation, which can be highly unpredictable for many Java applications. This can limit or destroy G1's ability to meet pause goals.

The switch that controls the core behavior of the collector is:

```
-XX:MaxGCPauseMillis=200
```

This means that the default pause time goal is 200 ms. In practice, pause times under 100 ms are very hard to achieve reliably, and such goals may not be met by the collector. One other option that may also be of use is the option of changing the region size, overriding the default algorithm:

```
-XX:G1HeapRegionSize=<n>
```

Note that <n> must be a power of 2, between 1 and 64, and indicates a value in MB. We will meet other G1 flags when we discuss tuning G1 in Chapter 8.

Overall, G1 is stable as an algorithm and is fully supported by Oracle (and recommended as of 8u40). For truly low-latency workloads it is still not as low-pause as CMS for most workloads, and it is unclear whether it will ever be able to challenge a collector like CMS on pure pause time; however, the collector is still improving and is the focus of Oracle's GC engineering efforts within the JVM team.

Shenandoah

As well as the Oracle-led effort to produce a next-generation, general-purpose collector, Red Hat has been working on its own collector, called *Shenandoah*, within the OpenJDK project. This is still an experimental collector and not ready for production use at the time of writing. However, it shows some promising characteristics and deserves at least an introduction.

Like G1, the aim of Shenandoah is to bring down pause times (especially on large heaps). Shenandoah's approach to this is to perform concurrent compaction. The resulting phases of collection in Shenandoah are:

1. Initial Mark (STW)
2. Concurrent Marking
3. Final Marking (STW)
4. Concurrent Compaction

These phases may initially seem similar to those seen in CMS and G1, and some similar approaches (e.g., SATB) are used by Shenandoah. However, there are some fundamental differences.

One of the most striking and important aspects of Shenandoah is its use of a *Brooks pointer*.[3] This technique uses an additional word of memory per object to indicate whether the object has been relocated during a previous phase of garbage collection and to give the location of the new version of the object's contents.

The resulting heap layout used by Shenandoah for its oops can be seen in Figure 7-7. This mechanism is sometimes called a "forwarding pointer" approach. If the object has not been relocated, then the Brooks pointer simply points at the next word of memory.

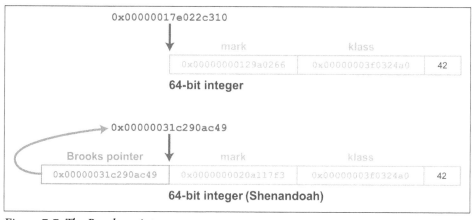

Figure 7-7. The Brooks pointer

---

3 Rodney Brooks, "Trading Data Space for Reduced Time and Code Space in Real-Time Garbage Collection on Stock Hardware," in LFP'84, *Proceedings of the 1984 ACM Symposium on LISP and Functional Programming* (New York: ACM, 1984), 256–262.

The Brooks pointer mechanism relies upon the availability of hardware compare-and-swap (CAS) operations to provide atomic updates of the forwarding address.

The Concurrent Marking phase traces through the heap and marks any live objects. If an object reference points to an oop that has a forwarding pointer, then the reference is updated to point directly at the new oop location. This can be seen in Figure 7-8.

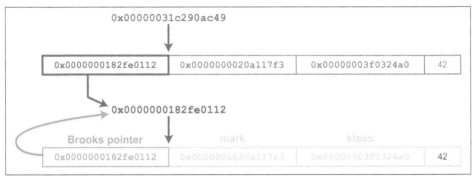

Figure 7-8. Updating the forwarding pointer

In the Final Marking phase, Shenandoah stops the world to rescan the root set, then copy and update roots to point to the evacuated copies.

Concurrent Compaction

The GC threads (which are running concurrently with app threads) now perform evacuation as follows:

1. Copy the object into a TLAB (speculatively).

2. Use a CAS operation to update the Brooks pointer to point at the speculative copy.

3. If this succeeds, then the compaction thread won the race, and all future accesses to this version of the object will be via the Brooks pointer.

4. If it fails, the compaction thread lost. It undoes the speculative copy, and follows the Brooks pointer left by the winning thread.

As Shenandoah is a concurrent collector, while a collection cycle is running, more garbage is being created by the application threads. Therefore, over an application run, collection has to keep up with allocation.

Obtaining Shenandoah

The Shenandoah collector is not currently available as part of a shipping Oracle Java build, or in most OpenJDK distributions. It is shipped as part of the IcedTea binaries in some Linux distros, including Red Hat Fedora.

For other users, compilation from source will be necessary (at the time of writing). This is straightforward on Linux, but may be less so on other operating systems, due to differences in compilers (macOS uses `clang` rather than `gcc`, for example) and other aspects of the operating environment.

Once a working build has been obtained, Shenandoah can be activated with this switch:

```
-XX:+UseShenandoahGC
```

A comparison of Shenandoah's pause times as compared to other collectors can be seen in Figure 7-9.

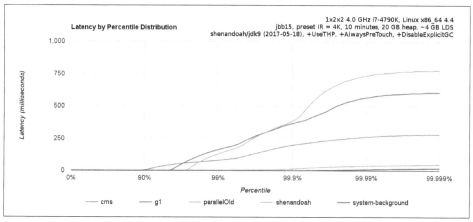

Figure 7-9. Shenandoah compared to other collectors (Shipilëv)

One aspect of Shenandoah that is underappreciated is that it is not a generational collector. As it moves closer to being a production-capable collector, the consequences of this design decision will become clearer, but this is a potential source of concern for performance-sensitive applications.

C4 (Azul Zing)

Azul Systems produces two different Java platform offerings. One of them, Zulu, is an OpenJDK-based FOSS solution available for multiple platforms. The other is Zing, which is a commercial and proprietary platform available for Linux only. It uses a version of the Java class libraries derived from OpenJDK (albeit under an Oracle proprietary license), but a completely different virtual machine.

One important aspect of Zing is that it was designed for 64-bit machines from the start, and never had any intention of supporting 32-bit architectures.

The Zing VM contains several novel software technologies, including the C4 (Continuously Concurrent Compacting Collector) garbage collector and some novel JIT technology, including ReadyNow and a compiler called Falcon.

Like Shenandoah, Zing uses a concurrent compaction algorithm, but it does not utilize a Brooks pointer. Instead, Zing's object header is a single 64-bit word (rather than the two-word header that HotSpot uses). The single header word contains a *kid*, which is a numeric klass ID (around 25 bits long) rather than a klass pointer.

In Figure 7-10 we can see the Zing object header, including the use of some of the oop reference bits for the loaded value barrier (LVB) rather than as address bits.

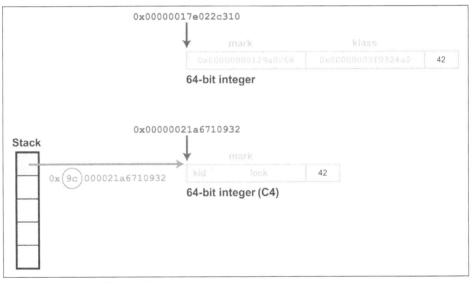

Figure 7-10. Object header layout in Zing

The bottom 32 bits of the header word are used for lock information. This includes the lock state, but also additional information depending on the state of the lock. For example, in the case of a *thin lock* this will be the owning thread ID for thin locks. See "Building Concurrency Libraries" on page 298 for more details about thin locks.

Zing does not support compressed oops or an equivalent technology, so for heaps smaller than ~30 GB the object headers are larger and will take up more space in the heap than in the equivalent HotSpot heap.

The design choice of implementing only on 64-bit architectures meant that Zing's metadata never needed to fit into 32 bits (or to allocate extended structures to be addressed via pointer indirection), thereby avoiding some of the pointer gymnastics present in 32-bit HotSpot.

The Loaded Value Barrier

In the Shenandoah collector, application threads can load references to objects that might have been relocated, and the Brooks pointer is used to keep track of their new location. The central idea of the LVB is to avoid this pattern, and instead provide a solution where every loaded reference is pointing directly at the current location of the object as soon as the load has completed. Azul refers to this as a *self-healing barrier*.

If Zing follows a reference to an object that has been relocated by the collector, then before doing anything else, the application thread updates the reference to the new location of the object, thus "healing" the cause of the relocation problem. This means that each reference is updated at most once, and if the reference is never used again, no work is done to keep it up to date.

As well as the header word, Zing's object references (e.g., from a local variable located on the stack to the object stored on the heap) use some of the bits of the reference to indicate metadata about the GC state of the object. This saves some space by using bits of the reference itself, rather than bits of the single header word.

Zing defines a `Reference` structure, which is laid out like this:

```
struct Reference {
    unsigned inPageVA : 21;      // bits 0-20
    unsigned PageNumber: 21;     // bits 21-41
    unsigned NMT : 1;            // bit 42
    unsigned SpaceID : 2;        // bits 43-44
    unsigned unused : 19;        // bits 45-63
};

int Expected_NMT_Value[4] = {0, 0, 0, 0};

// Space ID values:
// 00 NULL and non-heap pointers
// 01 Old Generation references
// 10 New Generation references
// 11 Unused
```

The NMT (Not Marked Through) metadata bit is used to indicate whether the object has already been marked in the current collection cycle. C4 maintains a target state that live objects should be marked as, and when an object is located during the mark, the NMT bit is set so that it is equal to the target state. At the end of the collection cycle, C4 flips the target state bit, so now all surviving objects are ready for the next cycle.

The overall phases of the GC cycle in C4 are:

1. Mark
2. Relocate
3. Remap

The Relocation phase, like with G1, will focus on the sparsest from-pages. This is to be expected, given that C4 is an evacuating collector.

C4 uses a technique called *hand-over-hand* compaction to provide continuous compaction. This relies upon a feature of the virtual memory system—the disconnect between physical and virtual addresses. In normal operation, the virtual memory subsystem maintains a mapping between a virtual page in the process address space and an underlying physical page.

 Unlike HotSpot, which does not use system calls to manage Java heap memory, Zing does make use of calls into the kernel as part of its GC cycle.

With Zing's evacuation technique, objects are relocated by being copied to a different page, which naturally corresponds to a different physical address. Once all objects from a page have been copied, the physical page can be freed and returned to the operating system. There will still be application references that point into this now-unmapped virtual page. However, the LVB will take care of such references and will fix them before a memory fault occurs.

Zing's C4 collector runs two collection algorithms at all times, one for young and one for old objects. This obviously has an overhead, but as we will examine in Chapter 8, when tuning a concurrent collector (such as CMS) it is useful for overhead and capacity planning reasons to assume that the collector may be in *back-to-back* mode when running. This is not so different from the continuously running mode that C4 exhibits.

Ultimately, the performance engineer should examine the benefits and tradeoffs of moving to Zing and the C4 collector carefully. The "measure, don't guess" philosophy applies to the choice of VM as much as it does anywhere else.

Balanced (IBM J9)

IBM produces a JVM called J9. This has historically been a proprietary JVM, but IBM is now in the process of open-sourcing it and renaming it Open J9. The VM has several different collectors that can be switched on, including a high-throughput collector similar to the parallel collector HotSpot defaults to.

In this section, however, we will discuss the Balanced GC collector. It is a region-based collector available on 64-bit J9 JVMs and designed for heaps in excess of 4 GB. Its primary design goals are to:

- Improve scaling of pause times on large Java heaps.
- Minimize worst-case pause times.
- Utilize awareness of non-uniform memory access (NUMA) performance.

To achieve the first goal, the heap is split into a number of regions, which are managed and collected independently. Like G1, the Balanced collector wants to manage at most 2,048 regions, and so will choose a region size to achieve this. The region size is a power of 2, as for G1, but Balanced will permit regions as small as 512 KB.

As we would expect from a generational region-based collector, each region has an associated age, with age-zero regions (Eden) used for allocation of new objects. When the Eden space is full, a collection must be performed. The IBM term for this is a *partial garbage collection* (PGC).

A PGC is an STW operation that collects all Eden regions, and may additionally choose to collect regions with a higher age, if the collector determines that they are worth collecting. In this manner, PGCs are similar to G1's mixed collections.

 Once a PGC is complete, the age of regions containing the surviving objects is increased by 1. These are sometimes referred to as *generational regions*.

Another benefit, as compared to other J9 GC policies, is that class unloading can be performed incrementally. Balanced can collect classloaders that are part of the current collection set during a PGC. This is in contrast to other J9 collectors, where classloaders could only be collected during a global collection.

One downside is that because a PGC only has visibility of the regions it has chosen to collect, this type of collection can suffer from floating garbage. To resolve this problem, Balanced employs a *global mark phase* (GMP). This is a partially concurrent operation that scans the entire Java heap, marking dead objects for collection. Once a GMP completes, the following PGC acts on this data. Thus, the amount of floating garbage in the heap is bounded by the number of objects that died since the last GMP started.

The final type of GC operation that Balanced carried out is *global garbage collection* (GGC). This is a full STW collection that compacts the heap. It is similar to the full collections that would be triggered in HotSpot by a concurrent mode failure.

J9 Object Headers

The basic J9 object header is a *class slot*, the size of which is 64 bits, or 32 bits when Compressed References is enabled.

 Compressed References is the default for heaps smaller than 57 GB and is similar to HotSpot's compressed oops technique.

However, the header may have additional slots depending on the type of object:

- Synchronized objects will have monitor slots.
- Objects put into internal JVM structures will have hashed slots.

In addition, the monitor and hashed slots are not necessarily adjacent to the object header—they may be stored anywhere in the object, taking advantage of otherwise wasted space due to alignment. J9's object layout can be seen in Figure 7-11.

Figure 7-11. J9 object layout

The highest 24 (or 56) bits of the class slot are a pointer to the class structure, which is off-heap, similarly to Java 8's Metaspace. The lower 8 bits are flags that are used for various purposes depending on the GC policy in use.

Large Arrays in Balanced

Allocating large arrays in Java is a common trigger for compacting collections, as enough contiguous space must be found to satisfy the allocation. We saw one aspect of this in the discussion of CMS, where free list coalescing is sometimes insufficient to free up enough space for a large allocation, and a concurrent mode failure results.

For a region-based collector, it is entirely possible to allocate an array object in Java that exceeds the size of a single region. To address this, Balanced uses an alternate representation for large arrays that allows them to be allocated in discontiguous chunks. This representation is known as *arraylets*, and this is the only circumstance under which heap objects can span regions.

The arraylet representation is invisible to user Java code, and instead is handled transparently by the JVM. The allocator will represent a large array as a central object, called the *spine*, and a set of array *leaves* that contain the actual entries of the array and which are pointed to by entries of the spine. This enables entries to be read with only the additional overhead of a single indirection. An example can be seen in Figure 7-12.

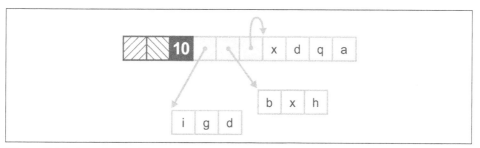

Figure 7-12. Arraylets in J9

> The arraylet representation is potentially visible through JNI APIs (although not from regular Java), so the programmer should be aware that when porting JNI code from another JVM, the spine and leaf representation may need to be taken into account.

Performing partial GCs on regions reduces average pause time, although overall time spent performing GC operations may be higher due to the overhead of maintaining information about the regions of a referrer and referent.

Crucially, the likelihood of requiring a global STW collection or compaction (the worst case for pause times) is greatly reduced, with this typically occurring as a last resort when the heap is full.

There is an overhead to managing regions and discontiguous large arrays, and thus, Balanced is suited to applications where avoiding large pauses is more important than outright throughput.

NUMA and Balanced

Non-uniform memory access is a memory architecture used in multiprocessor systems, typically medium to large servers. Such a system involves a concept of distance between memory and a processor, with processors and memory arranged into nodes. A processor on a given node may access memory from any node, but access time is significantly faster for local memory (that is, memory belonging to the same node).

For JVMs that are executing across multiple NUMA nodes, the Balanced collector can split the Java heap across them. Application threads are arranged such that they favor execution on a particular node, and object allocations favor regions in memory local to that node. A schematic view of this arrangement can be seen in Figure 7-13.

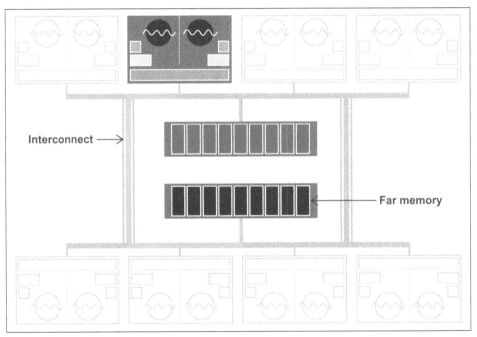

Figure 7-13. Non-uniform memory access

In addition, a partial garbage collection will attempt to move objects closer (in terms of memory distance) to the objects and threads that refer to them. This means the memory referenced by a thread is more likely to be local, improving performance. This process is invisible to the application.

Legacy HotSpot Collectors

In earlier versions of HotSpot, various other collectors were available. We mention them for completeness here, but none of them are recommended for production use anymore, and several combinations were deprecated in Java 8 and have been disallowed (or removed) as of Java 9.

Serial and SerialOld

The Serial and SerialOld collectors operated in a similar fashion to the Parallel GC and ParallelOld collectors, with one important difference: they only used a single CPU core to perform GC. Despite this, they were not concurrent collectors and were still fully STW. On modern multicore systems there is, of course, no possible performance benefit from using these collectors, and so they should not be used.

As a performance engineer, you should be aware of these collectors and their activation switches simply to ensure that if you ever encounter an application that sets them, you can recognize and remove them.

These collectors were deprecated as part of Java 8, so they will only ever be encountered on earlier legacy applications that are still using very old versions of Java.

Incremental CMS (iCMS)

The incremental CMS collector, normally referred to as iCMS, was an older attempt to do concurrent collection that tried to introduce into CMS some of the ideas that would later result in G1. The switch to enable this mode of CMS was:

```
-XX:+CMSIncrementalMode
```

Some experts still maintain that corner cases exist (for applications deployed on very old hardware with only one or two cores) where iCMS can be a valid choice from a performance point of view. However, virtually all modern server-class applications should not use iCMS and it was removed in Java 9.

 Unless extraordinary evidence exists that your workload will benefit from incremental mode, you should not use it, due to the safepointing behavior and other negatives.

Deprecated and Removed GC Combinations

The current usual cadence of deprecation and removal is that features are marked as deprecated in one Java version and then removed in the next version, or subsequently. Accordingly, in Java 8, the GC flag combinations in Table 7-1 were marked as deprecated, and were removed in Java 9.

Table 7-1. Deprecated GC combinations

Combination	Flags
DefNew + CMS	`-XX:-UseParNewGC -XX:+UseConcMarkSweepGC`
ParNew + SerialOld	`-XX:+UseParNewGC`
ParNew + iCMS	`-Xincgc`
ParNew + iCMS	`-XX:+CMSIncrementalMode -XX:+UseConcMarkSweepGC`
DefNew + iCMS	`-XX:+CMSIncrementalMode -XX:+UseConcMarkSweepGC -XX:-UseParNewGC`
CMS foreground	`-XX:+UseCMSCompactAtFullCollection`
CMS foreground	`-XX:+CMSFullGCsBeforeCompaction`
CMS foreground	`-XX:+UseCMSCollectionPassing`

You should consult this table when starting a new engagement, in order to confirm at the start that the application to be tuned is *not* using a deprecated configuration.

Epsilon

The Epsilon collector is not a legacy collector. However, it is included here because it *must not be used in production under any circumstances*. While the other collectors, if encountered within your environment, should be immediately flagged as extremely high-risk and marked for immediate removal, Epsilon is slightly different.

Epsilon is an experimental collector designed for testing purposes only. It is a *zero-effort* collector. This means it makes no effort to actually collect any garbage. Every byte of heap memory that is allocated while running under Epsilon is effectively a memory leak. It cannot be reclaimed and will eventually cause the JVM (probably very quickly) to run out of memory and crash.

> Develop a GC that only handles memory allocation, but does not implement any actual memory reclamation mechanism. Once available Java heap is exhausted, perform the orderly JVM shutdown.
>
> —Epsilon JEP

Such a "collector" would be very useful for the following purposes:

- Performance testing and microbenchmarks
- Regression testing
- Testing low/zero-allocation Java application or library code

In particular, JMH tests would benefit from the ability to confidently exclude any GC events from disrupting performance numbers. Memory allocation regression tests, ensuring that changed code does not greatly alter allocation behavior, would also become easy to do. Developers could write tests that run with an Epsilon configuration that accepts only a bounded number of allocations, and then fails on any further allocation due to heap exhaustion.

Finally, the proposed VM-GC interface would also benefit from having Epsilon as a minimal test case for the interface itself.

Summary

Garbage collection is a truly fundamental aspect of Java performance analysis and tuning. Java's rich landscape of garbage collectors is a great strength of the platform, but it can be intimidating for the newcomer, especially given the scarcity of documentation that considers the tradeoffs and performance consequences of each choice.

In this chapter, we have outlined the decisions that face performance engineers, and the tradeoffs that they must make when deciding on an appropriate collector to use for their applications. We have discussed some of the underlying theory and met a range of modern GC algorithms that implement these ideas.

In the next chapter, we will put some of this theory to work and introduce logging, monitoring, and tooling as a way to bring some scientific rigor to our discussion of performance-tuning garbage collection.

## CHAPTER 8

GC Logging, Monitoring, Tuning, and Tools

In this chapter, we will introduce the huge subject of GC logging and monitoring. This is one of the most important and visible aspects of Java performance tuning, and also one of the most often misunderstood.

Introduction to GC Logging

The GC log is a great source of information. It is especially useful for "cold case" analysis of performance problems, such as providing some insight into why a crash occurred. It can allow the analyst to work, even with no live application process to diagnose.

Every serious application should always:

- Generate a GC log.
- Keep it in a separate file from application output.

This is especially true for production applications. As we'll see, GC logging has no real observable overhead, so it should always be on for any important JVM process.

Switching On GC Logging

The first thing to do is to add some switches to the application startup. These are best thought of as the "mandatory GC logging flags," which should be on for any Java/JVM application (except, perhaps, desktop apps). The flags are:

```
-Xloggc:gc.log -XX:+PrintGCDetails -XX:+PrintTenuringDistribution
-XX:+PrintGCTimeStamps -XX:+PrintGCDateStamps
```

Let's look at each of these flags in more detail. Their usage is described in Table 8-1.

Table 8-1. Mandatory GC flags

Flag	Effect
`-Xloggc:gc.log`	Controls which file to log GC events to
`-XX:+PrintGCDetails`	Logs GC event details
`-XX:+PrintTenuringDistribution`	Adds extra GC event detail that is vital for tooling
`-XX:+PrintGCTimeStamps`	Prints the time (in secs since VM start) at which GC events occurred
`-XX:+PrintGCDateStamps`	Prints the wallclock time at which GC events occurred

The performance engineer should take note of the following details about some of these flags:

- The `PrintGCDetails` flag replaces the older `verbose:gc`. Applications should remove the older flag.

- The `PrintTenuringDistribution` flag is different from the others, as the information it provides is not easily usable directly by humans. The flag provides the raw data needed to compute key memory pressure effects and events such as premature promotion.

- Both `PrintGCDateStamps` and `PrintGCTimeStamps` are required, as the former is used to correlate GC events to application events (in application logfiles) and the latter is used to correlate GC and other internal JVM events.

This level of logging detail will not have a measurable effect on the JVM's performance. The amount of logs generated will, of course, depend on many factors, including the allocation rate, the collector in use, and the heap size (smaller heaps will need to GC more frequently and so will produce logs more quickly).

To give you some idea, a 30-minute run of the model allocator example (as seen in Chapter 6) produces ~600 KB of logs for a 30-minute run, allocating 50 MB per second.

In addition to the mandatory flags, there are also some flags (shown in Table 8-2) that control GC log rotation, which many application support teams find useful in production environments.

Table 8-2. GC log rotation flags

Flag	Effect
`-XX:+UseGCLogFileRotation`	Switches on logfile rotation
`-XX:+NumberOfGCLogFiles=<n>`	Sets the maximum number of logfiles to keep
`-XX:+GCLogFileSize=<size>`	Sets the maximum size of each file before rotation

The setup of a sensible log rotation strategy should be done in conjunction with operations staff (including devops). Options for such a strategy, and a discussion of appropriate logging and tools, is outside the scope of this book.

GC Logs Versus JMX

In "Monitoring and Tooling for the JVM" on page 29 we met the VisualGC tool, which is capable of displaying a real-time view of the state of the JVM's heap. This tool actually relies on the Java Management eXtensions (JMX) interface to collect the data from the JVM. A full discussion of JMX is outside the scope of this book, but as far as JMX impacts GC, the performance engineer should be aware of the following:

- GC log data is driven by actual garbage collection events, whereas JMX sourced data is obtained by sampling.
- GC log data is extremely low-impact to capture, whereas JMX has implicit proxying and Remote Method Invocation (RMI) costs.
- GC log data contains over 50 aspects of performance data relating to Java's memory management, whereas JMX has less than 10.

Traditionally, one advantage that JMX has had over logs as a performance data source is that JMX can provide streamed data out of the box. However, modern tools such as jClarity Censum (see "Log Parsing Tools" on page 175) provide APIs to stream GC log data, closing this gap.

 For a rough trend analysis of basic heap usage, JMX is a fairly quick and easy solution; however, for deeper diagnosis of problems it quickly becomes underpowered.

The beans made available via JMX are a standard and are readily accessible. The VisualVM tool provides one way of visualizing the data, and there are plenty of other tools available in the market.

Drawbacks of JMX

Clients monitoring an application using JMX will usually rely on sampling the runtime to get an update on the current state. To get a continuous feed of data, the client needs to poll the JMX beans in that runtime.

In the case of garbage collection, this causes a problem: the client has no way of knowing when the collector ran. This also means that the state of memory before and after each collection cycle is unknown. This rules out performing a range of deeper and more accurate analysis techniques on the GC data.

Analysis based on data from JMX is still useful, but it is limited to determining long-term trends. However, if we want to accurately tune a garbage collector we need to do better. In particular, being able to understand the state of the heap before and after each collection is extremely useful.

Additionally there is a set of extremely important analyses around memory pressure (i.e., allocation rates) that are simply not possible due to the way data is gathered from JMX.

Not only that, but the current implementation of the `JMXConnector` specification relies on RMI. Thus, use of JMX is subject to the same issues that arise with any RMI-based communication channel. These include:

- Opening ports in firewalls so secondary socket connections can be established
- Using proxy objects to facilitate `remove()` method calls
- Dependency on Java finalization

For a few RMI connections, the amount of work involved to close down a connection is minuscule. However, the teardown relies upon finalization. This means that the garbage collector has to run to reclaim the object.

The nature of the lifecycle of the JMX connection means that most often this will result in the RMI object not being collected until a full GC. See "Avoid Finalization" on page 273 for more details about the impact of finalization and why it should always be avoided.

By default, any application using RMI will cause full GCs to be triggered once an hour. For applications that are already using RMI, using JMX will not add to the costs. However, applications not already using RMI will necessarily take an additional hit if they decide to use JMX.

Benefits of GC Log Data

Modern-day garbage collectors contain many different moving parts that, put together, result in an extremely complex implementation. So complex is the implementation that the performance of a collector is seemingly difficult if not impossible to predict. These types of software systems are known as *emergent*, in that their final behavior and performance is a consequence of how all of the components work and perform together. Different pressures stress different components in different ways, resulting in a very fluid cost model.

Initially Java's GC developers added GC logging to help debug their implementations, and consequently a significant portion of the data produced by the almost 60 GC-related flags is for performance debugging purposes.

Over time those tasked with tuning the garbage collection process in their applications came to recognize that given the complexities of tuning GC, they also benefitted from having an exact picture of what was happening in the runtime. Thus, being able to collect and read GC logs is now an instrumental part of any tuning regime.

GC logging is done from within the HotSpot JVM using a nonblocking writing mechanism. It has ~0% impact on application performance and should be switched on for all production applications.

Because the raw data in the GC logs can be pinned to specific GC events, we can perform all kinds of useful analyses on it that can give us insights into the costs of the collection, and consequently which tuning actions are more likely to produce positive results.

Log Parsing Tools

There is no language or VM spec standard format for GC log messages. This leaves the content of any individual message to the whim of the HotSpot GC development team. Formats can and do change from minor release to minor release.

This is further complicated by the fact that, while the simplest log formats are easy to parse, as GC log flags are added the resulting log output becomes massively more complicated. This is especially true of the logs generated by the concurrent collectors.

All too often, systems with hand-rolled GC log parsers experience an outage at some point after changes are made to the GC configuration, that alter the log output format. When the outage investigation turns to examining the GC logs, the team finds that the homebrew parser cannot cope with the changed log format—failing at the exact point when the log information is most valuable.

It is not recommended that developers attempt to parse GC logs themselves. Instead, a tool should be used.

In this section, we will examine two actively maintained tools (one commercial and one open source) that are available for this purpose. There are others, such as GarbageCat, that are maintained only sporadically, or not at all.

Censum

The Censum memory analyzer is a commercial tool developed by jClarity. It is available both as a desktop tool (for hands-on analysis of a single JVM) and as a monitoring service (for large groups of JVMs). The aim of the tool is to provide best-available GC log parsing, information extraction, and automated analytics.

In Figure 8-1, we can see the Censum desktop view showing allocation rates for a financial trading application running the G1 garbage collector. Even from this simple view we can see that the trading application has periods of very low allocation, corresponding to quiet periods in the market.

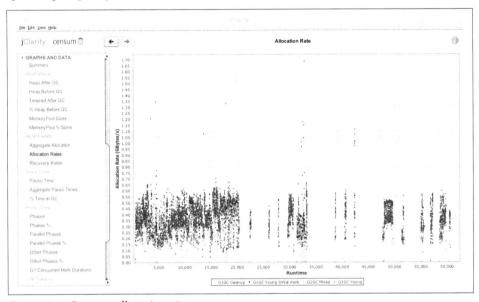

Figure 8-1. Censum allocation view

Other views available from Censum include the pause time graph, shown in Figure 8-2 from the SaaS version.

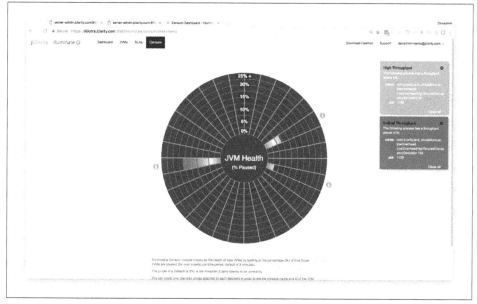

Figure 8-2. Censum pause time view

One of the advantages of using the Censum SAAS monitoring service is being able to view the health of an entire cluster simultaneously, as in Figure 8-3. For ongoing monitoring, this is usually easier than dealing with a single JVM at a time.

Figure 8-3. Censum cluster health overview

Censum has been developed with close attention to the logfile formats, and all check-ins to OpenJDK that could affect logging are monitored. Censum supports all versions of Sun/Oracle Java from 1.4.2 to current, all collectors, and the largest number of GC log configurations of any tool in the market.

As of the current version, Censum supports these automatic analytics:

- Accurate allocation rates
- Premature promotion
- Aggressive or "spiky" allocation
- Idle churn
- Memory leak detection
- Heap sizing and capacity planning
- OS interference with the VM
- Poorly sized memory pools

More details about Censum, and trial licenses, are available from the jClarity website (*https://www.jclarity.com/*).

GCViewer

GCViewer is a desktop tool that provides some basic GC log parsing and graphing capabilities. Its big positives are that it is open source software and is free to use. However, it does not have many features as compared to the commercial tools.

To use it, you will need to download the source (*https://github.com/chewiebug/GCViewer*). After compiling and building it, you can package into an executable JAR file.

GC logfiles can then be opened in the main GCViewer UI. An example is shown in Figure 8-4.

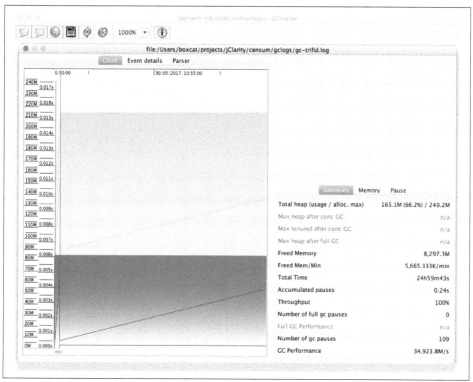

Figure 8-4. GCViewer

GCViewer lacks analytics and can parse only some of the possible GC log formats that HotSpot can produce.

It is possible to use GCViewer as a parsing library and export the data points into a visualizer, but this requires additional development on top of the existing open source code base.

Different Visualizations of the Same Data

You should be aware that different tools may produce different visualizations of the same data. The simple sawtooth pattern that we met in "The Role of Allocation" on page 134 was based on a sampled view of the overall size of the heap as the observable.

When the GC log that produced this pattern is plotted with the "Heap Occupancy after GC" view of GCViewer, we end up with the visualization shown in Figure 8-5.

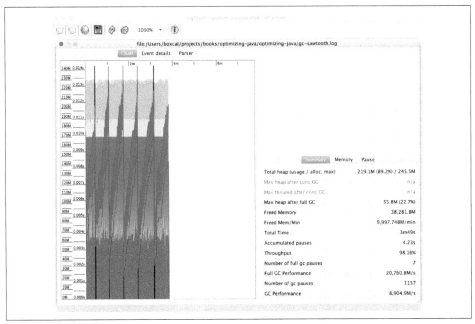

Figure 8-5. Simple sawtooth in GCViewer

Let's look at the same simple sawtooth pattern displayed in Censum. Figure 8-6 shows the result.

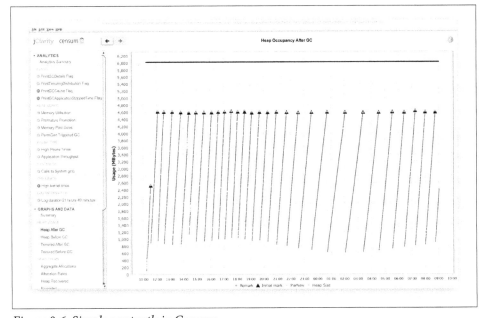

Figure 8-6. Simple sawtooth in Censum

While the images and visualizations are different, the message from the tool is the same in both cases—that the heap is operating normally.

Basic GC Tuning

When engineers are considering strategies for tuning the JVM, the question "When should I tune GC?" often arises. As with any other tuning technique, GC tuning should form part of an overall diagnostic process. The following facts about GC tuning are very useful to remember:

1. It's cheap to eliminate or confirm GC as the cause of a performance problem.
2. It's cheap to switch on GC flags in UAT.
3. It's not cheap to set up memory or execution profilers.

The engineer should also know that these four main factors should be studied and measured during a tuning exercise:

- Allocation
- Pause sensitivity
- Throughput behavior
- Object lifetime

Of these, allocation is very often the most important.

 Throughput can be affected by a number of factors, such as the fact that concurrent collectors take up cores when they're running.

Let's take a look at some of the basic heap sizing flags, listed in Table 8-3.

Table 8-3. GC heap sizing flags

Flag	Effect
`-Xms<size>`	Sets the minimum size reserved for the heap
`-Xmx<size>`	Sets the maximum size reserved for the heap
`-XX:MaxPermSize=<size>`	Sets the maximum size permitted for PermGen (Java 7)
`-XX:MaxMetaspaceSize=<size>`	Sets the maximum size permitted for Metaspace (Java 8)

The `MaxPermSize` flag is legacy and applies only to Java 7 and before. In Java 8 and up, the PermGen has been removed and replaced by Metaspace.

If you are setting `MaxPermSize` on a Java 8 application, then you should just remove the flag. It is being ignored by the JVM anyway, so it clearly is having no impact on your application.

On the subject of additional GC flags for tuning:

- Only add flags one at a time.
- Make sure that you fully understand the effect of each flag.
- Recall that some combinations produce side effects.

Checking whether GC is the cause of a performance issue is relatively easy, assuming the event is happening live. The first step is to look at the machine's high-level metrics using `vmstat` or a similar tool, as discussed in "Basic Detection Strategies" on page 48. First, log on to the box having the performance issue and check that:

- CPU utilization is close to 100%.
- The vast majority of this time (90+%) is being spent in user space.
- The GC log is showing activity, indicating that GC is currently running.

This assumes that the issue is happening right now and can be observed by the engineer in real time. For past events, sufficient historical monitoring data must be available (including CPU utilization and GC logs that have timestamps).

If all three of these conditions are met, GC should be investigated and tuned as the most likely cause of the current performance issue. The test is very simple, and has a nice clear result—either that "GC is OK" or "GC is not OK."

If GC is indicated as a source of performance problems, then the next step is to understand the allocation and pause time behavior, then tune the GC and potentially bring out the memory profiler if required.

Understanding Allocation

Allocation rate analysis is extremely important for determining not just how to tune the garbage collector, but whether or not you can actually tune the garbage collector to help improve performance at all.

We can use the data from the young generational collection events to calculate the amount of data allocated and the time between the two collections. This information can then be used to calculate the average allocation rate during that time interval.

Rather than spending time and effort manually calculating allocation rates, it is usually better to use tooling to provide this number.

Experience shows that sustained allocation rates of greater than 1 GB/s are almost always indicative of performance problems that cannot be corrected by tuning the garbage collector. The only way to improve performance in these cases is to improve the memory efficiency of the application by refactoring to eliminate allocation in critical parts of the application.

A simple memory histogram, such as that shown by VisualVM (as seen in "Monitoring and Tooling for the JVM" on page 29) or even jmap ("Introducing Mark and Sweep" on page 116), can serve as a starting point for understanding memory allocation behavior. A useful initial allocation strategy is to concentrate on four simple areas:

- Trivial, avoidable object allocation (e.g., log debug messages)
- Boxing costs
- Domain objects
- Large numbers of non-JDK framework objects

For the first of these, it is simply a matter of spotting and removing unnecessary object creation. Excessive boxing can be a form of this, but other examples (such as autogenerated code for serializing/deserializing to JSON, or ORM code) are also possible sources of wasteful object creation.

It is unusual for domain objects to be a major contributor to the memory utilization of an application. Far more common are types such as:

- char[]: The characters that comprise strings
- byte[]: Raw binary data
- double[]: Calculation data
- Map entries
- Object[]
- Internal data structures (such as methodOops and klassOops)

A simple histogram can often reveal leaking or excessive creation of unnecessary domain objects, simply by their presence among the top elements of a heap histogram. Often, all that is necessary is a quick calculation to figure out the expected data volume of domain objects, to see whether the observed volume is in line with expectations or not.

In "Thread-Local Allocation" on page 127 we met thread-local allocation. The aim of this technique is to provide a private area for each thread to allocate new objects, and thus achieve O(1) allocation.

The TLABs are sized dynamically on a per-thread basis, and regular objects are allocated in the TLAB, if there's space. If not, the thread requests a new TLAB from the VM and tries again.

If the object will not fit in an empty TLAB, the VM will next try to allocate the object directly in Eden, in an area outside of any TLAB. If this fails, the next step is to perform a young GC (which might resize the heap). Finally, if this fails and there's still not enough space, the last resort is to allocate the object directly in Tenured.

From this we can see that the only objects that are really likely to end up being directly allocated in Tenured are large arrays (especially byte and char arrays).

HotSpot has a couple of tuning flags that are relevant to the TLABs and the pretenuring of large objects:

```
-XX:PretenureSizeThreshold=<n>
-XX:MinTLABSize=<n>
```

As with all switches, these should not be used without a benchmark and solid evidence that they will have an effect. In most cases, the built-in dynamic behavior will produce great results, and any changes will have little to no real observable impact.

Allocation rates also affect the number of objects that are promoted to Tenured. If we assume that short-lived Java objects have a fixed lifetime (when expressed in wall-clock time), then higher allocation rates will result in young GCs that are closer together. If the collections become too frequent, then short-lived objects may not have had time to die and will be erroneously promoted to Tenured.

To put it another way, spikes in allocation can lead to the premature promotion problem that we met in "The Role of Allocation" on page 134. To guard against this, the JVM will resize survivor spaces dynamically to accommodate greater amounts of surviving data without promoting it to Tenured.

One JVM switch that can sometimes be helpful for dealing with tenuring problems and premature promotion is:

```
-XX:MaxTenuringThreshold=<n>
```

This controls the number of garbage collections that an object must survive to be promoted into Tenured. It defaults to 4 but can be set anywhere from 1 to 15. Changing this value represents a tradeoff between two concerns:

- The higher the threshold, the more copying of genuinely long-lived objects will occur.

- If the threshold is too low, some short-lived objects will be promoted, increasing memory pressure on Tenured.

One consequence of too low a threshold could be that full collections occur more often, due to the greater volume of objects being promoted to Tenured, causing it to fill up more quickly. As always, you should not alter the switch without a clear benchmark indicating that you will improve performance by setting it to a nondefault value.

Understanding Pause Time

Developers frequently suffer from cognitive bias about pause time. Many applications can easily tolerate 100+ ms pause times. The human eye can only process 5 updates per second of a single data item, so a 100–200 ms pause is below the threshold of visibility for most human-facing applications (such as web apps).

One useful heuristic for pause-time tuning is to divide applications into three broad bands. These bands are based on the application's need for responsiveness, expressed as the pause time that the application can tolerate. They are:

1. >1 s: Can tolerate over 1 s of pause

2. 1 s–100 ms: Can tolerate more than 200 ms but less than 1 s of pause

3. < 100 ms: Cannot tolerate 100 ms of pause

If we combine the pause sensitivity with the expected heap size of the application, we can construct a simple table of best guesses at a suitable collector. The result is shown in Table 8-4.

Table 8-4. Initial collector choice

Pause time tolerance			
>1 s	1 s–100 ms	<100 ms	< 2 GB
Parallel	Parallel	CMS	< 4 GB
Parallel	Parallel/G1	CMS	< 4 GB
Parallel	Parallel/G1	CMS	< 10 GB
Parallel/G1	Parallel/G1	CMS	< 20 GB
Parallel/G1	G1	CMS	> 20 GB

These are guidelines and rules of thumb intended as a starting point for tuning, not 100% unambiguous rules.

Looking into the future, as G1 matures as a collector, it is reasonable to expect that it will expand to cover more of the use cases currently covered by ParallelOld. It is also possible, but perhaps less likely, that it will expand to CMS's use cases as well.

 When a concurrent collector is in use, you should still reduce allocation before attempting to tune pause time. Reduced allocation means that there is less memory pressure on a concurrent collector; the collection cycles will find it easier to keep up with the allocating threads. This will reduce the possibility of a concurrent mode failure, which is usually an event that pause-sensitive applications need to avoid if at all possible.

Collector Threads and GC Roots

One useful mental exercise is to "think like a GC thread." This can provide insight into how the collector behaves under various circumstances. However, as with so many other aspects of GC, there are fundamental tradeoffs in play. These tradeoffs include that the scanning time needed to locate GC roots is affected by factors such as:

- Number of application threads
- Amount of compiled code in the code cache
- Size of heap

Even for this single aspect of GC, which one of these events dominates the GC root scanning will always depend on runtime conditions and the amount of parallelization that can be applied.

For example, consider the case of a large `Object[]` discovered in the Mark phase. This will be scanned by a single thread; no work stealing is possible. In the extreme case, this single-threaded scanning time will dominate the overall mark time.

In fact, the more complex the object graph, the more pronounced this effect becomes —meaning that marking time will get even worse the more "long chains" of objects exist within the graph.

High numbers of application threads will also have an impact on GC times, as they represent more stack frames to scan and more time needed to reach a safepoint. They also exert more pressure on thread schedulers in both bare metal and virtualized environments.

As well as these traditional examples of GC roots, there are also other sources of GC roots, including JNI frames and the code cache for JIT-compiled code (which we will meet properly in "The Code Cache" on page 220).

GC root scanning in the code cache is single-threaded (at least for Java 8).

Of the three factors, stack and heap scanning are reasonably well parallelized. Generational collectors also keep track of roots that originate in other memory pools, using mechanisms such as the RSets in G1 and the card tables in Parallel GC and CMS.

For example, let's consider the card tables, introduced in "Weak Generational Hypothesis" on page 125. These are used to indicate a block of memory that has a reference back into young gen from old gen. As each byte represents 512 bytes of old gen, it's clear that for each 1 GB of old gen memory, 2 MB of card table must be scanned.

To get a feel for how long a card table scan will take, consider a simple benchmark that simulates scanning a card table for a 20 GB heap:

```
@State(Scope.Benchmark)
@BenchmarkMode(Mode.Throughput)
@Warmup(iterations = 5, time = 1, timeUnit = TimeUnit.SECONDS)
@Measurement(iterations = 5, time = 1, timeUnit = TimeUnit.SECONDS)
@OutputTimeUnit(TimeUnit.SECONDS)
@Fork(1)
public class SimulateCardTable {

    // OldGen is 3/4 of heap, 2M of card table is required for 1G of old gen
    private static final int SIZE_FOR_20_GIG_HEAP = 15 * 2 * 1024 * 1024;

    private static final byte[] cards = new byte[SIZE_FOR_20_GIG_HEAP];

    @Setup
    public static final void setup() {
        final Random r = new Random(System.nanoTime());
        for (int i=0; i<100_000; i++) {
            cards[r.nextInt(SIZE_FOR_20_GIG_HEAP)] = 1;
        }
    }


    @Benchmark
    public int scanCardTable() {
        int found = 0;
        for (int i=0; i<SIZE_FOR_20_GIG_HEAP; i++) {
            if (cards[i] > 0)
                found++;
        }
        return found;
    }
}
```

```
    }
```

Running this benchmark results in an output similar to the following:

```
Result "scanCardTable":
  108.904 ±(99.9%) 16.147 ops/s [Average]
  (min, avg, max) = (102.915, 108.904, 114.266), stdev = 4.193
  CI (99.9%): [92.757, 125.051] (assumes normal distribution)


# Run complete. Total time: 00:01:46

Benchmark                         Mode  Cnt    Score    Error  Units
SimulateCardTable.scanCardTable   thrpt    5  108.904 ± 16.147  ops/s
```

This shows that it takes about 10 ms to scan the card table for a 20 GB heap. This is, of course, the result for a single-threaded scan; however, it does provide a useful rough lower bound for the pause time for young collections.

We've examined some general techniques that should be applicable to tuning most collectors, so now let's move on to look at some collector-specific approaches.

Tuning Parallel GC

Parallel GC is the simplest of the collectors, and so it should be no surprise that it is also the easiest to tune. However, it usually requires minimal tuning. The goals and the tradeoffs of Parallel GC are clear:

- Fully STW
- High GC throughput/computationally cheap
- No possibility of a partial collection
- Linearly growing pause time in the size of the heap

If your application can tolerate the characteristics of Parallel GC, then it can be a very effective choice—especially on small heaps, such as those under ~4 GB.

Older applications may have made use of explicit sizing flags to control the relative size of various memory pools. These flags are summarized in Table 8-5.

Table 8-5. Older GC heap sizing flags

Flag	Effect
`-XX:NewRatio=<n>`	(Old flag) Sets ratio of young gen to Heap
`-XX:SurvivorRatio=<n>`	(Old flag) Sets ratio of survivor spaces to young gen
`-XX:NewSize=<n>`	(Old flag) Sets min size of young gen
`-XX:MaxNewSize=<n>`	(Old flag) Sets max size of young gen
`-XX:MinHeapFreeRatio`	(Old flag) Sets min % of heap free after GC to avoid expanding
`-XX:MaxHeapFreeRatio`	(Old flag) Sets max % of heap free after GC to avoid shrinking

The survivor ratio, new ratio, and overall heap size are connected by the following formula:

```
Flags set:

-XX:NewRatio=N
-XX:SurvivorRatio=K

YoungGen = 1 / (N+1) of heap
OldGen = N / (N+1) of heap

Eden = (K - 2) / K of YoungGen
Survivor1 = 1 / K of YoungGen
Survivor2 = 1 / K of YoungGen
```

For most modern applications, these types of explicit sizing should not be used, as the ergonomic sizing will do a better job than humans in almost all cases. For Parallel GC, resorting to these switches is something close to a last resort.

Tuning CMS

The CMS collector has a reputation of being difficult to tune. This is not wholly undeserved: the complexities and tradeoffs involved in getting the best performance out of CMS are not to be underestimated.

The simplistic position "pause time bad, therefore concurrent marking collector good" is unfortunately common among many developers. A low-pause collector like CMS should really be seen as a last resort, only to be used if the use case genuinely requires low STW pause times. To do otherwise may mean that a team is lumbered with a collector that is difficult to tune and provides no real tangible benefit to the application performance.

CMS has a very large number of flags (almost 100 as of Java 8u131), and some developers may be tempted to change the values of these flags in an attempt to improve performance. However, this can easily lead to several of the antipatterns that we met in Chapter 4, including:

- Fiddling with Switches
- Tuning by Folklore
- Missing the Bigger Picture

The conscientious performance engineer should resist the temptation to fall prey to any of these cognitive traps.

 The majority of applications that use CMS will probably not see any real observable improvement by changing the values of CMS command-line flags.

Despite this danger, there are some circumstances where tuning is necessary to improve (or obtain acceptable) CMS performance. Let's start by considering the throughput behavior.

While a CMS collection is running, by default half the cores are doing GC. This inevitably causes application throughout to be reduced. One useful rule of thumb can be to consider the situation of the collector just before a concurrent mode failure occurs.

In this case, as soon as a CMS collection has finished, a new CMS collection immediately starts. This is known as a *back-to-back* collection, and in the case of a concurrent collector, it indicates the point at which concurrent collection is about to break down. If the application allocates any faster, then reclamation will be unable to keep up and the result will be a CMF.

In the back-to-back case, throughput will be reduced by 50% for essentially the entire run of the application. When undertaking a tuning exercise, the engineer should consider whether the application can tolerate this worst-case behavior. If not, then the solution may be to run on a host with more cores available.

An alternative is to reduce the number of cores assigned to GC during a CMS cycle. Of course, this is dangerous, as it reduces the amount of CPU time available to perform collection, and so will make the application less resilient to allocation spikes (and in turn may make it more vulnerable to a CMF). The switch that controls this is:

```
-XX:ConcGCThreads=<n>
```

It should be obvious that if an application cannot reclaim fast enough with the default setting, then reducing the number of GC threads will only make matters worse.

CMS has two separate STW phases:

Initial Mark

Marks the immediate interior nodes—those that are directly pointed at by GC roots

* Remark

Uses the card tables to identify objects that may require fixup work

This means that all app threads must stop, and hence safepoint, twice per CMS cycle. This effect can become important for some low-latency apps that are sensitive to safe-pointing behavior.

Two flags that are sometimes seen together are:

```
-XX:CMSInitiatingOccupancyFraction=<n>
-XX:+UseCMSInitiatingOccupancyOnly
```

These flags can be very useful. They also illustrate, once again, the importance of and dilemma presented by unstable allocation rates.

The initiating occupancy flag is used to determine at what point CMS should begin collecting. Some heap headroom is required so that there's spare space for objects to be promoted into from young collections that may occur while CMS is running.

Like many other aspects of HotSpot's approach to GC, the size of this spare space is controlled by the statistics collected by the JVM itself. However, an estimate for the first run of CMS is still required. The headroom size for this initial guess is controlled by the flag CMSInitiatingOccupancyFraction. The default for this flag means that the first CMS full GC will begin when the heap is 75% full.

If the UseCMSInitiatingOccupancyOnly flag is also set, then the dynamic sizing for the initiating occupancy is turned off. This should not be done lightly, and it is rare in practice to decrease the headroom (increase the parameter value above 75%).

However, for some CMS applications that have very bursty allocation rates, one strategy would be to increase the headroom (decrease the parameter value) while turning off the adaptive sizing. The aim here would be to try to reduce concurrent mode failures, at the expense of CMS concurrent GCs occurring more often.

Concurrent Mode Failures Due to Fragmentation

Let's look at another case where the data we need to perform a tuning analysis is only available in the GC logs. In this case we want to use the *free list statistics* to predict when the JVM might suffer from a CMF due to heap fragmentation. This type of CMF is caused by the free list that CMS maintains, which we met in "JVM Safepoints" on page 144.

We will need to turn on another JVM switch to see the additional output:

```
-XX:PrintFLSStatistics=1
```

The output that's produced in the GC log looks like this (detail of output statistics shown for a `BinaryTreeDictionary` benchmark):

```
Total Free Space: 40115394

Max Chunk Size: 38808526

Number of Blocks: 1360

Av. Block Size: 29496

Tree Height: 22
```

In this case we can get a sense of the size distribution of chunks of memory from the average size and the max chunk size. If we run out of chunks large enough to support moving a large live object into Tenured, then a GC promotion will degrade into this concurrent failure mode.

In order to compact the heap and coalesce the free space list, the JVM will fall back to Parallel GC, probably causing a long STW pause. This analysis is useful when performed in real time, as it can signal that a long pause is imminent. You can observe it by parsing the logs, or using a tool like Censum that can automatically detect the approaching CMF.

Tuning G1

The overall goal of tuning G1 is to allow the end user to simply set the maximum heap size and `MaxGCPauseMillis`, and have the collector take care of everything else. However, the current reality is still some way from this.

Like CMS, G1 comes with a large number of configuration options, some of which are still experimental and not fully surfaced within the VM (in terms of visible metrics for tuning). This makes it difficult to understand the impact of any tuning changes. If these options are needed for tuning (and currently they are for some tuning scenarios), then this switch must be specified:

```
-XX:+UnlockExperimentalVMOptions
```

In particular, this option must be specified if the options `-XX:G1NewSizePercent=<n>` or `-XX:G1MaxNewSizePercent=<n>` are to be used. At some point in the future, some of these options may become more mainstream and not require the experimental options flag, but there is no roadmap for this yet.

An interesting view of the G1 heap can be seen in Figure 8-7. This image was generated by the *regions* JavaFX application.

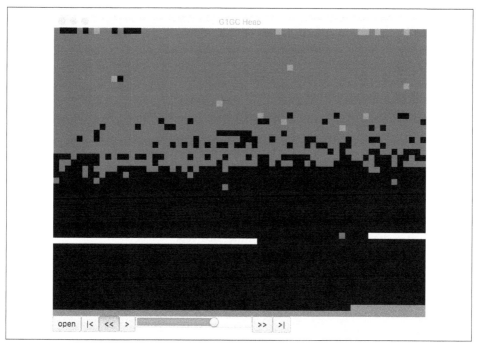

Figure 8-7. Visualizing G1's heap in regions

This is a small, open source Java FX application that parses a G1 GC log and provides a way to visualize the region layout of a G1 heap over the lifetime of a GC log. The tool was written by Kirk Pepperdine and can be obtained from GitHub (*https:// github.com/kcpeppe/regions*). At the time of writing it is still under active development.

One of the major issues with G1 tuning is that the internals have changed considerably over the early life of the collector. This has led to a significant problem with Tuning by Folklore, as many of the earlier articles that were written about G1 are now of limited validity.

With G1 becoming the default collector as of Java 9, performance engineers will surely be forced to address the topic of how to tune G1, but as of this writing it remains an often frustrating task where best practice is still emerging.

However, let's finish this section by focusing on where some progress has been made, and where G1 does offer the promise of exceeding CMS. Recall that CMS does not compact, so over time the heap can fragment. This will lead to a concurrent mode failure eventually and the JVM will need to perform a full parallel collection (with the possibility of a significant STW pause).

In the case of G1, provided the collector can keep up with the allocation rate, then the incremental compaction offers the possibility of avoiding a CMF at all. An application that has a high, stable allocation rate and which creates mostly short-lived options should therefore:

- Set a large young generation.
- Increase the tenuring threshold, probably to the maximum (15).
- Set the longest pause time goal that the app can tolerate.

Configuring Eden and survivor spaces in this way gives the best chance that genuinely short-lived objects are not promoted. This reduces pressure on the old generation and reduces the need to clean old regions. There are rarely any guarantees in GC tuning, but this is an example workload where G1 may do significantly better than CMS, albeit at the cost of some effort to tune the heap.

jHiccup

We already met HdrHistogram in "Non-Normal Statistics" on page 105. A related tool is *jHiccup*, available from GitHub (*https://github.com/giltene/jHiccup*). This is an instrumentation tool that is designed to show "hiccups" where the JVM is not able to run continuously. One very common cause of this is GC STW pauses, but other OS- and platform-related effects can also cause a hiccup. It is therefore useful not only for GC tuning but for ultra-low-latency work.

In fact, we have also already seen an example of how jHiccup works. In "Shenandoah" on page 156 we introduced the Shenandoah collector, and showcased a graph of the collector's performance as compared to others. The graph of comparative performance in Figure 7-9 was produced by JHiccup.

 jHiccup is an excellent tool to use when you are tuning HotSpot, even though the original author (Gil Tene) cheerfully admits that it was written to show up a perceived shortcoming of HotSpot as compared to Azul's Zing JVM.

jHiccup is usually used as a Java agent, by way of the `-javaagent:jHiccup.jar` Java command-line switch. It can also be used via the Attach API (like some of the other command-line tools). The form for this is:

```
jHiccup -p <pid>
```

This effectively injects jHiccup into a running application.

jHiccup produces output in the form of a histogram log that can be ingested by HdrHistogram. Let's take a look at this in action, starting by recalling the model allocation application introduced in "The Role of Allocation" on page 134.

To run this with a set of decent GC logging flags as well as jHiccup running as an agent, let's look at a small piece of shell scripting to set up the run:

```bash
#!/bin/bash

# Simple script for running jHiccup against a run of the model toy allocator

CP=./target/optimizing-java-1.0.0-SNAPSHOT.jar

JHICCUP_OPTS=
  -javaagent:~/.m2/repository/org/jhiccup/jHiccup/2.0.7/jHiccup-2.0.7.jar

GC_LOG_OPTS="-Xloggc:gc-jHiccup.log -XX:+PrintGCDetails -XX:+PrintGCDateStamps
  -XX:+PrintGCTimeStamps -XX:+PrintTenuringDistribution"

MEM_OPTS="-Xmx1G"

JAVA_BIN=`which java`

if [ $JAVA_HOME ]; then
    JAVA_CMD=$JAVA_HOME/bin/java
elif [ $JAVA_BIN ]; then
    JAVA_CMD=$JAVA_BIN
else
    echo "For this command to run, either $JAVA_HOME must be set, or java must be
    in the path."
    exit 1
fi

exec $JAVA_CMD -cp $CP $JHICCUP_OPTS $GC_LOG_OPTS $MEM_OPTS
  optjava.ModelAllocator
```

This will produce both a GC log and an *.hlog* file suitable to be fed to the `jHiccupLog Processor` tool that ships as part of jHiccup. A simple, out-of-the-box jHiccup view is shown in Figure 8-8.

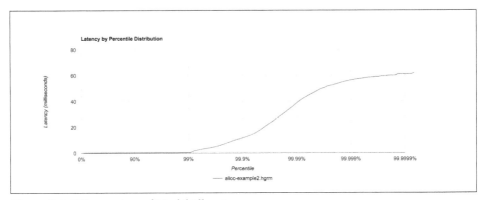

Figure 8-8. jHiccup view of ModelAllocator

This was obtained by a very simple invocation of jHiccup:

```
jHiccupLogProcessor -i hiccup-example2.hlog -o alloc-example2
```

There are some other useful switches—to see all the available options, just use:

```
jHiccupLogProcessor -h
```

It is very often the case that performance engineers need to comprehend multiple views of the same application behavior, so for completeness, let's see the same run as seen from Censum, in Figure 8-9.

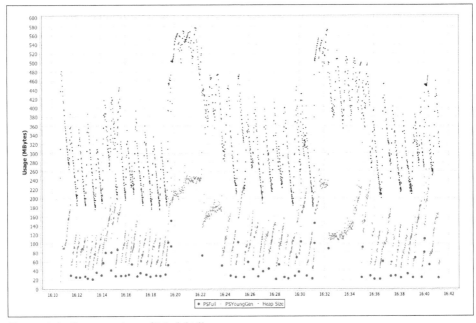

Figure 8-9. Censum view of ModelAllocator

This graph of the heap size after GC reclamation shows HotSpot trying to resize the heap and not being able to find a stable state. This is a frequent circumstance, even for applications as simple as ModelAllocator. The JVM is a very dynamic environment, and for the most part developers should avoid being overly concerned with the low-level detail of GC ergonomics.

Finally, some very interesting technical details about both HdrHistogram and jHiccup can be found in a great blog post by Nitsan Wakart (*http://psy-lob-saw.blogspot.in/2015/02/hdrhistogram-better-latency-capture.html*).

Summary

In this chapter we have scratched the surface of the art of GC tuning. The techniques we have shown are mostly highly specific to individual collectors, but there are some underlying techniques that are generally applicable. We have also covered some basic principles for handling GC logs, and met some useful tools.

Moving onward, in the next chapter we will turn to one of the other major subsystems of the JVM: execution of application code. We will begin with an overview of the interpreter and then proceed from there to a discussion of JIT compilation, including how it relates to standard (or "Ahead-of-Time") compilation.

## CHAPTER 9

Code Execution on the JVM

The two main services that any JVM provides are memory management and an easy-to-use container for execution of application code. We covered garbage collection in some depth in Chapters 6 through 8, and in this chapter we turn to code execution.

Recall that the Java Virtual Machine specification, usually referred to as the VMSpec, describes how a conforming Java implementation needs to execute code.

The VMSpec defines execution of Java bytecode in terms of an interpreter. However, broadly speaking, interpreted environments have unfavorable performance as compared to programming environments that execute machine code directly. Most production-grade modern Java environments solve this problem by providing dynamic compilation capability.

As we discussed in Chapter 2, this ability is otherwise known as *Just-in-Time compilation*, or just *JIT compilation*. It is a mechanism by which the JVM monitors which methods are being executed in order to determine whether individual methods are eligible for compilation to directly executable code.

In this chapter we start by providing a brief overview of bytecode interpretation and why HotSpot is different from other interpreters that you may be familiar with. We then turn to the basic concepts of profile-guided optimization. We discuss the code cache and then introduce the basics of HotSpot's compilation subsystem.

In the following chapter we will explain the mechanics behind some of HotSpot's most common optimizations, how they are used to produce very fast compiled methods, to what extent they can be tuned, and also their limitations.

Overview of Bytecode Interpretation

As we saw briefly in "Interpreting and Classloading" on page 15, the JVM interpreter operates as a stack machine. This means that, unlike with physical CPUs, there are no registers that are used as immediate holding areas for computation. Instead, all values that are to be operated on are placed on an *evaluation stack* and the stack machine instructions work by transforming the value(s) at the top of the stack.

The JVM provides three primary areas to hold data:

- The *evaluation stack*, which is local to a particular method
- *Local variables* to temporarily store results (also local to methods)
- The *object heap*, which is shared between methods and between threads

A series of VM operations that use the evaluation stack to perform computation can be seen in Figures 9-1 through 9-5, as a form of pseudocode that should be instantly recognizable to Java programmers.

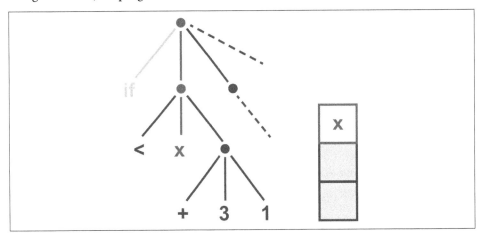

Figure 9-1. Initial interpretation state

The interpreter must now compute the righthand subtree to determine a value to compare with the contents of x.

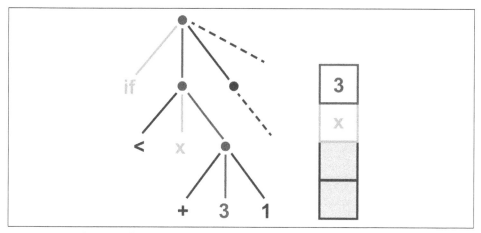

Figure 9-2. Subtree evaluation

The first value of the next subtree, an int constant 3, is loaded onto the stack.

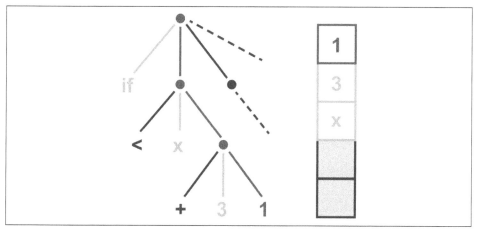

Figure 9-3. Subtree evaluation

Now another int value, 1, is also loaded onto the stack. In a real JVM these values will have been loaded from the constants area of the class file.

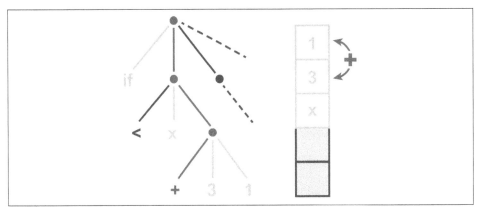

Figure 9-4. Subtree evaluation

At this point, the addition operation acts on the top two elements of the stack, removes them, and replaces them with the result of adding the two numbers together.

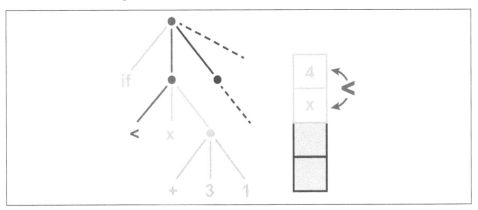

Figure 9-5. Final subtree evaluation

The resulting value is now available for comparison with the value contained in x, which has remained on the evaluation stack throughout the entire process of evaluating the other subtree.

Introduction to JVM Bytecode

In the case of the JVM, each stack machine operation code (opcode) is represented by 1 byte, hence the name *bytecode*. Accordingly, opcodes run from 0 to 255, of which roughly 200 are in use as of Java 10.

Bytecode instructions are typed, in the sense that iadd and dadd expect to find the correct primitive types (two int and two double values, respectively) at the top two positions of the stack.

Many bytecode instructions come in "families," with as many as one instruction for each primitive type and one for object references.

For example, within the store family, specific instructions have specific meanings: dstore means "store the top of stack into a local variable of type double," whereas astore means "store the top of stack into a local variable of reference type." In both cases the type of the local variable must match the type of the incoming value.

As Java was designed to be highly portable, the JVM specification was designed to be able to run the same bytecode without modification on both *big-endian* and *little-endian* hardware architectures. As a result, JVM bytecode has to make a decision about which endianness convention to follow (with the understanding that hardware with the opposite convention must handle the difference in software).

Bytecode is big-endian, so the most significant byte of any multi-byte sequence comes first.

Some opcode families, such as load, have *shortcut forms*. This allows the argument to be omitted, which saves the cost of the argument bytes in the class file. In particular, aload_0 puts the current object (i.e., this) on the top of the stack. As that is such a common operation, this results in a considerable savings in class file size.

However, as Java classes are typically fairly compact, this design decision was probably more important in the early days of the platform, when class files—often applets —would be downloaded over a 14.4 Kbps modem.

Since Java 1.0, only one new bytecode opcode (invokedynamic) has been introduced, and two (jsr and ret) have been deprecated.

The use of shortcut forms and type-specific instructions greatly inflates the number of opcodes that are needed, as several are used to represent the same conceptual operation. The number of assigned opcodes is thus much larger than the number of basic operations that bytecode represents, and bytecode is actually conceptually very simple.

Let's meet some of the main bytecode categories, arranged by opcode family. Note that in the tables that follow, c1 indicates a 2-byte constant pool index, whereas i1 indicates a local variable in the current method. The parentheses indicate that the family has some opcodes that are shortcut forms.

The first category we'll meet is the *load and store* category, depicted in Table 9-1. This category comprises the opcodes that move data on and off the stack—for example, by loading it from the constant pool or by storing the top of stack into a field of an object in the heap.

Table 9-1. Load and store category

Family name	Arguments	Description
load	(i1)	Loads value from local variable i1 onto the stack
store	(i1)	Stores top of stack into local variable i1
ldc	c1	Loads value from CP#c1 onto the stack
const		Loads simple constant value onto the stack
pop		Discards value on top of stack
dup		Duplicates value on top of stack
getfield	c1	Loads value from field indicated by CP#c1 in object on top of stack onto the stack
putfield	c1	Stores value from top of stack into field indicated by CP#c1
getstatic	c1	Loads value from static field indicated by CP#c1 onto the stack
putstatic	c1	Stores value from top of stack into static field indicated by CP#c1

The difference between ldc and const should be made clear. The ldc bytecode loads a constant from the constant pool of the current class. This holds strings, primitive constants, class literals, and other (internal) constants needed for the program to run.[1]

The const opcodes, on the other hand, take no parameters and are concerned with loading a finite number of true constants, such as aconst_null, dconst_0, and iconst_m1 (the latter of which loads -1 as an int).

The next category, the *arithmetic bytecodes*, apply only to primitive types, and none of them take arguments, as they represent purely stack-based operations. This simple category is shown in Table 9-2.

---

1 Recent versions of the JVM also permit more exotic constants to support modern advanced VM techniques.

Table 9-2. Arithmetic category

Family name	Description
add	Adds two values from top of stack
sub	Subtracts two values from top of stack
div	Divides two values from top of stack
mul	Multiplies two values from top of stack
(cast)	Casts value at top of stack to a different primitive type
neg	Negates value at top of stack
rem	Computes remainder (integer division) of top two values on stack

In Table 9-3, we can see the *flow control* category. This category represents the bytecode-level representation of the looping and branching constructs of source-level languages. For example, Java's for, if, while, and switch statements will all be transformed into flow control opcodes after source code compilation.

Table 9-3. Flow control category

Family name	Arguments	Description
if	(i1)	Branch to the location indicated by the argument, if the condition is true
goto	i1	Unconditional branch to the supplied offset
tableswitch		Out of scope
lookupswitch		Out of scope

A detailed description of how tableswitch and lookupswitch operate is outside the scope of this book.

The flow control category seems very small, but the true count of flow control opcodes is surprisingly large. This is due to there being a large number of members of the if opcode family. We met the if_icmpge opcode (*if-integer-compare-greater-or-equal*) in the javap example back in Chapter 2, but there are many others that represent different variations of the Java if statement.

The deprecated jsr and ret bytecodes, which have not been output by javac since Java 6, are also part of this family. They are no longer legal for modern versions of the platform, and so have not been included in this table.

One of the most important categories of opcodes is shown in Table 9-4. This is the *method invocation* category, and is the only mechanism that the Java program allows to transfer control to a new method. That is, the platform separates completely between local flow control and transfer of control to another method.

Table 9-4. Method invocation category

Opcode name	Arguments	Description
invokevirtual	c1	Invokes the method found at CP#c1 via virtual dispatch
invokespecial	c1	Invokes the method found at CP#c1 via "special" (i.e., exact) dispatch
invokeinterface	c1, count, 0	Invokes the interface method found at CP#c1 using interface offset lookup
invokestatic	c1	Invokes the static method found at CP#c1
invokedynamic	c1, 0, 0	Dynamically looks up which method to invoke and executes it

The JVM's design—and use of explicit *method call* opcodes—means that there is no equivalent of a `call` operation as found in machine code.

Instead, JVM bytecode uses some specialist terminology; we speak of a *call site*, which is a place within a method (the caller) where another method (the callee) is called. Not only that, but in the case of a nonstatic method call, there is always some object that we resolve the method upon. This object is known as the *receiver object* and its runtime type is referred to as the *receiver type*.

Calls to static methods are always turned into `invokestatic` and have no receiver object.

Java programmers who are new to looking at the VM level may be surprised to learn that method calls on Java objects are actually transformed into one of three possible bytecodes (`invokevirtual`, `invokespecial`, or `invokeinterface`), depending on the context of the call.

It can be a very useful exercise to write some Java code and see what circumstances produce each possibility, by disassembling a simple Java class with `javap`.

Instance method calls are normally turned into `invokevirtual` instructions, except when the static type of a receiver object is only known to be an interface type. In this case, the call is instead represented by an `invokeinterface` opcode. Finally, in the cases (e.g., private methods or superclass calls) where the exact method for dispatch is known at compile time, an `invokespecial` instruction is produced.

This begs the question of how invokedynamic enters the picture. The short answer is that there is no direct language-level support for invokedynamic in Java, even as of version 10.

In fact, when invokedynamic was added to the runtime in Java 7, there was no way at all to force javac to emit the new bytecode. In this old version of Java, the invoke dynamic technology had only been added to support long-term experimentation and non-Java dynamic languages (especially JRuby).

However, from Java 8 onward, invokedynamic has become a crucial part of the Java language and it is used to provide support for advanced language features. Let's take a look at a simple example from Java 8 lambdas:

```
public class LambdaExample {
    private static final String HELLO = "Hello";

    public static void main(String[] args) throws Exception {
        Runnable r = () -> System.out.println(HELLO);
        Thread t = new Thread(r);
        t.start();
        t.join();
    }
}
```

This trivial usage of a lambda expression produces bytecode as shown:

```
public static void main(java.lang.String[]) throws java.lang.Exception;
  Code:
     0: invokedynamic #2,  0  // InvokeDynamic #0:run:()Ljava/lang/Runnable;
     5: astore_1
     6: new            #3     // class java/lang/Thread
     9: dup
    10: aload_1
    11: invokespecial  #4     // Method java/lang/Thread.
                              //        "<init>":(Ljava/lang/Runnable;)V
    14: astore_2
    15: aload_2
    16: invokevirtual  #5     // Method java/lang/Thread.start:()V
    19: aload_2
    20: invokevirtual  #6     // Method java/lang/Thread.join:()V
    23: return
```

Even if we know nothing else about it, the form of the invokedynamic instruction indicates that some method is being called, and the return value of that call is placed upon the stack.

Digging further into the bytecode we discover that, unsurprisingly, this value is the object reference corresponding to the lambda expression. It is created by a platform factory method that is being called by the invokedynamic instruction. This invocation makes reference to extended entries in the constant pool of the class to support the dynamic runtime nature of the call.

This is perhaps the most obvious use case of invokedynamic for Java programmers, but it is not the only one. This opcode is extensively used by non-Java languages on the JVM, such as JRuby and Nashorn (JavaScript), and increasingly by Java frameworks as well. However, for the most part it remains something of a curiosity, albeit one that a performance engineer should be aware of. We will meet some related aspects of invokedynamic later in the book.

The final category of opcodes we'll consider are the *platform opcodes*. They are shown in Table 9-5, and comprise operations such as allocating new heap storage and manipulating the intrinsic locks (the monitors used by synchronization) on individual objects.

Table 9-5. Platform opcodes category

Opcode name	Arguments	Description
new	c1	Allocates space for an object of type found at CP#c1
newarray	prim	Allocates space for a primitive array of type prim
anewarray	c1	Allocates space for an object array of type found at CP#c1
arraylength		Replaces array on top of stack with its length
monitorenter		Locks monitor of object on top of stack
monitorexit		Unlocks monitor of object on top of stack

For newarray and anewarray the length of the array being allocated needs to be on top of the stack when the opcode executes.

In the catalogue of bytecodes there is a clear difference between "coarse" and "fine-grained" bytecodes, in terms of the complexity required to implement each opcode.

For example, arithmetic operations will be very fine-grained and are implemented in pure assembly in HotSpot. By contrast, coarse operations (e.g., operations requiring constant pool lookups, especially method dispatch) will need to call back into the HotSpot VM.

Along with the semantics of individual bytecodes, we should also say a word about safepoints in interpreted code. In Chapter 7 we met the concept of a JVM safepoint, as a point where the JVM needs to perform some housekeeping and requires a consistent internal state. This includes the object graph (which is, of course, being altered by the running application threads in a very general way).

To achieve this consistent state, all application threads must be stopped, to prevent them from mutating the shared heap for the duration of the JVM's housekeeping. How is this done?

The solution is to recall that every JVM application thread is a true OS thread.[2] Not only that, but for threads executing interpreted methods, when an opcode is about to be dispatched the application thread is definitely running JVM interpreter code, not user code. The heap should therefore be in a consistent state and the application thread can be stopped.

Therefore, "in between bytecodes" is an ideal time to stop an application thread, and one of the simplest examples of a safepoint.

The situation for JIT-compiled methods is more complex, but essentially equivalent barriers must be inserted into the generated machine code by the JIT compiler.

Simple Interpreters

As mentioned in Chapter 2, the simplest interpreter can be thought of as a `switch` statement inside a `while` loop. An example of this type can be found in the Ocelot project (*https://github.com/kittylyst/ocelotvm*), a partial implementation of a JVM interpreter designed for teaching. Version 0.1.1 is a good place to start if you are unfamiliar with the implementation of interpreters.

The `execMethod()` method of the interpreter interprets a single method of bytecode. Just enough opcodes have been implemented (some of them with dummy implementations) to allow integer math and "Hello World" to run.

A full implementation capable of handling even a very simple program would require complex operations, such as constant pool lookup, to have been implemented and work properly. However, even with only some very bare bones available, the basic structure of the interpreter is clear:

```java
public EvalValue execMethod(final byte[] instr) {
    if (instr == null || instr.length == 0)
        return null;

    EvaluationStack eval = new EvaluationStack();

    int current = 0;
    LOOP:
    while (true) {
        byte b = instr[current++];
        Opcode op = table[b & 0xff];
        if (op == null) {
```

---

2 At least in mainstream server JVMs.

```
                System.err.println("Unrecognized opcode byte: " + (b & 0xff));
                System.exit(1);
            }
            byte num = op.numParams();
            switch (op) {
                case IADD:
                    eval.iadd();
                    break;
                case ICONST_0:
                    eval.iconst(0);
                    break;
// ...
                case IRETURN:
                    return eval.pop();
                case ISTORE:
                    istore(instr[current++]);
                    break;
                case ISUB:
                    eval.isub();
                    break;
                // Dummy implementation
                case ALOAD:
                case ALOAD_0:
                case ASTORE:
                case GETSTATIC:
                case INVOKEVIRTUAL:
                case LDC:
                    System.out.print("Executing " + op + " with param bytes: ");
                    for (int i = current; i < current + num; i++) {
                        System.out.print(instr[i] + " ");
                    }
                    current += num;
                    System.out.println();
                    break;
                case RETURN:
                    return null;
                default:
                    System.err.println("Saw " + op + " : can't happen. Exit.");
                    System.exit(1);
            }
        }
    }
}
```

Bytecodes are read one at a time from the method, and are dispatched based on the code. In the case of opcodes with parameters, these are read from the stream as well, to ensure that the read position remains correct.

Temporary values are evaluated on the EvaluationStack, which is a local variable in execMethod(). The arithmetic opcodes operate on this stack to perform the calculation of integer math.

Method invocation is not implemented in the simplest version of Ocelot—but if it were, then it would proceed by looking up a method in the constant pool, finding the bytecode corresponding to the method to be invoked, and then recursively calling execMethod(). Version 0.2 of the code shows this case for calling static methods.

HotSpot-Specific Details

HotSpot is a production-quality JVM, and is not only fully implemented but also has extensive advanced features designed to enable fast execution, even in interpreted mode. Rather than the simple style that we met in the Ocelot training example, Hot-Spot is a *template interpreter*, which builds up the interpreter dynamically each time it is started up.

This is significantly more complex to understand, and makes reading even the inter-preter source code a challenge for the newcomer. HotSpot also makes use of a rela-tively large amount of assembly language to implement the simple VM operations (such as arithmetic) and exploits the native platform stack frame layout for further performance gains.

Also potentially surprising is that HotSpot defines and uses JVM-specific (aka pri-vate) bytecodes that do not appear in the VMSpec. These are used to allow HotSpot to differentiate common hot cases from the more general use case of a particular opcode.

This is designed to help deal with a surprising number of edge cases. For example, a final method cannot be overridden, so the developer might think an invokespecial opcode would be emitted by javac when such a method is called. However, the Java Language Specification 13.4.17 has something to say about this case:

> Changing a method that is declared final to no longer be declared final does not break compatibility with pre-existing binaries.

Consider a piece of Java code such as:

```
public class A {
    public final void fMethod() {
        // ... do something
    }
}

public class CallA {
    public void otherMethod(A obj) {
        obj.fMethod();
    }
}
```

Now, suppose javac compiled calls to final methods into invokespecial. The byte-code for CallA::otherMethod would look something like this:

```
public void otherMethod()
  Code:
    0: aload_1
    1: invokespecial #4                    // Method A.fMethod:()V
    4: return
```

Now, suppose the code for A changes so that fMethod() is made nonfinal. It can now be overridden in a subclass; we'll call it B. Now suppose that an instance of B is passed to otherMethod(). From the bytecode, the invokespecial instruction will be executed and the wrong implementation of the method will be called.

This is a violation of the rules of Java's object orientation. Strictly speaking, it violates the *Liskov Substitution Principle* (named for Barbara Liskov, one of the pioneers of object-oriented programming), which, simply stated, says that an instance of a subclass can be used anywhere that an instance of a superclass is expected. This principle is also the *L* in the famous SOLID principles of software engineering.

For this reason, calls to final methods must be compiled into invokevirtual instructions. However, because the JVM knows that such methods cannot be overridden, the HotSpot interpreter has a private bytecode that is used exclusively for dispatching final methods.

To take another example, the language specification says that an object that is subject to finalization (see "Avoid Finalization" on page 273 for a discussion of the finalization mechanism) must register with the finalization subsystem. This registration must occur immediately after the supercall to the Object constructor Object::<init> has completed. In the case of JVMTI and other potential rewritings of the bytecode, this code location may become obscured. To ensure strict conformance, HotSpot has a private bytecode that marks the return from the "true" Object constructor.

A list of the opcodes can be found in *hotspot/src/share/vm/interpreter/bytecodes.cpp* and the HotSpot-specific special cases are listed there as "JVM bytecodes."

AOT and JIT Compilation

In this section, we will discuss and compare Ahead-of-Time (AOT) and Just-in-Time (JIT) compilation as alternative approaches to producing executable code.

JIT compilation has been developed more recently than AOT compilation, but neither approach has stood still in the 20+ years that Java has been around, and each has borrowed successful techniques from the other.

AOT Compilation

If you have experience programming in languages such as C and C++ you will be familiar with AOT compilation (you may have just called it "compilation"). This is the process whereby an external program (the compiler) takes human-readable program source and outputs directly executable machine code.

 Compiling your source code ahead of time means you have only a single opportunity to take advantage of any potential optimizations.

You will most likely want to produce an executable that is targeted to the platform and processor architecture you intend to run it on. These closely targeted binaries will be able to take advantage of any processor-specific features that can speed up your program.

However, in most cases the executable is produced without knowledge of the specific platform that it will be executed upon. This means that AOT compilation must make conservative choices about which processor features are likely to be available. If the code is compiled with the assumption that certain features are available and they turn out not to be, then the binary will not run at all.

This leads to a situation where AOT-compiled binaries usually do not take full advantage of the CPU's capabilities, and potential performance enhancements are left on the table.

JIT Compilation

Just-in-Time compilation is a general technique whereby programs are converted (usually from some convenient intermediate format) into highly optimized machine code at runtime. HotSpot and most other mainstream production-grade JVMs rely heavily on this approach.

The technique gathers information about your program at runtime and builds a profile that can be used to determine which parts of your program are used frequently and would benefit most from optimization.

 This technique is known as *profile-guided optimization* (PGO).

The JIT subsystem shares VM resources with your running program, so the cost of this profiling and any optimizations performed needs to be balanced against the expected performance gains.

The cost of compiling bytecode to native code is paid at runtime and consumes resources (CPU cycles, memory) that could otherwise be dedicated to executing your program, so JIT compilation is performed sparingly and the VM collects statistics about your program (looking for "hot spots") to know where best to optimize.

Recall the overall architecture shown in Figure 2-3: the profiling subsystem is keeping track of which methods are running. If a method crosses a threshold that makes it eligible for compilation, then the emitter subsystem fires up a compilation thread to convert the bytecode into machine code.

 The design of modern versions of javac is intended to produce "dumb bytecode." It performs only very limited optimizations, and instead provides a representation of the program that is easy for the JIT compiler to understand.

In "Introduction to Measuring Java Performance" on page 86, we introduced the problem of JVM warmup as a result of PGO. This period of unstable performance when the application starts up has frequently led Java developers to ask questions such as "Can't we save the compiled code to disk and use it the next time the application starts up?" or "Isn't it very wasteful to rerun optimization and compilation decisions every time we run the application?"

The problem is that these questions contain some basic assumptions about the nature of running application code, and they are not usually correct. Let's look at an example from the financial industry to illustrate the problem.

US unemployment figures are released once a month. This *nonfarm payroll* (NFP) day produces traffic in trading systems that is highly unusual and not normally seen throughout the rest of the month. If optimizations had been saved from another day, and run on NFP day they would not be as effective as freshly calculated optimizations. This would have the end result of making a system that uses precomputed optimizations actually less competitive than an application using PGO.

This behavior, where application performance varies significantly between different runs of the application, is very common, and represents the kind of domain information that an environment like Java is supposed to protect the developer from.

For this reason, HotSpot does not attempt to save any profiling information and instead discards it when the VM shuts down, so the profile must be built again from scratch each time.

Comparing AOT and JIT Compilation

AOT compilation has the advantage of being relatively simple to understand. Machine code is produced directly from source, and the machine code that corresponds to a compilation unit is directly available as assembly. This, in turn, also offers the possibility of code that will have straightforward performance characteristics.

Offset against this is the fact that AOT means giving up access to valuable runtime information that could help inform optimization decisions. Techniques such as link-time optimization (LTO) and a form of PGO are now starting to appear in gcc and other compilers, but they are in the early stages of development compared to their counterparts in HotSpot.

Targeting processor-specific features during AOT compilation will produce an executable that is compatible only with that processor. This can be a useful technique for low-latency or extreme performance use cases; building on the exact same hardware as the application will run on ensures that the compiler can take advantage of all available processor optimizations.

However, this technique does not scale: if you want maximum performance across a range of target architectures, you will need to produce a separate executable for each one.

By contrast, HotSpot can add optimizations for new processor features as they are released and applications will not have to recompile their classes and JARs to take advantage of them. It is not unusual to find that program performance improves measurably between new releases of the HotSpot VM as the JIT compiler is improved.

At this point, let's address the persistent myth that "Java programs can't be AOT-compiled." This is simply not true: commercial VMs that offer AOT compilation of Java programs have been available for several years now and in some environments are a major route to deploying Java applications.

Finally, starting with Java 9 the HotSpot VM has begun to offer AOT compilation as an option, initially for core JDK classes. This is an initial (and quite limited) step toward producing AOT-compiled binaries from Java source, but it represents a departure from the traditional JIT environments that Java did so much to popularize.

HotSpot JIT Basics

The basic unit of compilation in HotSpot is a whole method, so all the bytecode corresponding to a single method is compiled into native code at once. HotSpot also supports compilation of a hot loop using a technique called *on-stack replacement* (OSR).

OSR is used to help the case where a method is not called frequently enough to be compiled but contains a loop that would be eligible for compilation if the loop body was a method in its own right.

HotSpot uses the vtables present in the klass metadata structure (which are pointed at by the klass word of the object's oop) as a primary mechanism to implement JIT compilation, as we'll see in the next section.

Klass Words, Vtables, and Pointer Swizzling

HotSpot is a multithreaded C++ application. This might seem a simplistic statement, but it is worth remembering that as a consequence, every executing Java program is actually always part of a multithreaded application from the operating system's point of view. Even single-threaded apps are always executing alongside VM threads.

One of the most important groups of threads within HotSpot are the threads that comprise the JIT compilation subsystem. This includes profiling threads that detect when a method is eligible for compilation and the compiler threads themselves that generate the actual machine code.

The overall picture is that when compilation is indicated, the method is placed on a compiler thread, which compiles in the background. The overall process can be seen in Figure 9-6.

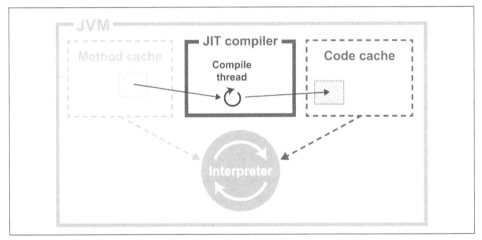

Figure 9-6. Simple compilation of a single method

When the optimized machine code is available, the entry in the vtable of the relevant klass is updated to point at the new compiled code.

This vtable pointer updating is given the slightly strange name of *pointer swizzling*.

This means that any new calls to the method will get the compiled form, whereas threads that are currently executing the interpreted form will finish the current invocation in interpreted mode, but will pick up the new compiled form on the next call.

OpenJDK has been widely ported to many different architectures with x86, x86-64, and ARM being the primary targets. SPARC, Power, MIPS, and S390 are also supported to varying degrees. Oracle officially supports Linux, macOS, and Windows as operating systems. There are open source projects to natively support a much wider selection, including BSDs and embedded systems.

Logging JIT Compilation

One important JVM switch that all performance engineers should know about is:

```
-XX:+PrintCompilation
```

This will cause a log of compilation events to be produced on STDOUT and will allow the engineer to get a basic understanding of what is being compiled.

For example, if the caching example from Example 3-1 is invoked like this:

```
java -XX:+PrintCompilation optjava.Caching 2>/dev/null
```

Then the resulting log (under Java 8) will look something like this:

```
56   1     3  java.lang.Object::<init> (1 bytes)
57   2     3  java.lang.String::hashCode (55 bytes)
58   3     3  java.lang.Math::min (11 bytes)
59   4     3  java.lang.String::charAt (29 bytes)
60   5     3  java.lang.String::length (6 bytes)
60   6     3  java.lang.String::indexOf (70 bytes)
60   7     3  java.lang.AbstractStringBuilder::ensureCapacityInternal (27 bytes)
60   8   n 0  java.lang.System::arraycopy (native)    (static)
60   9     1  java.lang.Object::<init> (1 bytes)
60   1     3  java.lang.Object::<init> (1 bytes)    made not entrant
61  10     3  java.lang.String::equals (81 bytes)
66  11     3  java.lang.AbstractStringBuilder::append (50 bytes)
67  12     3  java.lang.String::getChars (62 bytes)
68  13     3  java.lang.String::<init> (82 bytes)
74  14 %   3  optjava.Caching::touchEveryLine @ 2 (28 bytes)
74  15     3  optjava.Caching::touchEveryLine (28 bytes)
75  16 %   4  optjava.Caching::touchEveryLine @ 2 (28 bytes)
76  17 %   3  optjava.Caching::touchEveryItem @ 2 (28 bytes)
76  14 %   3  optjava.Caching::touchEveryLine @ -2 (28 bytes)    made not entrant
```

Note that as the vast majority of the JRE standard libraries are written in Java, they will be eligible for JIT compilation alongside application code. We should therefore not be surprised to see so many non-application methods present in the compiled code.

The exact set of methods that are compiled may vary slightly from run to run, even on a very simple benchmark. This is a side effect of the dynamic nature of PGO and should not be of concern.

The PrintCompilation output is formatted in a relatively simple way. First comes the time at which a method was compiled (in ms since VM start). Next is a number that indicates the order in which the method was compiled in this run. Some of the other fields are:

- n: Method is native
- s: Method is synchronized
- !: Method has exception handlers
- %: Method was compiled via on-stack replacement

The level of detail available from PrintCompilation is somewhat limited. To access more detailed information about the decisions made by the HotSpot JIT compilers, we can use:

    -XX:+LogCompilation

This is a diagnostic option we must unlock using an additional flag:

    -XX:+UnlockDiagnosticVMOptions

This instructs the VM to output a logfile containing XML tags representing information about the queuing and optimization of bytecode into native code. The LogCompilation flag can be verbose and generate hundreds of MB of XML output.

However, as we will see in the next chapter, the open source JITWatch tool can parse this file and present the information in a more easily digestible format.

Other VMs, such as IBM's J9 with the Testarossa JIT, can also be made to log JIT compiler information, but there is no standard format for JIT logging so developers must learn to interpret each log format or use appropriate tooling.

Compilers Within HotSpot

The HotSpot JVM actually has not one, but two JIT compilers in it. These are properly known as C1 and C2, but are sometimes referred to as the client compiler and the server compiler, respectively. Historically, C1 was used for GUI apps and other "client" programs, whereas C2 was used for long-running "server" applications. Modern Java apps generally blur this distinction, and HotSpot has changed to take advantage of the new landscape.

A compiled code unit is known as an *nmethod* (short for native method).

The general approach that both compilers take is to rely on a key measurement to trigger compilation: the number of times a method is invoked, or the *invocation count*. Once this counter hits a certain threshold the VM is notified and will consider queuing the method for compilation.

The compilation process proceeds by first creating an internal representation of the method. Next, optimizations are applied that take into account profiling information that has been collected during the interpreted phase. However, the internal representation of the code that C1 and C2 produce is quite different. C1 is designed to be simpler and have shorter compile times than C2. The tradeoff is that as a result C1 does not optimize as fully as C2.

One technique that is common to both is *single static assignment*. This essentially converts the program to a form where no reassignment of variables occurs. In Java programming terms, the program is effectively rewritten to contain only `final` variables.

Tiered Compilation in HotSpot

Since Java 6, the JVM has supported a mode called *tiered compilation*. This is often loosely explained as running in interpreted mode until the simple C1 compiled form is available, then switching to using that compiled code while C2 completes more advanced optimizations.

However, this description is not completely accurate. From the *advancedThresholdPolicy.hpp* source file, we can see that within the VM there are five possible levels of execution:

- Level 0: interpreter
- Level 1: C1 with full optimization (no profiling)
- Level 2: C1 with invocation and backedge counters
- Level 3: C1 with full profiling
- Level 4: C2

We can also see in Table 9-6 that not every level is utilized by each compilation approach.

Table 9-6. Compilation pathways

Pathway	Description
0-3-4	Interpreter, C1 with full profiling, C2
0-2-3-4	Interpreter, C2 busy so quick-compile C1, then full-compile C1, then C2
0-3-1	Trivial method
0-4	No tiered compilation (straight to C2)

In the case of the trivial method, the method starts off interpreted as usual but then C1 (with full profiling) is able to determine the method to be trivial. This means that it is clear that the C2 compiler would produce no better code than C2 and so compilation terminates.

Tiered compilation has been the default for some time now, and it is not normally necessary to adjust its operation during performance tuning. An awareness of its operation is useful, though, as it can frequently complicate the observed behavior of compiled methods and potentially mislead the unwary engineer.

The Code Cache

JIT-compiled code is stored in a memory region called the *code cache*. This area also stores other native code belonging to the VM itself, such as parts of the interpreter.

The code cache has a fixed maximum size that is set at VM startup. It cannot expand past this limit, so it is possible for it to fill up. At this point no further JIT compilations are possible and uncompiled code will execute only in the interpreter. This will have an impact on performance and may result in the application being significantly less performant than the potential maximum.

The code cache is implemented as a heap containing an unallocated region and a linked list of freed blocks. Each time native code is removed, its block is added to the free list. A process called the *sweeper* is responsible for recycling blocks.

When a new native method is to be stored, the free list is searched for a block large enough to store the compiled code. If none is found, then subject to the code cache having sufficient free space, a new block will be created from the unallocated space.

Native code can be removed from the code cache when:

- It is deoptimized (an assumption underpinning a speculative optimization turned out to be false).
- It is replaced with another compiled version (in the case of tiered compilation).
- The class containing the method is unloaded.

You can control the maximum size of the code cache using the VM switch:

```
-XX:ReservedCodeCacheSize=<n>
```

Note that with tiered compilation enabled, more methods will reach the lower compilation thresholds of the C1 client compiler. To account for this, the default maximum size is larger to hold these additional compiled methods.

In Java 8 on Linux x86-64 the default maximum sizes for the code cache are:

```
251658240 (240MB) when tiered compilation is enabled (-XX:+TieredCompilation)
 50331648  (48MB) when tiered compilation is disabled (-XX:-TieredCompilation)
```

Fragmentation

In Java 8 and earlier, the code cache can become fragmented if many of the intermediate compilations from the C1 compiler are removed after they are replaced by C2 compilations. This can lead to the unallocated region being used up and all of the free space residing in the free list.

The code cache allocator will have to traverse the linked list until it finds a block big enough to hold the native code of a new compilation. In turn, the sweeper will also have to more work to do scanning for blocks that can be recycled to the free list.

In the end, any garbage collection scheme that does not relocate memory blocks will be subject to fragmentation, and the code cache is not an exception.

Without a compaction scheme, the code cache can fragment and this can cause compilation to stop—it is just another form of cache exhaustion, after all.

Simple JIT Tuning

When undertaking a code tuning exercise, it is relatively easy to ensure that the application is taking advantage of JIT compilation.

The general principle of simple JIT compilation tuning is simple: "any method that wants to compile should be given the resources to do so." To achieve this aim, follow this simple checklist:

1. First run the app with the `PrintCompilation` switch on.
2. Collect the logs that indicate which methods are compiled.
3. Now increase the size of the code cache via `ReservedCodeCacheSize`.
4. Rerun the application.
5. Look at the set of compiled methods with the enlarged cache.

The performance engineer will need to take into account the slight nondeterminism inherent in the JIT compilation. Keeping this in mind, there are a couple of obvious tells that can easily be observed:

- Is the set of compiled methods larger in a meaningful way when the cache size is increased?

- Are all methods that are important to the primary transaction paths being compiled?

If the number of compiled methods does not increase (indicating that the code cache is not being fully utilized) as the cache size is increased, then provided the load pattern is representative, the JIT compiler is not short of resources.

At this point, it should be straightforward to confirm that all the methods that are part of the transaction hot paths appear in the compilation logs. If not, then the next step is to determine the root cause—why these methods are not compiling.

Effectively, this strategy is making sure that JIT compilation never shuts off, by ensuring that the JVM never runs out of code cache space.

We will meet more sophisticated techniques later in the book, but despite minor variations between Java versions, the simple JIT tuning approach can help provide performance boosts for a surprising number of applications.

Summary

The JVM's initial code execution environment is the bytecode interpreter. We have explored the basics of the interpreter, as a working knowledge of bytecode is essential for a proper understanding of JVM code execution. The basic theory of JIT compilation has also been introduced.

However, for most performance work, the behavior of JIT-compiled code is far more important than any aspect of the interpreter. In the next chapter, we will build on the primer introduced here and dive deep into the theory and practice of JIT compilation.

For many applications the simple tuning of the code cache shown in this chapter will be sufficient. Applications that are particularly performance-sensitive may require a deeper exploration of JIT behavior. The next chapter will also describe tools and techniques to tune applications that have these more stringent requirements.

## CHAPTER 10

Understanding JIT Compilation

In this chapter we will delve deeper into the inner workings of the JVM's JIT compiler. The majority of the material is directly applicable to HotSpot, and is not guaranteed to be the same for other JVM implementations.

Having said that, the general science of JIT compilation is quite well studied, and JIT implementations occur in many modern programming environments, not just the JVM. As a result, many of the same JIT techniques are applicable to other JIT compilers.

Due to the abstract and technically complex nature of the subject matter, we will rely upon tooling to help understand and visualize the inner workings of the JVM. The primary tool we will be using is JITWatch, and we introduce it at the start of the chapter. Following this, we will be able to explain specific JIT optimizations and features and show how the technique and its effects can be observed from JITWatch.

Introducing JITWatch

JITWatch is an open source JavaFX tool (*https://github.com/AdoptOpenJDK/jitwatch/*) designed and built by one of this book's authors (Chris Newland) as a personal project. The tool is now hosted under the AdoptOpenJDK initiative, as part of a program run by the London Java Community to improve the amount of community participation in the Java ecosystem.

JITWatch allows a development or devops team to better understand what HotSpot actually did to the bytecode during the execution of the application. It is possible to tune compilation switches to improve the performance of our applications, but it is essential that we have a mechanism of measuring any improvements we have made.

Any method that is to be analyzed must be used in a hot path and be eligible for compilation. Interpreted methods are not suitable targets for serious optimization.

JITWatch provides objective measurements for comparison. Without these measurements there is a real risk of falling into the Missing the Bigger Picture antipattern discussed in the section "Performance Antipatterns Catalogue" on page 69.

To function, JITWatch parses and analyzes the detailed HotSpot compilation log output from the running Java application and displays it in the JavaFX GUI. This means that in order to work the tool requires the application to be run with a certain set of flags.

As well as any flags required for normal runs of the application, the following flags must be added for JITWatch if they are not already present:

```
-XX:+UnlockDiagnosticVMOptions -XX:+TraceClassLoading -XX:+LogCompilation
```

With these flags switched on, the JVM will produce a log that can be fed into JIT-Watch.

Basic JITWatch Views

After the application run has finished, you can start JITWatch, load the log, and produce a view like that shown in Figure 10-1, based on the actual run of the application.

Figure 10-1. JITWatch main window

As well as loading logs from executed programs, JITWatch also provides an environment for experimenting with JIT behaviors called the *sandbox*. This view allows you to quickly prototype small programs and see the JIT decisions made by the JVM. A sample view is shown in Figure 10-2.

```
● ● ●                          Sandbox - Code, Compile, Execute, and Analyse JIT logs

New Editor   Open   Save   Configure Sandbox   Reset Sandbox   Java      ▾   Run   View Output                            📷

SimpleInliningTest.java ✕
    1      // The Sandbox is designed to help you learn about the HotSpot JIT compilers.
    2      // Please note that the JIT compilers may behave differently when isolating a method
    3      // in the Sandbox compared to running your whole application.
    4
    5      public class SimpleInliningTest
    6      {
    7          public SimpleInliningTest()
    8          {
    9              int sum = 0;
   10
   11              // 1_000_000 is F4240 in hex
   12              for (int i = 0 ; i < 1_000_000; i++)
   13              {
   14                  sum = this.add(sum, 99); // 63 hex
   15              }
   16
   17              System.out.println("Sum:" + sum);
   18          }
   19
   20          public int add(int a, int b)
   21          {
   22              return a + b;
   23          }
   24
   25          public static void main(String[] args)
   26          {

Sandbox ready
Disassembler available: /Library/Java/JavaVirtualMachines/jdk1.8.0_152.jdk/Contents/Home/jre/lib/server/hsdis-amd64.dylib
```

Figure 10-2. JITWatch sandbox

The sandbox workflow allows you to create or load a program written in Java or one of the other supported JVM languages, as an alternative to loading an existing logfile.

When you click the Run button, JITWatch will:

1. Compile your program into bytecode.
2. Execute the program on the JVM with JIT logging enabled.
3. Load the JIT logfile into JITWatch for analysis.

The sandbox is designed to allow fast feedback on the way small changes can affect the optimization choices made by the JVM. As well as Java, you can use the sandbox with Scala, Kotlin, Groovy, and JavaScript (Nashorn) by configuring their paths.

 The sandbox can be incredibly useful, so you should pay attention to the warning presented in the edit window. Always remember that code run inside the sandbox may behave very differently from that in a real application.

The sandbox also allows you to experiment with the VM switches that control the JIT subsystem (see Figure 10-3). For example, using the sandbox configurations setting, you can change JVM JIT behaviors including:

- Outputting disassembled native methods (requires a disassembly binary such as hsdis to be installed into your JRE) and choosing the assembly syntax.

- Overriding the JVM default setting for tiered compilation (using both C1 and C2 JIT compilers)

- Overriding compressed oops usage (disabling this can make the assembly easier to read by removing the address-shifting instructions)

- Disabling on-stack replacement

- Overriding the inlining default limits

Figure 10-3. JITWatch sandbox configuration

Changing these settings can have significant effects on JVM performance. Altering them is not recommended for a production system apart from in extreme edge cases. Even then they should not be changed without extensive testing.

Another way in which the sandbox differs from a regular run of a JVM application is that in a full-size application the JVM will have the ability to combine optimizations across a larger view of code, rather than just a sandbox snippet. Aggressive JIT compilers (such as C2) may even apply one set of optimizations as a first pass to broaden the scope of program code visible to the optimizer.

For example, the inlining technique collapses methods into their callers. This means that the optimizer can now consider further optimizations (such as more inlining, or other forms) that would not have been obvious before the initial inlining. In turn, this means that a toy application in the sandbox that has only trivial inlining behavior may be treated differently by the JIT compiler than a method from a real application with real inlining.

As a result, most practitioners prefer a more sophisticated view of application compilation than the sandbox. Fortunately, the primary view that JITWatch provides is a very capable view, known as the *TriView*. This view shows how the source code was compiled into both bytecode and assembly. An example is shown in Figure 10-4; it shows evidence of the JIT compiler removing some unnecessary object allocations—an important optimization in modern JVMs that we will meet later in this chapter.

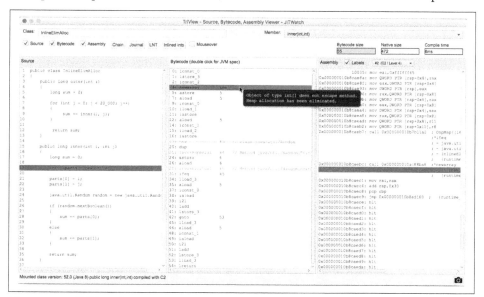

Figure 10-4. JITWatch TriView

JITWatch allows you to visualize where each compiled method is stored in the code cache. This is a relatively new feature and is still under active development, but the current view is shown in Figure 10-5.

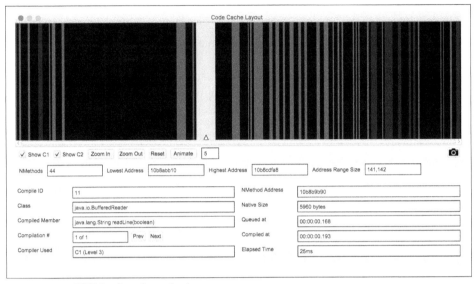

Figure 10-5. JITWatch code cache layout

In Java 8 and earlier, the code cache stores profiled compiled methods, nonprofiled compiled methods, and the VM's own native code in a single region.

Java 9 introduces a segmented code cache where these different types of native code are stored in different regions to reduce fragmentation and sweeper times and improve the locality of fully compiled code. We'll explore this feature fully in Chapter 15 when we discuss Java 9 features in depth.

Debug JVMs and hsdis

If you would like to delve deeper into tuning and obtaining statistics from the JIT subsystem, then you can do so with a *debug JVM*. This is one that has been built to produce debugging information beyond that available in a production JVM, and it will come at a cost in performance.

Debug VMs are not generally offered for download by the main JVM vendors, but a HotSpot debug JVM can be built from OpenJDK sources.

Debug VM binaries for the Linux x86_64 platform can be downloaded from the author's website (*https://chriswhocodes.com*).

If you want to inspect the disassembled native code produced by the JIT compilers, then you will need a disassembly binary such as hsdis. This can be built from the OpenJDK source code; instructions for doing so can be found in the JITWatch wiki article "Building hsdis" (*https://github.com/AdoptOpenJDK/jitwatch/wiki/Building-hsdis*).

To instruct the VM to output method assembly, add this VM switch:

```
-XX:+PrintAssembly
```

 Native code disassembly into readable assembly language is performed directly after the JIT compiler emits the method. It is an expensive operation that can impact the performance of your program and should be used carefully.

Now that we've introduced JITWatch, let's move on to look at some of the technical details of the HotSpot JIT compiler.

Introducing JIT Compilation

To complement the view of compiled code from the tool, it is necessary for the performance engineer to have a working knowledge of how the VM collects data and what optimizations it will carry out on an executing program.

We've already seen that HotSpot uses profile-guided optimization (PGO) to guide JIT compilation decisions. Under the hood, HotSpot stores profile data about the running program in structures called method data objects, or MDOs for short.

MDOs are used by the bytecode interpreter and the C1 compiler to record the information the JIT compilers use when determining what optimizations to make. MDOs store information such as methods invoked, branches taken, and types observed at call sites.

Counters that record the "hotness" of a profiled property are maintained, and the values in them are decayed during profiling. This ensures that methods are compiled only if they are still hot when they reach the head of the compilation queue.

Once this profiling data has been gathered and the decision has been made to compile, the specific details of the individual compiler take over. The compiler builds an internal representation of the code to be compiled; the exact nature of the representation depends on which compiler (C1 or C2) is in use.

From this internal representation, the compiler will heavily optimize the code. HotSpot's JIT compilers are able to perform a wide range of modern compiler optimization techniques, including:

- Inlining
- Loop unrolling
- Escape analysis
- Lock elision and lock coarsening
- Monomorphic dispatch
- Intrinsics
- On-stack replacement

In the following sections we will describe each in turn.

As you meet each technique, it is important to recall that the majority of these optimizations are partially or completely dependent on runtime information and support.

The two JIT compilers within HotSpot also use different subsets of the preceding techniques and have different philosophies about how compilation should be approached. In particular, C1 does not engage in *speculative optimization*. This is the use of optimizations that rely on an unproven assumption about the nature of the execution. Aggressive optimizers (e.g., C2) will make an assumption based on the observed runtime execution and will make an optimization based on that assumption. That simplifying assumption may allow large (sometimes very large) performance speedups to be made.

To protect against the case that the assumption was not actually correct and is later invalidated, a speculative optimization is always protected with a "sanity check" known as a *guard*. The guard ensures that the assumption still holds, and is checked just before each time the optimized code is run.

If the guard is ever failed, the compiled code is no longer safe and must be removed. HotSpot immediately *deoptimizes* and demotes the method to interpreted mode to prevent any incorrect code from ever being executed.

Inlining

Inlining is the process of taking a called method (the callee) and copying its contents to the place where it was called from (the call site).

This eliminates the overhead associated with calling a method, which is not large but can include:

- Setting up parameters to be passed
- Looking up the exact method to be called

- Creating new runtime data structures for the new call frame (such as local variables and an evaluation stack)
- Transferring control to the new method
- Possibly returning a result to the caller

Inlining is one of the first optimizations to be applied by the JIT compilers and is known as a *gateway optimization*, as it brings related code closer together by eliminating method boundaries.

Given the following code:

```
int result = add(a, b);

private int add(int x, int y) {
    return x + y;
}
```

The inlining optimization copies the body of the add() method to its call site, effectively giving:

```
int result = a + b;
```

HotSpot's inlining compiler optimization allows the developer to write well-organized and reusable code. It represents the view that a developer should not need to micro-optimize by hand. Instead, HotSpot uses automatic statistical analysis to determine when related code should be brought together. Inlining therefore broadens the horizon for other optimizations, including:

- Escape analysis
- Dead code elimination (DCE)
- Loop unrolling
- Lock elision

Inlining Limits

It is sometimes necessary for the VM to place limits on the inlining subsystem. For example, the VM may need to control:

- The amount of time the JIT compiler spends optimizing a method
- The size of native code produced (and hence its use of the code cache memory)

Without these constraints the compiler could become tied up inlining very deep call chains or filling up the code cache with huge native methods. The general principle—that JIT compilation resources are precious—comes into play again here.

HotSpot considers several factors when determining whether to inline a method, including:

- The bytecode size of the method to be inlined
- The depth of the method to be inlined in the current call chain
- The amount of space in the code cache already taken up by compiled versions of this method

In Figure 10-6 we can see JITWatch visualizing that the JIT compiler has inlined a chain of method calls into their ultimate caller but has rejected inlining a method created deliberately above the maximum default limit.

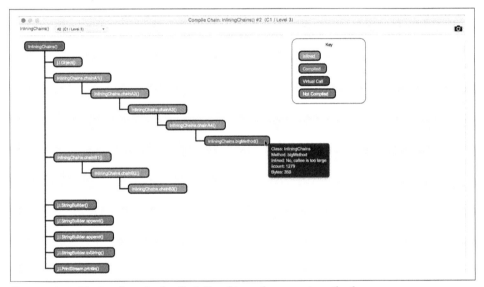

Figure 10-6. Chain of method calls inlined into the parent method

This depth of inlining is entirely typical and helps broaden the scope of the optimization.

Tuning the Inlining Subsystem

After we have determined that all important methods are being compiled, and adjusted the code cache to accommodate the application's most significant methods, the next step is to consider inlining. In Table 10-1 we can see the basic JVM switches used to control the behavior of the inlining subsystem. These switches can be used to extend the simple JIT tuning methodology shown in "Simple JIT Tuning" on page 221.

Table 10-1. Inlining switches

Switch	Default (JDK 8, Linux x86_64)	Explanation
`-XX:MaxInlineSize=<n>`	35 bytes of bytecode	Inline methods up to this size.
`-XX:FreqInlineSize=<n>`	325 bytes of bytecode	Inline "hot" (frequently called) methods up to this size.
`-XX:InlineSmallCode=<n>`	1,000 bytes of native code (non-tiered) 2,000 bytes of native code (tiered)	Do not inline methods where there is already a final-tier compilation that occupies more than this amount of space in the code cache.
`-XX:MaxInlineLevel=<n>`	9	Do not inline call frames deeper than this level.

If important methods are not being inlined (e.g., due to being "slightly too big" for inlining), then in some circumstances it may be appropriate to adjust JVM parameters to make these methods inline. Under these conditions, we would start by adjusting either `-XX:MaxInlineSize` or `-XX:FreqInlineSize` and verify whether such a change produces observable improvements.

Any such tuning exercise that adjusts these parameters must, as always, be informed by observed data. Failing to consider the actual data and to prove the worth of a parameter change is at the heart of the Fiddling with Switches antipattern (see "Fiddling with Switches" on page 81).

Loop Unrolling

Once any method calls within the loop have been inlined (where possible), the compiler has a better idea of the size and cost of each loop iteration. Based on this, it can consider *unrolling the loop* to reduce the number of times the execution has to jump back to the beginning.

Each *back branch* can have undesirable processor effects, as the CPU dumps its pipeline of incoming instructions due to the back branch. In general, the shorter the loop body, the higher the relative cost of the back branch. Therefore, HotSpot makes decisions on whether to unroll loops based on criteria including:

- The type of the loop counter variable (usually `int` or `long` rather than an object type)
- The loop stride (how the loop counter changes on each iteration)
- The number of exit points (`return` or `break`) within the loop

Consider some example methods that perform summation of data fetched sequentially from an array. This access pattern can be spotted in the assembly as [`base`, `index`, `offset`] addressing:

- `base register` contains the start address of data in the array.
- `index register` contains the loop counter (which gets multiplied by the data-type size).
- `offset` is used for offsetting each unrolled access.

```
add rbx, QWORD PTR [base register + index register * size + offset]
```

Loop unrolling behavior may vary between HotSpot versions and is highly architecture-dependent.

Given a loop over a `long[]` array, we can look at the conditions under which the loop will be unrolled. When a loop accesses an array, HotSpot can eliminate array bounds checks by splitting the loop into three sections, as shown in Table 10-2.

Table 10-2. Bounds elimination

Loop section	Bounds checks?	Explanation
Pre loop	Yes	Performs initial iterations with bounds checking.
Main loop	No	The loop stride is used to calculate the maximum number of iterations that can be performed without requiring a bounds check.
Post loop	Yes	Performs remaining iterations with bounds checking.

Here is some example setup code to create an array over which the loop will iterate:

```
private static final int MAX = 1_000_000;

private long[] data = new long[MAX];

private void createData()
{
    java.util.Random random = new java.util.Random();

    for (int i = 0; i < MAX; i++)
    {
        data[i] = random.nextLong();
    }
}
```

We can use a JMH benchmark to compare the performance of iterating over this same array using either an `int` counter or a `long` counter:

```
package optjava.jmh;
```

```
import org.openjdk.jmh.annotations.*;
import java.util.concurrent.TimeUnit;

@BenchmarkMode(Mode.Throughput)
@OutputTimeUnit(TimeUnit.SECONDS)
@State(Scope.Thread)
public class LoopUnrollingCounter
{
        private static final int MAX = 1_000_000;

        private long[] data = new long[MAX];

        @Setup
        public void createData()
        {
                java.util.Random random = new java.util.Random();

                for (int i = 0; i < MAX; i++)
                {
                        data[i] = random.nextLong();
                }
        }

        @Benchmark
        public long intStride1()
        {
                long sum = 0;
                for (int i = 0; i < MAX; i++)
                {
                        sum += data[i];
                }
                return sum;
        }

        @Benchmark
        public long longStride1()
        {
                long sum = 0;
                for (long l = 0; l < MAX; l++)
                {
                        sum += data[(int) l];
                }
                return sum;
        }
}
```

The results are as follows:

```
Benchmark                          Mode   Cnt     Score   Error  Units
LoopUnrollingCounter.intStride1    thrpt  200  2423.818 ± 2.547  ops/s
LoopUnrollingCounter.longStride1   thrpt  200  1469.833 ± 0.721  ops/s
```

The loop with the int counter performs nearly 64% more operations per second.

If we were to dive into the assembly, we would see that the body of a loop with a `long` counter will not be unrolled, and the loop will also contain a safepoint poll. These safepoint checks have been inserted by the JIT compiler to mitigate the possibility that compiled code runs for long periods without checking the safepoint flag (see "JVM Safepoints" on page 144).

Other microbenchmarks might include using a *variable stride*, where the increment is stored in a variable and is not a compile-time constant. With a variable stride, we see that the loop is not unrolled and a safepoint is inserted before the back branch.

Loop Unrolling Summary

HotSpot contains a number of specific optimizations for loop unrolling:

- It can optimize counted loops that use an `int`, `short`, or `char` loop counter.
- It can unroll loop bodies and remove safepoint polls.
- Unrolling a loop reduces the number of back branches and their associated branch prediction costs.
- Removing safepoint polls further reduces the work done each loop iteration.

You should always verify the effects yourself, though, rather than assume these examples hold true for all architectures and HotSpot versions.

Escape Analysis

HotSpot can perform a scope-based analysis for determining if work done within a method is visible or has side effects outside the boundary of that method. This *escape analysis* technique can be used to determine whether an object allocated within the method is visible outside of the method scope.

The escape analysis optimization is attempted after any inlining has taken place. Inlining copies the callee method body to the call site, which prevents objects that are passed only as method arguments from being marked as escaping.

During the escape analysis phase HotSpot categorizes potential escapee objects into three types. This piece of code from *hotspot/src/share/vm/opto/escape.hpp* details the different possible escape scenarios:

```
typedef enum {

    NoEscape      = 1, // An object does not escape method or thread and it is
                       // not passed to call. It could be replaced with scalar.
```

```
ArgEscape      = 2, // An object does not escape method or thread but it is
                    // passed as argument to call or referenced by argument
                    // and it does not escape during call.

GlobalEscape  = 3  // An object escapes the method or thread.
}
```

Eliminating Heap Allocations

Creating new objects within tight loops can put pressure on the memory allocation subsystem. Generating large numbers of short-lived objects will require frequent minor GC events to clean them up. It is possible for the allocation rate to be so high that the heap's young generation fills up and short-lived objects are prematurely promoted to the old generation. If this occurs, they will require a more expensive full GC event to clean them up.

HotSpot's escape analysis optimization is designed to allow developers to write idiomatic Java code without worrying about object allocation rates.

By proving that an allocated object does not escape the method (classed as a NoEscape), the VM can apply an optimization called *scalar replacement*. The fields in the object become scalar values, similar to if they had all been local variables instead of object fields. They can then be arranged into CPU registers by a HotSpot component called the *register allocator*.

 If there are not enough free registers available, then the scalar values can be placed onto the current stack frame (this is known as a *stack spill*).

The aim of escape analysis is to deduce whether the heap allocation can be avoided. If it can be, the object can be automatically allocated on the stack and thus GC pressure can be reduced by a small amount.

Let's look at an example of an object allocation that would be categorized as a NoEscape since the instance of MyObj does not leave the method scope:

```
public long noEscape() {
    long sum = 0;

    for (int i = 0; i < 1_000_000; i++) {
        MyObj foo = new MyObj(i); // foo does not escape the method (NoEscape)
        sum += foo.bar();
    }

    return sum;
}
```

Here is an example of an object allocation that would be categorized as an `ArgEscape` since the instance of `MyObj` is passed as an argument to the method `extBar()`.

```
public long argEscape() {
    long sum = 0;

    for (int i = 0; i < 1_000_000; i++) {
        MyObj foo = new MyObj(i);
        sum += extBar(foo); // foo is passed as an argument to extBar (ArgEscape)
    }

    return sum;
}
```

If the call to `extBar()` was inlined into the loop body before the escape analysis was performed, then `MyObj` would be categorized as a `NoEscape` and could avoid being allocated on the heap.

Locks and Escape Analysis

HotSpot is able to use escape analysis and some related techniques to optimize the performance of locks.

 This applies only to intrinsic locks (those that use `synchronized`). The locks from `java.util.concurrent` are not eligible for these optimizations.

The key lock optimizations that are available are:

- Removing locks on nonescaping objects (*lock elision*)
- Merging consecutive locked regions that share the same lock (*lock coarsening*)
- Detecting blocks where the same lock is acquired repeatedly without an unlock (*nested locks*)

When consecutive locks on the same object are encountered, HotSpot will check if it is possible to enlarge the locked region. To achieve this, when HotSpot encounters a lock it will search backward to try to find an unlock on the same object. If a match is found, then it will consider whether the two lock regions can be joined to produce a single larger region.

You can read more about this in the JVM specification (*http://docs.oracle.com/javase/specs/jvms/se7/html/jvms-3.html#jvms-3.14*). In Figure 10-7 we can see this effect directly in JITWatch.

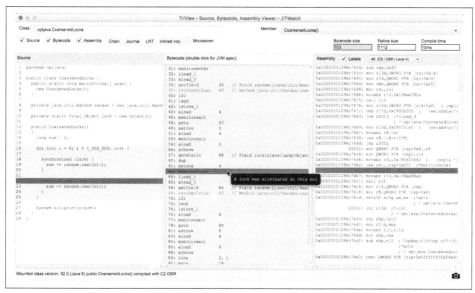

Figure 10-7. Lock coarsening

The lock coarsening optimization is enabled by default, but you can disable it using the VM switch -XX:-EliminateLocks to see its impact.

HotSpot is also able to detect nested locks that lock on the same object and remove the inner locks since the lock will already have been acquired by the thread.

> At the time of writing, the nested lock elimination in Java 8 appears to work with locks that are declared as static final and with locks on this.

The nested lock optimization is enabled by default but you can disable it using the VM switch -XX:-EliminateNestedLocks. Nested lock detection in JITWatch can be seen in Figure 10-8.

Figure 10-8. A nested lock is eliminated

HotSpot automatically calculates when it is safe to coarsen or eliminate locks. Tools such as JITWatch can visualize where locks have been optimized, and if you use a debug JVM you can output extra information on locks.

Limitations of Escape Analysis

Escape analysis, like other optimizations, is subject to tradeoffs since every allocation not made on the heap must happen somewhere, and the CPU registers and stack space are relatively scarce resources. One limitation in HotSpot is that by default, arrays of more than 64 elements will not benefit from escape analysis. This size is controlled by the following VM switch:

```
-XX:EliminateAllocationArraySizeLimit=<n>
```

Consider a hot code path that contains a temporary array allocation to read from a buffer. If the array does not escape the method scope, then escape analysis should prevent the heap allocation. However, if the array length is more than 64 elements (even if they are not all used), then it must be stored on the heap, which could quickly increase the allocation rate of this code.

In the following JMH benchmark, the test methods allocate nonescaping arrays of size 63, 64, and 65.

An array size of 63 is tested to ensure that 64 is not faster than 65 simply because of memory alignment.

In each test, only the first two array elements, a[0] and a[1], are used, but the limitation considers only the array length and not the maximum index used:

```java
package optjava.jmh;

import org.openjdk.jmh.annotations.*;
import java.util.concurrent.TimeUnit;

@State(Scope.Thread)
@BenchmarkMode(Mode.Throughput)
@OutputTimeUnit(TimeUnit.SECONDS)
public class EscapeTestArraySize {

    private java.util.Random random = new java.util.Random();

    @Benchmark
    public long arraySize63() {
        int[] a = new int[63];

        a[0] = random.nextInt();
        a[1] = random.nextInt();

        return a[0] + a[1];
    }

    @Benchmark
    public long arraySize64() {
        int[] a = new int[64];

        a[0] = random.nextInt();
        a[1] = random.nextInt();

        return a[0] + a[1];
    }

    @Benchmark
    public long arraySize65() {
        int[] a = new int[65];

        a[0] = random.nextInt();
        a[1] = random.nextInt();

        return a[0] + a[1];
    }
}
```

The results show a large drop in performance once the array allocation cannot benefit from the escape analysis optimization:

```
Benchmark                          Mode  Cnt       Score      Error  Units
EscapeTestArraySize.arraySize63    thrpt  200  49824186.696 ±  9366.780  ops/s
EscapeTestArraySize.arraySize64    thrpt  200  49815447.849 ±  2328.928  ops/s
EscapeTestArraySize.arraySize65    thrpt  200  21115003.388 ± 34005.817  ops/s
```

If you find that you do need to allocate a larger array in hot code, then you can instruct the VM to allow larger arrays to be optimized. Running the benchmark again with a limit of 65 elements shows that performance is restored:

```
$ java -XX:EliminateAllocationArraySizeLimit=65 -jar target/benchmarks.jar
```

```
Benchmark                          Mode  Cnt       Score      Error  Units
EscapeTestArraySize.arraySize63    thrpt  200  49814492.787 ± 2283.941  ops/s
EscapeTestArraySize.arraySize64    thrpt  200  49815595.566 ± 5833.359  ops/s
EscapeTestArraySize.arraySize65    thrpt  200  49818143.279 ± 2347.695  ops/s
```

Another important limitation is that HotSpot does not support *partial escape analysis* (also known as *flow-sensitive* escape analysis).

> The jRockit JVM did support partial escape analysis, but this technology was not carried over into HotSpot after the merging of the two JVMs.

If an object is found to escape the method scope on any branch, then the optimization to avoid allocating the object on the heap will not be applied. In the following example, if both branches are seen to be taken then the object can sometimes escape the methods and must be classed as an `ArgEscape`. This will increase the object allocation rate and put additional pressure on the GC.

```
for (int i = 0; i < 100_000_000; i++) {
    Object mightEscape = new Object(i);

    if (condition) {
        result += inlineableMethod(mightEscape);
    } else {
        result += tooBigToInline(mightEscape);
    }
}
```

If it is possible in your code to localize the object allocation to within a nonescaping branch, as shown here, then you will benefit from escape analysis on that path.

```
for (int i = 0; i < 100_000_000; i++) {

    if (condition) {
        Object mightEscape = new Object(i);
```

```
        result += inlineableMethod(mightEscape);
    } else {
        Object mightEscape = new Object(i);
        result += tooBigToInline(mightEscape);
    }
}
```

Monomorphic Dispatch

Many of the speculative optimizations that HotSpot's C2 compiler undertakes are based on empirical research. One example is the technique called *monomorphic dispatch* (*monomorphic* is derived from the Greek for "single form").

It relies on a strange, but powerful, observed fact: in human-authored code, very often only one runtime type is ever observed to be the type of the receiver object at any individual call site.

 This is generally understood to be a reflection of the way that humans design object-oriented software, rather than anything specific to Java or the JVM.

That is, when we're calling a method on an object, if we examine the runtime type of that object the first time we call that method, it is quite likely to always be the same type for every subsequent call.

If that speculative assumption is true, then the call to the method being invoked at that site can be optimized. In particular, the indirection of looking up methods in vtables can be eliminated. If it's always the same type, then we can compute the call target once and replace the `invokevirtual` instruction with a quick type test (the guard) and then a branch to the compiled method body.

Put another way, the virtual lookup and associated indirection through the klass pointer and vtable only needs to be done once and can be cached for future invocations at that call site.

 For an `invokevirtual` call site, the only possible types that can be seen are the base type that defines the method to be executed and any subtypes of it. This is the Liskov Substitution Principle in another guise.

Consider the following piece of code:

```
java.util.Date date = getDate();
System.out.println(date.toInstant());
```

If the getDate() method always returns an instance of java.util.Date, then the call to toInstant() can be assumed to be monomorphic. However, if after many iterations of this code, getDate() suddenly returns an instance of java.sql.Date, then the monomorphic assumption is no longer valid, as an entirely different implementation of toInstant() must now be called.

HotSpot's solution is to back out of the optimization and revert the call site to using full virtual dispatch. The guard that is used to protect the monomorphic call is very straightforward: it is a simple equality of klass words, and it is checked before every call instruction to ensure that no incorrect code is executed.

A very large number of calls in a typical application will be monomorphic. HotSpot also has another optimization, which is more rarely useful, called *bimorphic dispatch*. This allows two different types to be handled in a similar way to the monomorphic case, by caching two different klass words per call site.

Call sites that are not either monomorphic or bimorphic are known as *megamorphic* (Greek for "many forms"). If you find that you have a megamorphic call site with only a small number of observed types, you can use a trick to regain some performance. It works by "peeling" off types from the original call site using instanceof checks so that you leave only a bimorphic call site that observes two concrete types.

An example of this can be seen here:

```java
package optjava.jmh;

import org.openjdk.jmh.annotations.*;
import java.util.concurrent.TimeUnit;

interface Shape {
        int getSides();
}

class Triangle implements Shape {
        public int getSides() {
                return 3;
        }
}

class Square implements Shape {
        public int getSides() {
                return 4;
        }
}

class Octagon implements Shape {
        public int getSides() {
                return 8;
        }
}
```

```java
@State(Scope.Thread)
@BenchmarkMode(Mode.Throughput)
@OutputTimeUnit(TimeUnit.SECONDS)
public class PeelMegamorphicCallsite {

    private java.util.Random random = new java.util.Random();

    private Shape triangle = new Triangle();
    private Shape square = new Square();
    private Shape octagon = new Octagon();

    @Benchmark
    public int runBimorphic() {
        Shape currentShape = null;

        switch (random.nextInt(2))
        {
        case 0:
            currentShape = triangle;
            break;
        case 1:
            currentShape = square;
            break;
        }

        return currentShape.getSides();
    }

    @Benchmark
    public int runMegamorphic() {
        Shape currentShape = null;

        switch (random.nextInt(3))
        {
        case 0:
            currentShape = triangle;
            break;
        case 1:
            currentShape = square;
            break;
        case 2:
            currentShape = octagon;
            break;
        }

        return currentShape.getSides();
    }

    @Benchmark
    public int runPeeledMegamorphic() {
        Shape currentShape = null;
```

```
switch (random.nextInt(3))
{
case 0:
        currentShape = triangle;
        break;
case 1:
        currentShape = square;
        break;
case 2:
        currentShape = octagon;
        break;
}

// peel one observed type from the original call site
if (currentShape instanceof Triangle) {
        return ((Triangle) currentShape).getSides();
}
else {
        return currentShape.getSides(); // now only bimorphic
}
        }
    }
}
```

Running this benchmark produces the following output:

```
Benchmark                                Mode   Cnt    Score     Error  Units
PeelMega...Callsite.runBimorphic         thrpt  200  75844310 ±  43557  ops/s
PeelMega...Callsite.runMegamorphic       thrpt  200  54650385 ±  91283  ops/s
PeelMega...Callsite.runPeeledMegamorphic thrpt  200  62021478 ± 150092  ops/s
```

When two implementations are observed at the call site, bimorphic inlining occurs. This performs around 38% more operations per second than the megamorphic call site, which observes three implementations and where method dispatch remains a virtual call. Note that this is not a fair comparison, as the code is behaviorally different.

When one of the observed types is peeled off into a different call site, the program performs around 13% more operations per second than the megamorphic code.

The subject of method dispatch, and the resulting performance implications, is a deep one. Aleksey Shipilëv gives a master class in his blog post "The Black Magic of (Java) Method Dispatch" (*https://shipilev.net/blog/2015/black-magic-method-dispatch/*).

Intrinsics

An *intrinsic* is the name given to a highly tuned native implementation of a method that is preknown to the JVM rather than generated dynamically by the JIT subsystem. They are used for performance-critical core methods where the functionality is supported by specific features of the operating system or CPU architecture. This makes them platform-specific, and some intrinsics may not be supported on every platform.

When the JVM starts up, the CPU is probed at runtime and a list of the available processor features is built. This means that the decision about which optimizations to use can be deferred until runtime, and does not have to be made at code compilation time.

 Intrinsics can be implemented in the interpreter as well as the C1 and C2 JIT compilers.

Examples of some common intrinsics are shown in Table 10-3.

Table 10-3. Example intrinsified methods

Method	Description
`java.lang.System.arraycopy()`	Faster copying using vector support on the CPU.
`java.lang.System.currentTimeMillis()`	Fast implementations provided by most OSs.
`java.lang.Math.min()`	Can be performed without branching on some CPUs.
Other `java.lang.Math` methods	Direct instruction support on some CPUs.
Cryptographic functions (e.g., AES)	Hardware acceleration can give significant performance improvements.

The intrinsic templates are available to view in the HotSpot source code of OpenJDK. They are contained within *.ad* files (the suffix stands for "architecture dependent").

 Java 9 also introduces the `@HotSpotIntrinsicCandidate` annotation in the source code to indicate that an intrinsic may be available.

For the x86_64 architecture, they can be found in the file *hotspot/src/cpu/x86/vm/x86_64.ad*.

For example, to calculate the base 10 logarithm of a number, we can use the method from `java.lang.Math`:

```
public static double log10(double a)
```

On the x86_64 architecture this calculation can be performed with two instructions of the floating-point unit (FPU):

1. Calculate the base 10 logarithm of the constant 2.

2. Multiply this by the base 2 logarithm of your argument.

The intrinsic code for this is:

```
instruct log10D_reg(regD dst) %{
  // The source and result Double operands in XMM registers
  // match(Set dst (Log10D dst));
  // fldlg2      ; push log_10(2) on the FPU stack; full 80-bit number
  // fyl2x       ; compute log_10(2) * log_2(x)
  format %{ "fldlg2\t\t\t#Log10\n\t"
            "fyl2x\t\t\t# Q=Log10*Log_2(x)\n\t"
       %}
  ins_encode(Opcode(0xD9), Opcode(0xEC),
             Push_SrcXD(dst),

             Opcode(0xD9), Opcode(0xF1),
             Push_ResultXD(dst));
  ins_pipe( pipe_slow );
%}
```

If the source code of a core Java method appears nonoptimal, then check if the VM already has a platform-specific implementation via an intrinsic.

When considering adding a new intrinsic, you will need to evaluate the tradeoff of the additional complexity versus the likelihood of the intrinsic being useful.

For example, we could conceive of intrinsics that perform basic arithmetic identities, such as the sum of the first n numbers. Traditional Java code would require $O(n)$ operations to calculate this value, but it has a trivial formula that will calculate it in $O(1)$ time.

Should we implement an intrinsic to calculate the sum in constant time?

The answer depends on how many classes observed in the wild have a need to calculate such a sum—in this case, not many. Such an intrinsic would therefore clearly be of limited utility and almost certainly not worth the extra complexity in the JVM.

This underlines the point that intrinsics can have a large performance impact only for those operations that are genuinely seen frequently in real code.

On-Stack Replacement

Sometimes you will encounter code that contains a hot loop within a method that is not called enough times to trigger a compilation—for example, in a Java program's `main()` method.

HotSpot can still optimize this code using a technique called *on-stack replacement* (OSR). This trick counts the loop back branches in the interpreter; when these cross a threshold, the interpreted loop will be compiled and execution will switch to this compiled version.

The compiler is responsible for making sure any state changes, such as local variables and locks that were accessed within the interpreted loop, are made available to the compiled version. Once the compiled loop exits, all state changes must be visible at the point where execution continues.

For example, if we have this hot loop inside the `main()` method:

```
package optjava;

public class OnStackReplacement {
        // method called once
        public static void main(String[] args) {
                java.util.Random r = new java.util.Random();

                long sum = 0;

                // first long-running loop
                for (int i = 0; i < 1_000_000; i++) {
                        sum += r.nextInt(100);
                }

                // second long-running loop
                for (int i = 0; i < 1_000_000; i++) {
                        sum += r.nextInt(100);
                }

                System.out.println(sum);
        }
}
```

Then the method bytecode will look like this:

```
public static void main(java.lang.String[]);
  descriptor: ([Ljava/lang/String;)V
  flags: ACC_PUBLIC, ACC_STATIC
  Code:
    stack=4, locals=5, args_size=1
       0: new           #2       // class java/util/Random
       3: dup
       4: invokespecial #3       // Method java/util/Random."<init>":()V
       7: astore_1
       8: lconst_0
       9: lstore_2
      10: iconst_0
      11: istore        4
      13: iload         4
      15: ldc           #4       // int 1000000
      17: if_icmpge     36
      20: lload_2
      21: aload_1
      22: bipush        100
      24: invokevirtual #5       // Method java/util/Random.nextInt:(I)I
      27: i2l
      28: ladd
      29: lstore_2
      30: iinc          4, 1
      33: goto          13
      36: getstatic     #6       // Field java/lang/System.out:Ljava/io/PrintStream;
      39: lload_2
      40: invokevirtual #7       // Method java/io/PrintStream.println:(J)V
      43: return
```

The goto bytecode at index 33 returns the flow to the loop check at index 13.

A back branch happens when the loop reaches the end of its body, checks its exit condition, and—if the loop has not finished— branches back to the loop body start.

HotSpot can perform OSR compilation using both the C1 and C2 JIT compilers.

JITWatch can highlight which loop was OSR-compiled in the bytecode and source code, as can be seen in Figure 10-9.

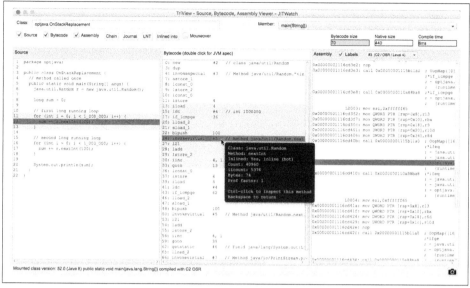

Figure 10-9. On-stack replacement

Safepoints Revisited

Before we leave the topic of JIT compilation, it makes sense to bring together a list of all the conditions in the JVM that require the VM to be at a safepoint. As well as GC STW events, the following activities require all threads to be at a safepoint:

- Deoptimizing a method
- Creating a heap dump
- Revoking a biased lock
- Redefining a class (e.g., for instrumentation)

In compiled code, the JIT compiler is responsible for emitting safepoint checks (as seen previously with loop unrolling) and in HotSpot it will generate them:

- At Loop back branches
- On Method return

This means that sometimes threads may take a certain amount of time to safepoint (e.g., if they are executing a loop containing a lot of arithmetic code without any method calls). If the loop is unrolled, then there may be an appreciable time before a safepoint is encountered.

The JIT compiler is free to emit speculative and out-of-order instructions as long as the semantics of your program are maintained. When the VM reaches a safepoint, the state of the compiled code will match the state of your program at that point. Debuggers rely on this behavior.

The compiler will try to balance the cost of safepoint polling checks with avoiding long Time to SafePoint (TTSP) durations where threads already at their safepoint have to wait for other threads to reach theirs.

 You can see the total time a program has spent at safepoints, including waiting for all threads to reach the safepoints, by using the VM switch -XX:+PrintGCApplicationStoppedTime. Combine this with -XX:+PrintSafepointStatistics for futher information on safepoints.

We will discuss safepoints again in Chapter 13, as they are a cross-cutting concern that has an impact on many of the JVM subsystems.

Core Library Methods

To conclude this chapter, let's take a quick look at some of the impacts of the size of JDK core library methods on JIT compilation.

Upper Method Size Limit for Inlining

Because inlining decisions are made on the bytecode size of a method, it is possible to identify methods that are too big for inlining using static analysis of class files.

The open source JarScan tool (part of the JITWatch distribution—its launch scripts are found in the JITWatch root folder) can identify all of the methods within a class folder or JAR file whose bytecode size is above a given threshold.

Running this tool over the Java 8 core libraries found in *jre/lib/rt.jar* with a command such as the following highlights some interesting results:

```
$ ./jarScan.sh --mode=maxMethodSize \
          --limit=325 \
          --packages=java.* \
          /path/to/java/jre/lib/rt.jar
```

In Java 8u152, on Linux x86_64, there are 490 methods in the *java.* package tree larger than 325 bytes of bytecode (the FreqInlineSize limit for that platform), some of which are methods that you would not be surprised to find in hot code.

For example, the methods toUpperCase() and toLowerCase() from the java.lang.String class weigh in at a surprisingly large 439 bytes of bytecode each—outside the normal range for inlining.

The reason for this size is that in some locales, converting the case of a character changes the number of char values needed to store it. The case-converting methods must therefore be able to detect this situation and resize and copy the underlying arrays backing the string, as demonstrated by the default implementation of the toUp perCase() method:

```java
public String toUpperCase(Locale locale) {
    if (locale == null) {
        throw new NullPointerException();
    }

    int firstLower;
    final int len = value.length;

    /* Now check if there are any characters that need to be changed. */
    scan: {
        for (firstLower = 0 ; firstLower < len; ) {
            int c = (int)value[firstLower];
            int srcCount;
            if ((c >= Character.MIN_HIGH_SURROGATE)
                    && (c <= Character.MAX_HIGH_SURROGATE)) {
                c = codePointAt(firstLower);
                srcCount = Character.charCount(c);
            } else {
                srcCount = 1;
            }
            int upperCaseChar = Character.toUpperCaseEx(c);
            if ((upperCaseChar == Character.ERROR)
                    || (c != upperCaseChar)) {
                break scan;
            }
            firstLower += srcCount;
        }
        return this;
    }

    /* result may grow, so i+resultOffset is the write location in result */
    int resultOffset = 0;
    char[] result = new char[len]; /* may grow */

    /* Just copy the first few upperCase characters. */
    System.arraycopy(value, 0, result, 0, firstLower);

    String lang = locale.getLanguage();
    boolean localeDependent =
            (lang == "tr" || lang == "az" || lang == "lt");
    char[] upperCharArray;
```

```
int upperChar;
int srcChar;
int srcCount;
for (int i = firstLower; i < len; i += srcCount) {
    srcChar = (int)value[i];
    if ((char)srcChar >= Character.MIN_HIGH_SURROGATE &&
        (char)srcChar <= Character.MAX_HIGH_SURROGATE) {
        srcChar = codePointAt(i);
        srcCount = Character.charCount(srcChar);
    } else {
        srcCount = 1;
    }
    if (localeDependent) {
        upperChar = ConditionalSpecialCasing.
                            toUpperCaseEx(this, i, locale);
    } else {
        upperChar = Character.toUpperCaseEx(srcChar);
    }
    if ((upperChar == Character.ERROR)
            || (upperChar >= Character.MIN_SUPPLEMENTARY_CODE_POINT)) {
        if (upperChar == Character.ERROR) {
            if (localeDependent) {
                upperCharArray =
                        ConditionalSpecialCasing.
                                toUpperCaseCharArray(this, i, locale);
            } else {
                upperCharArray = Character.toUpperCaseCharArray(srcChar);
            }
        } else if (srcCount == 2) {
            resultOffset += Character.toChars(upperChar,
                                            result, i + resultOffset)
                                            - srcCount;
            continue;
        } else {
            upperCharArray = Character.toChars(upperChar);
        }

        /* Grow result if needed */
        int mapLen = upperCharArray.length;
        if (mapLen > srcCount) {
            char[] result2 = new char[result.length + mapLen - srcCount];
            System.arraycopy(result, 0, result2, 0, i + resultOffset);
            result = result2;
        }
        for (int x = 0; x < mapLen; ++x) {
            result[i + resultOffset + x] = upperCharArray[x];
        }
        resultOffset += (mapLen - srcCount);
    } else {
        result[i + resultOffset] = (char)upperChar;
    }
}
```

```
        return new String(result, 0, len + resultOffset);
    }
```

Improve performance with a domain-specific method

If you can be sure that in your problem domain the character set of your inputs does not require this flexibility (perhaps all your inputs are in ASCII), then you could create a domain-specific version of `toUpperCase()` whose bytecode is easily within the inlining limits.

This ASCII-specific implementation compiles to just 69 bytes of bytecode:

```java
package optjava.jmh;

import org.openjdk.jmh.annotations.*;
import java.util.concurrent.TimeUnit;

@State(Scope.Thread)
@BenchmarkMode(Mode.Throughput)
@OutputTimeUnit(TimeUnit.SECONDS)
public class DomainSpecificUpperCase {

    private static final String SOURCE =
            "The quick brown fox jumps over the lazy dog";

    public String toUpperCaseASCII(String source) {
        int len = source.length();
        char[] result = new char[len];
        for (int i = 0; i < len; i++) {
            char c = source.charAt(i);
            if (c >= 'a' && c <= 'z') {
                c -= 32;
            }
            result[i] = c;
        }
        return new String(result);
    }

    @Benchmark
    public String testStringToUpperCase() {
        return SOURCE.toUpperCase();
    }

    @Benchmark
    public String testCustomToUpperCase() {
        return toUpperCaseASCII(SOURCE);
    }
}
```

Comparing the performance of the custom implementation against the core library's `String.toUpperCase()` method shows the following results:

```
Benchmark                                   Mode  Cnt      Score   Error  Units
DomainS...UpperCase.testCustomToUpperCase   thrpt  200  20138368 ± 17807  ops/s
DomainS...UpperCase.testStringToUpperCase   thrpt  200   8350400 ±  7199  ops/s
```

In this benchmark the domain-specific version performed approximately 2.4x the number of operations per second as the core library version.

Benefits of small methods

Another benefit of keeping methods small is that it increases the number of inlining permutations. Varying runtime data can result in different paths through the code becoming "hot."

By keeping methods small, we can build different inlining trees to optimize more of these hot paths. With larger methods, inlining size limits may be reached earlier, leaving some paths unoptimized.

Upper Method Size Limit for Compilation

There is one more limit inside HotSpot that we will now demonstrate. It is the byte-code size above which methods will not be compiled: 8,000 bytes. In the production JVM this limit cannot be changed, but if you are running a debug JVM you can use the switch -XX:HugeMethodLimit=<n> to set the maximum bytecode size for a method to be compilable.

Find these methods in the JDK core libraries using JarScan as follows:

```
./jarScan.sh --mode=maxMethodSize --limit=8000 /path/to/java/jre/lib/rt.jar
```

The results are as shown in Table 10-4.

Table 10-4. Outsized core library methods

Method	Size (bytes)
javax.swing.plaf.nimbus.NimbusDefaults.initializeDefaults()	23,103
sun.util.resources.LocaleNames.getContents()	22,832
sun.util.resources.TimeZoneNames.getContents()	17,818
com.sun.org.apache.xalan.internal.xsltc.compiler.CUP$XPathParser$actions.CUP$XPathParser$do_action()	17,441
javax.swing.plaf.basic,BasicLookAndFeel.initComponentDefaults()	15,361
com.sun.java.swing.plaf.windows.WindowsLookAndFeel.initComponentDefaults()	14,060
javax.swing.plaf.metal.MetalLookAndFeel.initComponentDefaults()	12,087

Method	Size (bytes)
com.sun.java.swing.plaf.motif.MotifLookAndFeel.initComponentDefaults()	11,759
com.sun.java.swing.plaf.gtk.GTKLookAndFeel.initComponentDefaults()	10,921
sun.util.resources.CurrencyNames.getContents()	8,578
javax.management.remote.rmi._RMIConnectionImpl_Tie()	8,152
org.omg.stub.javax.management.remote.rmi._RMIConnectionImpl_Tie()	8,152

None of these huge methods are likely to be found in hot code. They are mostly UI subsystem initializers or provide resources for lists of currencies, countries, or locale names.

To demonstrate the effect of losing JIT compilation, we will look at a benchmark of two near-identical methods, one just under the limit and one just over the HugeMethodLimit size:

```
private java.util.Random r = new java.util.Random();

@Benchmark
public long lessThan8000() {
    return r.nextInt() +
        r.nextInt() +
    ... // for a total method size of just under 8000 bytes of bytecode
}

@Benchmark
public long moreThan8000() {
    return r.nextInt() +
        r.nextInt() +
    ... // for a total method size of just over 8000 bytes of bytecode
}
```

This results in the following output:

```
Benchmark                  Mode   Cnt    Score    Error    Units
HugeMethod.lessThan8000    thrpt  100  89550.631 ±  77.703  ops/s
HugeMethod.moreThan8000    thrpt  100  44429.392 ± 102.076  ops/s
```

The method moreThan8000() was not JIT-compiled and ran at approximately half the speed of the method lessThan8000() that did get JIT-compiled. There are many reasons not to create such huge methods (e.g., readability, maintenance, debugging), but this gives you one more.

A real-world situation where huge methods may get created is in autogenerated code. Some software autogenerates code to represent queries on a data store. The query code is then compiled so that it can be executed on the JVM for performance. If a query were of a high enough complexity it could hit this HotSpot limit, so checking method sizes with a tool such as JarScan may be helpful.

While many of the JIT compiler settings are tunable, you should always benchmark your system before and after changing them as there could be unexpected side effects involving code cache space, JIT compiler queue lengths, and even GC pressure.

Summary

In this chapter, we have covered the basics of HotSpot's JIT compilation subsystem and examined how some of its optimizations are performed. We have looked at the parameters that can be used to tune the JIT compilers and inspected some of the assembly produced.

In terms of actionable, practical techniques, we can use the `-XX:+PrintCompilation` flag and the technique introduced in the last chapter to confirm the optimization of individual methods. The general principle of "write good code first, optimize only when required" definitely applies here. A knowledge of the limits for inlining and other compilation thresholds will allow developers to refactor and stay within those limits (or, in rare cases, alter the thresholds). Understanding the existence of mono-morphic dispatch and type sharpening means that applications can be written according to a classic principle: design for interfaces, even if there's just a single implementation. This gives the best of two approaches—the class can still be dummied up or mocked for testing, but the single implementation preserves monomorphic dispatch.

## CHAPTER 11

Java Language Performance Techniques

So far, we have explored the mechanisms by which the JVM takes the code written by a developer, converts it into bytecode, and optimizes it to high-performance compiled code.

It would be wonderful if every Java application were composed of top-quality, pristine code that was architected with performance in mind. The reality, however, is often quite different. Despite this, in many cases the JVM can take suboptimal code and make it work reasonably well—a testament to the power and robustness of the environment.

Even applications that have an insane code base and are difficult to maintain can often somehow be made to work adequately in production. Of course, no one wants to maintain or modify such applications. So what is left for the developer to consider when this type of code base needs to be tuned for performance?

After external application factors, such as network connectivity, I/O, and databases, one of the biggest potential bottlenecks for performance is the design of the code. Design is an incredibly difficult part to get right, and no design is ever perfect.

 Optimizing Java is complicated, and in Chapter 13, we'll look at how profiling tools can assist in finding code that is not performing as it should.

In spite of this, there are some basic aspects of code that the performance-conscious developer should keep in mind. For example, how data is stored in the application is incredibly important. And, as business requirements change, the way data is stored may also need to evolve. In order to understand the options available for data storage, it is important to familiarize yourself with the data structures available in the Java Collections API and their implementation details.

Selecting a data structure without knowing how it will be updated and queried is dangerous. Though some developers will reach straight for their favorite classes and use them without thinking about it, a conscientious developer considers how the data will be queried and which algorithms will most effectively query the data. There are many algorithms and operations that `java.lang.Collections` supplies in the form of static methods.

 Before writing an implementation of a common algorithm (e.g., a manually written bubble sort) for use in production code, check to see if there's something in `java.lang.Collections` that can be utilized.

Understanding domain objects and their lifetime within the system can have a significant impact on performance. There are several heuristics to consider, and the way that domain objects are used within an application can impact garbage collection and add overhead, which the JVM has to then manage (often unnecessarily) at runtime.

In this chapter, we will explore each of these concerns, starting with what the performance-conscious developer should know about collections.

Optimizing Collections

Most programming language libraries provide at least two general types of container:

- *Sequential containers* store objects at a particular position, denoted by a numerical index.
- *Associative containers* use the object itself to determine where the object should be stored inside the collection.

For certain container methods to work correctly, the objects being stored must have a notion of comparability and of equivalence. In the core Java Collections API this is usually expressed by the statement that the objects must implement `hashCode()` and `equals()`, in accordance with the contract popularized by Josh Bloch in his book *Effective Java* (Pearson).

As we saw in "Introducing the HotSpot Runtime" on page 119, fields of reference type are stored as references in the heap. Consequently, although we talk loosely about objects being stored sequentially, it is not the object itself that is stored in the container, but rather a reference to it. This means that you will not typically get the same performance as from using a C/C++-style array or vector.

This is an example of how Java's managed memory subsystem requires you to give up low-level control of memory in exchange for automatic garbage collection. The usual example of the low-level control being relinquished is manual control of allocation and release, but here we see that control of low-level memory layout is also given up.

 Another way to think about this issue is that Java has, as yet, no way to lay out the equivalent of an array of C structs.

Gil Tene (CTO of Azul Systems) often labels this limitation as one of the last major performance barriers between Java and C. The ObjectLayout website (*http://objectlay out.org*) has more information on how layout could be standardized, and the code there will work and compile on Java 7 and above. Its intention is that an optimized JVM would be able to take these types and lay out the structures correctly with the semantics described without breaking compatibility with other JVMs.

In Chapter 15 we will discuss the future of the Java environment and describe the effort to bring *value types* to the platform. This will go considerably further than is possible with the object layout code.

The Collections API defines a set of interfaces specifying the operations a container of that type must conform to. Figure 11-1 shows the basic type layout.

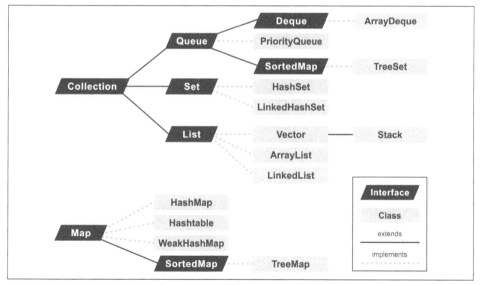

Figure 11-1. Class hierarchy from Java Collections API

In addition to the interfaces, there are several implementations of the collections available inside the JDK. Selecting the right implementation based on the design is the first part of the problem, but we also need to recognize that our choice may have an impact on the overall performance of the application.

Optimization Considerations for Lists

In core Java there are basically two options for representing a list, `ArrayList` and `LinkedList`.

 Although Java also has `Stack` and `Vector` classes, the former supplies additional semantics that are usually unwarranted and the latter is heavily deprecated. Your code should not use `Vector`, and you should refactor to remove any usage of it that you find.

Let's talk about each in turn, starting with the array-backed list.

ArrayList

`ArrayList` is backed by an array that has a fixed size. Entries can be added to the array up to the maximum size of the backing array. When the backing array is full, the class will allocate a new, larger array and copy the old values. The performance-conscious programmer must therefore weigh the cost of the resize operation versus the flexibility of not having to know ahead of time how big the lists will become. An `ArrayList` is initially backed by an empty array. On the first addition to the `Array List` a backing array of capacity 10 is allocated. We can prevent this resizing behavior by passing our preferred initial capacity value to the constructor. We can also use the ensureCapacity() to increase the capacity of the `ArrayList` to avoid resizing.

 It is wise to set a capacity whenever possible, as there is a performance cost to the resizing operation.

The following is a microbenchmark in JMH (as covered in "Introduction to JMH" on page 90) showing this effect:

```
@Benchmark
public List<String> properlySizedArrayList() {
        List<String> list = new ArrayList<>(1_000_000);
        for(int i=0; i < 1_000_000; i++) {
                list.add(item);
        }
        return list;
```

```
}

@Benchmark
public List<String> resizingArrayList() {
        List<String> list = new ArrayList<>();
        for(int i=0; i < 1_000_000; i++) {
                list.add(item);
        }
        return list;
}
```

 The microbenchmarks in this section are designed to be illustra-
tive, rather than authoritative. If your applications are genuinely
sensitive to the performance implications of these types of operations, you should explore alternatives to the standard collections.

This results in the following output:

Benchmark	Mode	Cnt	Score	Error	Units
ResizingList.properlySizedArrayList	thrpt	10	287.388	± 7.135	ops/s
ResizingList.resizingArrayList	thrpt	10	189.510	± 4.530	ops/s

The properlySizedArrayList test is able to perform around 100 extra operations per
second when it comes to insertion, as even though the cost of reallocation is amortized there is still an overall cost. Choosing a correctly sized ArrayList is always preferable when possible.

LinkedList

The LinkedList has a more dynamic growth scheme; it is implemented as a doubly
linked list and this means (among other things) that appending to the list will always
be O(1). Each time an item is added to the list, a new node is created and referenced
from the previous item. An example can be seen in Figure 11-2.

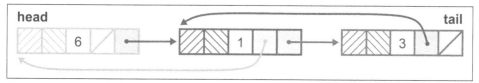

Figure 11-2. A LinkedList

ArrayList versus LinkedList

The real decision of whether to use an ArrayList or a LinkedList (or another nonstandard implementation of List) depends on the pattern of access and modification
of the data. Inserting at the end of a list in both ArrayList and LinkedList is a

constant-time operation (after the resize operations are amortized, in the case of `ArrayList`).

However, adding at an index in `ArrayList` requires all other elements to be shifted by one position to the right. `LinkedList`, on the other hand, has to traverse node references to find the position in the list where the insert is required, but the insert itself simply involves creating a new node and setting two references, one pointing to the node at the beginning of the list (the *first reference*) and the other to the next node in the list (the *next reference*). This benchmark shows the difference in performance of inserting at the beginning of each type of list:

```
Benchmark                       Mode  Cnt   Score     Error    Units
InsertBegin.beginArrayList      thrpt  10    3.402 ±  0.239   ops/ms
InsertBegin.beginLinkedList     thrpt  10  559.570 ± 68.629   ops/ms
```

List removal has a similar behavior; it is cheaper to remove from a `LinkedList`, at most two references need to change. In an `ArrayList`, all items to the right of the deletion need to shift one place to the left.

If the list is mainly accessed randomly `ArrayList` is the best choice, as any element can be accessed in O(1) time, whereas `LinkedList` requires navigation from the beginning to the index count. The costs of accessing the different types of list by a specific index are shown in the following simple benchmark:

```
Benchmark                       Mode  Cnt      Score        Error    Units
AccessingList.accessArrayList   thrpt  10  269568.627 ± 12972.927  ops/ms
AccessingList.accessLinkedList  thrpt  10       0.863 ±     0.030  ops/ms
```

In general it is recommended to prefer `ArrayList` unless you require the specific behavior of `LinkedList`, especially if you are using an algorithm that requires random access. If possible, size the `ArrayList` correctly ahead of time to avoid the charge of resizing. Collections in modern Java take the view that the developer should incur the synchronization costs for all accesses and should either use the concurrent collections or manually manage synchronization when necessary. In the `Collections` helper class there is a method called `synchronizedList()`, which is effectively a decorator that wraps all of the `List` method invocations in a `synchronized` block. In Chapter 12 we will discuss in more detail how to use `java.util.concurrent` for structures that can be used more effectively when you are writing multithreaded applications.

Optimization Considerations for Maps

A mapping in general describes a relationship between a key and an associated value (hence the alternative term *associative array*). In Java this follows the interface `java.util.Map<K,V>`. Both key and value must be of reference type, of course.

HashMap

In many ways, Java's HashMap can be seen as a classic introductory computer science hash table, but with a few additional embellishments to make it suitable for modern environments.

A cut-down version of the HashMap (eliding generics and a couple of key features, which we will return to) has some key methods that look like this:

```java
public Object get(Object key) {
    // SIMPLIFY: Null keys are not supported
    if (key == null) return null;

    int hash = key.hashCode();
    int i = indexFor(hash, table.length);
    for (Entry e = table[i]; e != null; e = e.next) {
        Object k;
        if (e.hash == hash && ((k = e.key) == key || key.equals(k)))
            return e.value;
    }

    return null;
}

private int indexFor(int h, int length) {
    return h & (length-1);
}

// This is a linked list node
static class Node implements Map.Entry {
    final int hash;
    final Object key;
    Object value;
    Node next;

    Node(int h, Object k, Object v, Entry n) {
        hash = h;
        key = k;
        value = v;
        next = n;
    }
}
```

In this case, the HashMap.Node class is restricted to package access in java.util; that is, it is a classic use case for a static class.

The layout of the HashMap is shown in Figure 11-3.

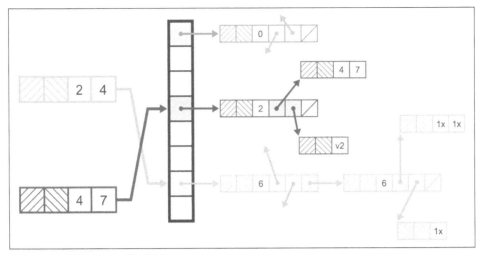

Figure 11-3. A simple HashMap

Initially the bucket entries will be stored in a list. When it comes to finding a value, the hash of the key is calculated and then the equals() method is used to find the key in the list. Because of the mechanics of hashing the key and using equality to find it in the list, duplicate keys are not permitted in a HashMap. Inserting the same key simply replaces the key currently stored in the HashMap.

In modern Java versions, one of the improvements is that indexFor() has been replaced by code that uses the hashCode() of the key object and applies a mask to spread higher bits in the hash downward.

This has been designed as a tradeoff to ensure that the HashMap takes into account higher bits when calculating which bucket a key hashes to. If this was not done, the higher bits might not be used in computing index calculations. This is problematic for a number of reasons, not least of which is that it violates Shannon's *Strict Avalanche Criteria*—the idea that even arbitrarily small changes in input data should produce potentially very large changes in the output of the hash function.

Two important variables impact the performance of a HashMap: initialCapacity and loadFactor, both of which can be set via parameters passed to the constructor. The capacity of a HashMap represents the current number of buckets that have been created, which defaults to 16. The loadFactor represents how full the hash table is allowed to get before the capacity is automatically increased. Increasing the capacity and recalculating hashes is a procedure known as *rehashing*, which doubles the number of buckets available and redistributes the data stored.

Setting the `initialCapacity` of a HashMap follows the same rules as for `ArrayList`: if you know up front roughly how much information will be stored, you should set it.

An accurate `initialCapacity` will avoid the need to automatically rehash as the table grows. It is also possible to tweak `loadFactor`, but `0.75` (the default) provides a good balance between space and time of access. A `loadFactor` of higher than `0.75` will reduce the rehashing requirement, but access will become slower as buckets will generally become fuller. Setting the `initialCapacity` to the maximum number of elements divided by the `loadFactor` will prevent a rehash operation from occurring.

The `HashMap` provides constant-time support for `get()` and `put()` operations, but iteration can be costly. As mentioned in the JavaDoc, setting the `initialCapacity` and `loadFactor` high will severely impact the iteration performance.

Another factor that impacts performance is a process known as *treeifying*. This relatively recent innovation is an internal implementation detail of `HashMap`, but is potentially useful for performance engineers.

Consider the case where a bucket becomes highly populated. If the bucket elements are implemented as a `LinkedList`, traversal to find an element becomes on average more expensive as the list grows.

To counteract this linear effect, modern implementations of `HashMap` have a new mechanism. Once a bucket reaches a `TREEIFY_THRESHOLD`, it is converted to a bin of `TreeNodes` (and behaves similar to a `TreeMap`).

Why not do this from the beginning? `TreeNodes` are about double the size of a list node, and therefore a space cost is paid. A well-distributed hashing function will rarely cause buckets to be converted to `TreeNodes`. Should this occur in your application, it is time to consider revisiting the hash function, `initialCapacity`, and `load Factor` settings for the `HashMap`.

As with everything else in performance, practical techniques are driven by tradeoffs and pragmatism, and you should adopt a similarly hardheaded and data-driven approach to the analysis of your own code.

LinkedHashMap

`LinkedHashMap` is a subclass of `HashMap` that maintains the insertion order of elements by using a doubly linked list running through the elements.

By default, using LinkedHashMap maintains the insertion order, but it is also possible to switch the mode to access order. LinkedHashMap is often used where ordering matters to the consumer, and it is not as costly as the usage of a TreeMap.

In most cases, neither the insertion order nor the access order will matter to the users of a Map, so there should be relatively few occasions in which LinkedHashMap is the correct choice of collection.

TreeMap

The TreeMap is, essentially, a red-black tree implementation. This type of tree is basically a binary tree structure with additional metadata (node coloring) that attempts to prevent trees from becoming overly unbalanced.

 For the nodes of the tree (TreeNodes) to be considered ordered it is necessary that keys use a comparator that is consistent with the equals() method.

The TreeMap is incredibly useful when a range of keys is required, allowing quick access to a submap. The TreeMap can also be used to partition the data from the beginning up to a point, or from a point to the end.

The TreeMap provides log(n) performance for the get(), put(), containsKey(), and remove() operations.

In practice, most of the time HashMap fulfills the Map requirement, but consider one example: the case where it is useful to process portions of a Map using streams or lambdas. Under these circumstances, using an implementation that understands partitioning of data—for example, TreeMap—may make more sense.

Lack of MultiMap

Java does not provide an implementation for MultiMap (a map that allows multiple values to be associated with a single key). The reason given in the documentation is that this is not often required and can be implemented in most cases as Map<K, List<V>>. Several open source implementations exist that provide a MultiMap implementation for Java.

Optimization Considerations for Sets

Java contains three types of sets, all of which have very similar performance considerations to Map.

In fact, if we start by taking a closer look at a version of HashSet (cut down for brevity), it is clear that it is implemented in terms of a HashMap (or LinkedHashMap in the case of LinkedHashSet):

```java
public class HashSet<E> extends AbstractSet<E> implements Set<E>, Serializable {
    private transient HashMap<E,Object> map;

    // Dummy value to associate with an Object in the backing Map
    private static final Object PRESENT = new Object();

    public HashSet() {
        map = new HashMap<>();
    }

    HashSet(int initialCapacity, float loadFactor, boolean dummy) {
        map = new LinkedHashMap<>(initialCapacity, loadFactor);
    }

    public boolean add(E e) {
        return map.put(e, PRESENT)==null;
    }
}
```

The behavior of a Set is to not allow duplicate values, which is exactly the same as a key element in a Map. In the add() method, the HashSet simply inserts the element E as a key in the HashMap and uses a dummy object, PRESENT, as the value. There is minimal overhead to this, as the PRESENT object will be created once and referenced. Hash Set has a second protected constructor that allows a LinkedHashMap; this can be used to mimic the same behavior while keeping track of the insert order. HashSet has O(1) insertion, removal, and contains operation time; it does not maintain an ordering of elements (unless used as a LinkedHashSet), and iteration cost depends on the initialCapacity and loadFactor.

A TreeSet is implemented in a similar way, leveraging the existing TreeMap previously discussed. Using a TreeSet will preserve the natural ordering of keys defined by the Comparator, making range-based and iteration operations far more suited to a TreeSet. A TreeSet guarantees log(n) time cost for insertion, removal, and contains operations and maintains the ordering of elements. Iteration and retrieval of subsets is efficient, and any range-based or ordering considerations would be better approached using TreeSet.

Domain Objects

Domain objects are the code that expresses the business concepts that matter to your applications. Examples might be an Order, an OrderItem, and a DeliverySchedule for an ecommerce site. They will typically have relationships between the types (so an Order has multiple OrderItem instances associated with it). For example:

```java
public class Order {
    private final long id;
    private final List<OrderItem> items = new ArrayList<>();
    private DeliverySchedule schedule;

    public Order(long id) {
        this.id = id;
    }

    public DeliverySchedule getSchedule() {
        return schedule;
    }

    public void setSchedule(DeliverySchedule schedule) {
        this.schedule = schedule;
    }

    public List<OrderItem> getItems() {
        return items;
    }

    public long getId() {
        return id;
    }
}

public class OrderItem {
    private final long id;
    private final String description;
    private final double price;

    public OrderItem(long id, String description, double price) {
        this.id = id;
        this.description = description;
        this.price = price;
    }

    @Override
    public String toString() {
        return "OrderItem{" + "id=" + id + ", description=" +
            description + ", price=" + price + '}';
    }
}

public final class DeliverySchedule {
    private final LocalDate deliveryDate;
    private final String address;
    private final double deliveryCost;
```

```java
    private DeliverySchedule(LocalDate deliveryDate, String address,
                double deliveryCost) {
        this.deliveryDate = deliveryDate;
        this.address = address;
        this.deliveryCost = deliveryCost;
    }

    public static DeliverySchedule of(LocalDate deliveryDate, String address,
                    double deliveryCost) {
        return new DeliverySchedule(deliveryDate, address, deliveryCost);
    }

    @Override
    public String toString() {
        return "DeliverySchedule{" + "deliveryDate=" + deliveryDate +
            ", address=" + address + ", deliveryCost=" + deliveryCost + '}';
    }
}
```

There will be ownership relationships between the domain types, as we can see in
Figure 11-4. Ultimately, however, the vast majority of the data items at the leaves of
the domain object graph will be simple data types such as strings, primitives, and
LocalDateTime objects.

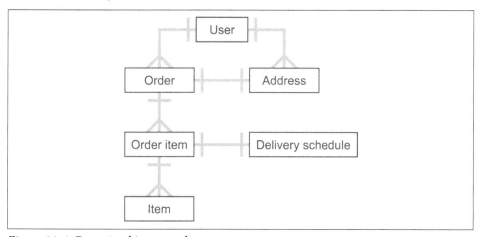

Figure 11-4. Domain objects graph

In "Introducing Mark and Sweep" on page 116, we encountered the jmap -histo
command. This provides a quick insight into the state of the Java heap, and equivalent functionality is available through GUI tools such as VisualVM. It is worth learning to use one of these very simple tools, as they can help diagnose a memory leak of
domain objects under some (limited, but fairly common) circumstances.

The domain objects of an application have a somewhat unique status. As they are the representations of the first-order business concerns of the application, they are highly visible when you are looking for bugs such as memory leaks.

To see why, we need to consider a couple of basic facts about the Java heap:

- The most commonly allocated data structures include strings, char arrays, byte arrays, and instances of Java collection types.
- Data that corresponds to a leak will show up as an anomalously large dataset in jmap.

That is, we expect the top entries by both memory volume and number of instances to be commonly occurring data structures from the core JDK. If application-specific domain objects appear in the top 30 or so entries generated by jmap, then this is a possible, but not conclusive, sign of a memory leak.

Another common behavior for leaking domain objects is the "all generations" effect. This effect occurs because objects of a specific type are not being collected when they should be. This means that they will eventually live long enough to become Tenured, and will show up with all possible values for the generational count after they survive enough collections.

If we plot a histogram of bytes per generational count (by data type), then we will see potentially leaking domain objects show up across all generations. This could be because they are being kept alive artificially beyond their natural lifetime.

One quick win is to look at the size of the dataset that corresponds to domain objects and see if this is reasonable and within the expected bounds for how many domain objects there should be in the working set.

At the other end of the spectrum, short-lived domain objects can be the cause of another form of the *floating garbage* problem that we have already met. Recall the SATB constraint for concurrent collectors—the idea that any objects, no matter how short-lived, are considered to be alive if they were allocated after a marking cycle started.

One occasionally observed feature of leaking domain objects is that they can show up as the culprit for high GC mark times. The root cause of this is that a single long-lived object is keeping alive an entire long chain of objects.

Domain objects can provide a useful "canary in the coal mine" for many applications; because they are the most obvious and natural representations of the business concerns, they seem to be more susceptible to leaks. Performance-conscious developers should ensure that they remain aware of their domain and the size of the relevant working sets.

Avoid Finalization

Java's finalize() mechanism is an attempt to provide automatic resource management, in a similar way to the *Resource Acquisition Is Initialization* (RAII) pattern from C++. In that pattern, a destructor method (known as finalize() in Java) is provided to enable automatic cleanup and release of resources when an object is destroyed.

The basic use case is thus fairly simple. When an object is created, it takes ownership of some resource, and the object's ownership of that resource persists for the lifetime of the object. Then, when the object dies, the ownership of the resource is automatically relinquished.

 Another way that this pattern can be described is as *Automatic Resource Management* (ARM).

The standard example for this approach is the observation that when the programmer opens a file handle, it is all too easy to forget to call the close() function when it is no longer required.

Let's look at a quick and simple C++ example that shows how to put an RAII wrapper around C-style file I/O:

```cpp
class file_error {};

class file {
  public:
    file(const char* filename) : _h_file(std::fopen(filename, "w+")) {
        if (_h_file == NULL) {
            throw file_error();
        }
    }

    // Destructor
    ~file() { std::fclose(_h_file); }

    void write(const char* str) {
        if (std::fputs(str, _h_file) == EOF) {
            throw file_error();
        }
    }
}
```

```
    void write(const char* buffer, std::size_t numc) {
        if (numc != 0 && std::fwrite(buffer, numc, 1, _h_file) == 0) {
            throw file_error();
        }
    }

private:
    std::FILE* _h_file;
};
```

This promotes good design, especially when the only reason for a type to exist is to act as a "holder" of a resource such as a file or network socket. In that case, strongly tying the resource ownership to the object lifetime makes sense. Getting rid of the object's resources automatically then becomes the responsibility of the platform, not the programmer.

War Story: Forgetting to Clean Up

Like many software war stories, this tale starts with production code that had been working fine for years. It was a service that connected via TCP to another service to establish permissions and entitlements information. The entitlements service was relatively stable and had good load balancing, usually responding instantly to requests. A new TCP connection was opened on each request—far from ideal in design.

One weekend a change happened that caused the entitlements system to be slightly slower in the response time. This caused the TCP connection to occasionally time out, a code path never previously seen in production. A TimeOutException was thrown and caught, nothing was logged, and there was no finally block—the close() function had previously been called from the success path.

Sadly, the problem did not end there. The close() function not being called meant that the TCP connection was left open. Eventually the production machine the application was running on ran out of file handles, which impacted other processes tenanted on that box. The resolution was to rewrite the code to first of all close the TCP connection and immediately patch, and second to pool the connection and not open a new connection for each resource.

Forgetting to call close() is an easy mistake to make, especially when using proprietary libraries.

Why Not Use Finalization to Solve the Problem?

Java initially offered the finalize() method, which lives on Object; by default, it is a no-op (and should usually remain that way). It is, however, possible to override finalize() and provide some behavior. The JavaDoc describes this as follows:

> Called by the garbage collector on an object when garbage collection determines that there are no more references to the object. A subclass overrides the `finalize()` method to dispose of system resources or to perform other cleanup.

The way that this is implemented is to use the JVM's garbage collector as the subsystem that can definitively say that the object has died. If a `finalize()` method is provided on a type, then all objects of that type receive special treatment. An object that overrides `finalize()` is treated specially by the garbage collector. The JVM implements this by registering individual finalizable objects on a successful return from the constructor body of `java.lang.Object` (which must be called at some point on the creation path of any object).

One detail of HotSpot that we need to be aware of at this point is that the VM has some special implementation-specific bytecodes in addition to the standard Java instructions. These specialist bytecodes are used to rewrite the standard ones in order to cope with certain special circumstances.

A complete list of the bytecode definitions, both standard Java and HotSpot special-case, can be found in *hotspot/share/interpreter/bytecodes.cpp*. For our purposes, we care about the special-case `return_register_finalizer` bytecode. This is needed because it is possible for, say, JVMTI to rewrite the bytecode for `Object.<init>()`. To precisely obey the standard, it is necessary to identify the point at which `Object.<init>()` completes (without rewriting), and the special-case bytecode is used to mark this point.

The code for actually registering the object as needing finalization can be seen in the HotSpot interpreter. The file *src/hotspot/cpu/x86/c1_Runtime.cpp* contains the core of the x86-specific port of the HotSpot interpreter. This has to be processor-specific because HotSpot makes heavy use of low-level assembly/machine code. The case `register_finalizer_id` contains the registration code.

Once the object has been registered as needing finalization, instead of being immediately reclaimed during the garbage collection cycle, the object follows this extended lifecycle:

1. Finalizable objects are moved to a queue.
2. After application threads restart, separate finalization threads drain the queue and run the `finalize()` method on each object.
3. Once the `finalize()` method terminates, the object will be ready for actual collection in the next cycle.

Overall, this means that all objects to be finalized must first be recognized as unreachable via a GC mark, then finalized, and then GC must run again in order for the data to be collected. This means that finalizable objects persist for one extra GC cycle at least. In the case of objects that have become Tenured, this can be a significant amount of time. The finalization queue processing can be seen in Figure 11-5.

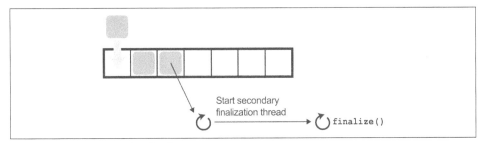

Figure 11-5. Draining the finalization queue

There are other problems with finalize(); for example, what would happen if the method throws an exception while it is being executed by a finalization thread? There is no context inside the user's application code at this point, so the exception is simply ignored. There is no way for the developer to know about or recover from a fault caused during finalization.

It is also possible that finalization could contain a blocking operation and therefore require the JVM to spawn a thread to run the finalize() method, with the inherent overhead of creating and running the new thread. Once again, the thread creation and management is outside of the developer's control but is necessary to avoid locking up the entire JVM subsystem.

The majority of the implementation for finalization actually takes place in Java. The JVM has separate threads to perform finalization that run at the same time as application threads for the majority of the required work. The core functionality is contained in the package-private class java.lang.ref.Finalizer, which should be fairly simple to read.

The class also provides some insight into how certain classes are granted additional privileges by the runtime. For example, it contains code like this:

```
/* Invoked by VM */
static void register(Object finalizee) {
    new Finalizer(finalizee);
}
```

Of course, in regular application code this would be nonsensical, as it creates an unused object. Unless the constructor has side effects (usually considered a bad design decision in Java), this would do nothing. In this case, the intent is to "hook" a new finalizable object.

The implementation of finalization also relies heavily on the FinalReference class. This is a subclass of java.lang.ref.Reference, which is a class that the runtime is

aware of as a special case. Like the better-known soft and weak references, `FinalRe`
`ference` objects are treated specially by the GC subsystem, comprising a mechanism
that provides an interesting interaction between the VM and Java code (both platform and user).

However, for all its technical interest the implementation is fatally flawed, due to differences in the memory management schemes of the two languages. In the C++ case,
dynamic memory is handled manually, with explicit lifetime management of objects
under the control of the programmer. This means that destruction can happen as the
object is deleted, and so the acquisition and release of resources is directly tied to the
lifetime of the object.

Java's memory management subsystem is a garbage collector that runs as needed, in
response to running out of available memory to allocate. It therefore runs at nondeterministic intervals and so the `finalize()` method is run only when the object is
collected, which will be at an unknown time.

Put another way, finalization does not safely implement automatic resource management, as the garbage collector does not run with any time guarantees. This means
that there is nothing in the mechanism that ties resource release to the lifetime of the
object, and so it is always possible to exhaust resources.

Finalization is not fit for its originally intended main purpose. The advice given to
developers by Oracle (and Sun) has, for many years, been to avoid finalization in
ordinary application code, and `Object.finalize()` has been deprecated in Java 9.

try-with-resources

Prior to Java 7 the responsibility of closing a resource was purely in the hands of the
developer. As discussed in "War Story: Forgetting to Clean Up" on page 274 it is easy
to forget and not notice the impact of this kind of omission until there is a production problem bearing down on you. The following code sample shows the responsibilities of a developer prior to Java 7:

```java
public void readFirstLineOld(File file) throws IOException {
    BufferedReader reader = null;
    try {
        reader = new BufferedReader(new FileReader(file));
        String firstLine = reader.readLine();
        System.out.println(firstLine);
    } finally {
        if (reader != null) {
            reader.close();
        }
    }
}
```

The developer must:

1. Create the `BufferedReader` and initialize it to `null` to ensure visibility from the `finally` block.

2. Throw or catch and handle the `IOException` (and possibly the `FileNotFound Exception` it hides).

3. Perform the business logic interacting with the external resource.

4. Check that the reader isn't `null`, and then close the resource.

This example uses only a single external resource, but the complexity increases dramatically when multiple external resources are handled. If you need a reminder, take a look at raw JDBC calls.

try-with-resources, a language-level construct added in Java 7, allows the creation of a resource to be specified in parentheses following the `try` keyword. Any object that implements the `AutoCloseable` interface can be used in the `try` parentheses. At the end of the scope of the `try` block, the `close()` method will be called automatically, rather than the developer having to remember to call the function. The following invocation of the `close()` method behaves just as in the preceding code example, and is run regardless of an exception being thrown in the business logic:

```
public void readFirstLineNew(File file) throws IOException {
    try (BufferedReader reader = new BufferedReader(new FileReader(file))) {
        String firstLine = reader.readLine();
        System.out.println(firstLine);
    }
}
```

Using `javap` we can compare the bytecode generated by the two versions. Here's the bytecode from the first example:

```
public void readFirstLineOld(java.io.File) throws java.io.IOException;
  Code:
     0: aconst_null
     1: astore_2
     2: new           #2  // class java/io/BufferedReader
     5: dup
     6: new           #3  // class java/io/FileReader
     9: dup
    10: aload_1
    11: invokespecial #4  // Method java/io/FileReader."<init>":
                          // (Ljava/io/File;)V
    14: invokespecial #5  // Method java/io/BufferedReader."<init>":
                          // (Ljava/io/Reader;)V
    17: astore_2
    18: aload_2
    19: invokevirtual #6  // Method java/io/BufferedReader.readLine:
                          // ()Ljava/lang/String;
```

```
22: astore_3
23: getstatic     #7   // Field java/lang/System.out:Ljava/io/PrintStream;
26: aload_3
27: invokevirtual #8   // Method java/io/PrintStream.println:
                       // (Ljava/lang/String;)V
30: aload_2
31: ifnull        54
34: aload_2
35: invokevirtual #9   // Method java/io/BufferedReader.close:()V
38: goto          54
41: astore        4
43: aload_2
44: ifnull        51
47: aload_2
48: invokevirtual #9   // Method java/io/BufferedReader.close:()V
51: aload         4
53: athrow
54: return
Exception table:
   from    to  target type
      2    30    41    any
     41    43    41    any
```

The equivalent bytecode from the try-with-resources version looks like this:

```
public void readFirstLineNew(java.io.File) throws java.io.IOException;
  Code:
     0: new           #2   // class java/io/BufferedReader
     3: dup
     4: new           #3   // class java/io/FileReader
     7: dup
     8: aload_1
     9: invokespecial #4   // Method java/io/FileReader."<init>":
                           // (Ljava/io/File;)V
    12: invokespecial #5   // Method java/io/BufferedReader."<init>":
                           // (Ljava/io/Reader;)V
    15: astore_2
    16: aconst_null
    17: astore_3
    18: aload_2
    19: invokevirtual #6   // Method java/io/BufferedReader.readLine:
                           // ()Ljava/lang/String;
    22: astore        4
    24: getstatic     #7   // Field java/lang/System.out:Ljava/io/PrintStream;
    27: aload         4
    29: invokevirtual #8   // Method java/io/PrintStream.println:
                           // (Ljava/lang/String;)V
    32: aload_2
    33: ifnull        108
    36: aload_3
    37: ifnull        58
    40: aload_2
    41: invokevirtual #9   // Method java/io/BufferedReader.close:()V
```

```
 44: goto         108
 47: astore       4
 49: aload_3
 50: aload        4
 52: invokevirtual #11 // Method java/lang/Throwable.addSuppressed:
                       // (Ljava/lang/Throwable;)V
 55: goto         108
 58: aload_2
 59: invokevirtual #9  // Method java/io/BufferedReader.close:()V
 62: goto         108
 65: astore       4
 67: aload        4
 69: astore_3
 70: aload        4
 72: athrow
 73: astore       5
 75: aload_2
 76: ifnull       105
 79: aload_3
 80: ifnull       101
 83: aload_2
 84: invokevirtual #9  // Method java/io/BufferedReader.close:()V
 87: goto         105
 90: astore       6
 92: aload_3
 93: aload        6
 95: invokevirtual #11 // Method java/lang/Throwable.addSuppressed:
                       // (Ljava/lang/Throwable;)V
 98: goto         105
101: aload_2
102: invokevirtual #9  // Method java/io/BufferedReader.close:()V
105: aload        5
107: athrow
108: return
Exception table:
   from    to  target type
     40    44     47  Class java/lang/Throwable
     18    32     65  Class java/lang/Throwable
     18    32     73  any
     83    87     90  Class java/lang/Throwable
     65    75     73  any
```

On the face of it, try-with-resources is simply a compiler mechanism to autogenerate boilerplate. However, when used consistently, it is a very useful simplification and can prevent classes from having to know how to release and clean up other classes. The result is to establish better encapsulation and bug-free code.

The try-with-resources mechanism is the recommended best practice for implementing something similar to the C++ RAII pattern. It does limit the use of the pattern to block-scoped code, but this is due to the Java platform's lack of low-level visibility into object lifetime. The Java developer must simply exercise discipline when dealing with resource objects and scope them as highly as possible—which is in itself a good design practice.

By now, it should be clear that these two mechanisms (finalization and try-with-resources), despite having the same design intent, are radically different from each other.

Finalization relies on assembly code far inside the runtime to register objects for special-case GC behavior. It then uses the garbage collector to kick off the cleanup using a reference queue and separate dedicated finalization threads. In particular, there is little if any trace of finalization in the bytecode, and the feature is provided by special mechanisms within the VM.

By contrast, try-with-resources is a purely compile-time feature that can be seen as syntactic sugar that simply produces regular bytecode and has no other special runtime behavior. The only possible performance effect of using try-with-resources is that because it leads to a large amount of automatically generated bytecode, it may impact the ability of the JIT compiler to effectively inline or compile methods that use this approach.

However, as with all other potential performance effects, the engineer should measure the effect of using try-with-resources on runtime performance and expend the effort to refactor only if it can be clearly shown that the feature is causing problems.

In summary, for resource management and in almost all other cases, finalization is not fit for purpose. Finalization depends on GC, which is itself a nondeterministic process. This means that anything relying on finalization has no time guarantee as to when the resource will be released.

Whether or not the deprecation of finalization eventually leads to its removal, the advice remains the same: do not write classes that override finalize(), and refactor any classes you find in your own code that do.

Method Handles

In Chapter 9 we met invokedynamic. This major development in the platform, introduced in Java 7, brings much greater flexibility in determining which method is to be executed at a call site. The key point is that an invokedynamic call site does not determine which method is to be called until runtime.

Instead, when the call site is reached by the interpreter, a special auxiliary method (known as a *bootstrap method*, or BSM) is called. The BSM returns an object that represents the actual method that should be called at the call site. This is known as the *call target* and is said to be *laced into* the call site.

In the simplest case, the lookup of the call target is done only once —the first time the call site is encountered—but there are more complex cases whereby the call site can be invalidated and the lookup rerun (possibly with a different call target resulting).

A key concept is the *method handle*, an object that represents the method that should be called from the invokedynamic call site. This is somewhat similar to concepts in reflection, but there are limitations inherent in reflection that make it inconvenient for use with invokedynamic.

Instead, Java 7 added some new classes and packages (especially java.lang.invoke.MethodHandle) to represent *directly executable* references to methods. These method handle objects have a group of several related methods that allow execution of the underlying method. Of these, invoke() is the most common, but there are additional helpers and slight variations of the primary invoker method.

Just as for reflective calls, a method handle's underlying method can have any signature. Therefore, the invoker methods present on method handles need to have a very permissive signature so as to have full flexibility. However, method handles also have a new and novel feature that goes beyond the reflective case.

To understand what this new feature is, and why it's important, let's first consider some simple code that invokes a method reflectively:

```
Method m = ...
Object receiver = ...
Object o = m.invoke(receiver, new Object(), new Object());
```

This produces the following rather unsurprising piece of bytecode:

```
17: iconst_0
18: new           #2  // class java/lang/Object
21: dup
22: invokespecial #1  // Method java/lang/Object."<init>":()V
25: aastore
26: dup
27: iconst_1
28: new           #2  // class java/lang/Object
31: dup
32: invokespecial #1  // Method java/lang/Object."<init>":()V
35: aastore
36: invokevirtual #3  // Method java/lang/reflect/Method.invoke
                      // :(Ljava/lang/Object;[Ljava/lang/Object;)
                      // Ljava/lang/Object;
```

The iconst and aastore opcodes are used to store the zeroth and first elements of the varadic arguments into an array to be passed to invoke(). Then, the overall signature of the call in the bytecode is clearly invoke:(Ljava/lang/Object;[Ljava/lang/Object;)Ljava/lang/Object;, as the method takes a single object argument (the receiver) followed by a varadic number of parameters that will be passed to the reflective call. It ultimately returns an `Object`, all of which indicates that nothing is known about this method call at compile time—we are punting on every aspect of it until runtime.

As a result, this is a very general call, and it may well fail at runtime if the receiver and `Method` object don't match, or if the parameter list is incorrect.

By way of a contrast, let's look at a similar simple example carried out with method handles:

```
MethodType mt = MethodType.methodType(int.class);
MethodHandles.Lookup l = MethodHandles.lookup();
MethodHandle mh = l.findVirtual(String.class, "hashCode", mt);

String receiver = "b";
int ret = (int) mh.invoke(receiver);
System.out.println(ret);
```

There are two parts to the call: first the lookup of the method handle, and then the invocation of it. In real systems, these two parts can be widely separated in time or code location; method handles are immutable stable objects and can easily be cached and held for later use.

The lookup mechanism seems like additional boilerplate, but it is used to correct an issue that has been a problem with reflection since its inception—access control.

When a class is initially loaded, the bytecode is extensively checked. This includes checks to ensure that the class does not maliciously attempt to call any methods that it does not have access to. Any attempt to call inaccessible methods will result in the classloading process failing.

For performance reasons, once the class has been loaded, no further checks are carried out. This opens a window that reflective code could attempt to exploit, and the original design choices made by the reflection subsystem (way back in Java 1.1) are not wholly satisfactory, for several different reasons.

The Method Handles API takes a different approach: the lookup context. To use this, we create a context object by calling `MethodHandles.lookup()`. The returned immutable object has state that records which methods and fields were accessible at the point where the context object was *created*.

This means that the context object can either be used immediately, or stored. This flexibility allows for patterns whereby a class can allow selective access to its private methods (by caching a lookup object and filtering access to it). By contrast, reflection only has the blunt instrument of the `setAccessible()` hack, which completely subverts the safety features of Java's access control.

Let's look at the bytecode for the lookup section of the method handles example:

```
 0: getstatic     #2  // Field java/lang/Integer.TYPE:Ljava/lang/Class;
 3: invokestatic  #3  // Method java/lang/invoke/MethodType.methodType:
                      // (Ljava/lang/Class;)Ljava/lang/invoke/MethodType;
 6: astore_1
 7: invokestatic  #4  // Method java/lang/invoke/MethodHandles.lookup:
                      // ()Ljava/lang/invoke/MethodHandles$Lookup;
10: astore_2
11: aload_2
12: ldc           #5  // class java/lang/String
14: ldc           #6  // String hashCode
16: aload_1
17: invokevirtual #7  // Method java/lang/invoke/MethodHandles$Lookup.findVirtual:
                      // (Ljava/lang/Class;Ljava/lang/String;Ljava/lang/invoke/
                      // MethodType;)Ljava/lang/invoke/MethodHandle;
20: astore_3
```

This code has generated a context object that can see every method that is accessible
at the point where the lookup() static call takes place. From this, we can use findVir
tual() (and related methods) to get a handle on any method visible at that point. If
we attempt to access a method that is not visible through the lookup context, then an
IllegalAccessException will be thrown. Unlike with reflection, there is no way for
the programmer to subvert or switch off this access check.

In our example, we are simply looking up the public hashCode() method on String,
which requires no special access. However, we must still use the lookup mechanism,
and the platform will still check whether the context object has access to the requested method. Next, let's look at the bytecode generated by invoking the method handle:

```
21: ldc           #8  // String b
23: astore        4
25: aload_3
26: aload         4
28: invokevirtual #9  // Method java/lang/invoke/MethodHandle.invoke
                      // :(Ljava/lang/String;)I
31: istore        5
33: getstatic     #10 // Field java/lang/System.out:Ljava/io/PrintStream;
36: iload         5
38: invokevirtual #11 // Method java/io/PrintStream.println:(I)V
```

This is substantially different from the reflective case because the call to invoke() is
not simply a one-size-fits-all invocation that accepts any arguments, but instead
describes the expected signature of the method that should be called at runtime.

> The bytecode for the method handle invocation contains better
> static type information about the call site than we would see in the
> corresponding reflective case.

In our case, the call signature is `invoke:(Ljava/lang/String;)I`, and nothing in the JavaDoc for `MethodHandle` indicates that the class has such a method.

Instead, the `javac` source code compiler has deduced an appropriate type signature for this call and emitted a corresponding call, even though no such method exists on `MethodHandle`. The bytecode emitted by `javac` has also set up the stack such that this call will be dispatched in the usual way (assuming it can be linked) without any boxing of varargs to an array.

Any JVM runtime that loads this bytecode is required to link this method call as is, with the expectation that the method handle will at runtime represent a call of the correct signature and that the `invoke()` call will be essentially replaced with a delegated call to the underlying method.

 This slightly strange feature of the Java language is known as *signature polymorphism* and applies only to method handles.

This is, of course, a very un-Java-like language feature, and the use case is deliberately skewed toward language and framework implementors (as was done with the C# `Dynamic` feature, for example).

For many developers, one simple way to think of method handles is that they provide a similar capability to core reflection, but done in a modern way with maximum possible static type safety.

Summary

In this chapter, we have discussed some performance aspects of the standard Java Collections API. We have also introduced the key concerns of dealing with domain objects.

Finally, we explored two other application performance considerations that are more concerned with the platform level: finalization and method handles. Both of these are concepts that many developers will not encounter every day. Nevertheless, for the performance-oriented engineer, a knowledge and awareness of them will be useful additions to the toolbox of techniques.

In the next chapter, we will move on to discuss several important open source libraries, including those that provide an alternative to the standard collections, as well as logging and related concerns.

## CHAPTER 12

Concurrent Performance Techniques

In the history of computing to date, software developers have typically written code in a sequential format. Programming languages and hardware generally only supported the ability to process one instruction at a time. In many situations a so-called "free lunch" was enjoyed, where application performance would improve with the purchase of the latest hardware. The increase in transistors available on a chip led to better and more capable processors.

Many readers will have experienced the situation where moving the software to a bigger or a newer box was the solution to capacity problems, rather than paying the cost of investigating the underlying issues or considering a different programming paradigm.

Moore's Law originally predicted the number of transistors on a chip would approximately double each year. Later the estimate was refined to every 18 months. Moore's Law held fast for around 50 years, but it has started to falter. The momentum we have enjoyed for 50 years is increasingly difficult to maintain. The impact of the technology running out of steam can be seen in Figure 12-1, a central pillar of "The Free Lunch Is Over," an article written by Herb Sutter that aptly describes the arrival of the modern era of performance analysis.[1]

---

1 Herb Sutter, "The Free Lunch Is Over: A Fundamental Turn Toward Concurrency in Software," *Dr. Dobb's Journal* 30 (2005): 202–210.

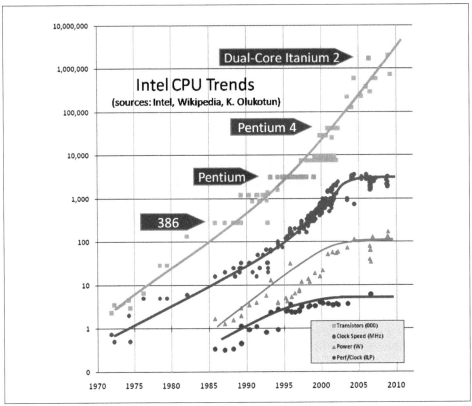

Figure 12-1. The Free Lunch Is Over (Sutter, 2005)

We now live in a world where multicore processors are commonplace. Well-written applications can (and increasingly, must) take advantage of distributing application processing over multiple cores. Application execution platforms such as the JVM are at a distinct advantage. This is because there are always VM threads that can take advantage of multiple processor cores for operations such as JIT compilation. This means that even JVM applications that only have a single application thread benefit from multicore.

To make full use of current hardware, the modern Java professional must have at least a basic grounding in concurrency and its implications for application performance. This chapter is a basic overview but is not intended to provide complete coverage of Java concurrency. Instead, a guide such as *Java Concurrency in Practice* by Brian Goetz et al. (Addison-Wesley Professional) should be consulted in addition to this discussion.

Introduction to Parallelism

For almost 50 years, single-core speed increased, and then around 2005 it began to plateau at about 3 GHz clock speed. In today's multicore world, however, *Amdahl's Law* has emerged as a major consideration for improving the execution speed of a computation task.

We introduced Amdahl's Law in "Reading Performance Graphs" on page 9, but we now need a more formal description. Consider a computing task that can be divided up into two parts—one part that can be executed in parallel, and one that has to run serially (for, e.g., collating results, or dispatching units of work for parallel execution).

Let's refer to the serial part as S and the total time needed for the task as T. We can use as many processors as we like for the task, so we denote the number of processors as N. This means that we should write T as a function of the number of processors, T(N). The concurrent part of the work is T - S, and if this can be shared equally among N processors, the overall time taken for the task is:

```
T(N) = S + (1/N) * (T - S)
```

This means that no matter how many processors are used, the total time taken can never be less than the serial time. So, if the serial overhead is, say, 5% of the total, then no matter how many cores are used, the effective speedup will never be more than 20x. This insight and formula is the underlying theory behind the introductory discussion of Amdahl's Law in Chapter 1. The impact can be seen in another way in Figure 12-2.

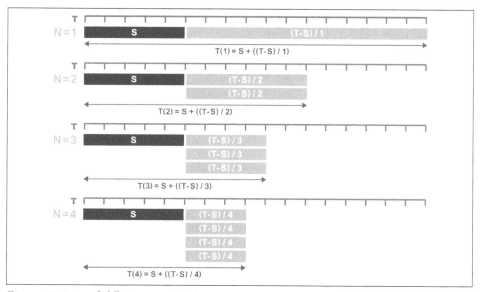

Figure 12-2. Amdahl's Law revisited

Only improvements in single-threaded performance, such as faster cores, can reduce the value of S. Unfortunately, trends in modern hardware mean that CPU clock speeds are no longer improving by any meaningful amount. As a consequence of single-core processors no longer getting faster, Amdahl's Law is often the practical limit of software scaling.

One corollary of Amdahl's Law is that if no communication between parallel tasks or other sequential processing is necessary, then unlimited speedup is theoretically possible. This class of workloads is known as *embarrassingly parallel*, and in this case, concurrent processing is fairly straightforward to achieve.

The usual approach is to subdivide the workload between multiple worker threads without any shared data. Once shared state or data is introduced between threads, the workload increases in complexity and inevitably reintroduces some serial processing and communication overhead.

> Writing correct programs is hard; writing correct concurrent programs is harder. There are simply more things that can go wrong in a concurrent program than in a sequential one.
>
> —*Java Concurrency in Practice*, Brian Goetz et al. (Addison-Wesley Professional)

In turn, this means that any workload with shared state requires correct protection and control. For workloads that run on the JVM, the platform provides a set of memory guarantees called the Java Memory Model (JMM). Let's look at some simple examples that explain the problems of Java concurrency before introducing the model in some depth.

Fundamental Java Concurrency

One of the first lessons learned about the counterintuitive nature of concurrency is the realization that incrementing a counter is not a single operation. Let's take a look:

```
public class Counter {
    private int i = 0;

    public int increment() {
        return i = i + 1;
    }

}
```

Analyzing the bytecode for this produces a series of instructions that result in loading, incrementing, and storing the value:

```
public int increment();
  Code:
   0: aload_0
   1: aload_0
   2: getfield      #2  // Field i:I
```

```
 5: iconst_1
 6: iadd
 7: dup_x1
 8: putfield      #2  // Field i:I
11: ireturn
```

If the counter is not protected by an appropriate lock and is accessed in a multithrea-ded way, it is possible a load could happen before another thread is stored. This prob-lem results in lost updates.

To see this in more detail, consider two threads, A and B, that are both calling the increment() method on the same object. For simplicity's sake, suppose they are run-ning on a machine with a single CPU and that the bytecode accurately represents low-level execution (so, no reordering, cache effects, or other details of real process-ors).

 As the operating system scheduler causes context switching of the threads at nondeterministic times, many different sequences of bytecodes are possible with even just two threads.

Suppose the single CPU executes the bytecodes as shown (note that there is a well-defined order of execution for the instructions, which would not be the case on an actual multiprocessor system):

```
A0: aload_0
A1: aload_0
A2: getfield #2 // Field i:I
A5: iconst_1
A6: iadd
A7: dup_x1
B0: aload_0
B1: aload_0
B2: getfield #2 // Field i:I
B5: iconst_1
B6: iadd
B7: dup_x1
A8: putfield #2 // Field i:I
A11: ireturn
B8: putfield #2 // Field i:I
B11: ireturn
```

Each thread will have a private evaluation stack from its individual entry into the method, so only the operations on fields can interfere with each other (because the object fields are located in the heap, which is shared).

The resulting behavior is that, if the initial state of i is 7 before either A or B starts executing, then if the execution order is precisely as just shown, both calls will return

8 and the field state will be updated to 8, despite the fact that increment() was called twice.

 This issue is caused by nothing other than OS scheduling—no hardware trickery was required to surface this problem, and it would be an issue even on a very old CPU without modern features.

A further misconception is that adding the keyword volatile will make the increment operation safe. By forcing the value to always be reread by the cache, volatile guarantees that any updates will be seen by another thread. However, it does not prevent the lost update problem just shown, as it is due to the composite nature of the increment operator.

The following example shows two threads sharing a reference to the same counter:

```java
package optjava;

public class CounterExample implements Runnable {

    private final Counter counter;

    public CounterExample(Counter counter) {
        this.counter = counter;

    }

    @Override
    public void run() {
        for (int i = 0; i < 100; i++) {
            System.out.println(Thread.currentThread().getName()
                    + " Value: " + counter.increment());
        }
    }

}
```

The counter is unprotected by synchronized or an appropriate lock. Each time a program runs, the execution of the two threads can potentially interleave in different ways. On some occasions the code will run as expected and the counter will increment fine. This is down to the programmer's dumb luck! On other occasions the interleaving may show repeated values in the counter due to lost updates, as seen here:

```
Thread-1 Value: 1
Thread-1 Value: 2
Thread-1 Value: 3
Thread-0 Value: 1
Thread-1 Value: 4
```

```
Thread-1 Value: 6
Thread-0 Value: 5
```

In other words, a concurrent program that runs successfully most of the time is not the same thing as a correct concurrent program. Proving it fails is as difficult as proving it is correct; however, it is sufficient to find one example of failure to demonstrate it is not correct.

To make matters worse, reproducing bugs in concurrent code can be extremely difficult. Dijkstra's famous maxim that "testing shows the presence, not the absence of bugs" applies to concurrent code even more strongly than to single-threaded applications.

To solve the aforementioned problems, we could use synchronized to control the updating of a simple value such as an int—and before Java 5, that was the only choice.

The problem with using synchronization is that it requires some careful design and up-front thought. Without this, just adding synchronization can slow down the program rather than speeding it up.

This is counter to the whole aim of adding concurrency: to increase throughput. Accordingly, any exercise to parallelize a code base must be supported by performance tests that fully prove the benefit of the additional complexity.

 Adding synchronization blocks, especially if they are uncontended, is a lot cheaper than in older versions of the JVM (but should still not be done if not necessary). More details can be found in "Locks and Escape Analysis" on page 238.

To do better than just a shotgun approach to synchronization, we need an understanding of the JVM's low-level memory model and how it applies to practical techniques for concurrent applications.

Understanding the JMM

Java has had a formal model of memory, the JMM, since version 1.0. This model was heavily revised and some problems were fixed in JSR 133,[2] which was delivered as part of Java 5.

---

2 The Java platform evolves through Java Specification Requests (JSRs) that track enhancements to the platform standards.

In the Java specifications the JMM appears as a mathematical description of memory. It has a somewhat formidable reputation, and many developers regard it as the most impenetrable part of the Java specification (except, perhaps, for generics).

The JMM seeks to provide answers to questions such as:

- What happens when two cores access the same data?
- When are they guaranteed to see the same value?
- How do memory caches affect these answers?

Anywhere shared state is accessed, the platform will ensure that the promises made in the JMM are honored. These promises fall into two main groups: guarantees related to ordering and those concerned with visibility of updates across threads.

As hardware has moved from single-core to multicore to many-core systems, the nature of the memory model has become increasingly important. Ordering and thread visibility are no longer theoretical issues, but are now practical problems that directly impact the code of working programmers.

At a high level, there are two possible approaches that a memory model like the JMM might take:

Strong memory model
> All cores always see the same values at all times.

Weak memory model
> Cores may see different values, and there are special cache rules that control when this may occur.

From the programming point of view, a strong memory model seems very appealing —not least because it doesn't require programmers to take any extra care when writing application code.

In Figure 12-3, we can see a (greatly) simplified view of a modern multi-CPU system. We saw this view in Chapter 3 and again in Chapter 7 (where it was discussed in the context of NUMA architectures).

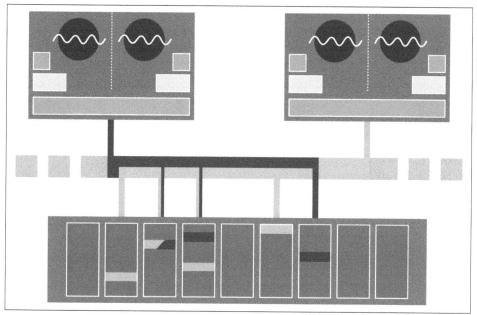

Figure 12-3. Modern multi-CPU system

If a strong memory model were to be implemented on top of this hardware, this would be equivalent to a writeback approach to memory. Notification of cache invalidation would swamp the memory bus, and effective transfer rates to/from main memory would nosedive. This problem would only get worse as the number of cores increases, which makes this approach fundamentally unsuitable for the many-core world.

It is also worth remembering that Java is designed to be an architecture-independent environment. This means that if the JVM were to specify a strong memory model, it would require additional implementation work to be done in software running on top of hardware that does not support a strong memory model natively. In turn, this would greatly increase the porting work required to implement a JVM on top of weak hardware.

In reality, the JMM has a very weak memory model. This fits better with trends in real CPU architecture, including MESI (described in "Memory Caches" on page 35). It also makes porting easier, as the JMM makes few guarantees.

It is very important to realize that the JMM is a minimum requirement only. Real JVM implementations and CPUs may do more than the JMM requires, as discussed in "Hardware Memory Models" on page 42.

This can lead to application developers being lulled into a false sense of security. If an application is developed on a hardware platform with a stronger memory model than the JMM, then undiscovered concurrency bugs can survive—because they do not manifest in practice due to hardware guarantees. When the same application is deployed onto weaker hardware, the concurrency bugs may become a problem as the application is no longer being protected by the hardware.

The guarantees provided by the JMM are based upon a set of basic concepts:

Happens-Before
    One event definitely happens before another.

Synchronizes-With
    The event will cause its view of an object to be synchronized with main memory.

As-If-Serial
    Instructions appear to execute in order outside of the executing thread.

Release-Before-Acquire
    Locks will be released by one thread before being acquired by another.

One of the most important techniques for handling shared mutable state is locking via synchronization. It is a fundamental part of the Java view of concurrency, and we will need to discuss it in some depth to work adequately with the JMM.

 For developers who are interested in performance, a passing acquaintance with the Thread class and the language-level basic primitives of Java's concurrency mechanism is not enough.

In this view, threads have their own description of an object's state, and any changes made by the thread have to be flushed to main memory and then reread by any other threads that are accessing the same data. This fits well with the write-behind view of hardware as discussed in the context of MESI, but in the JVM there is a considerable amount of implementation code that wraps the low-level memory access.

From this standpoint, it is immediately clear what the Java keyword synchronized refers to: it means that the local view of the thread holding the monitor has been Synchronized-With main memory.

Synchronized methods and blocks define touchpoints where threads must perform syncing. They also define blocks of code that must fully complete before other synchronized blocks or methods can start.

The JMM does not have anything to say about unsynchronized access. There are no guarantees about when, if ever, changes made on one thread will become visible to other threads. If such guarantees are required, then the write access must be protected by a synchronized block, triggering a writeback of the cached values to main memory. Similarly, the read access must also be contained within a synchronized section of code, to force a reread from memory.

Prior to the arrival of modern Java concurrency, using the Java keyword `synchronized` was the only mechanism of guaranteeing ordering and visibility of data across multiple threads.

The JMM enforces this behavior and offers various guarantees that can be assumed about Java and memory safety. However, the traditional Java `synchronized` lock has several limitations, which have become increasingly severe:

- All `synchronized` operations on the locked object are treated equally.
- Lock acquiring and releasing must be done on a method level or within a `synchronized` block within a method.
- Either the lock is acquired or the thread is blocked; there is no way to attempt to acquire the lock and carry on processing if the lock cannot be obtained.

A very common mistake is to forget that operations on locked data must be treated equitably. If an application uses `synchronized` only on write operations, this can lead to lost updates.

For example, it might seem as though a read does not need to lock, but it must use `synchronized` to guarantee visibility of updates coming from other threads.

 Java synchronization between threads is a cooperative mechanism and it does not work correctly if even one participating thread does not follow the rules.

One resource for newcomers to the JMM is the JSR-133 Cookbook for Compiler Writers (*http://gee.cs.oswego.edu/dl/jmm/cookbook.html*). This contains a simplified explanation of JMM concepts without overwhelming the reader with detail.

For example, as part of the treatment of the memory model a number of abstract barriers are introduced and discussed. These are intended to allow JVM implementors and library authors to think about the rules of Java concurrency in a relatively CPU-independent way.

The rules that the JVM implementations must actually follow are detailed in the Java specifications. In practice, the actual instructions that implement each abstract barrier may well be different on different CPUs. For example, the Intel CPU model automatically prevents certain reorderings in hardware, so some of the barriers described in the cookbook are actually no-ops.

One final consideration: the performance landscape is a moving target. Neither the evolution of hardware nor the frontiers of concurrency have stood still since the JMM was created. As a result, the JMM's description is an inadequate representation of modern hardware and memory.

In Java 9 the JMM has been extended in an attempt to catch up (at least partially) to the reality of modern systems. One key aspect of this is compatibility with other programming environments, especially C++11, which adapted ideas from the JMM and then extended them. This means that the C++11 model provides definitions of concepts outside the scope of the Java 5 JMM (JSR 133). Java 9 updates the JMM to bring some of those concepts to the Java platform and to allow low-level, hardware-conscious Java code to interoperate with C++11 in a consistent manner.

To delve deeper into the JMM, see Aleksey Shipilëv's blog post "Close Encounters of the Java Memory Model Kind" (*https://shipilev.net/blog/2016/close-encounters-of-jmm-kind/*), which is a great source of commentary and very detailed technical information.

Building Concurrency Libraries

Despite being very successful, the JMM is hard to understand and even harder to translate into practical usage. Related to this is the lack of flexibility that intrinsic locking provides.

As a result, since Java 5, there has been an increasing trend toward standardizing high-quality concurrency libraries and tools as part of the Java class library and moving away from the built-in language-level support. In the vast majority of use cases, even those that are performance-sensitive, these libraries are more appropriate than creating new abstractions from scratch.

The libraries in `java.util.concurrent` have been designed to make writing multi-threaded applications in Java a lot easier. It is the job of a Java developer to select the level of abstraction that best suits their requirements, and it is a fortunate confluence that selecting the well-abstracted libraries of `java.util.concurrent` will also yield better "thread hot" performance.

The core building blocks provided fall into a few general categories:

- Locks and semaphores
- Atomics
- Blocking queues
- Latches
- Executors

In Figure 12-4, we can see a representation of a typical modern concurrent Java application that is built up from concurrency primitives and business logic.

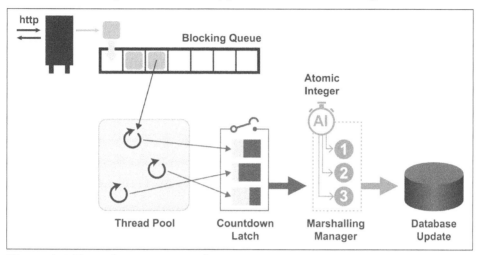

Figure 12-4. Example concurrent application

Some of these building blocks are discussed in the next section, but before we review them, let's take a look at some of the main implementation techniques used in the libraries. An understanding of how the concurrent libraries are implemented will allow performance-conscious developers to make the best use of them. For developers operating at the extreme edge, knowing how the libraries work will give teams who have outgrown the standard library a starting point for choosing (or developing) ultra-high-performance replacements.

In general, the libraries try to move away from relying upon the operating system and instead work more in user space where possible. This has a number of advantages, not least of which is that the behavior of the library is then hopefully more globally consistent, rather than being at the mercy of small but important variations between Unix-like operating systems.

Some of the libraries (notably locks and atomics) rely on low-level processor instructions and operating system specifics to implement a technique known as *Compare and Swap* (CAS).

This technique takes a pair of values, the "expected current value" and the "wanted new value," and a memory location (a pointer). As an atomic unit, two operations occur:

1. The expected current value is compared with the contents of the memory location.

2. If they match, the current value is swapped with the wanted new value.

CAS is a basic building block for several crucial higher-level concurrency features, and so this is a classic example of how the performance and hardware landscape has not stood still since the JMM was produced.

Despite the fact that the CAS feature is implemented in hardware on most modern processors, it does not form part of the JMM or the Java platform specification. Instead, it must be treated as an implementation-specific extension, and so access to CAS hardware is provided via the sun.misc.Unsafe class.

Unsafe

sun.misc.Unsafe is an internal implementation class, and as the package name suggests, it is not part of the standard API of the Java platform. Therefore, it is generally not to be used by application developers directly; the clue is in the class name. Any code that does use it is technically directly coupled to the HotSpot VM, and is potentially fragile.

 Unsafe is an unsupported, internal API and so technically could be withdrawn or modified at any time, without regard to user applications. It has been placed in the module jdk.unsupported in Java 9, as we will discuss later.

However, Unsafe has become a key part of the implementation of basically every major framework in one way or another. It provides ways to break the standard behavior of the JVM. For example, Unsafe allows such possibilities as:

- Allocate an object, but don't run its constructor.
- Access raw memory and the equivalent of pointer arithmetic.
- Use processor-specific hardware features (such as CAS).

These operations enable high-level framework features such as:

- Fast (de-)serialization
- Thread-safe native memory access (for example, off-heap or 64-bit indexed access)
- Atomic memory operations
- Efficient object/memory layouts
- Custom memory fences
- Fast interaction with native code

- A multi–operating system replacement for JNI
- Access to array elements with volatile semantics

While Unsafe is not an official standard for Java SE, its widespread popular usage in the industry has made it a de facto standard. In addition, it has become something of a dumping ground for nonstandard but necessary features. This landscape has been affected by the arrival of Java 9, however, and is expected to evolve significantly over the next few versions of Java.

Let's take a look at CAS in action, by exploring the atomic classes that were introduced with Java 5.

Atomics and CAS

Atomics have composite operations to add, increment, and decrement, which combine with a get() to return the affected result. This means that an operation to increment on two separate threads will return currentValue + 1 and currentValue + 2. The semantics of atomic variables are an extension of volatile, but they are more flexible as they can perform state-dependent updates safely.

Atomics do not inherit from the base type they wrap, and do not allow direct replacement. For example, AtomicInteger does not extend Integer—for one thing, java.lang.Integer is (rightly) a final class.

Let's look at how Unsafe provides the implementation of a simple atomic call:

```java
public class AtomicIntegerExample extends Number {

    private volatile int value;

    // setup to use Unsafe.compareAndSwapInt for updates
    private static final Unsafe unsafe = Unsafe.getUnsafe();
    private static final long valueOffset;

    static {
        try {
            valueOffset = unsafe.objectFieldOffset(
                AtomicIntegerExample.class.getDeclaredField("value"));
        } catch (Exception ex) {
            throw new Error(ex);
        }
    }

    public final int get() {
        return value;
    }

    public final void set(int newValue) {
        value = newValue;
```

```
        }

        public final int getAndSet(int newValue) {
            return unsafe.getAndSetInt(this, valueOffset, newValue);
        }
        // ...
```

This relies on some methods from `Unsafe`, and the key methods here are native and involve calling into the JVM:

```
        public final int getAndSetInt(Object o, long offset, int newValue) {
            int v;
            do {
                v = getIntVolatile(o, offset);
            } while (!compareAndSwapInt(o, offset, v, newValue));

            return v;
        }

        public native int getIntVolatile(Object o, long offset);

        public final native boolean compareAndSwapInt(Object o, long offset,
                                  int expected, int x);
```

The sample demonstrates the usage of a loop within `Unsafe` to repeatedly retry a CAS operation. It is vital for effective use of atomics that developers use the facilities provided and do not roll their own implementations of, say, an atomic increment operation using a loop, as the `Unsafe` implementation will already utilize that technique internally.

Atomics are lock-free and therefore cannot deadlock. Often atomics are accompanied by an internal retry loop, to deal with the situation of failure to compare and update. Usually this occurs when another thread just performed an update.

This retry loop produces a linear degradation of performance if multiple retries are required to update the variable. When considering performance, it is important to monitor the contention level to ensure throughput levels remain high.

Using `Unsafe` to provide access to lower-level hardware instructions is interesting, as Java usually allows the developer to be completely abstracted away from the machine. However, in this case the access to machine instructions is critical to enforcing the desired semantics of the atomic classes.

Locks and Spinlocks

The intrinsic locks that we have met up until now work by invoking the operating system in user code. The OS is used to put a thread into an indefinite wait until signaled. This can be a huge overhead if the contended resource is only in use for a very short period of time. In this case, it may be much more efficient to have the blocked thread stay active on a CPU, accomplish no useful work, and "burn CPU" retrying the lock until it becomes available.

This technique is known as a *spinlock* and is intended to be more lightweight than a full mutual-exclusion lock. In modern systems, spinlocks are usually implemented with CAS, assuming that the hardware supports it. Let's look at a simple example in low-level x86 assembly:

```
locked:
    dd      0

spin_lock:
    mov     eax, 1
    xchg    eax, [locked]
    test    eax, eax
    jnz     spin_lock
    ret

spin_unlock:
    mov     eax, 0
    xchg    eax, [locked]
    ret
```

The exact implementation of a spinlock varies between CPUs, but the core concept is the same on all systems:

- The "test and set" operation—implemented here by xchg—must be atomic.
- If there is contention for the spinlock, processors that are waiting execute a tight loop.

CAS essentially allows the safe updating of a value in one instruction if the expected value is correct. This helps us to form the building blocks for a lock.

Summary of Concurrent Libraries

We've seen an introduction to the low-level implementation techniques used to enable atomic classes and simple locks. Now, let's take a look at how the standard library uses these capabilities to create fully featured production libraries for general-purpose use.

Locks in java.util.concurrent

Java 5 reimagined locks and added a more general interface for a lock in `java.util.concurrent.locks.Lock`. This interface offers more possibilities than the behavior of intrinsic locks:

`lock()`

Traditionally acquires the lock and will block until the lock is available.

`newCondition()`

Creates conditions around the lock, which allows the lock to be used in a more flexible way. Allows a separation of concerns within the lock (e.g., a read and a write).

`tryLock()`

Tries to acquire the lock (with an optional timeout), allowing for a thread to continue the process in the situation where the lock does not become available.

`unlock()`

Releases the lock. This is the corresponding call following a `lock()`.

In addition to allowing different types of locks to be created, locks can now also span multiple methods, as it is possible to lock in one method and unlock in another. If a thread wants to acquire a lock in a nonblocking manner, it is able to do so using the `tryLock()` method and back out if the lock is not available.

The `ReentrantLock` is the main implementation of `Lock`, and basically uses a `compareAndSwap()` with an `int`. This means that the acquisition of the lock is lock-free in the uncontended case. This can dramatically increase the performance of a system where there is less lock contention, while also providing the additional flexibility of different locking policies.

 The idea of a thread being able to reacquire the same lock is known as *re-entrant locking*, and this prevents a thread from blocking itself. Most modern application-level locking schemes are re-entrant.

The actual calls to `compareAndSwap()` and the usage of `Unsafe` can be found in the static subclass `Sync`, which is an extension to `AbstractQueuedSynchronizer`. `AbstractQueuedSynchronizer` also makes use of the `LockSupport` class, which has methods that allow threads to be parked and resumed.

The `LockSupport` class works by issuing permits to threads, and if there isn't a permit available a thread must wait. The idea of permits is similar to the concept of issuing permits in semaphores, but here there is only a single permit (a binary semaphore). If a permit is not available a thread will be parked, and once a valid permit is available the thread will be unparked. The methods of this class replace the long-deprecated methods of `Thread.suspend()` and `Thread.resume()`.

There are three forms of `park()` that influence the following basic pseudocode.

```
    while (!canProceed()) { ... LockSupport.park(this); }}
```

They are:

park(Object blocker)
: Blocks until another thread calls unpark(), the thread is interrupted, or a spurious wakeup occurs.

parkNanos(Object blocker, long nanos)
: Behaves the same as park(), but will also return once the specified nano time elapses.

parkUntil(Object blocker, long deadline)
: Is similar to parkNanos(), but also adds a timeout to the scenarios that will cause the method to return.

Read/Write Locks

Many components in applications will have an imbalance between the number of read operations and write operations. Reads don't change the state, whereas write operations will. Using the traditional synchronized or ReentrantLock (without conditions) will follow a single lock strategy. In situations like caching, where there may be many readers and a single writer, the data structure may spend a lot of time unnecessarily blocking the readers due to another read.

The ReentrantReadWriteLock class exposes a ReadLock and a WriteLock that can be used within code. The advantage is that multiple threads reading do not cause other reading threads to block. The only operation that will block is a write. Using this locking pattern where the number of readers is high can significantly improve thread throughput and reduce locking. It is also possible to set the lock into "fair mode," which degrades performance but ensures threads are dealt with in order.

The following implementation for AgeCache would be a significant improvement over a version that uses a single lock:

```java
package optjava.ch12;

import java.util.HashMap;
import java.util.Map;
import java.util.concurrent.locks.Lock;
import java.util.concurrent.locks.ReentrantReadWriteLock;

public class AgeCache {
        private final ReentrantReadWriteLock rwl = new ReentrantReadWriteLock();
    private final Lock readLock = rwl.readLock();
    private final Lock writeLock = rwl.writeLock();
    private Map<String, Integer> ageCache = new HashMap<>();

    public Integer getAge(String name) {
```

```
    readLock.lock();
    try {
        return ageCache.get(name);
    } finally {
                    readLock.unlock();
            }
    }

    public void updateAge(String name, int newAge) {
        writeLock.lock();
        try {
            ageCache.put(name, newAge);
        } finally {
            writeLock.unlock();
        }
    }

}
```

However, we could make it even more optimal by considering the underlying data structure. In this example a concurrent collection would be a more sensible abstraction and yield greater thread hot benefits.

Semaphores

Semaphores offer a unique technique for allowing access to a number of available resources—for instance, threads in a pool or database connection objects. A semaphore works on the premise that "at most X objects are allowed access" and functions by having a set number of permits to control access:

```
// Semaphore with 2 permits and a fair model
private Semaphore poolPermits = new Semaphore(2, true);
```

Semaphore::acquire() reduces the number of available permits by one, and if there are no permits available will block. Semaphore::release() returns a permit and will release a waiting acquirer if there is one. Because semaphores are often used in a way where resources are potentially blocked or queued, it is most likely that a semaphore will be initialized as fair to avoid thread starvation.

A one-permit semaphore (binary semaphore) is equivalent to a mutex, but with one distinct difference. A mutex can only be released by a thread that the mutex is locked on, whereas a semaphore can be released by a nonowning thread. A scenario where this might be necessary would be forcing the resolution of a deadlock. Semaphores also have the advantage of being able to ask for and release multiple permits. If multiple permits are being used, it is essential to use fair mode; otherwise, there is an increased chance of thread starvation.

Concurrent Collections

In Chapter 11 we explored optimizations that could be considered for Java collections. Since Java 5, there have been implementations of the collections interfaces that have been specifically designed for concurrent uses. These concurrent collections have been modified and improved over time to give the best possible thread hot performance.

For example, the map implementation (ConcurrentHashMap) uses a split into buckets or segments, and we can take advantage of this structure to achieve real gains in performance. Each segment can have its own locking policy—that is, its own series of locks. Having both a read and a write lock enables many readers to be reading across the ConcurrentHashMap, and if a write is required the lock only needs to be on that single segment. Readers generally do not lock and can overlap safely with put()- and remove()-style operations. Readers will observe the happens-before ordering for a completed update operation.

It is important to note that iterators (and the spliterators used for parallel streams) are acquired as a sort of snapshot, meaning that they will not throw a ConcurrentModifi cationException. The table will be dynamically expanded when there are too many collisions, which can be a costly operation. It is worthwhile (as with the HashMap) to provide an approximate sizing if you know it at the time of writing the code.

Java 5 also introduced the CopyOnWriteArrayList and CopyOnWriteArraySet, which in certain usage patterns can improve multithreaded performance. With these, any mutation operation against the data structure causes a fresh copy of the backing array to be created. Any existing iterators can continue to traverse the old array, and once all references are lost the old copy of the array is eligible for garbage collection. Again, this snapshot style of iteration ensures that there is no ConcurrentModificationEx ception raised.

This tradeoff works well in systems where the copy-on-write data structure is accessed for reading many more times than mutating. If you are considering using this approach, make the change with a good set of tests to measure the performance improvement.

Latches and Barriers

Latches and barriers are useful techniques for controlling the execution of a set of threads. For example, a system may be written where worker threads:

1. Retrieve data from an API and parse it.
2. Write the results to a database.

3. Finally, compute results based on a SQL query.

If the system simply started all the threads running, there would be no guarantee on the ordering of events. The desired effect would be to allow all threads to complete task #1 and then task #2 before starting on task #3. One possibility would be to use a *latch*. Assuming we have five threads running, we could write code like the following:

```java
package optjava.ch12;

import                                        ;
import                                        ;
import                                        ;
import                                        ;

public class LatchExample implements Runnable {

    private final CountDownLatch latch;

    public LatchExample(CountDownLatch latch) {
        this.latch = latch;
    }

    @Override
    public void run() {
        // Call an API
        System.out.println(Thread.currentThread().getName() + " Done API Call");
        try {
            latch.countDown();
            latch.await();
        } catch (InterruptedException e) {
            e.printStackTrace();
        }
        System.out.println(Thread.currentThread().getName()
            + " Continue processing");
    }

    public static void main(String[] args) throws InterruptedException {
        CountDownLatch apiLatch = new CountDownLatch(5);

        ExecutorService pool = Executors.newFixedThreadPool(5);
        for (int i = 0; i < 5; i++) {
            pool.submit(new LatchExample(apiLatch));
        }
        System.out.println(Thread.currentThread().getName()
            +" about to await on main..");
        apiLatch.await();
        System.out.println(Thread.currentThread().getName()
            + " done awaiting on main..");
        pool.shutdown();
        try {
            pool.awaitTermination(5, TimeUnit.SECONDS);
        } catch (InterruptedException e) {
```

```
            e.printStackTrace();
        }
        System.out.println("API Processing Complete");
    }

}
```

In this example, the latch is set to have a count of 5, with each thread making a call to `countdown()` reducing the number by one. Once the count reaches 0, the latch will open, and any threads held on the `await()` function will be released to continue their processing.

It is important to realize that this type of latch is single-use only. This means that once the result is 0, the latch cannot be reused; there is no reset.

> Latches are extremely useful in examples such as cache population during startup and multithreaded testing.

In our example, we could have used two different latches: one for the API results to be finished and another for the database results to complete. Another option is to use a `CyclicBarrier`, which can be reset. However, figuring out which thread should control the reset is quite a difficult challenge and involves another type of synchronization. One common best practice is to use one barrier/latch for each stage in the pipeline.

Executors and Task Abstraction

In practice, most Java programmers should not have to deal with low-level threading concerns. Instead, we should be looking to use some of the `java.util.concurrent` features that support concurrent programming at a suitable level of abstraction. For example, keeping threads busy using some of the `java.util.concurrent` libraries will enable better thread hot performance (i.e., keeping a thread running rather than blocked and in a waiting state).

The level of abstraction that offers few threading concerns can be described as a *concurrent task*—that is, a unit of code or work that we require to run concurrently within the current execution context. Considering units of work as tasks simplifies writing a concurrent program, as the developer does not have to consider the thread lifecycle for the actual threads executing the tasks.

Introducing Asynchronous Execution

One way of fulfilling the task abstraction in Java is by using the `Callable` interface to represent a task that returns a value. The `Callable<V>` interface is a generic interface defining one function, `call()`, that returns a value of type `V` and throws an exception in the case that a result cannot be calculated. On the surface `Callable` looks very similar to `Runnable`; however, `Runnable` does not return a result and does not throw an exception.

 If `Runnable` throws an uncaught unchecked exception, it propagates up the stack and by default the executing thread stops running.

Dealing with exceptions in the lifetime of a thread is a difficult programming problem and can result in Java programs continuing to run in strange states if not managed correctly. It should also be noted that threads can be treated as OS-style processes, meaning they can be expensive to create on some operating systems. Getting hold of any result from `Runnable` can also add extra complexity, particularly in terms of coordinating the execution return against another thread, for instance.

The `Callable<V>` type provides us with a way to deal with the task abstraction nicely, but how are these tasks actually executed?

An `ExecutorService` is an interface that defines a mechanism for executing tasks on a pool of managed threads. The actual implementation of the `ExecutorService` defines how the threads in the pool should be managed and how many there should be. An `ExecutorService` can take either `Runnable` or `Callable` via the `submit()` method and its overloads.

The helper class `Executors` has a series of `new*` factory methods that construct the service and backing thread pool according to the selected behavior. These factory methods are the usual way to create new executor objects:

`newFixedThreadPool(int nThreads)`
> Constructs an `ExecutorService` with a fixed-size thread pool, in which the threads will be reused to run multiple tasks. This avoids having to pay the cost of thread creation multiple times for each task. When all the threads are in use, new tasks are stored in a queue.

`newCachedThreadPool()`
> Constructs an `ExecutorService` that will create new threads as required and reuse threads where possible. Created threads are kept for 60 seconds, after

which they will be removed from the cache. Using this thread pool can give better performance with small asynchronous tasks.

newSingleThreadExecutor()
Constructs an ExecutorService backed by a single thread. Any newly submitted tasks are queued until the thread is available. This type of executor can be useful to control the number of tasks concurrently executed.

newScheduledThreadPool(int corePoolSize)
Has an additional series of methods that allow a task to be executed at a point in the future that take Callable and a delay.

Once a task is submitted it will be processed asynchronously, and the submitting code can choose to block or poll for the result. The submit() call to the ExecutorService returns a Future<V> that allows a blocking get() or a get() with a timeout, or a non-blocking call using isDone() in the usual manner.

Selecting an ExecutorService

Selecting the right ExecutorService allows good control of asynchronous processing and can yield significant performance benefits if you choose the right number of threads in the pool.

It is also possible to write a custom ExecutorService, but this is not often necessary. One way in which the library helps is by providing a customization option: the ability to supply a ThreadFactory. The ThreadFactory allows the author to write a custom thread creator that can set properties on threads such as name, daemon status, and thread priority.

The ExecutorService will sometimes need to be tuned empirically in the settings of the entire application. Having a good idea of the hardware that the service will run on and other competing resources is a valuable part of the tuning picture.

One metric that is usually used is the number of cores versus the number of threads in the pool. Selecting a number of threads to run concurrently that is higher than the number of processors available can be problematic and cause contention. The operating system will be required to schedule the threads to run, and this causes a context switch to occur.

When contention hits a certain threshold, it can negate the performance benefits of moving to a concurrent way of processing. This is why a good performance model and being able to measure improvements (or losses) is imperative. Chapter 5 discusses performance testing techniques and antipatterns to avoid when undertaking this type of testing.

Fork/Join

Java offers several different approaches to concurrency that do not require developers to control and manage their own threads. Java 7 introduced the Fork/Join framework, which provides a new API to work efficiently with multiple processors. It is based on a new implementation of ExecutorService, called ForkJoinPool. This class provides a pool of managed threads, which has two special features:

- It can be used to efficiently process a subdivided task.
- It implements a *work-stealing* algorithm.

The subdivided task support is introduced by the ForkJoinTask class. This is a thread-like entity that is more lightweight than a standard Java thread. The intended use case is that potentially large numbers of tasks and subtasks may be hosted by a small number of actual threads in a ForkJoinPool executor.

The key aspect of a ForkJoinTask is that it can subdivide itself into "smaller" tasks, until the task size is small enough to compute directly. For this reason, the framework is suitable only for certain types of tasks, such as computation of pure functions or other "embarrassingly parallel" tasks. Even then, it may be necessary to rewrite algorithms or code to take full advantage of this part of Fork/Join.

However, the work-stealing algorithm part of the Fork/Join framework can be used independently of the task subdivision. For example, if one thread has completed all the work allocated to it and another thread has a backlog, it will steal work from the queue of the busy thread. This rebalancing of jobs across multiple threads is quite a simple but clever idea, yielding considerable benefit. In Figure 12-5, we can see a representation of work stealing.

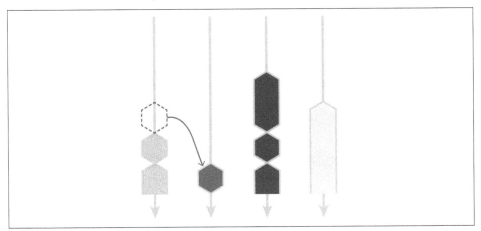

Figure 12-5. The work-stealing algorithm

`ForkJoinPool` has a static method, `commonPool()`, that returns a reference to the system-wide pool. This prevents developers from having to create their own pool and provides the opportunity for sharing. The common pool is lazily initialized so will be created only if required.

The sizing of the pool is defined by `Runtime.getRuntime().availableProcessors()` −1. However, this method does not always return the expected result.

Writing on the Java Specialists (*http://www.javaspecialists.eu/*) mailing list, Heinz Kabutz found a case where a 16-4-2 machine (16 sockets, each with 4 cores and 2 hyperthreads per core) returned the value 16. This seems very low; the naive intuition gained by testing on our laptops may have led us to expect the value to be 16 * 4 * 2 = 128. However, if we were to run Java 8 on this machine, it would configure the common Fork/Join pool to have a parallelism of only 15.

> The VM doesn't really have an opinion about what a processor is; it just asks the OS for a number. Similarly, the OS usually doesn't care either, it asks the hardware. The hardware responds with a number, usually the number of "hardware threads." The OS believes the hardware. The VM believes the OS.
>
> —Brian Goetz

Thankfully, there is a flag that allows the developer to programmatically set the desired parallelism:

```
-Djava.util.concurrent.ForkJoinPool.common.parallelism=128
```

As discussed in Chapter 5, though, be careful with magic flags. And as we will discuss with selecting the `parallelStream` option, nothing comes for free!

The work-stealing aspect of Fork/Join is becoming more utilized by library and framework developers, even without task subdivision. For example, the Akka framework, which we will meet "Actor-Based Techniques" on page 316, uses a `ForkJoin Pool` primarily for the benefits of work stealing. The arrival of Java 8 also raised the usage level of Fork/Join significantly, as behind the scenes `parallelStream()` uses the common Fork/Join pool.

Modern Java Concurrency

Concurrency in Java was originally designed for an environment where long-running blocking tasks could be interleaved to allow other threads to execute—for instance, I/O and other similar slow operations. Nowadays, virtually every machine a developer writes code for will be a multiprocessor system, so making efficient use of the available CPU resources is very sensible.

However, when the notion of concurrency was built into Java it was not something the industry had a great deal of experience with. In fact, Java was the first industry-standard environment to build in threading support at language level. As a result, many of the painful lessons developers have learned about concurrency were first encountered in Java. In Java the approach has generally been not to deprecate features (especially core features), so the Thread API is still a part of Java and always will be.

This has led to a situation where in modern application development, threads are quite low-level in comparison to the abstraction level at which Java programmers are accustomed to writing code. For example, in Java we do not deal with manual memory management, so why do Java programmers have to deal with low-level threading creation and other lifecycle events?

Fortunately, modern Java offers an environment that enables significant performance to be gained from abstractions built into the language and standard library. This allows developers to have the advantages of concurrent programming with fewer low-level frustrations and less boilerplate.

Streams and Parallel Streams

By far the biggest change in Java 8 (arguably the biggest change ever) was the introduction of lambdas and streams. Used together, lambdas and streams provide a sort of "magic switch" to allow Java developers to access some of the benefits of a functional style of programming.

Leaving aside the rather complex question of just how functional Java 8 actually is as a language, we can say that Java now has a new paradigm of programming. This more functional style involves focusing on data rather than the imperative object-oriented approach that it has always had.

A stream in Java is an immutable sequence of data items that conveys elements from a data source. A stream can be from any source (collection, I/O) of typed data. We operate on streams using manipulating operations, such as map(), that accept lambda expressions or function objects to manipulate data. This change from external iteration (traditional for loops) to internal iteration (streams) provides us with some nice opportunities to parallelize data and to lazily evaluate complicated expressions.

All collections now provide the stream() method from the Collection interface. This is a default method that provides an implementation to create a stream from any collection, and behind the scenes a ReferencePipeline is created.

A second method, parallelStream(), can be used to work on the data items in parallel and recombine the results. Using parallelStream() involves separating the work using a Spliterator and executing the computation on the common Fork/Join pool. This is a convenient technique to work on embarrassingly parallel problems, because stream items are intended to be immutable and so allow us to avoid the problem of mutating state when working in parallel.

The introduction of streams has yielded a more syntactically friendly way of working with Fork/Join than recoding using `RecursiveAction`. Expressing problems in terms of the data is similar to task abstraction in that it helps the developer avoid having to consider low-level threading mechanics and data mutability concerns.

It can be tempting to always use `parallelStream()`, but there is a cost to using this approach. As with any parallel computation, work has to be done to split up the task across multiple threads and then to recombine the results—a direct example of Amdahl's Law.

On smaller collections serial computation can actually be much quicker. You should always use caution and performance-test when using `parallelStream()`. Missing out on compute power could be disastrous, but the message of "measure, don't guess" applies here. In terms of using parallel streams to gain performance, the benefit needs to be direct and measurable, so don't just blindly convert a sequential stream to parallel.

Lock-Free Techniques

Lock-free techniques start from the premise that blocking is bad for throughput and can degrade performance. The problem with blocking is that it yields to the operating system to show that there is an opportunity to context-switch the thread.

Consider an application running two threads, t1 and t2, on a two-core machine. A lock scenario could result in threads being context-switched out and back onto the other processor. In addition, the time taken to pause and wake can be significant, meaning that locking can be a lot slower than a technique that is lock-free.

One modern design pattern that highlights the potential performance gains of lock-free concurrency is the Disruptor pattern, originally introduced by the London Multi Asset Exchange (LMAX). When benchmarked against an `ArrayBlockingQueue`, the Disruptor outperformed it by orders of magnitude. The GitHub project page (*https:// github.com/LMAX-Exchange/disruptor/wiki/Performance-Results*) shows some of these comparisons. One sample from the web page has the performance numbers listed in Table 12-1.

Table 12-1. LMAX performance statistics: Throughput in ops per second

	Array blocking queue	Disruptor
Unicast: 1P–1C	5,339,256	25,998,336
Pipeline: 1P–3C	2,128,918	16,806,157
Sequencer: 3P–1C	5,539,531	13,403,268
Multicast: 1P–3C	1,077,384	9,377,871

These astonishing results are achieved with a spinlock. The synchronization is effectively manually controlled between the two threads by way of a `volatile` variable (to ensure visibility across threads):

```
private volatile int proceedValue;

//...

while (i != proceedValue) {
    // busy loop
}
```

Keeping the CPU core spinning means that once data is received, it is immediately ready to operate on that core with no context switching required.

Of course, lock-free techniques also come at a cost. Occupying a CPU core is expensive in terms of utilization and power consumption: the computer is going to be busier doing nothing, but busier also implies hotter, which means more power will be required to cool down the core that's processing nothing.

Running applications that require this kind of throughput often requires the programmer to have a good understanding of the low-level implications of the software. This should be supplemented by a mechanical sympathy for how the code will interact with the hardware. It is not a coincidence that the term *mechanical sympathy* was coined by Martin Thompson, one of the originators of the Disruptor pattern.

> The name "mechanical sympathy" comes from the great racing driver Jackie Stewart, who was a three times world Formula 1 champion. He believed the best drivers had enough understanding of how a machine worked so they could work in harmony with it.
>
> —Martin Thompson

Actor-Based Techniques

In recent years, several different approaches to representing tasks that are somehow *smaller* than a thread have emerged. We have already met this idea in the `ForkJoin Task` class. Another popular approach is the *actor paradigm*.

Actors are small, self-contained processing units that contain their own state, have their own behavior, and include a mailbox system to communicate with other actors. Actors manage the problem of state by not sharing any mutable state and only communicating with each other via immutable messages. The communication between actors is asynchronous, and actors are reactive to the receipt of a message to perform their specified task.

By forming a network in which they each have specific tasks within a parallel system, actors take the view of abstracting away from the underlying concurrency model completely.

Actors can live within the same process, but are not required to. This opens up a nice advantage that actor systems can be multiprocess and even potentially span multiple machines. Multiple machines and clustering enables actor-based systems to perform effectively when a degree of fault tolerance is required. To ensure that actors work successfully in a collaborative environment, they typically have a fail-fast strategy.

For JVM-based languages, Akka is a popular framework for developing actor-based systems. It is written in Scala but also has a Java API, making it usable for Java and other JVM languages as well.

The motivation for Akka and an actor-based system is based on several problems that make concurrent programming difficult. The Akka documentation (*http:// doc.akka.io/docs/akka/2.5/java/guide/actors-motivation.html*) highlights three core motivations for considering the use of Akka over traditional locking schemes:

- Encapsulating mutable state within the domain model can be tricky, especially if a reference to the objects internals is allowed to escape without control.
- Protecting state with locks can cause significant reduction in throughput.
- Locks can lead to deadlock and other types of liveness problems.

Additional problems highlighted include the difficulty of getting shared memory usage correct and the performance problems this can introduce by forcing cache lines to be shared across multiple CPUs.

The final motivation discussed is related to failures in traditional threading models and call stacks. In the low-level threading API, there is no standard way to handle thread failure or recovery. Akka standardizes this, and provides a well-defined recovery scheme for the developer.

Overall, the actor model can be a useful addition to the concurrent developer's toolbox. However, it is not a general-purpose replacement for all other techniques. If the use case fits within the actor style (asynchronous passing of immutable messages, no shared mutable state, and time-bounded execution of every message processor), then it can be an excellent quick win. If, however, the system design includes request-response synchronous processing, shared mutable state, or unbounded execution, then careful developers may choose to use another abstraction for building their systems.

Summary

This chapter only scratches the surface of topics that you should consider before aiming to improve application performance using multithreading. When converting a single-threaded application to a concurrent design:

- Ensure that the performance of straight-line processing can be measured accurately.
- Apply a change and test that the performance is actually improved.
- Ensure that the performance tests are easy to rerun, especially if the size of data processed by the system is likely to change.

Avoid the temptation to:

- Use parallel streams everywhere.
- Create complicated data structures with manual locking.
- Reinvent structures already provided in `java.util.concurrent`.

Aim to:

- Improve thread hot performance using concurrent collections.
- Use access designs that take advantage of the underlying data structures.
- Reduce locking across the application.
- Provide appropriate task/asynchronous abstractions to prevent having to deal with threads manually.

Taking a step back, concurrency is key to the future of high-performance code. However:

- Shared mutable state is hard.
- Locks can be challenging to use correctly.
- Both synchronized and asynchronous state sharing models are needed.
- The JMM is a low-level, flexible model.
- The thread abstraction is very low-level.

The trend in modern concurrency is to move to a higher-level concurrency model and away from threads, which are increasingly looking like the "assembly language of concurrency." Recent versions of Java have increased the amount of higher-level classes and libraries available to the programmer. On the whole, the industry seems to be moving to a model of concurrency where far more of the responsibility for safe concurrent abstractions is managed by the runtime and libraries.

## CHAPTER 13

Profiling

The term *profiling* has a somewhat loose usage among programmers. There are in fact several different approaches to profiling that are possible, of which the two most common are:

- Execution
- Allocation

In this chapter, we will cover both of these topics. Our initial focus will be on execution profiling, and we will use this subject to introduce the tools that are available to profile applications. Later in the chapter we will introduce memory profiling and see how the various tools provide this capability.

One of the key themes that we will explore is just how important it is for Java developers and performance engineers to understand the way in which profilers in general operate. Profilers are very capable of misrepresenting application behavior and exhibiting noticeable biases.

Execution profiling is one of the areas of performance analysis where these biases come to the fore. The cautious performance engineer will be aware of this possibility and will compensate for it in various ways, including profiling with multiple tools in order to understand what's really going on.

It is equally important for engineers to address their own cognitive biases, and to not go looking for the performance behavior that they expect. The antipatterns and cognitive traps that we met in Chapter 4 are a good place to start when training ourselves to avoid these problems.

Introduction to Profiling

In general, JVM profiling and monitoring tools operate by using some low-level instrumentation and either feeding data back to a graphical console or saving it in a log for later analysis. The low-level instrumentation usually takes the form of either an agent loaded at application start or a component that dynamically attaches to a running JVM.

Agents were introduced in "Monitoring and Tooling for the JVM" on page 29; they are a very general technique with wide applicability in the Java tooling space.

In broad terms, we need to distinguish between *monitoring tools* (whose primary goal is observing the system and its current state), *alerting systems* (for detecting abnormal or anomalous behavior), and *profilers* (which provide deep-dive information about running applications). These tools have different, although often related, objectives and a well-run production application may make use of all of them.

The focus of this chapter, however, is profiling. The aim of (execution) profiling is to identify user-written code that is a target for refactoring and performance optimization.

Profiling is usually achieved by attaching a custom agent to the JVM executing the application.

As discussed in "Basic Detection Strategies" on page 48, the first step in diagnosing and correcting a performance problem is to identify which resource is causing the issue. An incorrect identification at this step can prove very costly.

If we perform a profiling analysis on an application that is not being limited by CPU cycles, then it is very easy to be badly misled by the output of the profiler. To expand on the Brian Goetz quote from "Introduction to JMH" on page 90, the tools will always produce a number—it's just not clear that the number has any relevance to the problem being addressed. It is for this reason that we introduced the main types of bias in "Cognitive Biases and Performance Testing" on page 79 and delayed discussion of profiling techniques until now.

A good programmer…will be wise to look carefully at the critical code; but only *after* that code has been identified.

—Donald Knuth

This means that before undertaking a profiling exercise, performance engineers should have already identified a performance problem. Not only that, but they should also have proved that application code is to blame. They will know this is the case if the application is consuming close to 100% of CPU in user mode.

If these criteria are not met, the engineer should look elsewhere for the source of the problem and should not attempt to diagnose further with an execution profiler.

Even if the CPU is fully maxed out in user mode (not kernel time), there is another possible cause that must be ruled out before profiling: STW phases of GC. As all applications that are serious about performance should be logging GC events, this check is a simple one: consult the GC log and application logs for the machine and ensure that the GC log is quiet and the application log shows activity. If the GC log is the active one, then GC tuning should be the next step—not execution profiling.

Sampling and Safepointing Bias

One key aspect of execution profiling is that it usually uses sampling to obtain data points (stack traces) of what code is running. After all, it is not cost-free to take measurements, so all method entries and exits are not usually tracked in order to prevent an excessive data collection cost. Instead, a snapshot of thread execution is taken— but this can only be done at a relatively low frequency without unacceptable overhead.

For example, the New Relic Thread Profiler (one of the tools available as part of the New Relic stack) will sample every 100 ms. This limit is often considered a best guess on how often samples can be taken without incurring high overhead.

The sampling interval represents a tradeoff for the performance engineer. Sample too frequently and the overhead becomes unacceptable, especially for an application that cares about performance. On the other hand, sample too infrequently and the chance of missing important behavior becomes too large, as the sampling may not reflect the real performance of the application.

By the time you're using a profiler it should be filling in detail—it shouldn't be surprising you.

—Kirk Pepperdine

Not only does sampling offer opportunities for problems to hide in the data, but in most cases sampling has only been performed at safepoints. This is known as *safepointing bias* and has two primary consequences:

- All threads must reach a safepoint before a sample can be taken.
- The sample can only be of an application state that is at a safepoint.

The first of these imposes additional overhead on producing a profiling sample from a running process. The second consequence skews the distribution of sample points, by sampling only the state when it is already known to be at a safepoint.

Most execution profilers use the `GetCallTrace()` function from HotSpot's C++ API to collect stack samples for each application thread. The usual design is to collect the samples within an agent, and then log the data or perform other downstream processing.

However, `GetCallTrace()` has a quite severe overhead: if there are N active application threads, then collecting a stack sample will cause the JVM to safepoint N times. This overhead is one of the root causes that set an upper limit on the frequency with which samples can be taken.

The careful performance engineer will therefore keep an eye on how much safepointing time is being used by the application. If too much time is spent in safepointing, then the application performance will suffer, and any tuning exercise may be acting on inaccurate data. A JVM flag that can be very useful for tracking down cases of high safepointing time is:

```
-XX:+PrintGCApplicationStoppedTime
```

This will write extra information about safepointing time into the GC log. Some tools (notably jClarity Censum) can automatically detect problems from the data produced by this flag. Censum can also differentiate between safepointing time and pause time imposed by the OS kernel.

One example of the problems caused by safepointing bias can be illustrated by a *counted loop*. This is a simple loop, of a similar form to this snippet:

```
for (int i = 0; i < LIMIT; i++) {
    // only "simple" operations in the loop body
}
```

We have deliberately elided the meaning of a "simple" operation in this example, as the behavior is dependent on the exact optimizations that the JIT compiler can perform. Further relevant details can be found in "Loop Unrolling" on page 233.

Examples of simple operations include arithmetic operations on primitives and method calls that have been fully inlined (so that no methods are actually within the body of the loop).

If LIMIT is large, then the JIT compiler will translate this Java code directly into an equivalent compiled form, including a back branch to return to the top of the loop. As discussed in "Safepoints Revisited" on page 251, the JIT compiler inserts safepoint checks at loop-back edges. This means that for a large loop, there will be an opportunity to safepoint once per loop iteration.

However, for a small enough LIMIT this will not occur, and instead the JIT compiler will unroll this loop. This means that the thread executing the small-enough counted loop will not safepoint until after the loop has completed.

Only sampling at safepoints has thus led directly to a biasing behavior that is sensitively dependent on the size of the loops and the nature of operations that we perform in them.

This is obviously not ideal for rigorous and reliable performance results. Nor is this a theoretical concern—loop unrolling can generate significant amounts of code, leading to long chunks of code where no samples will ever be collected.

We will return to the problem of safepointing bias, but it remains an excellent example of the kinds of tradeoffs that performance engineers need to be aware of.

Execution Profiling Tools for Developers

In this section we will discuss several different execution profiling tools with graphical UIs. There are quite a few tools available in the market, so we focus on a selection of the most common rather than attempting an exhaustive survey.

VisualVM Profiler

As a first example of a profiling tool, let's consider VisualVM (*https://visualvm.github.io/*). It includes both an execution and a memory profiler and is a very straightforward free profiling tool. It is quite limited in that it is rarely usable as a production tool, but it can be helpful to performance engineers who want to understand the behavior of their applications in dev and QA environments.

In Figure 13-1 we can see the execution profiling view of VisualVM.

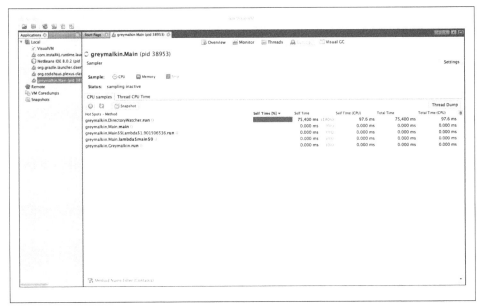

Figure 13-1. VisualVM memory profiler

This shows a simple view of executing methods and their relative CPU consumption. The amount of drilldown that is possible within VisualVM is really quite limited. As a result, most performance engineers quickly outgrow it and turn to one of the more complete tools on the market. However, it can be a useful first tool for performance engineers who are new to the art of and tradeoffs involved in profiling.

JProfiler

One popular commercial profiler is JProfiler (*https://www.ej-technologies.com/prod ucts/jprofiler/overview.html*) from ej-technologies GmbH. This is an agent-based profiler capable of running as a GUI tool as well as in headless mode to profile local or remote applications. It is compatible with a fairly wide range of operating systems, including FreeBSD, Solaris, and AIX, as well as the more usual Windows, macOS, and Linux.

When the desktop application is started for the first time, a screen similar to that shown in Figure 13-2 is displayed.

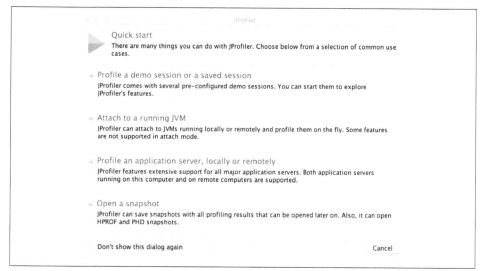

Figure 13-2. JProfiler startup wizard

Clearing this screen gives the default view show in Figure 13-3.

Figure 13-3. JProfiler startup screen

Clicking the Start Center button at the top left gives a variety of options, including Open Session (which contains some precanned examples to work with) and Quick Attach. Figure 13-4 shows the Quick Attach option, where we're choosing to profile the AsciidocFX application, which is the authoring tool in which much of this book was written.

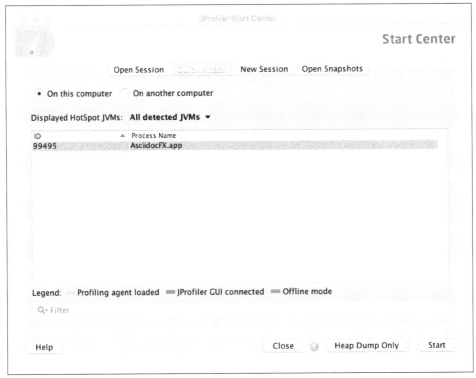

Figure 13-4. JProfiler Quick Attach screen

Attachment to the target JVM brings up a configuration dialog, as shown in Figure 13-5. Note that the profiler is already warning of performance tradeoffs in the configuration of the tool, as well as a need for effective filters and an awareness of the overhead of profiling. As discussed earlier in the chapter, execution profiling is very much not a silver bullet, and the engineer must proceed carefully to avoid confusion.

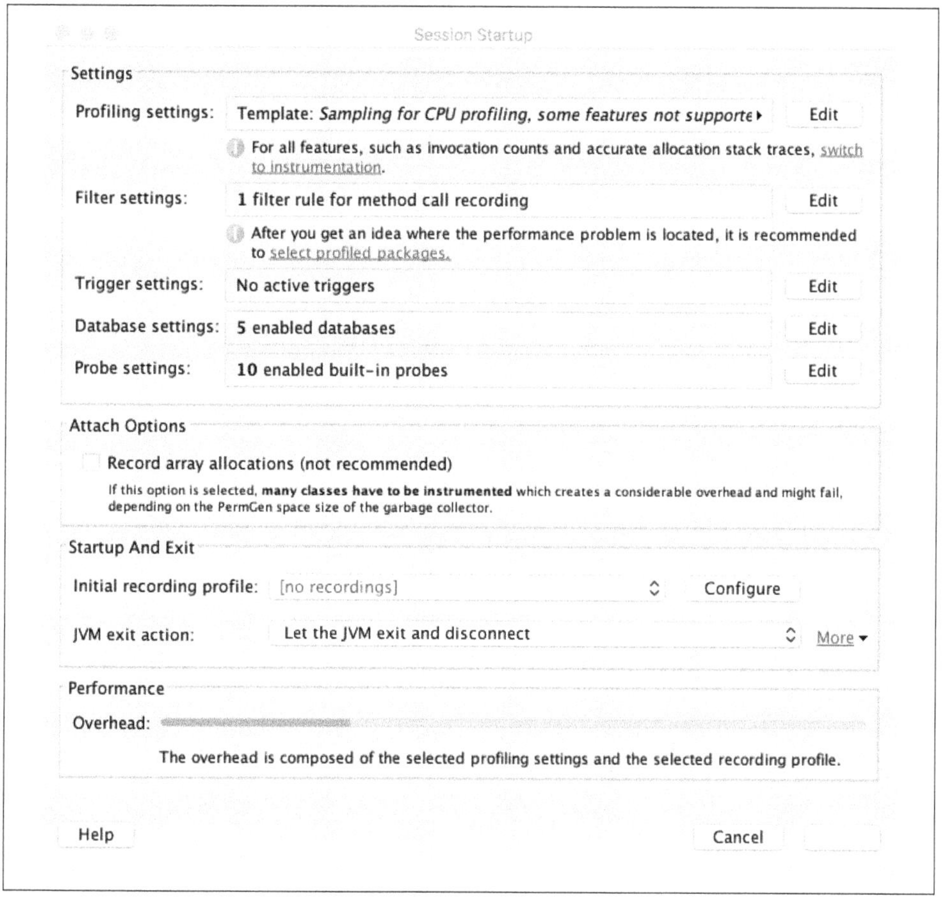

Figure 13-5. JProfiler attach configuration

After an initial scan, JProfiler springs into life. The initial screen shows a telemetry view similar to that of VisualVM, but with a scrolling display rather than the time-resizing view. This view is shown in Figure 13-6.

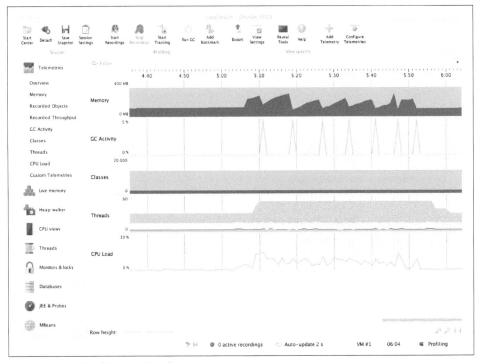

Figure 13-6. JProfiler simple telemetry

From this screen, all the basic views can be accessed, but without switching on some recordings not much can be seen. To see method timings, choose the Call Tree view and press the button to start recording. After a few seconds the results of profiling will start to show up. This should look something like Figure 13-7.

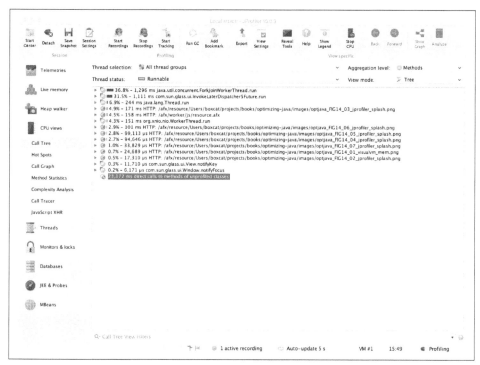

Figure 13-7. JProfiler CPU times

The tree view can be expanded to show the intrinsic time of methods that each method calls.

To use the JProfiler agent, add this switch to the run configuration:

```
-agentpath:<path-to-agent-lib>
```

In the default configuration, this will cause the profiled application to pause on startup and wait for a GUI to connect. The intent of this is to front-load the instrumentation of application classes at startup time, so that the application will then run normally.

For the case of production applications, it would not be normal to attach a GUI. In this case the JProfiler agent needs to be added with a configuration that indicates what data to record. These results are only saved to snapshot files to be loaded into the GUI later. JProfiler provides a wizard for configuring remote profiling and appropriate settings to add to the remote JVM.

Finally, the careful reader should note that in the screenshots we are showing the profile of a GUI app that is not CPU-bound, so the results are for demonstration purposes only. The CPU is nowhere near 100% utilized, so this is not a realistic use case for JProfiler (or any other profiling tool).

YourKit

The YourKit profiler (*https://www.yourkit.com/*) is another commercial profiler, produced by YourKit GmbH. The YourKit tool is similar to JProfiler in some ways, offering a GUI component as well as an agent that can either attach dynamically or be configured to run at application start.

To deploy the agent, use the following syntax (for 64-bit Linux):

```
-agentpath:<profiler-dir>/bin/linux-x86-64/libyjpagent.so
```

From the GUI perspective, it features similar setup and initial telemetry screens to those seen in VisualVM and JProfiler.

In Figure 13-8 we can see the CPU snapshot view, with drilldown into how the CPU is spending its time. This level of detail goes well beyond what is possible with VisualVM.

Figure 13-8. YourKit CPU times

In testing, the attach mode of YourKit occasionally displayed some glitches, such as freezing GUI applications. On the whole, though, the execution profiling features of YourKit are broadly on par with those offered by JProfiler; some engineers may simply find one tool more to their personal preference than the other.

If possible, profiling with both YourKit and JProfiler (although not at the same time, as this will introduce extra overhead) may reveal different views of the application that may be useful for diagnosis.

Both tools use the safepointing sampling approach discussed earlier, and so both tools are potentially subject to the same types of limitations and biases induced by this approach.

Flight Recorder and Mission Control

The Java Flight Recorder and Mission Control (JFR/JMC) tools (*https:// docs.oracle.com/javacomponents/index.html*) are profiling and monitoring technologies that Oracle obtained as part of its acquisition of BEA Systems. They were previously part of the tooling offering for BEA's JRockit JVM. The tools were moved to the commercial version of Oracle JDK as part of the process of retiring JRockit.

As of Java 8, Flight Recorder and Mission Control are commercial and proprietary tools. They are available only for the Oracle JVM and will not work with OpenJDK builds or any other JVM.

As JFR is available only for Oracle JDK, you must pass the following switches when starting up an Oracle JVM with Flight Recorder:

```
-XX:+UnlockCommercialFeatures -XX:+FlightRecorder
```

In September 2017, Oracle announced a major change to the release schedule of Java, moving it from a two-year release cycle to a six-month cadence. This was the result of the two previous releases (Java 8 and 9) being significantly delayed.

In addition to the decision to change the release cycle, Oracle also announced that post–Java 9, the primary JDK distributed by Oracle would become OpenJDK rather than Oracle JDK. As part of this change, Flight Recorder and Mission Control would become open source tools that are free to use.

At the time of writing, a detailed roadmap for the availability of JFR/JMC as free and open source features has not been announced. Neither has it been announced whether deployments of Java 8 or 9 will need to pay for production usage of JFR/ JMC.

 The initial installation of JMC consists of a JMX Console and JFR, although more plug-ins can easily be installed from within Mission Control.

JMC is the graphical component, and is started up from the jmc binary in *$JAVA_HOME/bin*. The startup screen for Mission Control can be seen in Figure 13-9.

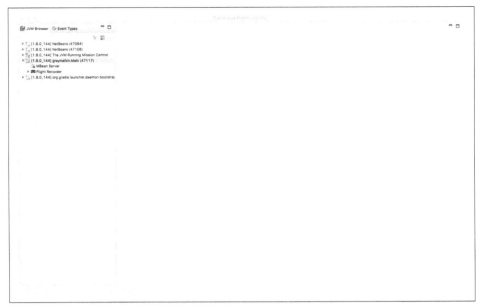

Figure 13-9. JMC startup screen

To profile, Flight Recorder must be enabled on the target application. You can achieve this either by starting with the flags enabled, or by dynamically attaching after the application has already started.

Once attached, enter the configuration for the recording session and the profiling events, as shown in Figures 13-10 and 13-11.

Figure 13-10. JMC recording setup

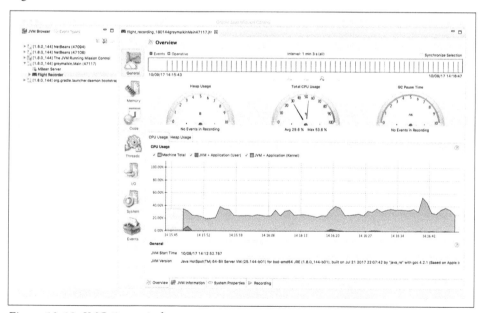

Figure 13-11. *JMC profiling event options*

When the recording starts, this is typically displayed in a time window, as shown in Figure 13-12.

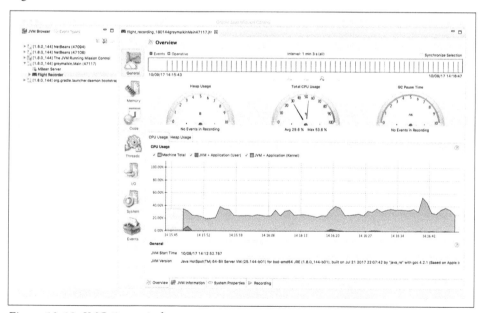

Figure 13-12. *JMC time window*

To support the port of JFR from JRockit, the HotSpot VM was instrumented to produce a large basket of performance counters similar to those collected in the Serviceability Agent.

Operational Tools

Profilers are, by their nature, developer tools used to diagnose problems or to understand the runtime behavior of applications at a low level. At the other end of the tooling spectrum are operational monitoring tools. These exist to help a team visualize the current state of the system and determine whether the system is operating normally or is anomalous.

This is a huge space, and a full discussion is outside the scope of this book. Instead, we'll briefly cover three tools in this space, two proprietary and one open source.

Red Hat Thermostat

Thermostat (*http://icedtea.classpath.org/thermostat/*) is Red Hat's open source serviceability and monitoring solution for HotSpot-based JVMs. It is available under the same license as OpenJDK itself, and provides monitoring for both single machines and clusters. It uses MongoDB to store historical data as well as point-in-time capabilities.

Thermostat is designed to be an open, extensible platform and consists of an agent and a client (typically a simple GUI). A simple Thermostat view can be seen in Figure 13-13.

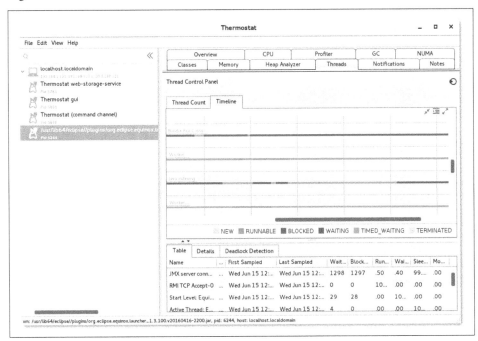

Figure 13-13. Red Hat Thermostat

Thermostat's architecture allows for extension. For example, you can:

- Collect and analyze your own custom metrics.
- Inject custom code for on-demand instrumentation.
- Write custom plug-ins and integrate tooling.

Most of Thermostat's built-in functionality is actually implemented as plug-ins.

New Relic

The New Relic (*https://newrelic.com/java*) tool is a SaaS product designed for cloud-based applications. It is a general-purpose toolset, covering much more than just JVMs.

In the JVM space, installation requires downloading an agent, passing a switch to the JVM, and restarting the server. Following this, New Relic will produce views similar to that shown in Figure 13-14.

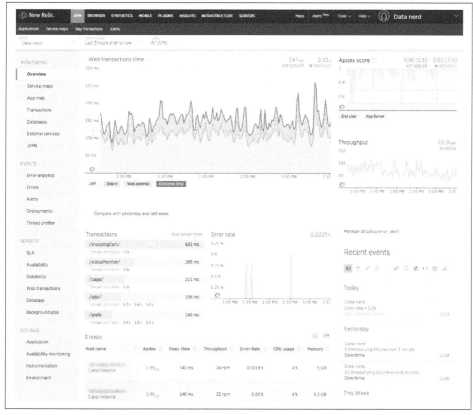

Figure 13-14. New Relic

The general monitoring and full-stack support provided by New Relic can make it an attractive operational and devops tool. However, being a general tool, it has no specific focus on JVM technologies and relies out of the box on the less sophisticated sources of data available from the JVM. This means that for deep-dive information on the JVM, it may need to be combined with more specific tooling.

New Relic provides a Java agent API (*https://docs.newrelic.com/docs/agents/java-agent/custom-instrumentation/java-agent-api*), or users can implement custom instrumentation (*https://docs.newrelic.com/docs/agents/java-agent/custom-instrumentation/java-custom-instrumentation*) to extend its base functionality.

It also suffers from the problem that it generates a huge amount of data, and as a result it can sometimes be difficult to spot anything other than obvious trends in the output.

jClarity Illuminate

A tool that provides a bridge between the developer profiling tools and operational monitoring is jClarity Illuminate (*https://www.jclarity.com/illuminate/*). This is not a traditional sampling profiler but instead operates in a monitoring mode with a separate out-of-process daemon that watches the main Java application. If it detects an anomaly in the behavior of the running JVM, such as a service-level agreement (SLA) being breached, Illuminate will initiate a deep-dive probe of the application.

Illuminate's machine learning algorithm analyzes data collected from the OS, GC logs, and the JVM to determine the root cause of the performance problem. It generates a detailed report and sends it to the user along with some possible next steps to fix the issue. The machine learning algorithm is based on the Performance Diagnostic Model (PDM) originally created by Kirk Pepperdine, one of the founders of jClarity.

In Figure 13-15 we can see the *triage* mode of Illuminate when it is investigating a problem that has been automatically spotted.

The tool is based on machine learning techniques and is focused on in-depth root-cause analysis, rather than the overwhelming "wall of data" sometimes encountered in monitoring tools. It also drastically reduces the amount of data it needs to collect, move over the network, and store, in an attempt to be a much lower-impact application performance monitoring tool than others in the space.

Figure 13-15. jClarity Illuminate

Modern Profilers

In this section we will discuss three modern open source tools that can provide better insight and more accurate performance numbers than traditional profilers. These tools are:

- Honest Profiler
- perf
- Async Profiler

Honest Profiler (*https://github.com/jvm-profiling-tools/honest-profiler*) is a relatively recent arrival to the profiling tool space. It is an open source project led by Richard Warburton, and derives from prototype code written and open-sourced by Jeremy Manson from the Google engineering team.

The key goals of Honest Profiler are to:

- Remove the safepointing bias that most other profilers have.
- Operate with significantly lower overhead.

To achieve this, it makes use of a private API call called `AsyncGetCallTrace` within HotSpot. This means, of course, that Honest Profiler will not work on a non-OpenJDK JVM. It will work with Oracle, Red Hat, and Azul Zulu JVMs as well as HotSpot JVMs that have been built from scratch.

The implementation uses the Unix OS signal SIGPROF to interrupt a running thread. The call stack can then be collected via the private `AsyncGetCallTrace()` method.

This only interrupts threads individually, so there is never any kind of global synchronization event. This avoids the contention and overhead typically seen in traditional profilers. Within the asynchronous callback the call trace is written into a lock-free ring buffer. A dedicated separate thread then writes out the details to a log without pausing the application.

> Honest Profiler isn't the only profiler to take this approach. For example, Flight Recorder also uses the `AsyncGetCallTrace()` call.

Historically, Sun Microsystems also offered the older Solaris Studio product, which also used the private API call. Unfortunately, the name of the product was rather confusing—it actually ran on other operating systems too, not just Solaris—and it failed to gain adoption.

One disadvantage of Honest Profiler is that it may show "Unknown" at the top of some threads. This is a side effect of JVM intrinsics; the profiler is unable to map back to a true Java stack trace correctly in that case.

To use Honest Profiler, the profiler agent must be installed:

```
-agentpath:<path-to-liblagent.so>=interval=<n>,logPath=<path-to-log.hpl>
```

Honest Profiler includes a relatively simple GUI for working with profiles. This is based on JavaFX and so will require installation of OpenJFX in order to run on an OpenJDK-based build (such as Azul Zulu or Red Hat IcedTea).

Figure 13-16 shows a typical Honest Profiler GUI screen.

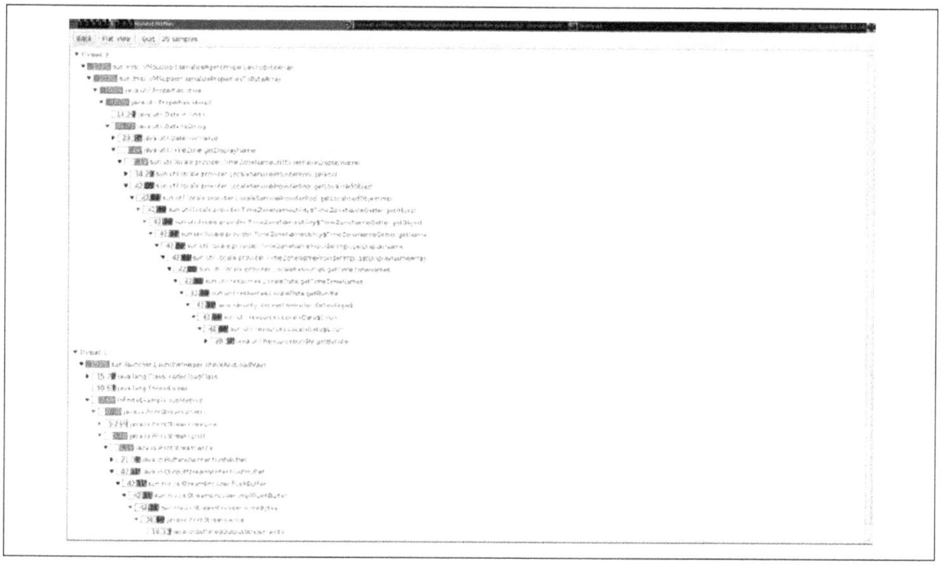

Figure 13-16. Honest Profiler

In practice, tools like Honest Profiler are more commonly run in headless mode as data collection tools. In this approach, visualization is provided by other tooling or custom scripts.

The project does provide binaries, but they are quite limited in scope—only for a recent Linux build. Most serious users of Honest Profiler will need to build their own binary from scratch, a topic which is out of scope for this book.

The perf tool (*https://perf.wiki.kernel.org/index.php/Main_Page*) is a useful lightweight profiling solution for applications that run on Linux. It is not specific to Java/JVM applications but instead reads hardware performance counters and is included in the Linux kernel, under *tools/perf*.

Performance counters are physical registers that count hardware events of interest to performance analysts. These include instructions executed, cache misses, and branch mispredictions. This forms a basis for profiling applications.

Java presents some additional challenges for perf, due to the dynamic nature of the Java runtime environment. To use perf with Java applications, we need a bridge to handle mapping the dynamic parts of Java execution.

This bridge is perf-map-agent (*https://github.com/jvm-profiling-tools/perf-map-agent*), an agent that will generate dynamic symbols for perf from unknown memory regions (including JIT-compiled methods). Due to HotSpot's dynamically created interpreter and jump tables for virtual dispatch, these must also have entries generated.

perf-map-agent consists of an agent written in C and a small Java bootstrap that attaches the agent to a running Java process if needed. In Java 8u60 a new flag was added to enable better interaction with perf:

```
-XX:+PreserveFramePointer
```

When using perf to profile Java applications, it is strongly advised that you are running on 8u60 or later, to give access to this flag.

> Using this flag disables a JIT compiler optimization, so it does decrease performance slightly (by up to 3% in tests).

One striking visualization of the numbers perf produces is the flame graph (*https://github.com/brendangregg/FlameGraph*). This shows a highly detailed breakdown of exactly where execution time is being spent. An example can be seen in Figure 13-17.

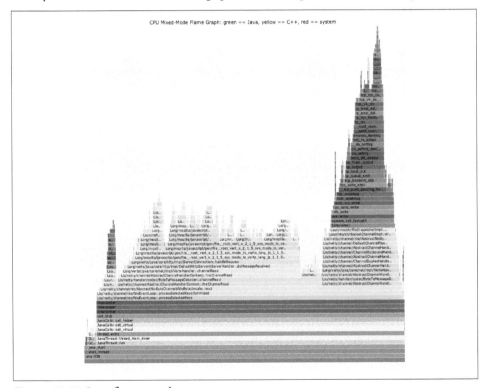

Figure 13-17. Java flame graph

The Netflix Technology Blog has some detailed coverage (*https://medium.com/netflix-techblog/java-in-flames-e763b3d32166*) of how the team has implemented flame graphs on its JVMs.

Finally, an alternative choice to Honest Profiler is Async Profiler (*https://github.com/jvm-profiling-tools/async-profiler*). It uses the same internal API as Honest Profiler, and is an open source tool that runs only on HotSpot JVMs. Its reliance on perf means that Async Profiler also works only on the operating systems where perf works (primarily Linux).

Allocation Profiling

Execution profiling is an important aspect of profiling—but it is not the only one! Most applications will also require some level of memory profiling, and one standard approach is to consider the allocation behavior of the application. There are several possible approaches to allocation profiling.

For example, we could use the `HeapVisitor` approach that tools like `jmap` rely upon. In Figure 13-18 we can see the memory profiling view of VisualVM, which uses this simple approach.

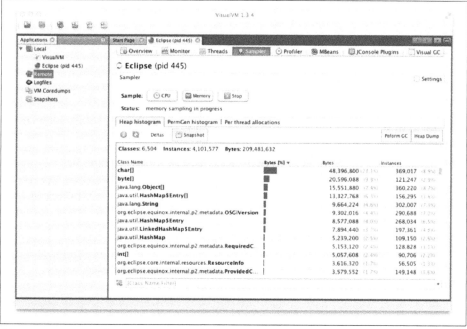

Figure 13-18. VisualVM memory profiler

A similar view can be seen in Figure 13-19, where we show the same capability using the YourKit allocation profiler.

Figure 13-19. YourKit memory profiler

For the JMC tool, the garbage collection statistics contain some values not available in the traditional Serviceability Agent. However, the vast majority of counters presented are duplicates. The advantage is that the cost for JFR to collect these values so they can be displayed in JMC is much cheaper than it is with the SA. The JMC displays also provide greater flexibility to the performance engineer in terms of how the details are displayed.

Another approach to allocation profiling is agent-based profiling. This can be done in several ways, one of the simplest of which is to instrument the bytecode. As seen in "Introduction to JVM Bytecode" on page 202, there are three bytecodes that instruct the JVM to allocate memory:

NEW
    Allocates space for a new object of a specified type

NEWARRAY
    Allocates space for an array of primitives

ANEWARRAY
    Allocates space for an array of objects of a specified type

These are the only bytecodes that need to be instrumented, as they are the only opcodes that can cause allocation to occur.

A simple instrumentation approach would consist of locating every instance of any of the allocation opcodes and inserting a call to a static method that logs the allocation before the allocation opcode executes.

Let's look at the skeleton of such an allocation profiler. We will need to set up the agent using the instrumentation API via a `premain()` hook:

```java
public class AllocAgent {

    public static void premain(String args, Instrumentation instrumentation) {
        AllocRewriter transformer = new AllocRewriter();
        instrumentation.addTransformer(transformer);
    }

}
```

To perform this sort of bytecode instrumentation it is usual to use a library, rather than trying to perform the transformations with hand-rolled code. One common bytecode manipulation library in wide use is ASM (*http://asm.ow2.org/*), which we will use to demonstrate allocation profiling.

To add the required allocation instrumentation code, we need a class rewriter. This provides the bridge between the instrumentation API and ASM and looks like this:

```java
public class AllocRewriter implements ClassFileTransformer {

    @Override
    public byte[] transform(ClassLoader loader, String className,
      Class<?> classBeingRedefined, ProtectionDomain protectionDomain,
      byte[] originalClassContents) throws IllegalClassFormatException {
        final ClassReader reader = new ClassReader(originalClassContents);
        final ClassWriter writer = new ClassWriter(reader,
            ClassWriter.COMPUTE_FRAMES | ClassWriter.COMPUTE_MAXS);
        final ClassVisitor coster = new ClassVisitor(Opcodes.ASM5, writer) {
            @Override
            public MethodVisitor visitMethod(final int access, final String name,
                final String desc, final String signature,
                final String[] exceptions) {
                final MethodVisitor baseMethodVisitor =
                    super.visitMethod(access, name, desc, signature, exceptions);
                return new AllocationRecordingMethodVisitor(baseMethodVisitor,
                    access, name, desc);
            }
        };
        reader.accept(coster, ClassReader.EXPAND_FRAMES);
        return writer.toByteArray();
    }

}
```

This uses a method visitor to inspect the bytecode and insert instrumentation calls to allow the allocation to be tracked:

```java
public final class AllocationRecordingMethodVisitor extends GeneratorAdapter {
    private final String runtimeAccounterTypeName =
        "optjava/bc/RuntimeCostAccounter";

    public AllocationRecordingMethodVisitor(MethodVisitor methodVisitor,
        int access, String name, String desc) {
        super(Opcodes.ASM5, methodVisitor, access, name, desc);
    }

    /**
     * This method is called when visiting an opcode with a single int operand.
     * For our purposes this is a NEWARRAY opcode.
     *
     * @param opcode
     * @param operand
     */
    @Override
    public void visitIntInsn(final int opcode, final int operand) {
        if (opcode != Opcodes.NEWARRAY) {
            super.visitIntInsn(opcode, operand);
            return;
        }

        // Opcode is NEWARRAY - recordArrayAllocation:(Ljava/lang/String;I)V
        // Operand value should be one of Opcodes.T_BOOLEAN,
        // Opcodes.T_CHAR, Opcodes.T_FLOAT, Opcodes.T_DOUBLE, Opcodes.T_BYTE,
        // Opcodes.T_SHORT, Opcodes.T_INT or Opcodes.T_LONG.
        final int typeSize;
        switch (operand) {
            case Opcodes.T_BOOLEAN:
            case Opcodes.T_BYTE:
                typeSize = 1;
                break;
            case Opcodes.T_SHORT:
            case Opcodes.T_CHAR:
                typeSize = 2;
                break;
            case Opcodes.T_INT:
            case Opcodes.T_FLOAT:
                typeSize = 4;
                break;
            case Opcodes.T_LONG:
            case Opcodes.T_DOUBLE:
                typeSize = 8;
                break;
            default:
                throw new IllegalStateException("Illegal op: to NEWARRAY seen: "
                    + operand);
        }
```

```
            super.visitInsn(Opcodes.DUP);
            super.visitLdcInsn(typeSize);
            super.visitMethodInsn(Opcodes.INVOKESTATIC, runtimeAccounterTypeName,
                "recordArrayAllocation", "(II)V", true);
            super.visitIntInsn(opcode, operand);
        }

        /**
         * This method is called when visiting an opcode with a single operand, that
         * is a type (represented here as a String).
         *
         * For our purposes this is either a NEW opcode or an ANEWARRAY.
         *
         * @param opcode
         * @param type
         */
        @Override
        public void visitTypeInsn(final int opcode, final String type) {
            // opcode is either NEW - recordAllocation:(Ljava/lang/String;)V
            // or ANEWARRAY - recordArrayAllocation:(Ljava/lang/String;I)V
            switch (opcode) {
                case Opcodes.NEW:
                    super.visitLdcInsn(type);
                    super.visitMethodInsn(Opcodes.INVOKESTATIC,
                        runtimeAccounterTypeName, "recordAllocation",
                        "(Ljava/lang/String;)V", true);
                    break;
                case Opcodes.ANEWARRAY:
                    super.visitInsn(Opcodes.DUP);
                    super.visitLdcInsn(8);
                    super.visitMethodInsn(Opcodes.INVOKESTATIC,
                    runtimeAccounterTypeName, "recordArrayAllocation",
                        "(II)V", true);
                    break;
            }

            super.visitTypeInsn(opcode, type);
        }
    }
}
```

This would also require a small runtime component:

```
public class RuntimeCostAccounter {
    private static final ThreadLocal<Long> allocationCost =
        new ThreadLocal<Long>() {
        @Override
        protected Long initialValue() {
            return 0L;
        }
    };

    public static void recordAllocation(final String typeName) {
        // More sophistication clearly necessary
```

```
            // E.g. caching approximate sizes for types that we encounter
            checkAllocationCost(1);
        }

        public static void recordArrayAllocation(final int length,
            final int multiplier) {
            checkAllocationCost(length * multiplier);
        }

        private static void checkAllocationCost(final long additional) {
            final long newValue = additional + allocationCost.get();
            allocationCost.set(newValue);
            // Take action? E.g. failing if some threshold has been exceeded.
        }

        // This could be exposed, e.g. via a JMX counter
        public static long getAllocationCost() {
            return allocationCost.get();
        }

        public static void resetCounters() {
            allocationCost.set(0L);
        }
    }
```

The aim of these two pieces is to provide simple allocation instrumentation. They use the ASM bytecode manipulation library (a full description of which is unfortunately outside the scope of this book). The method visitor adds in a call to a recording method prior to each instance of the bytecodes NEW, NEWARRAY, and ANEWARRAY.

With this transformation in place, whenever any new object or array is created, the recording method is called. This must be supported at runtime by a small class, the RuntimeCostAccounter (which must be on the classpath). This class maintains per-thread counts of how much memory has been allocated in the instrumented code.

This bytecode-level technique is rather crude, but it should provide a starting point for interested readers to develop their own simple measurements of how much memory is being allocated by their threads. For example, this could be used in a unit or regression test to ensure that changes to the code are not introducing large amounts of extra allocation.

However, for full production usage this approach may not be suitable. There are additional method calls occurring every time memory is allocated, leading to a huge amount of extra calls. JIT compilation will help, as the instrumented calls will be inlined, but the overall effect is likely to have a highly significant effect on performance.

Another approach to allocation profiling is TLAB exhaustion. For example, Async Profiler features TLAB-driven sampling. This uses HotSpot-specific callbacks to receive notifications:

- When an object is allocated in a newly created fresh TLAB
- When an object is allocated outside of a TLAB (the "slow path")

As a result, not every object allocation is counted. Instead, in aggregate, allocations every n KB are recorded, where n is the average size of the TLAB (recall that the size of a TLAB can change over time).

This design aims to make heap sampling cheap enough to be suitable for production. On the other hand, the collected data has been sampled and so may not be complete. The intent is that in practice it will reflect the top allocation sources, at least enough of the time to be useful to the performance engineer.

To use the TLAB sampling feature, a HotSpot JVM with version 7u40 or later is required, because this version is where the TLAB callbacks first appeared.

Heap Dump Analysis

A technique related to allocation profiling is *heap dump analysis*. This is the use of tool to examine a snapshot of an entire heap and determine salient facts, such as the live set and numbers and types of objects, as well as the shape and structure of the object graph.

With a heap dump loaded, performance engineers can then traverse and analyze the snapshot of the heap at the time the heap dump was created. They will be able to see live objects and any objects that have died but not yet been collected.

The primary drawback of heap dumps is their sheer size. A heap dump can frequently be 300–400% the size of the memory being dumped. For a multigigabyte heap this is substantial. Not only must the heap be written to disk, but for a real production use case, it must be retrieved over the network as well. Once retrieved, it must then be loaded on a workstation with sufficient resources (especially memory) to handle the dump without introducing excessive delays to the workflow. Working with large heap dumps on a machine that can't load the whole dump at once can be very painful, as the workstation pages parts of the dump file on and off disk.

Production of a heap file also requires an STW event while the heap is traversed and the dump written out.

YourKit supports capturing memory snapshots in both hprof and a proprietary format. Figure 13-20 shows a view of the heap dump analyzer.

Figure 13-20. YourKit memory dump profiler

Among the commercial tools, YourKit provides a good selection of filters and other views of a heap dump. This includes being able to break it down by classloader and web app, which can lead to faster diagnosis of heap problems.

The Allocations view of JMC/JFR is also worth considering as a tool. It is capable of displaying the TLAB allocation view that is also used by Async Profiler. Figure 13-21 shows a sample image of JMC's view of allocations.

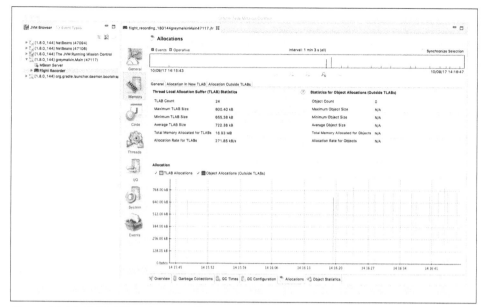

Figure 13-21. JMC Allocations profiling view

Allocation and heap profiling are of interest for the majority of applications that need to be profiled, and performance engineers are encouraged not to overfocus on execution profiling at the expense of memory.

hprof

The `hprof` profiler has shipped with the JDK since version 5. It is largely intended as a reference implementation for the JVMTI technology rather than as a production-grade profiler. Despite this, it is frequently referred to in documentation, and this has led some developers to consider `hprof` a suitable tool for actual use.

As of Java 9 (JEP 240), `hprof` is being removed from the JDK. The removal JEP has this to say on the subject:

> The `hprof` agent was written as demonstration code for the JVM Tool Interface and not intended to be a production tool.

In addition, the code and documentation for `hprof` contain a number of statements of the general form:

> This is demonstration code for the JVM TI interface and use of BCI; it is not an official product or formal part of the JDK.

For this reason, `hprof` should not be relied upon except as a legacy format for heap snapshots. The ability to create heap dumps will continue to be maintained in Java 9 and for the foreseeable future.

Summary

The subject of profiling is one that is often misunderstood by developers. Both execution and memory profiling are necessary techniques. However, it is very important that performance engineers understand what they are doing, and *why*. Simply using the tools blindly can produce completely inaccurate or irrelevant results and waste a lot of analysis time.

Profiling modern applications requires the use of tooling, and there are a wealth of options to choose from, including both commercial and open source options.

## CHAPTER 14

High-Performance Logging and Messaging

When compared to languages such as C++, the use of Java and the JVM is sometimes considered a tradeoff. Java has achieved increased productivity by reducing the number of lower-level concerns a developer must deal with in day-to-day development. The perceived tradeoff is higher-level language abstraction, leading to increased developer productivity at the expense of low-level control and raw performance.

C++ takes the approach that regardless of any new language features, performance must never be compromised. The C++ philosophy leads to a sophisticated level of control, at the cost that every developer has to manage resources manually or conform to appropriate idioms.

The Java platform takes the approach that the developer should be free from concerns about the low-level details. The benefit of automatic memory management should not be underestimated as a huge productivity boost—the authors have spent many years witnessing the mistakes that can be made and damage done by an unwitting C++ developer, and still have the scars.

However, garbage collection and other higher-level managed abstractions on the JVM can cause a level of unpredictability where performance is concerned. This nondeterminism is, naturally, something that should be minimized in latency-sensitive applications.

Does this mean that Java and the JVM is not a suitable platform for high-performance systems?

This chapter aims to explore some common concerns that developers need to address when considering high-performance, latency-sensitive applications. It also looks at the design approaches and requirements placed on low-latency systems. Two considerations that are central to low-latency, high-performance systems are logging and messaging.

Logging should be a concern of any Java developer, as a maintainable Java system usually contains a high number of log messages. However, for the latency-conscious developer, logging can take on a special significance. Fortunately, logging is an area where much development and research have been conducted, which we will explore in this chapter.

Messaging systems have provided one of the most successful architectural patterns in recent years. As a result, they are usually at the forefront of low-latency systems and are typically measured in number of messages processed per second. The number of messages a system is capable of processing is often critical to gaining a competitive advantage. The ability to tie a tangible value to throughput (e.g., trades per second) means that this is an area that is heavily researched and funded. We will discuss some modern messaging approaches later in the chapter.

Logging

For many developers, the logging library is not considered an important part of the project, and its selection is a "path of least resistance" process. This is in contrast to many of the other libraries that are introduced into a project, where time is committed to researching their features and perhaps even to reviewing some performance benchmarks.

A few antipatterns surrounding the selection of a production-grade logging system include:

The "10-year logger"
    Someone once configured the logger successfully. It is much easier to borrow that config than to recreate it.

The "project-wide logger"
    Someone once wrapped the logger to avoid having to reconfigure the logger in each part of the project.

The "firm-wide logger"
    Someone once created a logger for the entire firm to use.

Of course, *someone* is never intentionally trying to create a future problem. There is usually a valid case for logging architecture choices—for example, integration with other functions in an organization, leading to the firm-wide logger. The problem is often around maintenance of the logging system, as it is typically not seen as business-critical. This neglect leads to a technical debt that has the potential to reach across the entire organization. Despite loggers not being exciting and their selection frequently following one of the preceding antipatterns, they are central to all applications.

In many high-performance environments, processing accuracy and reporting are as important as speed. There is no point doing things quickly and incorrectly, and often there can be audit requirements to accurately report processing. Logs help to identify production issues, and should log enough that teams will be able to investigate a problem after the fact. It is important that the logger is not treated simply as a cost but rather like any other component in the system—one that requires careful control and thoughtful inclusion in the project.

Logging Microbenchmarks

This section will explore a set of microbenchmarks intended to fairly compare the performance of the three most popular loggers (Logback, Log4j, and `java.util.log ging`) using various log patterns.

The statistics are based on an open source project by Stephen Connolly and can be found on GitHub (*https://github.com/stephenc/java-logging-benchmarks*). The project is well designed and presented in a runnable benchmark suite, with multiple logger runs with various configurations.

These benchmarks explore each logger combined with different logging formats to give us an idea of the logging framework's overall performance and whether the pattern has any impact on performance.

At this point it is essential that we explicitly explain why we are using a microbenchmark approach. When discussing the details of these specific technologies, we faced a similar problem to a library author: we wanted to get an idea of the performance of different loggers based on different configurations, but we knew it would be really tricky to find a good corpus of applications using the exact configurations of logging we needed and produce results that would provide a meaningful comparison.

In this situation, where the code will run in many different applications, a microbenchmark provides an estimate of how that code will perform. This is the "general-purpose, no meaningful corpus exists" use case for microbenchmarks.

The figures give us an overall picture, but it's imperative to profile the application before and afterward to get a true perspective of the changes before implementing them in a real application.

That said, let's take a look at the results and how they were achieved.

No logging

No logging is a test conducted by the benchmark to measure the cost of a no-op log in the situation where the log message is below the threshold at which the logger is currently active. This can be thought of as the experiment's control group.

Logback format

```
14:18:17.635 [Name Of Thread] INFO  c.e.NameOfLogger - Log message
```

The benchmarks used version 1.2.1 of logback.

java.util.logging format

```
Feb 08, 2017 2:09:19 PM com.example.NameOfLogger nameOfMethod
INFO: Log message
```

Log4j format

```
2017-02-08 14:16:29,651 [Name Of Thread] INFO com.example.NameOfLogger - message
```

The benchmarks used version 2.7 of Log4j.

Measurements

For purposes of comparison the benchmarks have been run on an iMac and on an AWS (Amazon Web Services) EC t2.2xlarge instance (see Tables 14-1 and 14-2). Profiling on macOS can cause problems due to various power-saving techniques, and AWS has the disadvantage that other containers can impact the results of the benchmark. No environment is perfect: there is always noise, and as discussed in Chapter 5, microbenchmarks are full of perils. Hopefully comparison between two datasets of the benchmarks will help uncover useful patterns for guidance in profiling real applications. Remember Feynman's "you must not fool yourself" principle whenever experimental data needs to be handled.

Table 14-1. Benchmarks executed on iMac (ns/op)

	No logging	Logback format	java.util.logging format	Log4j format
Java util logger	158.051 (±0.762)	42404.202 (±541.229)	86054.783 (±541.229)	74794.026 (±2244.146)
Log4j	138.495 (±94.490)	8056.299 (±447.815)	32755.168 (±27.054)	5323.127 (±47.160)
Logback	214.032 (±2.260)	5507.546 (±258.971)	27420.108 (±37.054)	3501.858 (±47.873)

The Java util logger performs its logging operations at between 42,404 ns and 86,054 ns per operation. The worst-case performance for this logger is using the java.util.logging format—over 2.5× worse than using the same format on Log4j.

Overall Logback offers the best performance from this benchmark run on the iMac, performing best using the Log4j style of logging formatter.

Table 14-2. Benchmarks executed on AWS EC t2.2xlarge (ns/op)

	No logging	Logback format	java.util.logging format	Log4j format
Java util logger	1376.597 (±106.613)	54658.098 (±516.184)	144661.388 (±10333.854)	109895.219 (±5457.031)
Log4j	1699.774 (±111.222)	5835.090 (±27.592)	34605.770 (±38.816)	5809.098 (±27.792)
Logback	2440.952 (±159.290)	4786.511 (±29.526)	30550.569 (±39.951)	5485.938 (±38.674)

Looking at the benchmarks for AWS, we can see the results show a similar overall pattern to the iMac results. Logback is slightly quicker than Log4j. There are some key takeaways from these results.

 The correct way to measure the impact to the application is to profile the application before and after the configuration is changed on production hardware. The benchmarks that have been run here should be repeated on a configuration that mirrors your specific production machine and not taken as is.

AWS, though, has noticeably quicker execution speeds overall, which could be due to power saving kicking in on the iMac or other factors that have not been captured.

Logger results

The benchmarks reveal that there is a range of results depending on the logging format that is used, the logging framework, and the configuration used. Util logging generally offers the worst performance across the board in terms of execution time. The Log4j format appears to give the most consistent results across the board, with Logback executing the log statement in the best time.

In real systems, it is worth testing execution time performance on production kit, especially when the numbers are this close. Real systems are murky, and only the clearest of signals should be taken as evidence of anything underlying; a few tens of percent is not normally enough.

The danger with microbenchmarks, as discussed in Chapter 5, is that looking at the problem in the small can potentially disguise its impact on our application as a whole. We could make a decision based on these microbenchmarks that would influence the application in other unexpected ways.

The amount of garbage generated by a logging framework might be one such consideration, as would the amount of CPU time spent logging instead of processing business-critical parallel tasks. The design of the logging library and the mechanism by which it works are just as important as the straight-line execution results in the microbenchmarks.

Designing a Lower-Impact Logger

Logging is a critical component of any application, but in low-latency applications it is essential that the logger does not become a bottleneck for business logic performance. Earlier in the chapter, we explored the idea that there is often no conscious process for the developer in selecting an appropriate logger, and no benchmarking. In many circumstances logging surfaces as a problem only when it becomes a large or dominant cost in the application.

> To date, I've rarely run into a customer whose system wasn't somehow negatively impacted by logging. My extreme case is a customer that was facing a 4.5-second time budget where logging accounted for 4.2 seconds.
>
> —Kirk Pepperdine

The Log4j 2.6 release aims to address the concerns Kirk voiced by introducing a steady-state garbage-free logger.

The documentation highlights a simple test, consisting of running the application in Java Flight Recorder to sample logging a string as often as possible over 12 seconds. The logger was configured to be asynchronous via a `RandomAccessFile` appender with the pattern `%d %p %c{1.} [%t] %m %ex%n`.

Figure 14-1 demonstrates a non-steady-state garbage collector and a sample profile for comparison. This is not intended to be an accurate microbenchmark but rather an overview of profiling the behavior of logging. The profiler shows significant GC cycles: 141 collections with an average pause time of around 7 ms and a maximum pause time of 52 ms.

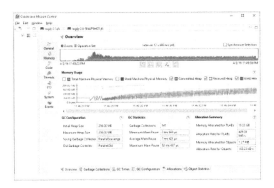

Figure 14-1. Sample running Log4j 2.5 (https://logging.apache.org/log4j/2.x/manual/garbagefree.html)

Comparing this to Figure 14-2 shows the difference that Log4j 2.6 provides, with 0 GC cycles kicking in during the same time period.

Figure 14-2. Sample running Log4j 2.6 (https://logging.apache.org/log4j/2.x/manual/garbagefree.html)

Log4j 2.6 provides some clear advantages when configured to run as in Figure 14-2. However, there are some limitations due to the way the zero-allocation logger is implemented—as always, there are no free lunches!

Log4j achieves the performance observed by reusing objects, rather than creating temporary objects on each log message. This is a classic use of the Object Pool pattern, with all of the consequences that come along with it. Log4j 2.6 reuses objects by using ThreadLocal fields and by reusing buffers for converting strings to bytes.

 This is one of the outcomes that we could not have deduced by looking solely at the microbenchmark. As always, the design and the big picture must be considered.

ThreadLocal objects can be problematic in web containers, in particular when web applications are loaded into and unloaded from the container. Log4j 2.6 won't use ThreadLocal when running inside a web container, but it will still use some shared and cached structures to help improve performance.

If an application is already using an older version of Log4j, directly upgrading to 2.6 and reviewing the configuration should be a consideration. Log4j reduces the number of allocations by using varargs, creating a temporary array for parameters being passed in to the log statement. If Log4j is used via SLF4J, the facade will still only support two parameters; using more via SLF4J would require not using a garbage-free approach or refactoring the code base to use Log4j2 libraries directly.

Low Latency Using Real Logic Libraries

Real Logic (*https://real-logic.co.uk*) is a UK-based company founded by Martin Thompson. Martin is known for pioneering the approach of mechanical sympathy, based on an understanding of how lower-level details influence high-performance design. One of Martin's best-known contributions to the Java space is the Disruptor pattern (*https://lmax-exchange.github.io/disruptor/*).

> Martin's blog (*http://mechanical-sympathy.blogspot.co.uk*), also called Mechanical Sympathy, and the associated mailing list (*https://groups.google.com/forum/?fromgroups#!forum/mechanical-sympathy*) are great resources for developers who want to push the performance envelope of their applications.

Real Logic's GitHub page (*https://github.com/real-logic*) houses several popular open source projects that build on the expertise of Martin and the other contributors, including:

Agrona
High-performance data structures and utility methods for Java

Simple Binary Encoding (SBE)
A high-performance message codec

Aeron
An efficient reliable UDP unicast, UDP multicast, and IPC message transport

Artio
A resilient, high-performance, FIX gateway

The following sections will explore these projects and the design philosophy that enables these libraries to push the bounds of Java performance.

> Real Logic also hosts a resilient high-permanence FIX gateway utilizing these libraries. However, this will not be something we explore further in this chapter.

Agrona

Project Agrona (*https://github.com/real-logic/agrona*) (which derives its name from Celtic mythology in Wales and Scotland) is a library containing building blocks for low-latency applications. In "Building Concurrency Libraries" on page 298, we discussed the idea of using `java.util.concurrent` at the appropriate level of abstraction to not reinvent the wheel.

Agrona provides a similar set of libraries for truly low-latency applications. If you have already proved that the standard libraries do not meet your use case, then a reasonable next step would be to evaluate these libraries before rolling your own. The project is well unit-tested and documented and has an active community.

Buffers

Richard Warburton has written an excellent article (*http://insightfullogic.com/ 2015/Apr/18/agronas-threadsafe-offheap-buffers/*) on buffers and the problems with buffers in Java.

Broadly, Java offers a `ByteBuffer` (*https://docs.oracle.com/javase/8/docs/api/java/nio/ ByteBuffer.html*) class, which offers an abstraction for a buffer that is either direct or nondirect.

A direct buffer lives outside of the usual Java heap (but still within the "C heap" of the overall JVM process). As a result, it can often have slower allocation and deallocation rates as compared to an on-heap (nondirect) buffer. The direct buffer has the advantage that the JVM will attempt to invoke instructions directly on that structure without an intermediate mapping.

The main problem with `ByteBuffer` is the generalized use case, meaning that optimizations specific to the type of buffer are not applied. For example, they don't support atomic operations, which is a problem if you want to build a producer/ consumer-style model across a buffer. `ByteBuffer` requires that every time you wrap a different structure a new underlying buffer is allocated. In Agrona the copy is avoided, and it supports four types of buffer with different characteristics, allowing you to define and control the interactions possible with each buffer object:

- The `DirectBuffer` interface provides the ability to read only from the buffer and forms the top level of the hierarchy.
- The `MutableDirectBuffer` interface extends `DirectBuffer` and adds write access to the buffer.
- The `AtomicBuffer` interface extends `MutableDirectBuffer`, offering ordering behavior.
- `UnsafeBuffer` is the class that uses `Unsafe` to implement `AtomicBuffer`.

Figure 14-3 shows the inheritance hierarchy of buffer classes for Agrona's buffers.

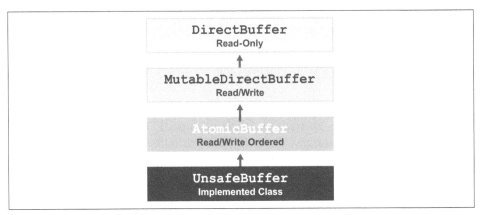

Figure 14-3. Agrona buffers

The code in Agrona, as you might imagine, is very low-level and uses Unsafe extensively, including in this code fragment:

```
// This horrible filth is to encourage the JVM to call memset()
// when address is even.
// TODO: check if this still applies when Java 9 is out!!!
UNSAFE.putByte(byteArray, indexOffset, value);
UNSAFE.setMemory(byteArray, indexOffset + 1, length - 1, value);
```

This is not to say that Agrona is *hacky* in any way—quite the opposite. The need for this code was to bypass an old optimization that was applied inside the JVM that is now an antioptimization. The library has gone down to this level of detail in ensuring maximum performance can be gained.

Agrona buffers allow access to the underlying data through various get methods—for example, getLong(int index). Even though the buffer is wrapped, it is up to the developer to know at what point the index of their data resides. In addition, put operations allow putting the long value at a specific point on the buffer. Note that the buffer is not of any single type; it is down to the developer to select and manage the appropriate structure for their data. Bounds checking can be enabled/disabled, so dead code can be optimized away by the JIT compiler.

Lists, maps, and sets

Agrona provides a series of list implementations that are backed by arrays of ints or long primitives. As mentioned in "Optimizing Collections" on page 260, Java does not have a mechanism of laying out objects side by side in an array, and in standard collections the result is an array of references. Forcing the usage of an object rather than a primitive in standard collections results in autoboxing and unboxing, in addition to the size overhead of the object itself. Agrona also supplies ArrayList utilities that allow fast removal from an ArrayList but spoil the ordering.

Agrona's map and set implementations store keys and values side by side in a hash table structure. If a collision of keys occurs, the next value is stored immediately after that position in the table. This kind of structure lends itself well to quick access of primitive mappings present on the same cache line.

Queues

Agrona has its own concurrent package that contains useful concurrent utilities and structures including queues and ring buffers.

Queues follow the standard `java.util.Queue` interface, and they can be used in place of a standard queue implementation. Agrona queues also implement the `org.agrona.concurrent.Pipe` interface, which adds support for a container processed in sequence. In particular, `Pipe` adds support for counting, capacity, and draining operations, to interact easily with consumers of the queue. The queues are all lockless and use `Unsafe` to make them appropriate for use in low-latency systems. The `org.agrona.concurrent.AbstractConcurrentArrayQueue` provides the first level of support for a series of queues that will provide different producer/consumer models. One interesting part of this API are these classes:

```
/**
 * Pad out a cache line to the left of a producer fields
 * to prevent false sharing.
 */
class AbstractConcurrentArrayQueuePadding1
{
    @SuppressWarnings("unused")
    protected long p1, p2, p3, p4, p5, p6, p7, p8, p9, p10, p11, p12,
        p13, p14, p15;
}

/**
 * Values for the producer that are expected to be padded.
 */
class AbstractConcurrentArrayQueueProducer
        extends AbstractConcurrentArrayQueuePadding1
{
    protected volatile long tail;
    protected long headCache;
    protected volatile long sharedHeadCache;
}

/**
 * Pad out a cache line between the producer and consumer fields to prevent
 * false sharing.
 */
class AbstractConcurrentArrayQueuePadding2
        extends AbstractConcurrentArrayQueueProducer
{
```

```
    @SuppressWarnings("unused")
    protected long p16, p17, p18, p19, p20, p21, p22, p23, p24, p25,
        p26, p27, p28, p29, p30;
}

/**
 * Values for the consumer that are expected to be padded.
 */
class AbstractConcurrentArrayQueueConsumer
        extends AbstractConcurrentArrayQueuePadding2
{
    protected volatile long head;
}

/**
 * Pad out a cache line between the producer and consumer fields to
 * prevent false sharing.
 */
class AbstractConcurrentArrayQueuePadding3
    extends AbstractConcurrentArrayQueuePadding2
{
    @SuppressWarnings("unused")
    protected long p31, p32, p33, p34, p35, p36, p37, p38, p39, p40,
        p41, p42, p43, p44, p45;
}

/**
 * Leftover immutable queue fields.
 */
public abstract class AbstractConcurrentArrayQueue<E>
    extends AbstractConcurrentArrayQueuePadding3
    implements QueuedPipe<E> {...}
```

It is worth noting that sun.misc.contended (or jdk.internal
.vm.annotation.Contended) may be made available to generate
this kind of cache line padding in the future.

The code fragment from AbstractConcurrentArrayQueue shows a clever (forced)
arrangement of the queue memory to avoid false sharing when the queue is accessed
by the consumer and producer concurrently. The reason that we require this padding
is because the layout of fields in memory is not guaranteed by Java or the JVM.

Putting the producer and consumer on separate cache lines ensures that the structure
can adequately perform in a low-latency, high-throughput situation. Cache lines are
used to access memory, and if the producer and consumer shared the same cache
line, problems would occur when the cache line was accessed concurrently.

There are three concrete implementations, and separating out the implementation in this way enables coordination in code only where necessary:

OneToOneConcurrentArrayQueue

If we choose one producer and one consumer, we are opting into a policy that the only concurrent access occurring is when the producer and consumer are accessing the structure at the same time. The main point of interest is the head and tail positions, as these are only updated by one thread at a time.

The head can only be updated by a poll or drain operation to take from the queue, and the tail can only be updated by a put() operation. Selecting this mode avoids unnecessary loss of performance due to additional coordination checks, which are required by the other two types of queue.

ManyToManyConcurrentArrayQueue

Alternatively, if we choose to have many producers, then additional controls are required for the updating of the tail position (as this may have been updated by another producer). Using Unsafe.compareAndSwapLong in a while loop until the tail is updated ensures a lock-free way of updating the queue tail safely. Again, there is no such contention on the consumer side, as we are guaranteeing one consumer.

ManyToOneConcurrentArrayQueue

Finally, if we choose to have many producers and consumers, then coordination controls are needed for the update of the head or the tail. This level of coordination and control is achieved by a while loop wrapping a compareAndSwap. This will require the most coordination of all of the alternatives and so should be used only if that level of safety is required.

Ring buffers

Agrona provides org.agrona.concurrent.RingBuffer as an interface for exchanging binary-encoded messages for interprocess communication. It uses a Direct Buffer to manage the storage of the message off-heap. Thanks to some ASCII art in the source code, we can see that messages are stored in a RecordDescriptor structure:

```
*   0                   1                   2                   3
*   0 1 2 3 4 5 6 7 8 9 0 1 2 3 4 5 6 7 8 9 0 1 2 3 4 5 6 7 8 9 0 1
*   +-+-+-+-+-+-+-+-+-+-+-+-+-+-+-+-+-+-+-+-+-+-+-+-+-+-+-+-+-+-+-+-+
*   |R|                        Length                             |
*   +-+-------------------------------------------------------------+
*   |                          Type                               |
*   +---------------------------------------------------------------+
*   |                       Encoded Message                      ...
*   ...                                                           |
*   +---------------------------------------------------------------+
```

There are two types of ring buffer implemented in Agrona, the `OneToOneRingBuffer` and the `ManyToOneRingBuffer`. The write operation takes a source buffer to write a message to the buffer, whereas read operations are called back on an `onMessage` style of handler. Where many producers are writing in the `ManyToOneRingBuffer`, a call to `Unsafe.storeFence()` manually controls memory synchronization. The store fence "ensures lack of reordering of stores before the fence with loads or stores after the fence."

Agrona has many low-level structures and interesting aspects. If the software system that you are looking to build is at this level of detail, this project is a great first step to experiment with.

There are other projects available, such as JCTools (*https://github.com/JCTools/JCTools*), that also provide variations for concurrent queue structures. Unless a very specific use case is required, developers should not ignore the existence of these open source libraries and should avoid reinventing the wheel.

Simple Binary Encoding

SBE was developed to meet the need for a binary encoding representation suitable for low-latency performance. The encoding was created specifically for the FIX protocol used in financial systems.

> Simple Binary Encoding (SBE) provides different characteristics than other binary encodings. It is optimized for low latency. This new FPL binary encoding complements the existing only binary encoding developed in 2005 (FAST) with a focus on reducing bandwidth utilization for market data.
>
> —Simple Binary Encoding specification Release Candidate 1

SBE is an application-layer concern used for encoding and decoding messages; the buffers that are used in SBE are from Agrona. SBE has been optimized to allow low-latency messages to pass through the data structure without triggering GC and optimizing concerns such as memory access. It was designed specifically for the high-frequency trading environment, where responding to market events often must happen in micro- or nanoseconds.

 The SBE encoding was defined within the FIX protocol organization only in contrast to competing proposals to encode FIX with Google Protocol Buffers and ASN.1.

Another key nonfunctional requirement of high-frequency trading is that operation should be consistently fast. One of the authors has witnessed a system that would process messages at a reasonably high throughput, then suddenly would pause for two minutes due to a GC bug. This kind of pause would be completely unacceptable in a low-latency application, and avoiding garbage collection altogether is one way to ensure consistent performance. These types of performance issues will be identified via a soak test or other long-running performance exercise.

The goal of low-latency applications is to squeeze every possible measure of performance out of the application. This can lead to an "arms race" where teams at competing trading firms try to outdo each other in reducing latency through a trading application's critical path.

The authors of SBE proposed a series of design principles (*https://github.com/real-logic/simple-binary-encoding/wiki/Design-Principles*) to reflect these concerns and explain their thinking. We will explore some of the design decisions and how they relate to low-latency system design in the following sections.

Copy-free and native type mapping

Copying comes at a cost, and anyone who has done any programming in C++ will probably have been caught out from time to time copying objects accidentally. Copying isn't expensive when objects are small, but as the size of objects increases so does the cost of the copy.

High-level Java programmers may not always consider this problem, as they are so used to working with references and having memory automatically managed. The copy-free technique in SBE is designed to ensure that no intermediate buffers are used when encoding or decoding messages.

Writing to the underlying buffer directly does, however, come at a design cost: larger messages that cannot fit in the buffer aren't supported. In order to support them, a protocol would have to be built in to segment the messages and reassemble them.

Types that natively map to sensible assembly instructions also help when you are working with a copy-free design. Having a mapping that corresponds to a good selection of assembly operations dramatically improves the performance of field retrieval.

Steady-state allocation

Allocating objects in Java introduces a natural problem where low-latency applications are concerned. The allocation itself requires CPU cycles (even if it's very small, such as a TLAB allocation), and then there's the problem of deleting the object after the usage is complete.

GC is often stop-the-world, which introduces a pause. This is true even of more advanced collectors that work mostly concurrently. Even when limiting the absolute pause time, the process of GC can introduce a meaningful variance in the performance model.

It might seem natural to think that C++ could help to resolve that problem, but allocation and deallocation mechanisms can also introduce problems. In particular, some memory pools may employ a locking mechanism that damages performance.

SBE is allocation-free because it uses the flyweight pattern over the underlying buffer.

Streaming access and word-aligned access

Access to memory is something that we would not normally have control over in Java. In "Optimizing Collections" on page 260, we discussed ObjectLayout, which is a proposal to store objects in alignment like in C++ vectors. Normally arrays in Java are arrays of references, meaning reading in memory sequentially would not be possible.

SBE is designed to encode and decode messages in a forward progression that also is framed correctly to allow for good word alignment. Without good alignment, performance issues can start to occur at the processor level.

Working with SBE

SBE messages are defined as XML schema files specifying the layout of the messages. Although XML is nowadays quite generally disliked, schemas do give us a good mechanism for specifying a message interface accurately. XML also has instant toolchain support in IDEs such as Eclipse and Intellij.

SBE provides sbe-tool, a command-line tool that, when given a schema, allows you to generate the appropriate encoders and decoders. The steps to get this to work are as follows:

```
# Fork or clone the project
git clone git@github.com:real-logic/simple-binary-encoding.git

# Build the project using your favorite build tool
gradle

# The sbe-tool will be created in
sbe-tool/build/libs

# Run the sbe-tool with a schema-a sample schema is provided at
# https://github.com/real-logic/simple-binary-encoding/blob/master/
    sbe-samples/src/main/resources/example-schema.xml
java -jar sbe-tool-1.7.5-SNAPSHOT-all.jar message-schema.xml

# When this command completes it will generate a series of .java files in the
    baseline directory
$ ls
BooleanType.java            GroupSizeEncodingEncoder.java
BoostType.java              MessageHeaderDecoder.java
BoosterDecoder.java         MessageHeaderEncoder.java
```

```
BoosterEncoder.java          MetaAttribute.java
CarDecoder.java              Model.java
CarEncoder.java              OptionalExtrasDecoder.java
EngineDecoder.java           OptionalExtrasEncoder.java
EngineEncoder.java           VarStringEncodingDecoder.java
GroupSizeEncodingDecoder.java  VarStringEncodingEncoder.java
```

It is important to remember that one of the core parts of the SBE protocol is that the messages must be read in order, which means essentially as defined in the schema. The tutorial to start working with these messages is outlined in the SBE Java Users Guide (*https://github.com/real-logic/simple-binary-encoding/wiki/Java-Users-Guide*).

Although this demonstration has used the SBE tool on the command line, it is more likely that this tool would be integrated into a build pipeline.

Aeron

Aeron is the final product in the Real Logic stack that we will explore. It should be no surprise that we've left this until last, as it builds upon both SBE and Agrona. Aeron is a UDP (User Datagram Protocol) unicast, multicast, and IPC (inter-process communication) message transport written for Java and C++. It is media layer–agnostic, which means that it will also work nicely with InfiniBand.

Essentially, this is a general, all-encompassing messaging protocol that you can use to get applications to speak to each other via IPC on the same machine or over the network. Aeron is designed to have the highest throughput possible and aims to achieve the lowest and most predictable latency results (consistency being important, as we discussed in "Simple Binary Encoding" on page 364). This section explores the Aeron API and discusses some of the design decisions.

Why build something new?

One of the primary reasons for building a new product such as Aeron is that some products in the market have become more general. This is not meant as a criticism, but when customers demand features (and are usually paying for them), it can push a product in a particular direction. The products can become bloated and provide many more features than originally intended, perhaps even becoming frameworks.

Messaging systems in low-level Java are quite fun to build and may start life as a pet project inside a company or in the open source community. The potential problem is that a lack of experience with what is needed from a low-latency perspective can make it hard to take these pet projects and make them production-ready. Ensuring that a product is built for low latency from the ground up without sacrificing performance remains a difficult challenge.

As this chapter has highlighted, the strong design principle behind Aeron is that it is built as a library of components. This means that you are not bound to a framework, and if you only require a low-level data structure then Agrona will provide that, without the need to bring in many other dependencies.

Publishers

Before we discuss Aeron in depth, it is useful to understand some of the higher-level components depicted in Figure 14-4.

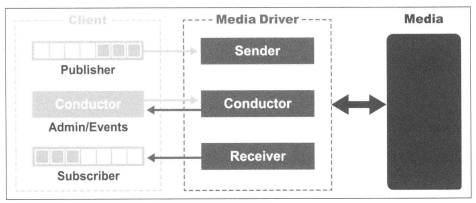

Figure 14-4. Architecture overview of Aeron's major components

Specifically:

- *Media* refers to the mechanism over which Aeron will communicate; for example, this could be UDP or IPC. It could also be InfiniBand or another medium. The main point is Aeron as a client has an abstraction away from this.

- The *media driver* refers to the connection between the media and Aeron, allowing configuration to be set and communication to occur with that transport.

- The *conductor* is responsible for administration, such as setting up the buffers and listening to requests for new subscribers and publishers. It will also look for NAKs (Negative Acknowledgments) and arrange for retransmission. The conductor allows the sender and receiver to just deal with shifting bytes for maximum throughput.

- The *sender* reads data from producers and sends it out on sockets.

- The *receiver* reads data from the sockets and forwards it on to the corresponding channel and session.

The media driver is usually a separate process that provides the buffers to be used for transmitting and receiving messages. Different media drivers can be used to exploit optimizations on different hardware deployments; the MediaDriver.Context is the configuration that sets up the optimizations for that media driver. The media driver can also be launched in an embedded way within the same process; the embedded process can be configured with a context or through system properties. Starting up an embedded media driver can be done as follows:

```
final MediaDriver driver = MediaDriver.launch();
```

The Aeron applications need to connect to the media driver as either publishers or subscribers. The `Aeron` class makes this fairly straightforward. Aeron also has an inner `Context` class that can be used to configure the settings:

```
final Aeron.Context ctx = new Aeron.Context();
```

Aeron can then connect a publication to communicate over a given channel and stream. Because a `Publication` is `AutoClosable`, it will be automatically cleaned up when the `try` block finishes executing:

```
try (Publication publication = aeron.addPublication(CHANNEL, STREAM_ID))
{...}
```

To send a message a buffer is offered to the publisher, with the result of the offer determining the state of the message. `Publication` has a series of long constants that represent a mapping of errors that can be compared to the `long` result from the `offer()` method:

```
final long result = publication.offer(BUFFER, 0, messageBytes.length);
```

Sending a message is as simple as that, but in order for this to be of any use a subscriber should be listening to the same media driver.

Subscribers

The subscriber's startup is similar to the publisher's: the media driver needs to be accessed and then the Aeron client connects. The components of a consumer mirror the image shown in Figure 14-4. The consumer registers a callback function that is triggered when a message is received:

```
final FragmentHandler fragmentHandler =
    SamplesUtil.printStringMessage(STREAM_ID);

try (Aeron aeron = Aeron.connect(ctx);
     Subscription subscription = aeron.addSubscription(CHANNEL, STREAM_ID))
{
    SamplesUtil.subscriberLoop(fragmentHandler,
        FRAGMENT_COUNT_LIMIT, running).accept(subscription);

}
```

These examples have just explored the basic setup; the Aeron project has samples (*https://github.com/real-logic/aeron/tree/master/aeron-samples/src/main/java/io/aeron/samples*) that explore more advanced examples.

The Design of Aeron

Martin Thompson's talk at Strange Loop (*https://youtu.be/tM4YskS94b0*) provides an extremely good introduction to Aeron and the reason why it was built. This section will explore some of the discussion in the video, in conjunction with the open documentation.

Transport requirements

Aeron is an OSI layer 4 transport for messaging, which means it has a series of responsibilities that it must comply with:

Ordering
> Packets will be received out of order from lower-level transports, and it is responsible for reordering out-of-sequence messages.

Reliability
> Problems will occur when data is lost, and it must make a request to retransmit that data. While the request for old data is in progress, the process of receiving new data should not be impeded. Reliability in this context refers to connection-level reliability rather than session-level reliability (e.g., fault tolerance over multiple process restarts).

Back pressure
> Subscribers will come under pressure under high-volume scenarios, so the service must support flow control and back-pressure measures.

Congestion
> This is a problem that can occur on saturated networks, but if a low-latency application is being built it should not be a primary concern. Aeron provides an optional feature to activate congestion control; users that are on low-latency networks can turn it off and users sensitive to other traffic can turn it on. Congestion control can impact a product that in the optimal path has adequate network capacity.

Multiplexing
> The transport should be capable of handling multiple streams of information across a single channel without compromising the overall performance.

Latency and application principles

Aeron is driven by eight design principles, as outlined on the Aeron Wiki (*https:// github.com/real-logic/aeron/wiki/Design-Principles*):

Garbage-free in steady-state running
GC pauses are a large cause of latency and unpredictability in Java applications. Aeron has been designed to ensure steady state to avoid GC, which means it can be included in applications that also observe this same design decision.

Apply Smart Batching in the message path
Smart Batching is an algorithm that is designed to help handle the situation when burst messages are received. In many messaging systems, it is incorrect to assume that messages will be received steadily throughout the day. It is more likely that messages are received in bursts due to business-based events. While processing a message, if another message is received it can also be bundled into the same network packet, up to capacity. Using appropriate data structures, Aeron enables this batching to work without stalling producers writing to the shared resource.

Lock-free algorithms in the message path
Locking introduces contention where threads can be blocked while other threads run; even parking and waking from locks can slow down an application. Avoiding locks prevents the slowdowns that they can cause. Locks and lock-free techniques are discussed in more detail in Chapter 14.

Nonblocking I/O in the message path
Blocking I/O can block a thread, and the cost of waking is high. Using nonblocking I/O avoids these costs.

No exceptional cases in the message path
Applications spend the majority of their time executing primary scenarios and not smaller edge-case scenarios. Edge-case scenarios should be handled, but not at the cost of the execution speed of the primary scenarios.

Apply the Single Writer Principle
As discussed with the `ManyToOneConcurrentArrayQueue` in "Queues" on page 361, having multiple writers involves a high degree of control and coordination to access the queue. Establishing a single writer significantly simplifies this policy and reduces contention on writing. Aeron publication objects are thread-safe and support multiple writers, but subscribers are not thread-safe—one is required per thread that you want to subscribe on.

Prefer unshared state
A single writer solves the problem of contention on the queue, but also introduces another point at which mutable data has to be shared. Maintaining private or

local state is far preferred in all walks of software design, as it considerably simplifies the data model.

Avoid unnecessary data copies

As we have mentioned, data is normally cheap to copy, but the invalidation of cache lines and potential to evict other data causes a problem in both Java and C++. Minimizing copies helps to prevent this accidental churn of memory.

How it works under the hood

Many existing protocols introduce complicated data structures, such as skip lists, to try to build effective message processing systems. This complexity, mainly due to indirection of pointers, leads to systems that have unpredictable latency characteristics.

> Fundamentally Aeron creates a replicated persistent log of messages.
>
> —Martin Thompson

Aeron was designed to provide the cleanest and simplest way of building a sequence of messages in a structure. Although it might not seem like the most likely choice initially, Aeron makes significant use of the concept of a file. Files are structures that can be shared across interested processes, and using the memory-mapped file feature of Linux directs all calls to the file to memory rather than a physical file write.

 Aeron by default maps to *tmpfs* (which is volatile memory mounted like a file). The performance is significantly better than with a disk-memory-mapped file.

The tail pointer is used to keep track of where the last message was written. Figure 14-5 shows a single message has been written into our current file along with the header.

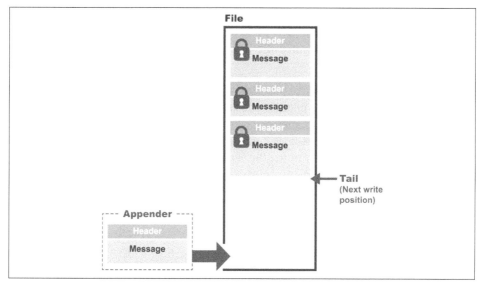

Figure 14-5. Messages written to a file

The sequencing of events is quite interesting here. The tail pointer reserves the space for the message in the file. The increment of the tail is atomic, and therefore the writer knows the beginning and end of its section.

The Critical Patch Update intrinsic to making this increment atomic was added as part of Java 8.

This allows multiple writers to update the file in a lock-free manner, which is what effectively establishes the file writing protocol. The message is then written, but how can we tell that it's finished? The header is the last thing to be written atomically to the file. Its presence tells us that the message is complete.

Files are persistent structures that grow when written and do not mutate. Reading records from the file does not require locks, as the file can be opened and read only by an observing process. But is it possible to simply have a file that grows infinitely?

This introduces a lot of problems due to page faults and page churn being introduced in our previously nicely memory-mapped file. We address this concern by having three files: *active*, *dirty*, and *clean*. Active represents the file currently being written to, dirty is the file that was previously written to, and clean is the next file for writing to. The files are rotated to avoid latency caused by bigger files.

Messages are never allowed to go across files. If the tail is pushed off the end of the active file, the insertion process pads the remainder of the file and writes the message into the clean file. From the dirty file it is possible to archive and deep-store the transaction log permanently.

The mechanism for handling missing messages is also really clever and avoids the skip lists and other structures mentioned earlier. The header of the message contains the message's ordering. When a message is inserted, if it comes out of order a space is left for the previous messages(s). When the missing message is received, it can be inserted in the correct position in the file. This gives an ever-increasing series of messages with no gaps or other structures involved. Ordering data incrementally also has the added benefit of being incredibly quick to work with from a mechanical sympathy perspective.

A watermark represents the current position of the last received message. If the watermark and tail end up being different for a period of time, it indicates missing messages. To resolve the missing messages, NAKs are sent to request them. A NAK can be sent for a message and populated once the message is received.

One interesting side effect of this protocol is that every message received has a unique way of identifying the bytes in each message, based on the `streamId`, `sessionId`, `termId`, and `termOffset`. The Aeron Archive (*https://github.com/real-logic/aeron/wiki/Aeron-Archive*) can be used to record and replay messaging streams. By combining the archive and this unique representation it is possible to uniquely identify all messages throughout the history.

The logfile is at the heart of Aeron's ability to maintain speed and state. It is also a simple, elegantly executed design that allows the product to compete with—and in many cases beat—well-established (and pricey) multicast products.

Summary

Logging is an unavoidable part of all production-grade applications, and the type of logger used can have a significant impact on overall application performance. It is important to consider the application as a whole when it comes to logging (not just the execution of the log statement), as well as the impact it has on other JVM subsystems such as thread usage and garbage collection.

This chapter contains some simple examples of low-latency libraries, starting from the lowest level and progressing all the way up to a full messaging implementation. It is clear that the goals and objectives of low-latency systems need to be applied throughout the software stack, right from the lowest level of queues up to the higher-level usage. Low-latency, high-throughput systems require a great deal of thought, sophistication, and control, and many of the open source projects discussed here have been built from a huge wealth of experience. When you are creating a new low-latency system, these projects will save you days, if not weeks, of development time, provided you adhere to the low-level design goals up to the top-level application.

The chapter started by asking to what extent Java and the JVM can be used for high-throughput applications. Writing low-latency, high-throughput applications is hard in any language, but Java provides some of the best tooling and productivity of any language available. Java and the JVM do, however, add another level of abstraction, which needs to be managed and in some cases circumvented. It is important to consider the hardware, the JVM performance, and much lower-level concerns.

These lower-level concerns are not normally surfaced during day-to-day Java development. Using newer logging libraries that are allocation-free, and the data structures and messaging protocols discussed in this chapter, significantly lowers the barrier to entry, as much of the complexity has been solved by the open source community.

## CHAPTER 15

Java 9 and the Future

While this book was being written, Java 9 was in active development. The new release contains a number of performance-related features and enhancements that are relevant to the Java/JVM application engineer.

In the first part of this chapter, we survey the new and modified aspects of the platform that a performance engineer should know about in Java 9.

The truth is, for most developers, Java 9 really does consist of "modules and then everything else." Just as Java 8 was all about lambdas and their consequences (streams, default methods, and small aspects of functional programming), so Java 9 is mostly about modules.

Modules are a new way of building and deploying software and are not easy to adopt piecemeal. They represent a very modern way to build well-architected apps. However, it may take teams and projects a while to see the long-term benefits of adopting modules. For our purposes modules are not of any real performance significance, and so we make no attempt to discuss them in any detail and instead focus on the smaller but performance-relevant changes.

 Readers interested in Java 9 modules should consult an appropriate reference, such as *Java 9 Modularity* by Sander Mak and Paul Bakker (O'Reilly).

The majority of this chapter is taken up with a discussion of the future, as it exists at the time of writing. The Java platform ecosystem has a number of initiatives under way that have the potential to radically reshape the performance landscape for JVM applications. To conclude the book, we will take a look at these projects and their relevance to Java performance professionals.

Small Performance Enhancements in Java 9

This section discusses the enhancements made in Java 9 that are relevant to performance. Some of them are quite small, but could be significant for some applications. In particular, we will discuss changes such as:

- The segmented code cache
- Compact strings
- New string concatenation
- C2 compiler improvements
- G1 changes

Segmented Code Cache

One improvement delivered in Java 9 is to split the code cache (*http:// openjdk.java.net/jeps/197*) into separate regions for:

- Nonmethod code such as the interpreter
- Profiled code (Level 2 and Level 3 from the client compiler)
- Nonprofiled code (Level 1 and Level 4)

This should result in shorter sweeper times (the nonmethod region will not require sweeping) and better code locality for fully optimized code. The downside of a segmented code cache is the possibility of one region filling up while there is space available in other regions.

Compact Strings

In Java, the contents of a string have always been stored as a char[]. As char is a 16-bit type, this means that roughly twice as much space is used to store ASCII strings than is actually required. The platform has always treated this overhead as a price worth paying to simplify Unicode handling.

With Java 9 comes the possibility of *compact strings*. This is a per-string opportunity to optimize. If the string can be represented in Latin-1, then it is represented as a byte array (with the bytes understood to correspond to Latin-1 characters), and the empty zero bytes of the char representation are saved. In the source code of the Java 9 String class, this change looks like this:

```
private final byte[] value;

/**
 * The identifier of the encoding used to encode the bytes in
 * {@code value}. The supported values in this implementation are
 *
 * LATIN1
 * UTF16
 *
 * @implNote This field is trusted by the VM, and is a subject to
 * constant folding if String instance is constant. Overwriting this
 * field after construction will cause problems.
 */
private final byte coder;

static final byte LATIN1 = 0;
static final byte UTF16  = 1;
```

In Java 9, the value field is now byte[] rather than char[] as in earlier versions.

 You can disable or enable this feature by passing -XX:-CompactStrings or -XX:+CompactStrings (which is the default).

This change will have the most pronounced effect on applications that have a large heap containing a lot of string data that is Latin-1 (or ASCII) only—for example, ElasticSearch, caches, and other related components. For these applications, it may be worth moving to a Java 9 runtime for this improvement alone.

New String Concatenation

Consider this simple bit of Java:

```
public class Concat {
  public static void main(String[] args) {
    String s = "("+ args[0] + " : "+ args[1] +")";
    System.out.println(s);
  }
}
```

Since Java 5, this language feature has been desugared into a series of method calls involving the StringBuilder type. This produces a fairly large amount of bytecode:

```
public static void main(java.lang.String[]);
  Code:
     0: new           #2      // class java/lang/StringBuilder
     3: dup
     4: invokespecial #3      // Method java/lang/StringBuilder."<init>":()V
     7: ldc           #4      // String (
```

```
    9: invokevirtual #5        // Method java/lang/StringBuilder.append:
                               // (Ljava/lang/String;)Ljava/lang/StringBuilder;
   12: aload_0
   13: iconst_0
   14: aaload
   15: invokevirtual #5        // Method java/lang/StringBuilder.append:
                               // (Ljava/lang/String;)Ljava/lang/StringBuilder;
   18: ldc           #6        // String  :
   20: invokevirtual #5        // Method java/lang/StringBuilder.append:
                               // (Ljava/lang/String;)Ljava/lang/StringBuilder;
   23: aload_0
   24: iconst_1
   25: aaload
   26: invokevirtual #5        // Method java/lang/StringBuilder.append:
                               // (Ljava/lang/String;)Ljava/lang/StringBuilder;
   29: ldc           #7        // String )
   31: invokevirtual #5        // Method java/lang/StringBuilder.append:
                               // (Ljava/lang/String;)Ljava/lang/StringBuilder;
   34: invokevirtual #8        // Method java/lang/StringBuilder.toString:
                               // ()Ljava/lang/String;
   37: astore_1
   38: getstatic     #9        // Field java/lang/System.out:
                               // Ljava/io/PrintStream;
   41: aload_1
   42: invokevirtual #10       // Method java/io/PrintStream.println:
                               // (Ljava/lang/String;)V
   45: return
```

However, under Java 9, the compiler produces radically different bytecode:

```
public static void main(java.lang.String[]);
  Code:
     0: aload_0
     1: iconst_0
     2: aaload
     3: aload_0
     4: iconst_1
     5: aaload
     6: invokedynamic #2,  0   // InvokeDynamic #0:makeConcatWithConstants:
                               // (Ljava/lang/String;Ljava/lang/String;)
                               // Ljava/lang/String;
    11: astore_1
    12: getstatic     #3       // Field java/lang/System.out:
                               // Ljava/io/PrintStream;
    15: aload_1
    16: invokevirtual #4       // Method java/io/PrintStream.println:
                               // (Ljava/lang/String;)V
    19: return
```

This relies on invokedynamic, which was introduced in "Introduction to JVM Bytecode" on page 202. By looking at the verbose output from javap we can see the bootstrap method in the constant pool:

```
0: #17 REF_invokeStatic java/lang/invoke/StringConcatFactory.
   makeConcatWithConstants:(Ljava/lang/invoke/MethodHandles$Lookup;Ljava/
   lang/String;Ljava/lang/invoke/MethodType;Ljava/lang/String;
   [Ljava/lang/Object;)Ljava/lang/invoke/CallSite;
```

This uses a factory method called `makeConcatWithConstants()` from the `StringConcatFactory` to produce a recipe for concatenation. This technique can use a number of different strategies, including writing bytecode for a new custom method. It is similar in some ways to using a prepared statement for SQL execution rather than naive string assembly.

The overall performance impact of this small change is not expected to be very significant for many applications. However, the change does indicate the broader use of `invokedynamic` and illustrate the general direction of the evolution of the platform.

C2 Compiler Improvements

The C2 compiler is now quite mature, and it is widely believed (by companies such as Twitter, and even by experts such as Cliff Click) that no more major enhancements are possible within the current design. This means that any improvements are, of necessity, somewhat marginal. However, one area that would potentially allow better performance is the use of *Single Instruction, Multiple Data* (SIMD) extensions present on modern CPUs.

When compared to other programming environments, Java and the JVM are in a good position to exploit these due to the following platform features:

- Bytecode is platform-agnostic.
- The JVM performs CPU probing at startup, so it knows the capabilities of the hardware it executes on at runtime.
- JIT compilation is dynamic code generation, so can use all instructions available on the host.

As discussed in "Intrinsics" on page 246, the route to implement these improvements is the area of VM intrinsics.

> A method is intrinsified if the HotSpot VM replaces the annotated method with hand-written assembly and/or handwritten compiler IR—a *compiler intrinsic* to improve performance.
>
> —@HotSpotIntrinsicCandidate JavaDoc

HotSpot already supports some of x86 SIMD instructions, including:

- Automatic vectorization of Java code
- Superword optimizations in C2 to derive SIMD code from sequential code

- JVM SIMD intrinsics, including array copying, filling, and comparison

The Java 9 release contains a number of fixed issues that implement improved or new intrinsics to take even better advantage of SIMD and related processor features. From the release notes, the following issues are closed as fixed, due to the addition of enhanced intrinsics:

- Masked vector post loops
- SuperWord loop unrolling analysis
- Multiversioning for range check elimination
- Support for vectorizing double-precision `sqrt`
- Improved vectorization of parallel streams
- SuperWord enhancement to support vector conditional move (CMovVD) on Intel AVX CPUs

In general, intrinsics should be recognized as point fixes and not general techniques. They have the advantage that they are powerful, lightweight, and flexible, but have potentially high development and maintenance costs as they must be supported across multiple architectures. The SIMD techniques are useful and welcome, but are clearly an approach offering only diminishing returns to performance engineers.

New Version of G1

As discussed in "G1" on page 152, G1 is designed to solve several problems at once, offering features such as easier tuning and better control of pause times. In Java 9, it became the default garbage collector. This means that applications moving from Java 8 to 9 that do not explicitly set their choice of collector will experience a change of collection algorithm. Not only that, but the version of G1 that ships in Java 9 is different from the version in Java 8.

Oracle has claimed that in its benchmarks, the new version performs substantially better than the version present in Java 8. This has not been supported by the public publication of any results or studies, however, and for now we have only anecdotal community evidence at best.

Hopefully most applications will not be negatively impacted by this change of algorithm. However, all applications moving to Java 9 should do a full performance test if they are impacted by the switch (i.e., if they use Java 8 with default collection or G1).

Java 10 and Future Versions

Java 9 has just been released at the time of writing. As a result, development effort on the platform has now fully switched to the next version, Java 10. In this section, we'll discuss the new release model that will be in effect as of the next version before looking at what is known about Java 10 at this point.

New Release Process

Mere days before the release of Java 9, Oracle announced a brand new release model for Java, starting with Java 10. Releases had historically been feature-driven; major changes were targeted for a specific release, and if necessary the release was delayed until the feature was ready. This approach caused significant delays to the release of Java 9, and also impacted Java 8.

The feature-driven release cycle also had far deeper implications for the overall speed of development of the Java platform. Keystone features actually acted as a blocker on other smaller features, due to the long cycles needed to produce and fully test a release. Delaying a release close to the end of the development cycle means that the source repos are in a locked-down or semi-locked-down form for a much higher percentage of the available development cycle.

From Java 10 onward, the project has moved to a strict time-based model. A new version of Java, containing new features, will ship every six months. These releases are to be known as *feature releases*, and are the equivalent of major releases in the old model.

> Feature releases will not typically contain as many new features or as much change as a major Java release did in the old model. However, major features will still sometimes arrive in a feature release.

Oracle will also offer *Long-Term Support* (LTS) releases for some of the feature releases. These will be the only releases that Oracle will make as a proprietary JDK. All other releases will be OpenJDK binaries, under the GNU Public License (GPL) with the Classpath exemption—the same license that has always been used for open source Java builds. Other vendors may also offer support for their binaries, and may decide to support releases other than LTS versions.

Java 10

At the time of writing, the scope for Java 10 is still being confirmed and locked down. As a result, there is still the possibility of significant changes to its scope and content between now and the release. For example, in the few weeks immediately after the release of Java 9, there was a public debate about the version numbering scheme that would be used going forward.

New JVM features or enhancements are tracked through the Java Enhancement Process (*http://openjdk.java.net/jeps/1*). Each JDK Enhancement Proposal (JEP) has a number that it can be tracked under. These are the major features that shipped as part of Java 10, not all of which are performance-related or even directly developer-facing:

- 286: Local-Variable Type Inference
- 296: Consolidate the JDK Forest into a Single Repository
- 304: Garbage-Collector Interface
- 307: Parallel Full GC for G1
- 310: Application Class-Data Sharing
- 312: Thread-Local Handshakes

JEP 286 allows the developer to reduce boilerplate in local variable declarations, so that the following becomes legal Java:

```
var list = new ArrayList<String>();   // infers ArrayList<String>
var stream = list.stream();           // infers Stream<String>
```

This syntax will be restricted to local variables with initializers and local variables in for loops. It is, of course, implemented purely in the source code compiler and has no real effect on bytecode or performance. Nevertheless, the discussion of and reaction to this change illustrates one important aspect of language design, known as *Wadler's Law* after the functional programmer and computer scientist Philip Wadler:

> The emotional intensity of debate on a language feature increases as one moves down the following scale: Semantics, Syntax, Lexical Syntax, Comments.

Of the other changes, JEP 296 is purely housekeeping and JEP 304 increases code isolation of different garbage collectors and introduces a clean interface for garbage collectors within a JDK build. Neither of these has any impact on performance either.

The remaining three changes all have some impact, albeit potentially small, on performance. JEP 307 solves a problem with the G1 garbage collector that we have not previously addressed; if it ever has to fall back to a full GC, then a nasty performance shock awaits. As of Java 9, the current implementation of the full GC for G1 uses a single-threaded (i.e., serial) mark-sweep-compact algorithm. The aim of JEP 307 is to parallelize this algorithm so that in the unlikely event of a G1 full GC the same number of threads can be used as in the concurrent collections.

JEP 310 extends a feature called *Class-Data Sharing* (CDS), which was introduced in Java 5. The idea is that the JVM records a set of classes and processes them into a shared archive file. This file can then be memory-mapped on the next run to reduce startup time. It can also be shared across JVMs and thus reduce the overall memory footprint when multiple JVMs are running on the same host.

As of Java 9, CDS only allows the Bootstrap classloader to load archived classes. The aim of this JEP is to extend this behavior to allow the application and custom class-loaders to make use of archive files. This feature exists, but is currently available only in Oracle JDK, not OpenJDK. This JEP therefore essentially moves the feature into the open repo from the private Oracle sources.

Finally, JEP 312 lays the groundwork for improved VM performance, by making it possible to execute a callback on application threads without performing a global VM safepoint. This would mean that the JVM could stop individual threads and not just all of them. Some of the improvements that this change will enable include:

- Reducing the impact of acquiring a stack trace sample
- Enabling better stack trace sampling by reducing reliance on signals
- Improving biased locking by only stopping individual threads for revoking biases
- Removing some memory barriers from the JVM

Overall, Java 10 is unlikely to contain any major performance improvements, but instead represents the first release in the new, more frequent and gradual release cycle.

Unsafe in Java 9 and Beyond

No discussion of the future of Java would be complete without mention of the contro-versy surrounding the class sun.misc.Unsafe and the associated fallout. As we saw in "Building Concurrency Libraries" on page 298, Unsafe is an internal class that is not a part of the standard API, but as of Java 8 has become a de facto standard.

From the point of view of the library developer, Unsafe contains a mixture of features of varying safety. Methods such as those used to access CAS hardware are basically entirely safe, but nonstandard. Other methods are not remotely safe, and include such things as the equivalent of pointer arithmetic. However, some of the "not remotely safe" functionality cannot be obtained in any other way. Oracle refers to these capabilities as *critical internal APIs*, as discussed in the relevant JEP (*http:// openjdk.java.net/jeps/260*).

The main concern is that without a replacement for some of the features in sun.misc.Unsafe and friends, major frameworks and libraries will not continue to function correctly. This in turn indirectly impacts every application using a wide range of frameworks, and in the modern environment, this is basically every applica-tion in the ecosystem.

In Java 9, the --illegal-access runtime switch has been added to control runtime accessibility to these APIs. The critical internal APIs are intended to be replaced by supported alternatives in a future release, but it was not possible to complete this before Java 9 shipped. As a result, access to the following classes has had to be maintained:

- `sun.misc.{Signal,SignalHandler}`
- `sun.misc.Unsafe`
- `sun.reflect.Reflection::getCallerClass(int)`
- `sun.reflect.ReflectionFactory`
- `com.sun.nio.file.{ExtendedCopyOption,ExtendedOpenOption,` Extended `WatchEventModifier,SensitivityWatchEventModifier}`

In Java 9, these APIs are defined in and exported by the JDK-specific module `jdk.unsupported`, which has this declaration:

```
module jdk.unsupported {
    exports sun.misc;
    exports sun.reflect;
    exports com.sun.nio.file;

    opens sun.misc;
    opens sun.reflect;
}
```

Despite this temporary (and rather grudging) support from Oracle, many frameworks and libraries are having problems moving to Java 9, and no announcement has been made as to when the temporary support for critical internal APIs will be withdrawn.

Having said that, definite progress has been made in creating alternatives to these APIs. For example, the `getCallerClass()` functionality is available in the stack-walking API defined by JEP 259 (*http://openjdk.java.net/jeps/259*). There is also one other very important new API that aims to start replacing functionality from `Unsafe`; we'll look at that next.

VarHandles in Java 9

We have already met method handles in Chapter 11 and `Unsafe` in Chapter 12.

Method handles provide a way to manipulate directly executable references to methods, but the original functionality was not 100% complete for fields as only getter and setter access was provided. This is insufficient, as the Java platform provides access modes for data that go beyond those simple use cases.

In Java 9, method handles have been extended to include *variable handles*, defined in JEP 193 (*http://openjdk.java.net/jeps/193*). One intent of this proposal was to plug these gaps and, in doing so, provide safe replacements for some of the APIs in

Unsafe. The specific replacements include CAS functionality and access to volatile fields and arrays. Another goal is to allow low-level access to the memory order modes available in JDK 9 as part of the updates to the JMM.

Let's look at a quick example that shows how we might approach replacing Unsafe:

```java
public class AtomicIntegerWithVarHandles extends Number {

    private volatile int value = 0;
    private static final VarHandle V;

    static {
        try {
            MethodHandles.Lookup l = MethodHandles.lookup();
            V = l.findVarHandle(AtomicIntegerWithVarHandles.class, "value",
                int.class);
        } catch (ReflectiveOperationException e) {
            throw new Error(e);
        }
    }

    public final int getAndSet(int newValue) {
        int v;
        do {
            v = (int)V.getVolatile(this);
        } while (!V.compareAndSet(this, v, newValue));

        return v;
    }
    // ....
```

This code is essentially equivalent to the example of the atomic integer that we saw in "Building Concurrency Libraries" on page 298 and demonstrates how a VarHandle can replace the usage of unsafe techniques.

At the time of writing, the actual AtomicInteger class has not been migrated to use the VarHandle mechanism (due to cyclic dependencies) and still relies on Unsafe. Nevertheless, Oracle strongly advises all libraries and frameworks to move to the new supported mechanisms as soon as possible.

Project Valhalla and Value Types

The mission statement of Project Valhalla (*https://wiki.openjdk.java.net/display/ valhalla/Main*) is to be "a venue to explore and incubate advanced Java VM and Language feature candidates." The major goals of the project are explained as:

- Aligning JVM memory layout behavior with the cost model of modern hardware
- Extending generics to allow abstraction over all types, including primitives, values, and even void

- Enabling existing libraries, especially the JDK, to compatibly evolve to fully take advantage of these features

Buried within this description is a mention of one of the most high-profile efforts within the project: exploring the possibility of *value types* within the JVM.

Recall that, up to and including version 9, Java has had only two types of values: primitive types and object references. To put this another way, the Java environment deliberately does not provide low-level control over memory layout. As a special case, this means that Java has no such thing as structs, and any composite data type can only be accessed by reference.

To understand the consequences of this, let's look at the memory layout of arrays. In Figure 15-1 we can see an array of primitive ints. As these values are not objects, they are laid out at adjacent memory locations.

Figure 15-1. Array of ints

By contrast, the boxed integer is an object and so is referred to by reference. This means that an array of Integer objects will be an array of references. This is shown in Figure 15-2.

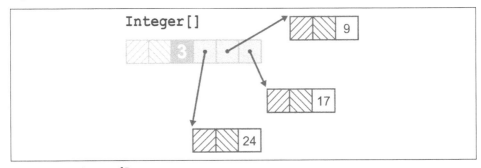

Figure 15-2. Array of Integers

For over 20 years, this memory layout pattern has been the way that the Java platform has functioned. It has the advantage of simplicity, but has a performance tradeoff— dealing with arrays of objects involves unavoidable indirections and attendant cache misses.

As a result, many performance-oriented programmers would like the ability to define types that can be laid out in memory more effectively. This would also include removing the overhead of needing a full object header for each item of composite data.

For example, a point in three-dimensional space, a `Point3D`, really only comprises the three spatial coordinates. As of Java 9, such a type can only be represented as an object type with three fields:

```
public final class Point3D {
    private final double x;
    private final double y;
    private final double z;

    public Point3D(double a, double b, double c) {
        x = a;
        y = b;
        c = z;
    }

    // Getters and other boilerplate elided
}
```

Therefore, an array of points will have the memory layout shown in Figure 15-3.

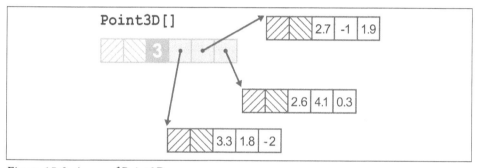

Figure 15-3. Array of Point3Ds

When this array is being processed, each entry must be accessed via an additional indirection to get the coordinates of each point. This has the potential to cause a cache miss for each point in the array, for no real benefit.

It is also the case that object identity is meaningless for the `Point3D` types. That means that they are equal if and only if all their fields are equal. This is broadly what is meant by a *value type* in the Java ecosystem.

If this concept can be implemented in the JVM, then for simple types such as spatial points, a memory layout such as that shown in Figure 15-4 (effectively an array of `structs`) would be far more efficient.

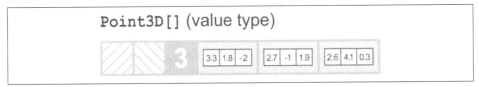

Figure 15-4. Array of "struct-like" Point3Ds

Not only this, but then other possibilities (such as user-defined types that behave in a similar way to built-in primitive types) also emerge.

However, there are some key conceptual difficulties in this area. One important problem is related to the design decisions made as part of the addition of generic types in Java 5. This is the fact that the Java type system lacks a *top type*, so there is no type that is the supertype of both `Object` and `int`. We can also say that the Java type system is not *single-rooted*.

As a consequence of this, Java's generics range only over reference types (subtypes of `Object`), and there is no obvious way to construct a consistent meaning for, say, `List<int>`. Java uses *type erasure* to implement backward-compatible generic types over reference types, but this much-hated mechanism is not responsible for the lack of a top type and the resulting lack of primitive collections.

If the Java platform is to be extended to include value types, then the question naturally arises as to whether value types can be used as type parameter values. If not, then this would seem to greatly limit their usefulness. Therefore, the design of value types has always included the assumption that they will be valid as values of type parameters in an enhanced form of generics.

At the time of writing, this has led to a design (*http://cr.openjdk.java.net/~dlsmith/ values-notes.html*) in which there should be three different *shapes* of JVM class and interface types:

- Reference types (R), which represent references to an instance of a class that has an identity or is `null`
- Value types (Q), which are instances of *value classes* that lack identity
- Universal types (U), which can be either R or Q

This begs the question, "How should type information in existing class files be understood?" That is, are the existing L types (that correspond to current types in Java 9 class files) actually R types, or are they really U types, and it's simply the case that we've never seen a Q type before?

For compatibility reasons, and to allow us to extend the definition of generics to include Q types, L types are understood to be U types, rather than R types.

This is quite an early prototype, and there are still plenty of design issues to be worked out—for example, the question of whether value types will require variable-width values at VM level.

In Java 9, at VM level all types have fixed-width values. Primitive types are either 1, 2, 4, or 8 bytes wide and object references are pointers (so they are 1 machine word wide). On modern hardware this means that references are either 32- or 64-bit depending on the hardware architecture of the machine.

Will the addition of value types mean the bytecode will need to accommodate variable-width types? Is there space in the bytecode for the instructions needed for this? Currently, it is believed that only two new opcodes need to be added:

- `vdefault`, which produces the default Q-typed instance of a value class
- `withfield`, which produces a new value of the input type and throws an exception on nonvalue or `null` inputs

Some bytecodes will also need some retrofitting to handle the new Q types. Above the VM level, extensive work is also needed to allow the core libraries to evolve in a compatible manner.

> Valhalla may be motivated by performance considerations, but a better way to view it is as enhancing abstraction, encapsulation, safety, expressiveness, and maintainability—*without* giving up performance.
>
> —Brian Goetz

Due to the changes to the release schedule, it is unclear which release of Java will eventually introduce value types as a production feature. The authors' best guess is that they will arrive in one of the 2019 releases, but this is unconfirmed by Oracle.

Graal and Truffle

The C2 compiler present in HotSpot has been enormously successful. However, it has been delivering obvious diminishing returns in recent years, and no major improvements have been implemented in the compiler in the last several years. For all intents and purposes, C2 has reached the end of its lifecycle and must now be replaced.

The current direction of research intended to lead to new shipping products is based around *Graal* and *Truffle*. The former is a specialized JIT compiler, and the latter is an interpreter generator for hosting languages on the JVM runtime.

One avenue of potential improvement for the JIT compiler is that the C2 compiler is written in C++, which exposes some potentially serious issues. C++, is, of course, an unsafe language that uses manual memory management, so errors in C2's code can crash the VM. Not only that, but the code in C2 has been modified and iterated on repeatedly and as a result has become very hard to maintain and extend.

To make progress, Graal is trying a different approach; it is a JIT compiler for the JVM written in Java. The interface that the JVM uses to talk to Graal is called the JVM Compiler Interface (JVMCI) and was added to the platform as JEP 243. This lets you plug in a Java interface as a JIT compiler, in a similar way to how Java agents can be plugged into the JVM.

The view taken by the project is that a JIT compiler really just needs to be able to accept JVM bytecode and produce machine code. At a low level, the compiler just transforms a byte[] (bytecode) into another byte[] (machine code), so there is no reason why this couldn't be implemented in Java.

This Java-in-Java approach has a number of benefits, including simplicity, memory safety, and being able to use a standard Java toolchain such as IDEs and debuggers rather than requiring compiler developers to have skills in an esoteric dialect of C++.

These advantages are enabling powerful new optimizations such as partial escape analysis (as mentioned in "Limitations of Escape Analysis" on page 240) to be implemented in Graal rather than C2. One additional advantage is that Graal enables teams to modify parts of it for their own applications, such as developing custom intrinsics (e.g., for custom hardware) or optimization passes.

Truffle is a framework for developing interpreters for languages on the JVM. It is designed to work in concert with Graal as a library to automatically generate a high-performance JIT compiler for the input language from just the interpreter, using an academic technique called the *Futamuru projection*. This is a technique from the area of academic computer science known as *partial specialization* that has recently become more practical to use in real systems (although some of the ideas have been used in the Python PyPy implementation for several years).

Truffle is an alternative to the approach of generating bytecode at runtime that is used by existing language implementations on the JVM, such as JRuby, Jython, and Nashorn. The performance measurements so far indicate that the combination of Truffle and Graal can potentially deliver much higher performance than previously seen.

The umbrella project for all of this work is the new *Project Metropolis*. This is an effort to rewrite more of the VM in Java, starting with HotSpot's JIT compilers and possibly the interpreter.

The Metropolis/Graal technology is present and shipping in Java 9, although it is still very much experimental. The switches to enable a new JIT compiler to be used are:

```
-XX:+UnlockExperimentalVMOptions -XX:+EnableJVMCI -XX:+UseJVMCICompiler
```

There is one other way in which Graal can be used in Java 9: the Ahead-of-Time compiler mode. This compiles Java directly into machine code, in a similar way to C and

C++. Java 9 includes a `jatoc` command that uses Graal and has the sole goal of speeding up startup time until the normal tiered compilation can take over. The tool currently supports only the `java.base` module on a single platform (Linux/ELF), but support is expected to expand over the next few releases of Java.

To create the binaries from Java class files, we use the new `jaotc` tool as follows:

```
jaotc --output libHelloWorld.so HelloWorld.class
jaotc --output libjava.base.so --module java.base
```

Finally, *SubstrateVM* is a research project (also using Graal) to take this functionality further and to compile a whole JVM written in Java along with a Java application to produce a single, statically linked native executable. The aim is that this will produce native binaries that do not need any form of JVM installed and can be as small as a few kilobytes and start in a few milliseconds.

Future Directions in Bytecode

One of the biggest changes in the VM has been the arrival of `invokedynamic`. This new bytecode has opened the door to a rethinking of how JVM bytecode can be written. There is now an attempt to extend the technology used in this opcode to provide even more flexibility to the platform.

For example, recall the distinction between `ldc` and `const` in "Overview of Bytecode Interpretation" on page 200. There is rather more to this than is obvious at first sight. Let's look at a simple bit of code:

```
public static final String HELLO = "Hello World";
public static final double PI = 3.142;

public void showConstsAndLdc() {
    Object o = null;
    int i = -1;
    i = 0;
    i = 1;
    o = HELLO;
    double d = 0.0;
    d = PI;
}
```

This produces the following rather straightforward bytecode sequence:

```
public void showConstsAndLdc();
  Code:
     0: aconst_null
     1: astore_1
     2: iconst_m1
     3: istore_2
     4: iconst_0
     5: istore_2
```

```
 6: iconst_1
 7: istore_2
 8: ldc              #3                    // String Hello World
10: astore_1
11: dconst_0
12: dstore_3
13: ldc2_w           #4                    // double 3.142d
16: dstore_3
17: return
```

There are now also some extra entries that show up in the constant pool:

```
#3 = String              #29            // Hello World
#4 = Double              3.142d
...
  #29 = Utf8             Hello World
```

The basic pattern is clear: the "true constants" show up as const instructions, while loads from the constant pool are represented by ldc instructions.

The former are a small finite set of constants, such as the primitives 0, 1, and null. In contrast, any immutable value can be considered a constant for ldc, and recent Java versions have greatly increased the number of different constant types that can live in the constant pool.

For example, consider this piece of Java 7 (or above) code that makes use of the Method Handles API we met in "Method Handles" on page 281:

```
public MethodHandle getToStringMH() throws NoSuchMethodException,
    IllegalAccessException {
    MethodType mt = MethodType.methodType(String.class);
    MethodHandles.Lookup lk = MethodHandles.lookup();
    MethodHandle mh = lk.findVirtual(getClass(), "toString", mt);

    return mh;
}

public void callMH() {
    try {
        MethodHandle mh = getToStringMH();
        Object o = mh.invoke(this, null);
        System.out.println(o);
    } catch (Throwable e) {
        e.printStackTrace();
    }
}
```

To see the impact of method handles on the constant pool, let's add this simple method to our previous trivial ldc and const example:

```
public void mh() throws Exception {
    MethodType mt = MethodType.methodType(void.class);
    MethodHandle mh = MethodHandles.lookup().findVirtual
```

```
                    (BytecodePatterns.class, "mh", mt);
    }
```

This produces the following bytecode:

```
public void mh() throws java.lang.Exception;
  Code:
     0: getstatic      #6   // Field java/lang/Void.TYPE:Ljava/lang/Class;
     3: invokestatic   #7   // Method java/lang/invoke/MethodType.methodType:
                            // (Ljava/lang/Class;)Ljava/lang/invoke/MethodType;
     6: astore_1
     7: invokestatic   #8   // Method java/lang/invoke/MethodHandles.lookup:
                            // ()Ljava/lang/invoke/MethodHandles$Lookup;
    10: ldc            #2   // class optjava/bc/BytecodePatterns
    12: ldc            #9   // String mh
    14: aload_1
    15: invokevirtual  #10  // Method java/lang/invoke/MethodHandles$Lookup.
                            // findVirtual:(Ljava/lang/Class;Ljava/lang/
                            // String;Ljava/lang/invoke/MethodType;)Ljava/
                            // lang/invoke/MethodHandle;
    18: astore_2
    19: return
}
```

This contains an additional ldc, for the BytecodePatterns.class literal, and a work-around for the void.class object (which must live as a houseguest in the java.lang.Void type). However, class constants are only a little more interesting than strings or primitive constants.

This is not the whole story, and the impact on the constant pool once method handles are in play is very significant. The first place we can see this is in the appearance of some new types of pool entry:

```
#58 = MethodHandle  #6:#84  // invokestatic java/lang/invoke/LambdaMetafactory.
                            // metafactory:(Ljava/lang/invoke/MethodHandles
                            // $Lookup;Ljava/lang/String;Ljava/lang/invoke/
                            // MethodType;Ljava/lang/invoke/MethodType;Ljava/
                            // lang/invoke/MethodHandle;Ljava/lang/invoke/
                            // MethodType;)Ljava/lang/invoke/CallSite;
#59 = MethodType    #22     // ()V
#60 = MethodHandle  #6:#85  // invokestatic optjava/bc/BytecodePatterns.
                            // lambda$lambda$0:()V
```

These new types of constant are required to support invokedynamic, and the direction of the platform since Java 7 has been to make greater and greater use of the technology. The overall aim is to make calling a method via invokedynamic as performant and JIT-friendly as the typical invokevirtual calls.

Other directions for future work include the possibility of a "constant dynamic" capability—an analog of invokedynamic, but for constant pool entries that are unresolved at link time but calculated when first encountered.

It is expected that this area of the JVM will continue to be a very active topic of research in forthcoming Java versions.

Future Directions in Concurrency

As we discussed in Chapter 2, one of Java's major innovations was to introduce automatic memory management. These days, virtually no developer would even try to defend the manual management of memory as a positive feature that any new programming language should use.

We can see a partial mirror of this in the evolution of Java's approach to concurrency. The original design of Java's threading model is one in which all threads have to be explicitly managed by the programmer, and mutable state has to be protected by locks in an essentially cooperative design. If one section of code does not correctly implement the locking scheme, it can damage object state.

 This is expressed by the fundamental principle of Java threading: "Unsynchronized code does not look at or care about the state of locks on objects and can access or damage object state at will."

As Java has evolved, successive versions have moved away from this design and toward higher-level, less manual, and generally safer approaches—effectively toward *runtime-managed concurrency*.

One aspect of this is the recently announced *Project Loom*. This project deals with supporting JVM concurrency at a lower level than has been done on the JVM until now. The essential problem with core Java threads is that every thread has a stack. These are expensive and are not endlessly scalable; once we have, say, 10,000 threads, the memory that is devoted to them amounts to gigabytes.

One solution is to take a step back and consider a different approach: execution units that are not directly schedulable by the operating system, have a lower overhead, and may be "mostly idle" (i.e., don't need to be executing a high percentage of the wall-clock time).

This chimes well with the approach taken by other languages (both JVM-based and not). In many cases they have lower-level cooperative constructs, such as goroutines, fibers, and continuations. These abstractions must be cooperative rather than preemptive, as they are operating below the visibility of the operating system and do not constitute schedulable entities in their own right.

Following this approach requires two basic components: a representation of the called code (e.g., as a `Runnable` or similar type) and a scheduler component. Ironically, the

JVM has had a good scheduling component for these abstractions since version 7, even if the other parts were not in place.

The Fork/Join API (described in "Fork/Join" on page 312) arrived in Java 7 and was based on two concepts—the idea of recursive decomposition of executable tasks and that of work stealing, where idle threads can take work from the queues of busier threads. The ForkJoinPool executor is at the heart of these two concepts, and is responsible for implementing the work-stealing algorithm.

It turns out that recursive decomposition is not all that useful for most tasks. However, the executor thread pool with work stealing can be applied to many different situations. For example, the Akka actor framework has adopted ForkJoinPool as its executor.

It is still very early days for Project Loom, but it seems entirely possible that the Fork JoinPool executor will also be used as the scheduling component for these lightweight execution objects. Once again, standardizing this capability into the VM and core libraries greatly reduces the need to use external libraries.

Conclusion

Java has changed a huge amount since its initial release. From not being explicitly designed as a high-performance language, it has very much become one. The core Java platform, community, and ecosystem have remained healthy and vibrant even as Java has expanded into new areas of applicability.

Bold new initiatives, such as Project Metropolis and Graal, are reimagining the core VM. invokedynamic has enabled HotSpot to break out of its evolutionary niche and reinvent itself for the next decade. Java has shown that it is not afraid to undertake ambitious changes, such as adding value types and returning to tackle the complex issue of generics.

Java/JVM performance is a very dynamic field, and in this chapter we have seen that advances are still being made in a large number of areas. There are numerous other projects that we did not have time to mention, including Java/native code interaction (Project Panama) and new garbage collectors such as Oracle's ZGC.

As a result, this book is nowhere near complete, as there is simply so much to comprehend as a performance engineer. Nevertheless, we hope that it has been a useful introduction to the world of Java performance and has provided some signposts for readers on their own performance journey.

Index

Symbols

constant dynamic capability, 395
constant pool, 19
constants
    impact of method handles on constant pool, 394
    ldc and const bytecodes, 393
context switches, 46
    detecting CPU utilization problems from, 50
Continuously Concurrent Compacting Collector (see C4 garbage collector)
copying, 365
CopyOnWriteArrayList, 307
CopyOnWriteArraySet, 307
correlation, spurious, in measurements, 103
counter, incrementing, 290-293
CPU clock speeds, increases in, 34
CPU utilization, 7, 48
    analysis for Java application running on Unix system, 49

D

DataLite antipattern, 78
debug JVMs, 228
    setting maximum method byte size for compilation, 256
degradation
    about, 7
    connections with other performance observables, 8
degradation tests, 62
deprecated and removed GC combinations, 168
Dijkstra, Edsger, 143, 293
Disruptor pattern, 315, 358
Distracted by Shiny (antipattern), 69
Distracted by Simple (antipattern), 70
distributions
    non-normal, 106
    normal (or Gaussian), 102, 105
domain objects, 183, 269-273
    diagnosing memory leaks, 271
    short-lived, causing floating garbage problem, 272

E

Eden region (memory), 125
    configuration in G1 tuning, 194
    in G1 algorithm, 154
    management of, 127

young GC and, 135
efficiency, 7
Ellsberg's Paradox, 82
embarrassingly parallel workloads, 290
emergent behavior of complex systems, 80
endianness, 203
endurance tests, 62
Epsilon garbage collector, 168
equals method, 260
error margin in benchmarkng code, 89
errors in performance analysis, 100
    random error, 102
    systematic error, 101
escape analysis, 236-242
    eliminating heap allocations, 237
    limitations of, 240
    optimizing lock performance, 238
evacuating collectors, 119, 127
    compacting collectors vs., 131
    hemispheric evacuating collector, 128
evaluation stack, 200
exact GC scheme, 118
exception handling in thread lifetime, 310
Exclusive state (caches), 37
execution profiling, 319
    tools for developers, 323-336
executors and task abstraction, 309-313
    asynchronous execution, 310
    Fork/Join framework, 312
    selecting an ExecutorService, 311
Executors class, new* factory methods, 310
ExecutorService, 310
    selecting, 311
explicit method call opcodes, 206
Extension classloader, 16

F

Fiddle with Switches antipattern, 81, 122
final methods changed to be nonfinal, invocation by HotSpot interpreter, 211
finalization, avoiding, 273-281
    forgetting to clean up, 274
    problems with finalization, 274
    try-with-resources, 277-281
finalize method, 274
FinalReference class, 277
fine-grained bytecodes, 208
fixed-width values for Java types, 391
Flichel, Carey (blog post), 67

S

safepoints
    activities requiring, 251
    in interpreted code, 208
    JIT compiler emitting safepoint checks, 251
    safepointing bias of profilers, 322
    tracking down cases of high safepointing
        time, 322
safepoints (application threads), 144
Sampler tab (VisualVM), 32
sampling data
    in non-normal distributions, 106
    in profiling, 321
SATB (snapshot at the beginning), 146
scalability
    about, 7
    Amdahl's Law, 10
    connections with other performance
        observables, 8
scheduler (process), 43
SDLC (software development life cycle), perfor-
    mance testing in, 66
semaphores, 306
sender (Aeron), 368
sequential containers, 260
Serial and SerialOld garbage collectors, 167
Serviceability Agent (SA), 30
sets
    Agrona library, 361
    optimization considerations, 268
Shannon's Strict Avalanche Criteria, 266
Shared state (caches), 37
Shenandoah garbage collector, 156-159
    concurrent compaction, 158
    obtaining, 159
    phases, 157
signature polymorphism, 285
Simple Binary Encoding (SBE), 364-367
    copy-free and native type mapping, 365
    steady-state allocation, 365
    streaming access and word-aligned access,
        366
    working in, 366
simplest parts of a system, targeting, 70
Single Instruction-Multiple Data (SIMD)
    extensions, 381
single static assignment, 219
snapshot at the beginning (SATB), 146

software development life cycle (SDLC), perfor-
    mance testing in, 66
speculative execution in modern CPUs, 41
speculative optimization, 230
spinlocks, 303, 316
Spliterator, 314
Stack class, 262
stack samples, collecting for application
    threads, 322
stack-based interpreted machine (JVM), 15
state
    and controlling state, in JMH framework, 95
    MESI states for lines in a cache, 37
statistics
    for JVM performance, 99-108
        interpretation of, 109-113
        non-normal statistics, 105
        spurious correlations, 103
        systematic error, 101
        types of error, 100
    naive techniques, inappropriate use for
        Java/JVM performance, 4
stop-the-world (STW) pauses, 118
    in CMS collection, 190
    in parallel collectors, 132
    nondeterministic nature of, 143
    ruling out before profiling, 321
streams, 314
    parallel streams, 314
stress tests, 61
StringConcatFactory, 381
strings
    compact strings in Java 9, 378
    new string concatenation in Java 9, 379
strong memory model, 294
SubstrateVM research project, 393
sun.misc.Unsafe class, 300
superhero types in development teams, 71
survivor spaces, 128
    configuration in G1 tuning, 194
    in G1 algorithm, 154
Sync class, 304
synchronization
    controlling between threads using volatile
        variable, 316
    controlling updating of a counter, 292
    locking via, handling shared mutable state,
        296
    synchronizes-with in JMM, 296

V

value types, 261
    Project Valhalla and, 387-391
VarHandles in Java 9, 386
variable-width types, 391
variables
    local variable offsets, 21
    single static assignment in C1 and C2 compilers, 219
Vector class (deprecated), 262
virtual addressing of memory, in memory management unit (MMU), 43
Virtual Dynamically Shared Objects (vDSO), 47
virtualization, 54
VisualGC plug-in for VisualVM, 118
    GC debugging tool, 129
    survivor spaces in, 128
VisualVM, 30, 271, 323
    memory profiler, 341
    Overview, Monitor, Threads, Sampler, and Profiler tabs, 32
VMSpec, 199
vmstat utility, 49
volatile keyword, 292
    atomic variables and, 301
    volatile variable controlling thread synchronization, 316
vtables, 216
    method lookup in, eliminating, 243

W

Wadler's Law, 384
walls (in performance), 95

weak generational hypothesis, 125
weak memory model, 294
"Why Developers Keep Making Bad Technology Choices", 67
Windows systems
    os::javaTimeMillis() function implementation, 46
    process scheduler, 45
work-stealing algorithm, Fork/Join framework, 312
write barrier, 147
write walls, protecting against in benchmarking, 95
write-back behavior, 38
write-through behavior, 38
WriteLock, 305

X

-Xms and -Xmx options (VM), 88

Y

YourKit
    allocation profiler, 342
    execution profiler, 330
    memory dump profiler, 347

Z

zero-overhead principle, 22
Zing, 159
    (see also C4 garbage collector)
Zing JVM, 27
Zulu, 27

About the Authors

Ben Evans is the cofounder of and Technology Fellow at jClarity, a startup that delivers performance tools to help development and ops teams. He helps to organize the London Java Community, and represents them on the Java Community Process Executive Committee, where he works to define new standards for the Java ecosystem. Ben is a Java Champion and JavaOne Rockstar, coauthor of *The Well-Grounded Java Developer* (Manning), and a regular public speaker on the Java platform, performance, concurrency, and related topics.

James (Jim) Gough is a Java developer and author. Jim first became interested in Java during his degree program at the University of Warwick, and after graduating he became a member of the London Java Community. Community has remained central to Jim's contributions, which include working on the design and testing of JSR-310 and serving on the Java Community Process Executive Committee for several years. Jim is a regular conference speaker and is currently focused on building customer facing technology at Morgan Stanley. He spent four years teaching Java and C++ in various countries around the world.

Chris Newland is a senior developer at ADVFN using Java to process stock market data in real time. He is the author of the JITWatch project, an open source log analyzer to visualize and inspect Just-in-Time compilation decisions made by the HotSpot JVM. Chris is a Java Champion and has presented on JIT compilation techniques at several conferences.

Colophon

The animal on the cover of *Optimizing Java* is a markhor goat (*Capra falconeri*). This species of wild goat is distinguished by its Merlin-esque beards and twisting, towering horns. Found in the mountainous regions of western and central Asia, these goats inhabit high-altitude monsoon forests and can be found between 600–3,600 meters in elevation.

The markhor are herbivores that primarily graze on a variety of vegetation including grasses, leaves, herbs, fruits, and flowers. Like other wild goats, the markhor play a valuable role within their ecosystem as they munch the leaves from the low-lying trees and scrub, spreading the seeds in their dung.

The mating season takes place in winter, during which the males fight each other by lunging, locking horns, and attempting to push each other off balance. The subsequent births occur from late April to early June and result in one or two kids. Adult males are largely solitary and prefer the forest while the females and their young live in flocks on the rocky ridges high above.

Learn from experts.
Find the answers you need.

Sign up for a **10-day free trial** to get **unlimited access** to all of the content on Safari, including Learning Paths, interactive tutorials, and curated playlists that draw from thousands of ebooks and training videos on a wide range of topics, including data, design, DevOps, management, business—and much more.

Start your free trial at:

oreilly.com/safari

(No credit card required.)

Milton Keynes UK
Ingram Content Group UK Ltd.
UKHW050234200924
448528UK00002B/2